Indigenous People, Crime and Punishment

Thalia Anthony

Routledge
Taylor & Francis Group
a GlassHouse Book

First published 2013
by Routledge
2 Park Square, Milton Park, Abingdon, Oxon OX14 4RN

Simultaneously published in the USA and Canada
by Routledge
711 Third Avenue, New York, NY 10017

Routledge is an imprint of the Taylor & Francis Group, an informa business

British Library Cataloguing in Publication Data
A catalogue record for this book is available from the British Library

Library of Congress Cataloging in Publication Data
A catalog record for this book has been requested

ISBN 978-0-415-66844-6 (hbk)
ISBN 978-0-203640296 (ebk)

Typeset in Baskerville
by Keystroke, Station Road, Codsall, Wolverhampton

MIX
Paper from responsible sources
FSC www.fsc.org FSC® C013056

Printed and bound in Great Britain by
TJ International Ltd, Padstow, Cornwall

Contents

Foreword

In a recent interview, the Nobel Laureate civil rights activist Toni Morrison revealed the struggle of a marginalized culture to gain recognition. Based on her background as an African-American, she experienced the distorted representations of black personality, black culture and, more insidious than these, the depiction of anything non-white as a danger to decency, functionality and even to the safety of the dominant race. While there is always the danger of cultural generalization in making the parallel between the recognition of African-Americans and Indigenous peoples, the universal desire for recognition is a driver behind worldwide Indigenous emancipation.

The recognition process can be viewed as a struggle for personal and cultural, even historic, identity, against diverse and sovereign forces of control. Thalia Anthony advances the issue of recognition as one of institutionalized subordination. Recognition, she argues, reinforces cultural values of the dominant order, but more than this provides a platform for unpacking these values against an appreciation of non-regulation and mis-regulation as essential in defining Indigenous offenders *and* their communities as both the essence of disorder, and the challenge to ordering in all its postcolonial forms.

Applied to the criminal justice system, *Indigenous People, Crime and Punishment* is concerned with particularizing and historicizing the recognition of the colonized, and how criminalization and colonization are intricately connected. In particular, Chapter 2 is a historical account of the criminalization of Indigenous peoples, with such an intent at the forefront, while Chapters 4 and 5 are concerned with the particular recognition of the colonized in terms of culture and laws. The book constantly reiterates how historical specificity is essential in conceiving the recognition problem as a critical analytical tool. In applying recognition as a profound critical device, one needs to generalize its analytical capacity while at the same time emphasizing the historical particularity of its application.

In an Australian context, post *Mabo*, recognition has come to mean a challenge for engagement, albeit in largely white-men's terms. The land rights battle necessitated for Indigenous people the reluctant acceptance of imposed law and justice as a framework for obtaining limited fundamental rights. It even required Indigenous Australians to talk of land as alienable property which is anathema to Indigenous custom, if only to secure some qualified and begrudging acceptance of their power to again free their land to be as they believe it should be. Recognition in this scenario has not meant the distillation of *truth* for either side, but rather it has been a discourse which has endorsed the dominion of one culture in order to save some fragile essence for the other. Recognition as it stands is a two-way street which relies on one party in the relationship having dominion over the legitimacy of recognition.

What we need to know much more about, particularly beyond political rhetoric, is how recognition, and the law's role in its facilitation, nuances individual integrity and cultural survival. In this book, Dr Anthony employs the analytical device of recognition to address similar concerns through the focus on criminal justice sentencing. Two apparent claims to originality and value for this endeavour are the sentencing paradigm, and the manner in which recognition is seen as a mechanism of mutual meaning manufacturing. On the first, the critical literature on Indigenous/European relations in Australia is heavily concerned with criminal justice discrimination, but almost entirely with a policing perspective. While admittedly these individual encounters of power and domination are a much broader and immediate evidencing of postcolonial oppression, the construction of judicial reasoning and narrative reveals a much more powerful normative story about the way in which crime and justice are employed in Australia as a bedrock of Indigenous social engineering. On the second claim, I believe the true value of this book is founded. The manner in which recognition restructures meaning, through intricate layers of acceptance and rejection, requires the conceptual and empirical unpacking that we are offered in what follows, in order that the contemporary story of Indigenous Australia may be understood beyond the oversimplification of racism or misguided paternalism.

The choice of sentencing and judicial narrative as the frame for analyzing recognition in a socio-political context obsessed from its inception with law and order is inspired. I say this for several reasons. It enables the enunciation of authority regarding the state's role in regulating the individual and his or her community. Judicial narrative represents a form of reasoning which if not essentially principled and logical, then available for deconstruction in its effort to rationalize competing matters of justice. Add to this the developmental nature of common law sentencing and the manner in which its jurisprudence is much more expansive than that on determining liability, and it provides a rich source for analyzing the words and workings of state power.

I cannot do justice to the sophistication or empirical conviction of Dr Anthony's analytical achievement with a short summary of her approaches to recognition. However, it is revealing at least to highlight their intersection. As the book's introduction appropriately starts out, the reader is introduced to the ways in which Indigenous offenders and their communities recognize and respond to delinquency in their midst. In this sense, the central place of community and tradition stand in stark contrast to the depersonalizing process of Western criminal justice with its professionalized abstraction.

However, we are promptly reminded that Indigenous people do not have autonomy over such things. In this respect any assertion that there currently exists in Australia an Indigenous criminal justice in any viable sense is misguided, not because it is not possible, but because it is not recognized as autonomous. The inevitable question is how will white law and justice accommodate communitarian resolutions outside its province?

Here Thalia enters into an intricate deconstruction of meaning creation. Judges interpret Indigenous resolutions as complementary but supplementary, or as a challenge to the nature and purpose of introduced criminal justice. There has been a historical fluctuation between both polar representations and Thalia questions this beyond the individual idiosyncrasies of individual judges. There are clear signals – political and social – that can explain such shifts. These are contexts in which externalities which may have nothing to do with the offence and the offender become the critical history of Indigenous encounters with white justice.

A more confounding paradox is contained in the book's interrogation of the judicial homily. This pronouncement has always been used to speak out more than the morality of the law. When it is turned on Indigenous offenders, it clearly becomes a tool for individual and communal denunciation. At both levels the homily ignores structural inequalities in which the introduced system of criminal justice is complicit and should stand accused.

Judicial pronouncements declare and reinforce the *peculiar* representation of the Indigenous offender ranging from genetically infirmed to morally and socially depraved. Even when these *peculiarities* of race and character are interpreted in mitigation, they are founded on *mis-representations* which make possible the wider responsibility of Indigenous communities in the fall from grace.

Potentially much more destructive and resonant with recent conservative political attacks on Indigenous communities as criminogenic and depraved, are the judicial pronouncements on the failings of Indigenous culture. Dr Anthony highlights both the dysfunctional and *non-functional* judicial representations of Indigenous culture and the way in which these are employed to widen the reach of *governing through crime.*

The recognition conundrum is then thrown back to us. Is it white Australian culture which is the society in denial and are the judges our wavering mouthpiece? This allegation would not be so powerful were it not for the postcolonial history of criminal justice as an agent for exterminating Indigenous culture and tradition in our name.

The book is pervaded by what the author coins as metaphoric control. Judicial narrative as a crucial mechanism in the authority of meaning creation gives power to the state to control recognition. Through this power and the core control over *knowledge* which benefits from judicial determination, Foucault's revelation of knowledge as the disciplining force in the power to punish is writ large.

In her conclusion, Thalia concedes that it is not possible for judges to reorder the terms of recognition if justice is to be provided for Indigenous peoples. Her argument is that recognition needs to be mutually provided by Indigenous and non-Indigenous peoples. This aspiration of mutuality involves restructuring the social order so Indigenous people can recognize the entry points into the Anglo-Australian criminal justice system. Recognition thus needs to be deconstructed with a positive intention. The final passages of the book suggest how the operation of Indigenous laws and the empowerment of communities would redress the asymmetry between the recognizer and the recognized.

A cynic might criticize such 'big picture' reconciliation, motivated through judicial intervention (thus far much of the problem) as resembling the Thomas Mathiessen paradox between prison reform and abolition (*The Politics of Abolition*). However, Dr Anthony lays out a new approach to recognition with dignity as a phased process rather than some 'all or nothing' approach to macro structural reform.

Beyond critique, in detailing the positive potential of common law and the state frameworks of sentencing, this book challenges judges to actively recognize *the terms of Indigeneity* as a critical determinant of Australian criminal justice, and from there to accept and engage with a profoundly enabling judicial intersection. Only in this way can judges and their narrative rise to their role as restorative voices in a new and respectful age of recognition through genuine criminal justice.

Mark Findlay

Preface

Re-imagining the Indigenous criminal

In 2006, in response to a moral panic over sexual offences in remote Indigenous settlements in the Northern Territory of Australia, the federal government launched an intervention into these communities that involved a broad range of restrictions. The first of these was a restriction on cultural and customary law considerations in sentencing (Crimes Act 1914, s. 16A(2A)). The government told two stories to support its policy: that there was an epidemic of culturally condoned sexual assaults in Indigenous communities, and that leniency in criminal sentencing underlies the crime problem. With such impugnation of Indigenous communities and the judiciary, the idea for this book was born. I was intrigued to explore the ways in which judiciaries have historically represented the Indigenous criminal, changing influences on their decisions, and how these factors have affected the punishment received by Indigenous people.

Since colonization, Indigenous criminality has been a scapegoat for many coercive policies imposed on Indigenous people in Australia and other British colonies. Settlers inflicted violent punishment on Indigenous people for alleged crimes of trespass and cattle killing. In the nineteenth and twentieth centuries, laws imposed on Indigenous peoples to control their daily lives had criminal penalties attached. Resistance to land takeovers and assimilation was met with harsh penalties. Dispensing the criminal law was a vehicle for punishing and containing Indigenous people through a seemingly neutral mechanism. Violence dressed up as 'punishment' created a logic that it was a normal response to Indigenous people on the frontier and beyond. Punishment for crimes meant that the repression and restraint of Indigenous people was not an abuse of power, but a justification for the use of power.

In this context, sentencing courts have occasionally provided clemency for Indigenous offenders, especially over the past 50 years – the period from which the key sources for this book are drawn. Indigenous offenders sought lesser sentences by submitting a range of circumstances particular to their group, including culture, Indigenous law, poverty, alcoholism and racism. The courts accepted these submissions in recognizing that Indigenous communities provide unique conditions for the offender. However, such recognition did not undermine the pervasiveness of the common law or state sovereignty. Rather, leniency would often be cited to justify the fairness of Anglo-Australian institutions. Indigenous 'difference' therefore lies in the shadow of the overarching Anglo-Australian legal order.

Governments and the media characterized 'benevolent' courts who granted leniency to Indigenous offenders as a chink in the coercive armoury of the state, especially over the past decade. Courts were criticised for compromising state punishment, whereas the police and prosecutors were perceived as carrying out their duty of being tough on crime. Nonetheless, the main work of toning down judicial benevolence was not done by the state, but by the courts themselves. The higher courts from the late 1990s reoriented the sentencing principles to focus on the interests of the wider community, the need for deterrence and the seriousness of the harm. The effect of the harm on the Indigenous victim also became a more frequent consideration, but without reference to her or his actual sentiments or cultural context. This punitive turn in sentencing Indigenous offenders, as I regard it, has been most confronting with the increased judicial condemnation of Indigenous communities for their supposed complicity in crime and dysfunctionality. Accordingly, a central focus of my research and this book is how the judicial recognition of Indigeneity has been as much a burden as a benefit for Indigenous people.

I use sentencing narratives to provide texture to an understanding of how a postcolonial system engages with Indigenous people through punishment processes. They provide insights into the shift in Indigenous affairs policy and the increasing paternalism of the state since the late 1990s. Accordingly, I have supplemented my analysis of sentencing materials with references to legislation, government statements and media reports to paint this bigger picture. In addition, my reading of these textual sources has been enhanced by my time spent in a number of Indigenous communities, including as a young child and teenager as well as more recently in a research capacity. I refer to some of my published research arising from my fieldwork in Northern Territory communities and incorporate Indigenous views where possible.

From 2008 I have had the privilege to visit Northern Territory communities where Indigenous laws and cultures are central in the lives of their Indigenous members. When I first visited Lajamanu in the Tanami Desert, for example, I was struck by the leading role of its Warlpiri members in deciding important law matters, organizing ceremonies and cultural activities for young people, planning the Milpirri festival and meeting with senior politicians from the Northern Territory government to discuss breaches of their laws by Anglo-Australian officers (albeit often with little effect). Indigenous laws, especially in governing relationships, were palpable in shaping day-to-day routines, roles and senses of place. Often, Indigenous laws are referred to as 'customary law' to denigrate their lawful status, but my experiences showed me that Indigenous laws retain their authority in Indigenous communities in very practical ways. Despite policies of segregation, dispossession and assimilation, Indigenous laws have displayed remarkable resilience. They have weathered the increasing influx of government bureaucrats, which has produced a growing sense of disillusionment with government policy. These impressions of Indigenous laws stayed with me during my short visits to other communities, including Daguragu, Kalkarindji and Yuendumu.

Contrasting with the powerful roles that I saw Warlpiri people play in managing their laws and community were my observations of their role in Anglo-Australian courts. My observations of magistrates' courts in Lajamanu and Yuendumu were that Warlpiri people were sidelined. There were some small exceptions, including one community court in Yuendumu where I witnessed the Elders involved in sentencing, and a pre-sentencing meeting in Lajamanu where the Elders deliberated over advice they would provide to the magistrate on sentences they felt were appropriate for offenders. However, in the main, Warlpiri people were excluded from the sentencing process. Magistrates did not discuss the significance, if there was any, of the sentencing recommendations of the community. Rather, they concentrated on the court's exclusive disciplinary role in delivering sentences.

For many Indigenous people, the question of judicial punishment is not central to the issue of community safety. Rather, what is central to this issue is their ongoing claims to self-governance and to the practice of their laws. One aspect of Indigenous legal practice followed by this book is the ongoing dispensation of Indigenous punishment (including exile, shaming and spearing) to uphold Indigenous law and reconcile relations in the community. In Lajamanu, the Warlpiri community boasts low crime rates due to the strength of their laws and its enforcement through Indigenous punishment. The courts have recognized Indigenous punishment that has been administered by the Indigenous community on the defendant. In the past, it has served as a basis for reducing sentences and providing bail. However, this recognition has not provided a sound basis for legal recognition, especially as courts increasingly doubt the functionality of Indigenous laws. For Anglo-Australian institutions to comprehensively recognize Indigenous laws, there need to be protections for Indigenous laws and their related governance structures, land connections, family relationships, language and ceremonies (Napaljarri and Cataldi 2003: xvii). I review approaches to how this may be realized towards the end of this book.

In writing this book, I have had particular regard to the terminology. First, the term 'Indigenous people' is used in this book to generally refer to the traditional owners of Australian land. However, I have also reverted to this term where I have not known the particular Indigenous society or particular Indigenous background of a person. Otherwise, I have attempted to use the name of the relevant Indigenous nation or peoples. In Australia, there are hundreds of Indigenous groups with different languages, cultures, identities, land connections and histories. Therefore, general reference to 'Indigenous people' is invoked to contrast Anglo-Australian law and culture rather than simplify the diversity of Indigenous laws, cultures and communities. At times in Chapter 2 on the history of Indigenous criminalization, I use the term 'Aboriginal' to reflect its contemporary usage in the nineteenth and most of the twentieth century.

Second, for Indigenous people living in communities far from major cities or towns, I use the common term 'remote communities'. This is notwithstanding that the word 'remote' may in fact reinforce the core-periphery relationship established by the colonizer which attempts to decentre Indigenous homelands. Conversely, for Indigenous people, their communities are the centre of their lives, and the major towns and cities are the communities of outsiders. Also, when I use the term 'culture', I do not seek to imply that it has fixed parameters. Rather, I appreciate that culture is a dynamic experience that abounds in non-Indigenous societies as much as in Indigenous societies. Furthermore, the terms 'white' or 'whiteness' are used herein to signify the dominant non-Indigenous culture. 'Whiteness' is a historical construct which conveys the European monopolization of culture. This is buttressed by the historical construct of the 'Indigenous Other' (Hage 2003: 49–50, 1998: 58–9).

Finally, I use the term 'postcolonial' to communicate the ongoing experience of colonization for Indigenous peoples, and not to simply mean 'after' colonization. Postcolonial is referred to in this book in relation to Anglo-Australian institutions that have continued to subjugate Indigenous people and their laws. This subjugation has occurred long after the British Empire relinquished official control of Australia's institutions (bar the head of state) and over Australia's Indigenous peoples and their lands. The continuation of colonization manifests itself in the continued subjection of Indigenous people to Anglo-Australian rules and governments. However, as postcolonial studies remind us, within this colonizing paradigm, Indigenous people also continue to use their agency to resist and renegotiate the boundaries of contested space. This book reveals as much about Indigenous challenges to sovereignty as the assertion of Anglo-Australian authority.

Acknowledgements

Some of the questions and conclusions in this book may appear ambitious, and it is only with the support and feedback of various people that I have been able to take on the challenge. These people have also given me hope that we can achieve an alternative to the justice system as it currently exists. They include Amanda Porter, Dorothea Anthony, Harry Blagg, Michelle Burgis, Honni van Rijswijk, Richard Edney, Pat O'Malley, Ian Dennis, David Brown, Ralph Henman and Mark Findlay. Amanda's astute comments and continuous reading of drafts and re-drafts were particularly valuable. She also provided an Indigenous perspective that enhanced the writing of this book.

This book came to life with my experiences in Warlpiri communities in the Northern Territory, which were initially made possible with the assistance of Robert Chapman. My experiences strengthened my sense of the communities' cohesiveness and Indigenous legal authority. The busy and vibrant life in these communities – filled with meetings, ceremonies, the organization of festivals and community activities, and interactions with government officials – gave me an appreciation of Indigenous communities' great capacity to create justice for their members.

Access to many of the earlier sentencing remarks as well as court statistics was made possible due to the librarians at the Northern Territory Supreme Court, who went beyond the call of duty. I am grateful for the assistance from Frieda Evans, Rayleen Dalziel, Bronwyn King, Kate Verus and Malika Okeil. I also thank Patrick O'Mara for his support in locating cases in the University of Sydney library collection. For their help in providing access to historical sources on Indigenous policies and directives and colonial accounts of Indigenous Australians, I thank the archival staff at the Northern Territory Archives Service, Mortlock Library (Adelaide), National Archives (Darwin and Canberra) and the National Library of Australia (Canberra).

The research for this book was greatly supported by funds provided by the Faculty of Law at the University of Sydney and the University of Technology, Sydney. I would like to thank my colleagues in the Institute of Criminology, University of Sydney with whom I worked during the early stages of this book. I would like to give thanks for the advice and encouragement from my colleagues at the University of Technology, Sydney law faculty, including Nicole Graham, Shaunnagh Dorsett, Lesley Hitchens and Bronwyn Olliffe. The completion of this book was facilitated by Jumbunna (Indigenous) Research Centre at the University of Technology, Sydney, which provided me with an inspiring work environment in the final writing phase. I was nurtured by the collegiality of Larissa Behrendt, Nicole Watson, Amanda Porter, Jason de Santolo, Raema Behrendt and Annette Munro. I am very appreciative of the confidence that Colin Perrin and Melanie Fortmann-Brown from Routledge placed in this book as well as the generous feedback by the anonymous referees who provided valuable direction in developing the ideas in this book.

Thank you to Jennifer Turner-Walker for the inspired cover to this book. In Jennifer's words, the cover image is of country locked behind the windows of the High Court of Australia and underlying the court's water feature. The image represents that the basis of Indigenous law is the relationship with country. Whitefella law is a wafer-thin overlay, which is as poorly understood by Indigenous peoples as Indigenous law is understood to whitefella law-makers.

Some of my initial thinking for this book was conveyed in articles published in a different form and framework, namely, 'The Punitive Turn in Postcolonial Sentencing and the Judicial Will to Civilise' *Waikato Law Review* (2011) 19(2): 66–85 and 'Moral Panics and Misgivings over Indigenous Punishment: Sentencing Cultural Crimes in Australia's Northern Territory' *Cambrian Law Review* (2011) 42: 91–112. Substantial parts of Chapter 6 were originally published in 'Is There Social Justice in Sentencing Indigenous Offenders?' *University of New South Wales Law Journal* (2012) 35(2): 563–97. I'd like to thank that latter journal's editor, Robert Woods, for useful suggestions about the application of Nancy Fraser's concept of recognition. Chapter 7 also reproduces a large portion of 'Sentencing Indigenous Riot Offenders in a Spatial Fantasy' *Griffith Law Review* (2011) 20(2): 385–420. I am grateful to the editors and anonymous referees of the above-mentioned journals for their useful guidance, which has enhanced subsequent iterations in this book.

Finally, I owe a great debt to Mark O'Donnell, whose loving support as well as comments on draft chapters made my incessant approach to research and writing seem like a natural part of our family life. The recent arrival of our daughter, Rosemary Anthony, added to the completeness of this picture, which will only be enhanced with the imminent birth of our expected child. To them I write this book in hope that you grow up in a just society where humanity supplants subordination.

Table of legislation

Aboriginal and Torres Strait Islander Affairs Act 1965 (Qld).
Aboriginal and Torres Strait Islanders (Queensland Reserves and Communities Self-Management) Act 1978 (Cth).
Aboriginal Land Act 1991 (Qld).
Aboriginal Land Rights Act 1976 (Cth).
Aboriginal Land Rights Act 1983 (NSW).
Aboriginal Lands Act 1970 (Vic).
Aboriginal Lands Act 1995 (Tas).
Aboriginal Native Offenders Act 1849 (SA).
Aboriginal Offenders Amendment Act 1892 (WA).
Aboriginal Protection Act 1869 (Vic).
Aboriginals Ordinance 1911 (Cth).
Aboriginals Ordinance 1918 (Cth).
Aboriginals Protection and Restriction of the Sale of Opium Act 1897 (Qld).
Aborigines Act 1905 (WA).
Aborigines Act 1911 (SA).
Aborigines Protection Act 1886 (WA).
Aborigines Protection Act 1909 (NSW).
Australian Courts Act 1828 (Imp).
Bail Act 1982 (NT).
Breach of Contract Act 1842 (SA).
Capital Punishment Amendment Act 1871 (WA).
Care and Protection of Children Act 2007 (NT).
Commonwealth of Australia Constitution Act 1901 (Cth).
Community Services (Aborigines) Act 1984 (Qld).
Crimes Act 1914 (Cth).
Crimes (Sentencing) Act 2005 (ACT).
Crimes (Sentencing Procedure) Act 1999 (NSW).
Criminal Code Act (NT).
Criminal Code RSC, 1985 (Canada).
Criminal Law (Sentencing Act) 1988 (SA).
Criminal Procedure Act 1986 (NSW).

Families, Community Services and Indigenous Affairs and Other Legislation Amendment (Northern Territory National Emergency Response and Other Measures) Act 2007 (Cth).
Imperial Acts Application Act 1969 (NSW).
Law Reform (Gender, Sexuality and De Facto Relationships) Act 2003 (NT).
Liquor Act (NT).
Magistrates' Court Act 1989 (Vic).
Maralinga Tjarutja Land Rights Act 1984 (SA).
Master and Servants Act 1842 (WA).
Motor Vehicle Act (NT).
New South Wales Act 1823 (Imp).
Northern Territory (Administration) Act 1910 (Cth).
Northern Territory National Emergency Response Act 2007 (Cth).
Penalties and Sentences Act 1992 (Qld).
Pitjantjatjara Land Rights Act 1981 (SA).
Racial Discrimination Act 1975 (Cth).
Sentencing Act 1991 (Vic).
Sentencing Act 1995 (NT).
Sentencing Act 1995 (WA).
Sentencing Act 1997 (Tas).
Social Security and Other Legislation Amendment (Welfare Payment Reform) Act 2007 (Cth).
Stronger Futures in the Northern Territory Act 2012 (Cth).
Summary Trial and Punishment of Native Offenders Ordinance 1849 (WA).
Supreme Court Ordinance 1911 (Cth).
Torres Strait Islander Land Act 1991 (Qld).
Traffic Act (NT).
Waste Lands Act 1842 (SA).
Welfare Ordinance 1953 (Cth).
Youth Justice Act 2005 (NT).

Table of cases and inquests

A v. *The Queen* [2010] NTCCA 14.
Aboriginal Areas Protection Authority v. *S & R Building & Construction Pty Ltd* [2011] NTSC 3.
Alderson v. *The Queen* [2002] NTCCA 10.
Amagula v. *Chambers* [2007] NTSC 59.
Amagula v. *White* [1998] NTSC (Unreported, 7 January).
Anderson v. *The Queen* [2008] NSWCCA 211.
Andrews v. *The Queen* [2007] NSWCCA 68.
Anthony (2004) 142 A Crim R 440.
Atkinson & Another v. *Walkely* (1984) 27 NTR 34.
Attorney-General v. *Brown* (1847) 2 Legge 312.
Barnes (1997) 96 A Crim R 593.
Bellas v. *The Queen* [2006] NTCCA 8.
Bryce Jabaltjari Spencer v. *The Queen* [2005] NTCCA 3.
Carr v. *The Queen* [2009] NSWSC 995.
Ceissman (2001) 119 A Crim R 535.
Coe v. *Commonwealth* (1979) 53 ALJR 403.
Coe v. *Commonwealth* (1993) 118 ALR 193.
Cook v. *Chute* [1997] NTSC 76.
Cooper v. *Stuart* (1889) 14 App Cas 286.
Crawford v. *Laverty* [2008] ACTSC 107.
Croaker v. *The Queen* [2008] NSWCCA 232.
DPP v. *Terrick*, *DPP* v. *Marks*, *DPP* v. *Stewart* [2009] VSCA 220.
DPP v. *Wilson* [2002] VSC 299.
Eatock v. *Bolt* (2011) 283 ALR 505.
Fernando (1992) 76 A Crim R 58.
Gadatjiya v. *Lethbridge* (1992) 106 FLR 265.
Gibbs v. *Capewell* (1995) 128 ALR 577.
Gillon v. *R.* [2009] NSWCCA 277.
GJ v. *The Queen* [2006] HCA Trans 252.
Green v. *The Queen* (2006) 19 NTLR 1.
Hales v. *Jamilmira* (2003) 142 NTR 1.

Ingomar v. *Police* [1998] SASC 6875.
Inkamala v. *R.* [2005] NTCCA 6.
Inquest into the Death of Mulrunji (2006) Office of the State Coroner, C. Clements, Brisbane. Available http://www.courts.qld.gov.au/__data/assets/pdf_file/0008/86642/cif-doomadgee-mulrunji-20060927.pdf (accessed 6 January 2013).
Jabaltjari v. *Hammersley* (1977) 15 ALR 94.
Jabarula & Others v. *Jambajimba & Others* (1989) 68 NTR 26.
Jadurin v. *The Queen* (1982) 7 A Crim R 182.
Jones v. *Hales & Rigby* [2003] 4 NTSC 63.
Joshua v. *Thomson* [1994] NTSC (Unreported, 27 May).
Juli v. *R.* (1990) 50 A Crim R 31.
Jurisic (1998) 45 NSWLR 209.
Leering v. *Nayda* [1997] NTSC 4.
Lofty v. *The Queen* [1999] NTSC 73.
Mabo v. *State of Queensland (No. 2)* (1992) 175 CLR 1.
Mamarika v. *Murphy & Another* [2007] NTSC 58.
Markarian v. *R.* (2005) 228 CLR 357.
Members of the Yorta Yorta Aboriginal Community v. *The State of Victoria* (2002) 214 CLR 422.
Milirrpum v. *Nabalco Pty Ltd* (1971) 17 FLR 141.
Mungatopi v. *R.* (1991) 57 A Crim R 341.
Munungurr v. *The Queen* (1994) 4 NTLR 63.
Mununggurr v. *The Queen* [2006] NTCCA 16.
Neal v. *The Queen* (1982) 149 CLR 305.
Parmbuk v. *Garner* [1999] NTSC 108 (Unreported, 14 October).
Parker v. *DPP* (1992) 28 NSWLR 282.
Pascoe v. *Hales* [2002] NTSC (Unreported, 8 October).
Police v. *Abdulla* (1999) 74 SASR 337.
Police v. *Bernard Wurramurra* [1977] Northern Territory Court of Summary Jurisdiction (Unreported, 27 July).
Police v. *Dickenson & Others* [2010] Alice Springs Court of Summary Jurisdiction (Unreported, 1 December, Magistrate Bamber).
R. v. *Aboriginal Charlie Mulparinga* (1953) 28 NTJ 219.
R. v. *Ah-See* [2004] NSWCCA 202.
R. v. *Anderson* (1954) 36 NTJ 240.
R. v. *Bashford* [2007] NSWSC 1380.
R. v. *Benny Lee* [1974] NTSC 221.
R. v. *Blow* [2010] NSWCCA 294.
R. v. *Boney* [1991] NSWCCA (Unreported, 22 July, No. 60342/91).
R. v. *Bulmer* (1987) 25 A Crim R 155.
R. v. *Cargill* [2005] NSWDC (Unreported, 6 January, Audio recording of proceedings).
R. v. *Charlie Limbiari Jagamara* [1984] NTSC (Unreported, 28 May).

R. v. *Churchill* [2000] WASCA 230.
R. v. *Daniel* (1998) 1 Qld R 499.
R. v. *Davey* (1980) 2 A Crim R 254.
R. v. *Downes* [2001] NTSC (Unreported, 10 October).
R. v. *Dylan Jagamarra Charles* [2004] NTSC (Unreported, 26 May).
R. v. *F.A.P.* [2007] NSWSC 905.
R. v. *Fernando* [2002] NSWCCA 28.
R. v. *Friday* (1985) 14 A Crim R 471.
R. v. *Fuller-Cust* (2002) 6 VR 496.
R. v. *Gibuma & Anau* (1991) 54 A Crim R 347.
R. v. *GJ* (2005) 196 FLR 233.
R. v. *Goldsmith* (1995) 65 SASR 373.
R. v. *Gorey* [1978] NTSC (Unreported, 20 June).
R. v. *Helmhout & Another* [2000] NSWSC 651.
R. v. *Herbert & Others* (1983) 23 NTR 22.
R. v. *Hickey* [1994] NSWCCA (Unreported, 27 September).
R. v. *Iginiwuni* [1975] NTCCA 6.
R. v. *Ipeelee* (2012) SCC 13.
R. v. *Jinjair* [2003] NTSC (Unreported, 28 November).
R. v. *Job Warusam* [1993] NTSC (Unreported, 24 March).
R. v. *Jungarai* (1981) 9 NTR 30.
R. v. *Kelly* [2005] NSWCCA 280.
R. v. *Knight* [2004] NSWSC 498.
R. v. *Knight* [2005] NSWCCA 241.
R. v. *Lane, Hunt & Smith* [1980] NTSC (Unreported, 29 May).
R. v. *Long* [1995] NTSC (Unreported, 13 February).
R. v. *Mamarika* (1982) 5 A Crim R 354.
R. v. *McCormack & Others* [1981] VR 104.
R. v. *Minor* (1992) 105 FLR 180.
R. v. *Miyatatawuy* (1996) 87 A Crim R 574.
R. v. *Morgan* (2003) 57 NSWLR 533.
R. v. *Mungurala* [1974] NTSC (Unreported, 18 April).
R. v. *Murray, R* v. *Bates* [1992] NSWCCA (Unreported, 6 April, CCA 60322 of 1991, CCA 60343 of 1991).
R. v. *Murrell & Bummaree* [1836] NSWSC 35 (5 February 1836) and related archival materials. Available http://www.austlii.edu.au/au/cases/nsw/NSWSupC/1836/35.html (accessed 6 January 2013).
R. v. *Mustey* [2001] VSC 68.
R. v. *Newman, R* v. *Simpson* (2004) 145 A Crim R 361.
R. v. *Njana* [1998] WASC (Unreported, 13 March).
R. v. *Pitt* [2001] NSWCCA 156.
R. v. *Poulson* (2001) 122 A Crim R 388.
R. v. *Poynter, Norman & Parker; ex parte A-G (Qld)* [2006] QCA 517.
R. v. *Rictor* [2002] WASC (Unreported, 30 April).

R. v. *Riley* (2006) 161 A Crim R 414.
R. v. *Rindjarra* [2008] NTCCA 9.
R. v. *Shannon* (1991) 56 A Crim R 56.
R. v. *Smith* [2003] SASC 263.
R. v. *Stone* (1995) 84 A Crim R 218.
R. v. *Taylor* [2005] VSCA 222.
R. v. *Thompson* [2001] WASC (Unreported, 20 February).
R. v. *Tjami* [2000] SASC 311.
R. v. *Trindall* [2005] NSWCCA 446.
R. v. *Walter & Thompson* [2004] NSWCCA 304.
R. v. *Wanambi* [2001] NTSC (Unreported, 7 December).
R. v. *Way* (2004) 60 NSWLR 168.
R. v. *Wheeler* [1959] 36 NTSC 231 (Unreported, 13 August).
R. v. *Wheeler* [1959a] 36 NTSC 275 (Unreported, 19 August).
R. v. *Whyte* (2002) 55 NSWLR 252.
R. v. *William Davey* [1980a] NTSC (Unreported, 30 June).
R. v. *Williams* [1976] SASC (Unreported, 14 May).
R. v. *Wilson* (1995) 81 A Crim R 270.
R. v. *Woodley, Boonga & Charles* (1994) 76 A Crim R 302.
R. v. *Wordie* [2003] VSCA 107.
R. v. *Wotton* [2007] QDC 181.
R. v. *Wunungmurra* (2009) 231 FLR 180.
Robertson v. *Flood* (1992) 111 FLR 177.
Rogers & Murray v. *R* (1989) 44 A Crim R 301.
Russell v. *The Queen* [2010] NSWCCA 248.
Sargeant v. *Verity* [2009] NTSC 39.
Shaw & Another v. *Wolf & Others* (1999) 163 ALR 205.
The Queen v. *Aiden Kelly* [2010] NTSC (Unreported, SC 20920376).
The Queen v. *Bara* [2006] NTCCA 17.
The Queen v. *Berida* [1990] NTSC (Unreported, 5 April).
The Queen v. *Booth* [2005] NTSC (Unreported, 22 September).
The Queen v. *GJ* [2005a] NTSC (Unreported, 11 August).
The Queen v. *Inkamala* [2006] NTCCA 11.
The Queen v. *Linda Nabarula Wilson* [2006] NTSC (Unreported, 19 May).
The Queen v. *MC* [2012] NTSC (Unreported, 24 July).
The Queen v. *Redford* [2007] NTSC (Unreported, 26 March).
The Queen v. *Sims & Walker* [2012] NTSC (Unreported, 27 February).
The Queen v. *Tewedy Maxwell* [2011] NTSC (Unreported, SCC 21023768).
The Queen v. *Turner* [2011] NTSC (Unreported, 8 April).
The Queen v. *Walker* [1994] 46 NTSC 1.
The Queen v. *Walker* [2007] NTSC (Unreported, 26 September).
The Queen v. *Webb* [2003] NTSC (Unreported, 21 February).
The Queen v. *Wotton* [2008] Townsville District Court (Unreported, 7 November).
Thorpe v. *Commonwealth (No. 3)* (1997) 144 ALR 677.

Tuckiar v. *The King* (1934) 52 CLR 332.
Veen v. *The Queen (No. 2)* (1988) 164 CLR 465.
Walker v. *State of New South Wales* (1994) 182 CLR 45.
Waters v. *R.* [2007] NSWCCA 219.
Wik Peoples v. *State of Queensland* (1996) 187 CLR 1.
Wong v. *The Queen* (2001) 207 CLR 584.
Wurramara (1999) 105 A Crim R 512.
Wynbyne v. *Marshall* (1997) 117 NTR 11.
Yougie (1987) 33 A Crim R 301.

Chapter 1

Introduction to Indigenous representations in criminal sentencing

> Australian courts have opted for a rather weak version of cultural relativism which accepts that the general legal system is presumptively applicable but will make concessions to specific cultural arguments.
>
> (Zdenkowski 1994: 27)

Recognition of the 'Other'

On 6 October 1994, an Indigenous woman from Milingimbi – a Northern Territory island community in the Arafura Sea – stabbed her husband while she was drunk. He suffered a stab wound to his chest, puncturing his lung, and a laceration of the biceps. Jane Miyatatawuy admitted guilt. The response was several meetings held among clan groups and families on Milingimbi and surrounding communities to discuss the circumstances of the offence and possible resolutions, including spearing through the thigh. Miyatatawuy had to undergo the distressing situation of facing the clans and families at the meetings. The clans ultimately imposed a 2-year cultural good behavioural bond under Yolŋu law, which would be enforced by the Milingimbi Indigenous community. This was Miyatatawuy's trial and punishment. Afterwards she would go before the Anglo-Australian courts (see *R.* v. *Miyatatawuy* 1996).

A few years earlier, on 13 February 1991, Stanley Fernando stabbed his one-time partner, causing deep lacerations to her leg, upper arm and neck. Fernando was an Indigenous man from north-western New South Wales. He and his victim lived in the town of Walgett, which is beleaguered by socio-economic disadvantage. Non-Indigenous society in Walgett has drawn bold lines between its space and Indigenous space in the town. Fernando's story is not unusual in this part of the world: he received little formal education, was removed from his family by the Welfare Department and sent to an isolated property. He had taken to excessive drinking, and crime had followed. His criminal record was drenched with drops of alcohol. Like many others in his predicament, Fernando from a young age had been caught up in the Anglo-Australian criminal justice system in a self-perpetuating cycle (see *Fernando* 1992).

These two cases presented the Northern Territory and New South Wales supreme courts with distinct challenges in sentencing the offenders: how to take into account 'traditional' Indigenous punishment (hereinafter, 'Indigenous punishment') where the offender was immersed in the laws of his or her Indigenous community, and how to take into account disadvantage and alcoholism where the Indigenous offender had experienced disadvantage and dispossession at the hands of Anglo-Australian postcolonial society. These cases nonetheless converge on the judicial recognition of Indigenous law and society and its attendant limitations. This book examines the various manifestations of judicial recognition of a colonized population in criminal sentencing, primarily in relation to the Northern Territory, but also in New South Wales and Queensland. It regards judicial recognition of Indigeneity as a form of cultural representation and argues that the judiciary ebbs and flows between tolerance and exclusion in recognizing the 'other' and its alternative system of law. The continually shifting ground is typified by the higher courts' changing characterization of the Indigenous offender over the past decade – from an object of sympathy to an object of risk. This change has cohered with a punitive turn for Indigenous offenders, but with a twist: the Indigenous community has simultaneously been impugned as *dysfunctional* (where social norms and order has been broken down) or *non-functional* (where the community is seen as not Indigenous enough to be recognized). This *misrecognition* or *non-recognition* locates the offender in failed communities, which are helpless in assisting victims or otherwise incapable of being defined as Indigenous due to their assimilation. Such views have also arisen in media and governmental discourses to justify 'governing through crime', whereby crime has been a vehicle for coercive controls over Indigenous welfare recipients, parents, community councils and traditional land owners as well as restrictions placed on sentencing discretion (see Simon 2007).

Due to the recognition process in the criminal justice system being, at best, a blunt instrument for Indigenous justice, or at worst, a sharp instrument for injustice; *Indigenous People, Crime and Punishment* is ultimately a call to restructure the criminal justice system to empower Indigenous domains in the Anglo-Australian legal system. Postcolonial theory informs us of the possibilities of coexisting spaces of authority. Blagg (2008) describes the space where Indigenous law and Anglo-Australian law intersect as a 'liminal space' where there is cultural hybridity, compromise and contestation. This space resists the Anglo-Australian legal system's classifications and stigmatization of Indigenous people (2008: 31). The value of Blagg's work and postcolonial theory more generally is that it refuses to view colonization as a completed project and stresses the constant cultural interactions in these 'interstitial spaces' (Bhabha 1994: 2). While judicial recognition can be an expression of cultural hybridity, it is constantly undercut by postcolonial practices that create intricate 'structures of attitude and reference' to uphold white privilege and normalize white possession (Said 1994: 23). The sentencer's recognition of Indigenous circumstances mirrors white norms and values and therefore precludes 'a genuine relationship' between Indigenous and non-Indigenous peoples and laws (Dodson 1994: 9). Recognition of identities creates and perpetuates the imaginary order of the subject (Lacan 1977). It produces a general frame of reference to bind society through a shared language (Berger and Luckmann 1966: 35–40; Barthes 1972: 11; Bourdieu 1991: 43–65). Through recognition, the objectified Indigene lives outside of this order. Courts refashion, reconstitute and redefine Indigenous identities and cultures to make them 'quite distinct from [their] social existence' in order to reinforce their outsider status (Pollock 1988: 6).

The effect of misrecognition or non-recognition of Indigeneity is much deeper than degrading or dehumanizing 'their' identity. It reproduces institutional subordination of Indigenous peoples, cultures and laws. Fraser (2004: 29) refers to its role in entrenching 'institutionalized patterns of cultural value'. In its beneficent countenance, judicial recognition fosters sympathy and valorization of the Indigene – manufacturing a fantasy of 'magical' native qualities (JanMohammed 1985: 86). This gives rise to lighter sentences and accommodates Indigenous community submissions. In her concept of social justice, Fraser (1997: 24) refers to this type of recognition as an 'affirmative remedy' that provides some relief for the marginalized, but leaves intact subjugated identities and underlying 'group differentiations'. It buttresses the Anglo-Australian legal system by providing a sense-making paradigm for the system's 'whiteness'. The candour of this racializing process appears when recognition takes on a maleficent form. Judicial recognition can slide into condemning portrayals of the 'Indigenous other' and tougher punishment.

This book is concerned with how Indigenous people are represented in the sentencing process. It examines the judicial construction of Indigeneity as a product of 'symbolic interactions' in the courtroom, which reflects 'the symbolic vision' of the recognizer and breathes meaning into the identity to the deviant (Downes and Rock 2007: 165, 187).[1] In interpreting evidence of Indigenous circumstances from lawyers and Indigenous community members, the court draws on pre-existing racial ideologies and legitimizes dominant institutional discourses (Denzin 2001: 246; Berger and Luckmann 1966: 85). Indigenous alterity is infused in sentencing to construct the Other as a counterpoint to the superior position of the white Self (Fanon 1967: 97). In this version, alterity is an artefact of whiteness rather than a mirror of blackness (1967: 113). The judiciary excludes, obscures or inferiorizes the Other to militate similarities between the groups and convey a sense of homogeneous whiteness (1967: 14; Hage 1998: 155). Sentencers are agents of 'white' fantasy-fulfilment. Their production of cultural meaning reflects the normative universe where symbols of language shape power (Cover 1983–4: 4; Travers 2006: 455, 458). *Indigenous People, Crime and Punishment* elucidates how these meanings shift according to different

1 Symbolic Interactionism is concerned with the relationship between social interaction and identity and how meanings are derived and modified through interpretation (Blumer 1969; Mead and Morris 1934).

situations, places and times and in response to punitive imperatives (Charon 2007: 49–50). Performances of tolerant 'whiteness' in sentencing (where accommodation of 'difference' provides clemency) can give way to protective 'whiteness' (where penalty is exerted to protect victims of Indigenous barbarism), notwithstanding that the nature of the offence remains consistent. The various intonations of whiteness provide cues in the script for sentencing Indigenous offenders (Goffman 1958: 15–17).

Recognition in a society of denial

This book explores the *recognition dilemma* in criminal sentencing: how courts recognize Indigenous alterity in the Anglo-Australian legal order while upholding its whiteness. Such a dilemma arises because Anglo-Australian law has otherwise excluded the operation of Indigenous laws in its criminal justice system. Since the earliest New South Wales Supreme Court decisions in the 1830s, the common law has renounced Indigenous societies and laws. This has been a pervasive feature of property law that has asserted exclusive Crown title to all land. In justifying British Crown sovereignty over New South Wales land, Stephen CJ in *Attorney-General* v. *Brown* (1847: 317) claimed that Britain found Australia as a 'newly-discovered country'. Thus, the settlement of British subjects rendered valid the Crown's 'occupancy' and 'executive authority' (1847: 318). Reliance on a notion of *terra nullius* (land belonging to no one, where the 'one' is of recognizable legal character) nullified the need for the British to enter into treaties with Australian Indigenous peoples and severed Indigenous rights to land and sovereignty. By the time the first Australian native claim was made by the Yolŋu people of east Arnhem land in the Northern Territory, in *Milirrpum* v. *Nabalco* (1971), the Federal Court held that the common law did not have the capacity to recognize Indigenous title. This was despite the court finding that Yolŋu society comprised 'a government of laws, and not of men' (1971: 267). Thus, the court recognized the existence of Indigenous laws, but was unable to accommodate them because of the Crown's exclusive title to land. Paradoxically, exclusive title was only secured in the first instance because Indigenous people and laws were not recognized.

The denial of an alternative system of Indigenous laws also emerged in the colonial criminal law, which has cast long shadows over the exercise of jurisdiction. The New South Wales Supreme Court conferred exclusive authority to the colonial courts to try and punish British subjects, including Indigenous defendants. This was due to the Crown's occupation of the land and the fact that, in the court's eyes, Indigenous people did not possess a system of laws. Consequently, Indigenous defendants before the Supreme Court who sought to be dealt with by their own laws were met with the assertion of colonial jurisdiction. In the case of *R.* v. *Murrell & Bummaree* (1836), the Indigenous defendants sought to have their killings dealt with by 'tribal' law and punishment. The Supreme Court determined that Indigenous Australians were too low on the evolutionary scale to be afforded legal recognition: 'the various tribes had not attained at the first settlement of the English people amongst them to such a position in point of numbers and civilization, and to such a form of Government and laws, as to be entitled to be recognized as so many sovereign states governed by laws of their own' (1836: [211]). The court then articulated that the British state had taken into 'actual possession' half of the Australian continent and 'obtained and exercised for many years the rights of Domain and Empire over the country' (1836: [211]). This is despite the fact that the British had not explored most of that land by the 1830s and colonial courts did not try Indigenous defendants until several decades after colonization (Ford 2010: 200).

Indigenous laws continued to operate despite the common law's jurisdiction. Therefore, in 1994 the contention by an Indigenous defendant that he should be punished according to his own laws rather than the laws of Anglo-Australian society was put to the High Court of Australia in *Walker* v. *New South Wales* (1994). The case was brought in light of the *Mabo* v. *Queensland (No. 2)* (1992) (hereinafter, '*Mabo*') decision that for the first time recognized native title rights in Australian common law.[2] In *Mabo*, the High Court as a matter of obiter ruled out the recognition of Indigenous rights to self-governance beyond native title. Brennan J. noted that Indigenous traditions will be observed in so far as they do not fracture the 'skeleton' of the common law and, furthermore, as an 'act of state', the High Court could not challenge state sovereignty because it would threaten the courts of the state (*Mabo* 1992: 44–5). In *Walker* v. *New South Wales* (1994), the defendant argued that the right to practise criminal law on his land was commensurate to the right to exercise native title rights. The High Court held that rights to Indigenous criminal laws cannot be analogized with native title. It reasoned that extending native title recognition to the criminal jurisdiction would encroach on the 'inherently universal' nature of the criminal law (1994: 50). This universality of postcolonial law does not allow for coexisting criminal laws: 'English criminal law did not, and Australian criminal law does not, accommodate an alternative body of law operating alongside it' (1994: 50; see also Yeo 1994; Dorsett 2002: 58). Therefore, the judiciary perceived an antinomy between Indigenous laws and the Anglo-Australian criminal law, which aborted claims to legal pluralism.

In another case that sought to apply *Mabo* to an Indigenous claim to sovereignty, *Coe* v. *Commonwealth* (1993: 199), the High Court rejected 'subsisting Aboriginal claim[s] to sovereignty'. It sought to maintain its legal hierarchy by positing that '*Mabo* is entirely at odds with the notion that sovereignty adverse to the Crown resides in the Aboriginal people of Australia' (1993: 200). The court referred to its reasoning in an earlier case also brought by Indigenous rights campaigner Paul Coe for sovereignty over Wiradjuri land in New South Wales (*Coe* v. *Commonwealth* 1979: 408). There it was stated that the annexation of the

2 Native title is a creature of common law that provides rights for Indigenous peoples to use their lands. It places a burden on the radical title of the Crown: *Mabo* (1992). Native title is one of the major forms of Indigenous recognition in the Australian common law.

east coast of Australia by Captain Cook and subsequent acts of Crown possession could not be challenged. Further, it is *not* possible to say that Indigenous people are organized as a 'distinct political society separated from others' (1979: 408). Most recently, in *Thorpe* v. *Commonwealth (No. 3)* (1997), the High Court held that it did not have jurisdiction to decide an Indigenous sovereignty claim. This reasoning has been described as a piece of 'circuitous logic' in which the authority of the court was unable to be challenged for being unlawful on the grounds that the state had unchallengeable authority over Indigenous people (Flynn and Stanton 1997: 19). These cases show that 'recognition' is tied to the maintenance of the common law. It is a contingent gift bestowed on Indigenous people where it safeguards the common law's legal dominion, and denied where it challenges its authority. In discussing *Coe* v. *Commonwealth* (1993), Motha (2005: 120, 125) argues that recognition reinforces the 'monistic conception of sovereignty', 'imperial absolutism and hegemony'.

Within the common law's self-proclaimed legal exclusivity in the criminal domain, it has identified spaces in sentencing to account for Indigenous 'difference'. Recognition of Indigeneity in sentencing does not challenge the purported monologism of Anglo-Australian criminal law because it operates within conventional legal frameworks and sentencing principles rather than undercutting those principles. The judiciary uses its discretion to afford 'individualized justice' by taking into account, where it deems relevant, Indigenous community expectations, cultural practices, alternative modes of punishment, socio-economic disadvantage and 'racial' grievances. It can also account for the positive role played by the defendant in the Indigenous community. The common law jurisprudence on these factors is nonetheless vulnerable to being subsumed by general sentencing principles or prohibited by legislation. Furthermore, the 'recognition space' offered by criminal sentencing is an end-point of the criminalization process. The Anglo-Australian law has well and truly been imposed on Indigenous persons by the time they reach the sentencing court, including through reprimand, arrest, investigation, bail refusal, the trial and a determination of guilt. After these 'punishing processes', sentencing abruptly throws up opportunities for the Indigenous defendant to explain his or her crime with reference to Indigenous background, community and circumstances (Feeley 1992). Hay (1975: 41, 44) asserts that discretion in the sentencing phase allows the legal system to represent the conviction stage as belonging to a neutral order where factors such as race are invisible. It also conveys the humanity of the judge after a conviction (1975: 47). Recognition of Indigeneity at this stage does not threaten the structure of the common law or undermine the application of criminal laws, but can enhance the fantasy of 'whiteness' as humane.

Recognition as metaphoric control

Recognition of Indigeneity is an institutional expression that asserts control through objectifying the Indigene. While there may be a degree of accommodation of the 'Other', including through allowing Indigenous communities to submit evidence on the nature of their culture and laws, the 'white' court is the ultimate arbiter of acceptable Indigeneity. Michael Dodson, a Yawuru man from Broome, Western Australia, maintains that recognition is a tool of the colonizer:

> In the construction of 'Aboriginality' we have been objects to be manipulated and used to further the aspirations of other peoples. We are constantly defined as 'other', but we are never permitted to be genuinely independent, genuinely different. In fact, far from being recognised in our difference, in our own terms, we are always defined in terms of the colonising or defining culture.
>
> (Dodson 1994: 8)

Representations create their own meaning beyond their object, including meanings about the subject (the recognizer) (Berger and Luckmann 1966: 96). Recognition is a metaphor for the power of the colonizer over the colonized. Pollock (1988: 6) argues that representation is not a mirror of the world, but refashioned and coded for social ordering. Without these representations, the colonizers' exclusive claim to govern loses its foundation. Representations of Indigenous people are a crutch for ongoing domination where the colonial order is incomplete. They arise from an anxiety about governance where there continues to exist competing claims to authority by Indigenous people. Psychoanalyst Kristeva (1991) observes that the strangeness of the 'Other' is the strangeness of the Self. In the Australian polity, this strangeness arises from the failure to reconcile Indigenous sovereign societies to the postcolonial legal system and government. Therefore, representations of the strange 'Other' are matched with fantasises of the universal and normal white Self (Hage 1998; Kristeva 1991).

Judicial representations of 'difference' are not simply constructed in relation to the Indigenous offender, but also the Indigenous community of which the offender is a member. In the courtroom the judge addresses the offender, but their representations of the Indigenous offender have much broader ideological meaning. Through their construction of Indigenous 'difference', sentencing courts provide a statement on the legitimacy of the Indigenous community. They variously liken the Indigenous community to a romantic ideal akin to the noble savage; deprive the community of its Indigenous status because it does not meet the classic Indigenous markers such as remoteness, or represent the community as so 'excessively' Indigenous that they offend non-Indigenous standards. In these respects, recognition is a screen for white civility, universality and righteousness.

Critiques of Indigenous recognition emerge in debates on native title (Dorsett 2002: 52; Young 2008; Amankwah 1994: 32; McLaughlin 1996; Povinelli 2002; Biber 2004), but are less developed in relation to criminal sentencing, notwithstanding the breadth and depth of Indigenous representations in sentencing precedent (e.g. *Neal* v. *The Queen* 1982; *R.* v. *Minor* 1992; *Fernando* 1992; *Wurramara* 1999). This is possibly because the purpose of sentencing is not to allocate rights, but to punish with greater or lesser severity. However, sentencing remarks are fertile sources for examining the contours of cultural legitimacy because crime provides a powerful metaphor for the control of the state over the Other. Punishment is a reaction to threats to social order *and* a means by which social order is constructed in the first place. This dual role of political power and affective legitimating of the legal system affirms the core beliefs of the normative society (Duff and Garland 1994: 32). Punishment thus asserts instrumental and epistemological control over the Other. The effect of punishment is to uphold the legitimacy of the white community and delegitimize the Indigenous community. The punishment of the Indigenous offender is a commanding 'crime metaphor' of the repressive relationship between the postcolonial state and the Indigene (Simon 2001–2: 1053).

The inscribing of Indigenous identity in sentencing remarks arises from multiple symbolic interactions between the judge and actors, including imagined participants, within and outside of the court. First, the judge collaborates with a class of professionals – lawyers, witnesses and experts – to determine the boundaries of Indigenous evidence. The establishment of Aboriginal legal services in the 1970s influenced these considerations, as did the ability for Indigenous people to serve as experts on their culture at this time (Faine 1993: 30; O'Shane 1992: 4; Douglas 2009: 181). However, their evidence was invariably filtered by the judiciary and constrained by laws on evidence and procedure. Second, the judge conducts a personal, one-way conversation with the offender. In handing down a sentence, the judge speaks directly and paternalistically to the offender, and often publishes remarks in the grammatical second person. In doing so, the judge may speak through the Indigenous community, such as stating that 'the community will be disappointed in your actions'. Third, the judge engages the public through the public theatre of sentencing and publication of reasons, which make sentencing 'probably the most public face of the criminal justice process' (Ashworth 2002: 1077). Judges increasingly seek to represent the public in handing down harsh sentences, which they communicate as something the public demands of them. Finally, in recent years judges communicate directly to the Indigenous community, especially where issues of Indigenous cultural practices, laws or political struggles have arisen. In the case of *The Queen* v. *GJ* (2005a), Martin CJ delivered his sentencing remarks in the Indigenous community of Yarralin to convey a message about the wrongfulness of the cultural practice of customary marriage (see Chapter 4).[3] These judicial interactions are compelling metaphors for the control of the court over Indigenous communities.

3 Subsequent to *The Queen* v. *GJ*, the judge publicly apologized for the leniency of the sentence, although not for his reasoning (Martin 2005: 12).

Same difference in sentencing: common law and statutory frameworks for recognition

Judicial recognition of Indigenous 'difference' arises from the same common law and statutory sentencing principles that apply to all (non-Indigenous) offenders. Where leniency is provided to Indigenous offenders because of their low socio-economic status, cultural practices or laws, it works within the Anglo-Australian legal framework rather than challenges it. Matters of culpability arising from group membership apply to all offenders 'with equal force' (*R.* v. *Gibuma & Anau* 1991: 349; *Rogers & Murray* v. *R.* 1989: 307). Recognition therefore involves the imposition of the common law while maintaining its relevance in a society of dependent cultures. Bourdieu (1987: 826, 845) considers that the *incremental* change within the common law historicizes the norm, while tying 'the present continuously to the past'. New information on Indigeneity is interpreted with orthodox sentencing principles (Shapiro 1972: 131). Accordingly, the long-standing principle in Australian common law of 'individualized justice' enables Indigenous factors to be recognized in the same way the courts take into account all relevant factors (*Wong* v. *The Queen* 2001: 611). This straddles a common law commitment to judicial discretion to account for all 'circumstances of the offence and the offender' (*R.* v. *Whyte* 2002: 276). The High Court notes that Indigenous 'difference' operates like any other variable in a judge's repertoire of sentencing considerations:

> The same sentencing principles are to be applied, of course, in every case, irrespective of the identity of a particular offender or his membership of an ethnic or other group. But in imposing sentences courts are bound to take into account, in accordance with those principles, all material facts including those facts which exist only by reason of the offender's membership of an ethnic or other group. So much is essential to the even administration of criminal justice.
>
> (*Neal* v. *The Queen* 1982: 326)

Discretion is applied on a case-by-case basis to determine whether Indigenous factors are relevant to reducing a sentence (*R.* v. *Woodley, Boonga & Charles* 1994). There is no special right of an Indigenous offender to receive leniency by virtue of Indigenous status alone (*Neal* v. *The Queen* 1982: 326). Courts invoke Indigenous factors only when the offender is a member of an Indigenous community *and* his or her offence or punishment reflects that membership (*Fernando* 1992: 63; *R.* v. *Minor* 1992: 190). In his article 'Customary Law: Is It Relevant?', Mildren J. (2008: 75) of the Northern Territory Supreme Court stresses that the court only considers Indigenous matters that are relevant to 'ordinary' sentencing principles. He describes the court's reasoning and process in the following way:

> Customary law or cultural practices sometimes provide relevant background material of a secondary fact to prove a primary fact which has traditionally

> been regarded as a mitigatory fact. For example, in cases involving 'pay-back' [Indigenous punishment], the relevant primary fact is that the accused has already been punished or in the future will be punished by others for his or her offence. The principle being invoked in such cases is that, to ignore this, it would expose the offender to an element of double punishment. In such cases the court applies exactly the same sentencing principles when sentencing an Aboriginal person as anyone else.
>
> (Mildren 2008: 73–4)

Against this common law backdrop, legislation across Australia enshrines normative sentencing principles, such as punishment, deterrence, rehabilitation of the offender, offender accountability, denunciation of the offender's conduct, community protection, and recognition of the seriousness of the offence and harm to the victim (see Crimes Act 1914 (Cth) s. 16A; Crimes (Sentencing Procedure) Act 1999 (NSW) s. 3A; Sentencing Act 1995 (NT) s. 5(1); Penalties and Sentences Act 1992 (Qld) s. 9(1); Crimes (Sentencing) Act 2005 (ACT) s. 7; Criminal Law (Sentencing Act) 1988 (SA) s. 10; Sentencing Act 1997 (Tas) s. 3; Sentencing Act 1991 (Vic) s. 5(1); and Sentencing Act 1995 (WA) s. 6 (hereinafter referred to by their abbreviated jurisdiction)). Courts are obliged to take into account these principles when sentencing the offender. The statutes also particularize some of the matters that judicial officers must take into account when passing a sentence. The statutes vary, but most include the maximum penalty for the offence, the nature of and harm caused by the offence, the identity and age of the victim, the offender's criminal record, character, age, intellectual capacity, prospects of rehabilitation and remorse (Cth s. 16A; NSW s. 21A; NT s. 6A; Qld s. 9(2); ACT s. 33; SA s. 10; Tas s. 9; and WA ss. 7 and 8).

Legislation gives courts wide discretion to take into account aggravating and mitigating factors relevant to the offender and the offence (Cth s. 16A(2); NSW s. 21A(1); NT ss. 5(2)(s), 6 and 6A; Qld s. 9(2)(r); SA s. 10(1)(o); and Vic s. 5(2)(g)). These factors increase or reduce a sentence respectively, and their content may or may not be specified in legislation. Indigenous background is not listed as a mitigating or aggravating factor in any statute, but may be relevant in interpreting the listed factors. Courts achieve a balance between legal and extra-legal factors (including Indigenous circumstances), based on an 'instinctive synthesis' whereby the sentencer performs a balancing act (*Wong* v. *The Queen* 2001: 611).[4] Australian legislation, along with common law principle (*Parker* v. *DPP* 1992), provides that imprisonment is a sanction of last resort (Cth s. 17A(1); NSW s. 5(1); Qld s. 9(2)(a); SA s. 11; Vic s. 5(4); and WA s. 6(4)). However, unlike

4 The notion of 'instinctive synthesis' accepts that there is not a decisive sentencing principle or factors in every case and the sentencing court subjectively and intuitively assesses the various sentencing principles and factors to 'take account of *all* relevant factors and to arrive at a single result which takes due account of all of them' (*Wong* v. *R.* 2001: 611; see also Edney and Bagaric 2007: 20).

in Canada, legislation does not promote non-prison sentences specifically for Indigenous offenders (see Criminal Code RSC, 1985 s. 718.2(e)).

In three Australian jurisdictions, legislation refers specifically to the offender's cultural background.[5] The ACT legislation provides that the court must consider whether the cultural background of the offender is relevant (ACT s. 33(m)). Courts in Queensland, when sentencing an Indigenous person, must have regard to submissions made by a representative of the community justice group in the offender's community, including 'any cultural considerations' (Qld s. 9(2)(p)). In the Northern Territory, a sentencing court may receive information about an aspect of Indigenous customary law, or the views of members of an Indigenous community, but only where certain procedural requirements have been fulfilled (NT s. 104A). More recently, and contrary to principles of individualized justice, in 2006 and 2007 the Australian Government passed the Crimes Act 1914 (Cth), s. 16A(2A) and the Northern Territory National Emergency Response Act 2007 (hereinafter, NTER Act) (Cth), ss. 90–1, which prohibit the use of 'customary law or cultural practice' in sentencing and bail considerations in Commonwealth and Northern Territory jurisdictions.[6] Notwithstanding these legislative restrictions, the Northern Territory Supreme Court has retained its discretion to consider cultural evidence by narrowly interpreting the legislation to apply only to establishing the objective seriousness of the crime, and not to establishing whether the offender had the predisposition to commit the crime and was of good character, likely to reoffend or be rehabilitated (*R.* v. *Wunungmurra* 2009). This indicates an attempt by the court to hold onto its tool to metaphorically govern Indigenous communities.[7]

Because judicial recognition of Indigeneity arises from sentencing principles provided by the common law and statutes, it is prone to misrecognition or non-recognition, as indicated by the prohibitions in the NTER Act as well as the courts' own reassessment of Indigenous circumstances. Indigeneity may also be deemed insignificant in light of increases to maximum penalties, mandatory sentences or the introduction of guideline sentences by the courts or parliaments. In the first instance, courts are required to give 'careful attention' to maximum penalties (*Markarian* v. *R.* 2005: 372). Where maximum penalties have increased, courts are expected to give effect to the legislature's intention that penalties should increase (*R.* v. *Way* 2004: 182). Second, mandatory prison sentences are

5 Different legislation applies to juvenile offenders, which tends to specifically accommodate Indigenous offenders. For example, the Youth Justice Act 2005 (NT) s. 4 requires courts to hand down sentences that are culturally appropriate, involves the youth's Indigenous community and provides young people with an opportunity to maintain their cultural identity. Section 81 provides that the youth's cultural background is considered in sentencing.

6 In 2012 the Federal Government repealed the NTER Act and inserted the equivalent prohibitive sections into the Crimes Act 1914 (Cth) s. 16AA.

7 However, the Northern Territory Supreme Court's narrow reading of the prohibitive section has not enabled cultural evidence to be taken into account to extend sentences where white people have intruded on Indigenous sacred sites (*Aboriginal Areas Protection Authority* v. *S & R Building & Construction* 2011).

part of the statutory framework in the Northern Territory and Western Australia, which precludes considerations of individual offender circumstances. In Western Australia, a person convicted of home burglary who is a repeat offender must be sentenced to at least 12 months' imprisonment and that sentence must not be suspended (WA s. 401(4)). In the Northern Territory, offenders convicted of aggravated property offences, certain violent offences and sexual offences must be sentenced to imprisonment (NT ss. 78B–78BB). Finally, provision for guidelines on prison sentences (also referred to as 'standard non-parole periods' or 'tariffs'[8]), which structure the incarceration period according to the type of offence and harm, exists in New South Wales (ss. 37–37A, 39A, Pt 4 Div. 1A Table; and see *Jurisic* 1998), Western Australia (ss. 6(5), 143–143A) and South Australia (ss. 29A–B). These guidelines have had the effect of increasing prison sentences and discounting exculpating factors (Findlay 2006: 200–1).

While mandatory and guideline sentencing boldly registers the universalizing agenda of the criminal justice system, this agenda also emerges in the application of the same sentencing principles to Indigenous offenders as non-Indigenous offenders and generally through the universal application of the Anglo-Australian criminal jurisdiction. As early as *R.* v. *Murrell & Bummaree* (1836), the New South Wales Supreme Court regarded Indigenous and non-Indigenous people as equally bound to the colonial jurisdiction. The court averred that although 'the Blacks were generally considered as beasts of the forest', in the presence of 'the Almighty God' they are 'under the same divine protection as Europeans'. This mindset also emerges in ideas of assimilation that seek to integrate Indigenous people into a white normativity. Motha (1998: 86) maintains that recognition of Indigenous difference at law subsuming the particular Other in the general Self: 'The other is transported/transferred into an imagined we, a community wrought on the back of the erasure of particularity in the name of a universal, abstract commonality'. Asserting the same legal principles posits Indigenous law systems as just another sentencing factor, and furnishes a metaphor of a singular and universal white legal order.

Interplay between discretion to recognize and sentencing statutes

While statutes influence the length of sentences, courts are responsible for the ever-changing content of Indigenous recognition. Where punitive pressures for imprisonment prevail, the courts refashion the content of their discretion rather than dispense with it (Tata 2007: 437). They enable punitive discourses in recognizing Indigenous circumstances, allowing them to lengthen Indigenous

8 A 'tariff' presupposes that there is a normal range of sentences for a particular offence. Where such a tariff exists, sentences to be imposed by different judges or magistrates should fall within that range, unless the circumstances of the offence or of the offender are exceptional (Northern Territory Supreme Court 2009: 6).

sentences as much as shorten them. In sentencing Indigenous offenders, the courts respond to and shape the penal mood of Anglo-Australian society and attitudes towards alterity. They give expression to statutory objectives in the process of reinventing the Other. Therefore, discretion in sentencing does not defy statutory rules, as Kritzer (2007) and Aas (2005: 15) posture, but is inherent in the application of rules (Hogarth 1971: 360).

Moreover, where statutes impose restrictions on sentencing discretion, the courts jealously guard their liberty to recognize individual factors, especially where the restrictions appear impenetrable as with the NTER Act, s. 91 (see *R.* v. *Wunungmurra* 2009). However, they reserve the right not to recognize Indigenous background where the offender does not meet the courts' criteria for relevant Indigenous identity or where the court deems other sentencing principles (such as the seriousness of the offence) to be of greater importance. By leaving their 'personal signature' on the sentence and the boundaries of Indigeneity, the courts retain their authoritative role (Tata 2007: 426, 437). The next section evaluates the various and changing attempts by sentencers in the higher courts in the Northern Territory, New South Wales and Queensland to recognize Indigenous circumstances.

The guises of recognition

Recognition of disparate Indigenous experiences

The sentencing jurisprudence on Indigeneity has tended to polarize Indigenous experiences between those who have culture and those who have no culture. It overlooks the diversity of Indigenous cultural experiences (see Behrendt and Vivian 2010: 22). Tata and Hutton (1998: 354) claim that sentencers conceptualize cases according to 'familiar narratives' rather than the nuanced facts. Themes in Indigenous sentencing narratives reflect 'stock stories' – which are 'a set of standard, typical or familiar stories held in reserve to explain racial dynamics' – to sustain the status quo (Bell 2010: 29). When Indigenous circumstances are grounds for mitigation, because they reduce the moral culpability of the offender, courts draw on stock stories of the 'traditional' Indigenous person who practises pre-colonial culture or, alternatively, of the modern offender who is an outcast in postcolonial society by virtue of idleness, poverty and alcoholism. *Indigenous People, Crime and Punishment* explores both of these divergent stock stories in sentencing narratives. It bridges the schism between scholars on Indigenous sentencing who either focus on offenders from remote communities (e.g. Finnane 2006; Douglas 2009) or offenders from urban areas (e.g. Flynn 2005; Edney 2005). By addressing the various categories of Indigenous 'material facts', it is possible to reveal how the judiciary relies on notions of too little or too much culture. The recognized material facts are grouped accordingly:

- the existence of Indigenous laws and cultural practices;
- the dispensation of Indigenous law punishment by community members;

- severe disadvantage, endemic alcohol abuse and cultural breakdown;
- the detrimental impact of over-policing in Indigenous communities and its ensuing collective resistance.

Although these features of Indigenous communities emerge across various geographies, their recognition is tied to particular places and jurisdictions. The most extensive and long-standing sentencing jurisprudence on the practice of Indigenous laws and cultural practices is located in the Northern Territory, notwithstanding that these cases constitute less than 1 per cent of Northern Territory Supreme Court sentencing submissions (Goldflam 2012: 8).[9] The relatively late and sparse 'white' occupation of the Northern Territory in the 1860s and the moderate 'white' legal surveillance of Indigenous societies meant that Indigenous laws, including punishment systems, survived into the twenty-first century and shape the everyday experiences and social relationships of their members (Northern Territory Law Reform Committee 2003). Furthermore, the hundreds of Northern Territory remote Indigenous communities are isolated from Anglo-Australian influences, lying hundreds of kilometres out of cities and white towns.[10] The vast majority of their populations are Indigenous and primarily speak an Indigenous language. In terms of the postcolonial Indigenous experiences of dispossession and socio-economic disadvantage, the most cited precedent is in New South Wales in the form of the *Fernando* (1992) principles with respect to urban offenders. These conditions nonetheless pervade remote communities with increasing intensity and have precipitated a body of relevant jurisprudence in the Northern Territory. Finally, Indigenous political resistance, especially to police violence, is an issue in leading cases in New South Wales and Queensland due to the long and tense relations between Indigenous communities and police. These relations arise from the tight control of Indigenous people on colonial reserves and over-policing of contemporary Indigenous communities, culminating in deaths in custody. Each jurisdiction is affected by its own sentencing legislation and, as Downes and Rock (2007: 167) remind us, unique symbolic interactions in their particular court settings. Nonetheless, the purpose of this book is to convey changes in the particular recognition fact over time based on shifting penal paradigms.

Shifting penality

Sentencing discourses reveal a reconceptualization of Indigeneity since the late 1990s. This book seeks to compare this period with the preceding decades. In

9 The decisions of the South Australian, Western Australian and Victorian Supreme Courts are alluded to where relevant, but given their late development in Indigenous sentencing jurisprudence and their smaller case profile, a coherent body of jurisprudence is harder to isolate.

10 In the Northern Territory there are approximately 77 official Indigenous communities and 800 other Indigenous communities with populations of between 5 and 100 people (Northern Territory Road Safety Taskforce 2006: 38).

the case of the Northern Territory, the starting point is the 1950s when Indigenous culture was first regarded as a circumstance of mitigation, although the full potential of recognition was not articulated until the 1970s. In relation to New South Wales, its genesis was is in the 1970s, although reached its highpoint with *Fernando* (1992). Before the late 1990s, higher courts recognized that Indigenous community circumstances could reduce the offender's culpability, and therefore the severity of a penalty. Indigenous 'difference' was treated as a legitimate burden on social norms, but a burden nonetheless. Indigenous communities were imagined as objects of sympathy due to their primitive (yet cohesive) culture, uncivilized (yet restorative) punishment, hopeless economic conditions and political frustrations. However, in the past 10 years the higher courts have re-imagined Indigenous offenders and communities as dysfunctional or so entrenched in postcolonial society that they are no longer Indigenous. This condemning and concealing approach has been matched with more punitive sentences to emphasize the seriousness of the crime, to reinstate the interests of the wider community in imprisonment and to send a message of deterrence to the Indigenous community.

Lenience and the tolerant guise

The earlier mode of recognition expressed a tolerance, and sometimes celebration, of Indigenous 'difference'. Indigeneity was understood as a disadvantage for the offender who could not benefit from the social norms or economic opportunities of non-Indigenous society, caught in the cultural crossfire or prone to alcoholism. Alternatively, Indigenous cultures and laws were valorized where they could provide punishment that would return the offender to his or her noble, native roots and provide salvation. The courts placed Indigeneity in this light in order to rationalize the application of mitigatory principles. Culpability is reduced where the Indigenous circumstances disadvantaged the offender or reconciled the offender with his or her 'tradition'. Douglas's (2009) study on early Indigenous sentencing jurisprudence in the Northern Territory revealed how it germinated from the perception of cultural backwardness. The sole judge of the Northern Territory Supreme Court in the 1950s, Kriewaldt J., represented Indigenous culture as uncivilized. Accordingly, 'traditional' Indigenous offenders received more lenient sentences because their culture was perceived as 'a disability' that precluded 'self-control' (2009: 185, 80). At the same time, the court assumed non-Indigenous people to be in-control. While this dichotomy is inferred in 'cultural practice' cases, it explicitly emerges in 'riot' cases where the New South Wales and Queensland courts present Indigenous offenders as acting out a rage in response to over-policing and deaths in custody, while the courts conjure a fantasy of a reasonable and humane 'whiteness'. These courts romanticize the earlier days of protectionism where 'whites' controlled Indigenous people and kept their rage in check.

Returning to the Northern Territory, whereas Kriewaldt J. regarded 'civilized' Indigenous offenders, who had been exposed to Anglo-Australian culture, as unable to receive sentencing mitigation because they had benefited from that culture, his successors on the Supreme Court sympathized with the adverse effects of cultural *breakdown* and therefore factored it into mitigation (Douglas 2009: 170). The Bench considered civilisation as having brought 'social devastation' to Indigenous communities (2009: 170). This was especially from the 1970s when Aboriginal legal services began to represent Indigenous defendants and present submissions of this nature. By the early 1990s, this jurisprudence was also well established in New South Wales and other Australian states on socio-economic disadvantage as an explanatory factor for Indigenous crime. The synergies between Indigenous disadvantage and alcoholism were underlined by judiciaries across Australia. They regarded alcohol abuse as plaguing communities, and it became a signpost for 'Aboriginal cultural breakdown, social devastation and disadvantage' (2009: 170). This judicial imagining reinforces an iconic image of the 'drunken aborigine' that is a powerful tool of condescension. It frames Indigenous people as lacking control, discipline and civilisation (Langton 1993: 205). These representations also position Indigenous peoples as victims who are denied agency and capacity to manage their own affairs. Cowlishaw (1991: 107–8) asserts that arousing sympathy for Indigenous disadvantage entrenches 'dependence' rather than assists cross-cultural dialogue. Indeed, it maintains a fantasy of a tolerant whiteness bestowing kindness on a depraved Other.

Stronger penalties and the exclusionary guise

Since the late 1990s the higher courts have retreated from recognizing Indigenous 'difference' as a mitigating circumstance. Representations of Indigenous circumstances have been channelled into a concern that Indigenous communities present a *risk* to their members who are putative victims. This requires more severe sentences to reflect the seriousness of crimes in these 'dysfunctional' communities and deter their behaviours. Higher courts have privileged normative sentencing principles above moral culpability to subjugate Indigenous factors. In line with punitive ideologies that isolate offending from social context, these courts have increasingly cited the *seriousness of the offence* (hereinafter, 'seriousness') as the foremost sentencing principle. The definition of seriousness is not clearly stated in principle or legislation (Edney and Bagaric 2007), but for Indigenous offenders it is progressively associated with harm or potential harm (e.g. *Wurramara* 1999). It is referred to as 'objective seriousness' to imply a rational calculation of the scale of harm (*The Queen* v. *Bara* 2006: [24]; *Mamarika* v. *Murphy* 2007: [80]; *R.* v. *Morgan* 2003: 542). It resonates with Bentham's (1962: 579–80) argument that punishment should be imposed through sanctions that are infinitely gradable to match seriousness.

Alternatively, criminologists and earlier judiciaries posit that culpability is a 'central dimension of seriousness' and 'racial' context can thus reduce seriousness (von Hirsch 2004: 361; *Neal* v. *The Queen* 1982: 325; Easton and Piper 2005: 60; *Veen* v. *The Queen (No. 2)* 1988: 477). Otherwise, seriousness based exclusively on harm presumes individuals to be autonomous and rational agents and neglects the fact that 'strong social disadvantages may be at the root of much offending' (Ashworth 2005: 86; Duff 1998: 149; Ashworth 2002: 1106). Correlating seriousness with harm coheres with the current judicial emphasis on deterrence that assumes 'more prison equals less crime', and neglects factors impinging on choice (Lacey 1988: 59–61; Bauman 2000: 137; Hudson 2006b). The doctrines of seriousness and deterrence are not so much rational as they are rationalizing by enforcing the criminal law's blind universality (Norrie 2001). Indigenous considerations are a casualty of the harm-based approach that relies on decontextualized sentencing approaches. Offenders whose behaviour is shaped by cultural values or community pressures fit uncomfortably in a model that assumes individual autonomy.

A parallel sentencing principle, which crystallizes seriousness, is the interests of the victim. Pratt (2008: 271–2) asserts that 'victimisation is seen as a particularly authentic expression' of a 'new mode of knowledge'. Victimization is measured by the 'objective' harm to the victim, making it inseparable from the notion of seriousness. However, victimization provides an emotive tone to the sentencing process, not conveyed by seriousness. It incites empathy and shocks the senses by symbolizing the victim's harm as inflicted on 'one of us' (Garland 2001: 11). The victims invoked to justify greater penal severity are 'ideal victims' who are 'a category of individuals who – when hit by crime – most readily are given the complete and legitimate status of being a victim' (Christie 1986: 18). They are signified by weakness and have a virtuous character (Crenshaw 1991: 1278). When raised in Indigenous cases, the ideal victim embodies the morality of the white community who is affected by the risk of the Indigene.

While principles of seriousness, deterrence and victimization have long-featured in sentencing, in recent years they have been applied to recast the recognition of Indigenous community influences. The effect has been not only to undermine Indigenous factors in reducing culpability, but also to ascribe harmfulness to Indigenous cultures and communities in the following ways:

1. The practice of 'traditional' Indigenous cultures in remote communities is perceived as violent and victimizing, thus requiring a special deterrent message through harsher sentencing (see Chapter 4).
2. 'Traditional' Indigenous punishment is regarded as inimical to the maintenance of law or restoration of Indigenous communities and is more akin to retributive practices and contributes to their problem of violence, requiring a deterrence message (see Chapter 5).
3. Indigenous community circumstances pose harm to police in 'riot' cases (see Chapter 7) or harm to potential helpless victims in 'dysfunctional' communities (see Chapter 6).
4. Offenders from urban Indigenous communities are sufficiently 'assimilated' to know better than offenders from remote communities to commit crime, and due to their awareness, their crimes are grave (see Chapter 6).

Across these re-imaginings of Indigeneity there is a tendency for the higher courts to perceive the Indigenous community to either conform to Anglo-Australian social norms by expressing too much culture, or reject Indigeneity for failing to meet the Indigenous cultural preconditions set by Anglo-Australian courts. In other words, the courts are either *refusing the tradition* of the Indigenous community because it is not appropriate or *denying the tradition* because it is 'not really traditional' (O'Malley 1996: 319). Motha (2005: 119) has argued that Indigenous culture is either prone to a view that it is too 'repugnant' to be recognized or otherwise prone to disappearance because it does not meet the 'condition-precedent' for recognition. This is the paradox, or 'cunning', of recognition gestures that expect Indigenous people to alter their 'problematic culture' to fit 'modern' legal norms while ensuring their culture is 'traditional' (Motha 2007: 80; Povinelli 2002). In relation to the first requirement of a proper culture, the courts have painted a picture of Indigenous cultures as affronting the social and moral order of the wider community. Courts have shifted from depicting Indigenous communities as functional and legitimate and towards portraying them as dysfunctional and harmful. Offenders are cast as both a product of and contributor to the dysfunction. The extenuating effect of Indigenous community circumstances on sentences has been diminished because these communities require deterrence messages that are delivered through imprisoning the offender. Any beneficial effect that Indigenous cultures and laws have on restoring the offender and community are dismissed in favour of a view that they have a criminogenic effect and the community is without regard for its victims. In doing so, the courts also reinforce the dominant white narrative about Indigenous inferiority and barbarism. This view coincides with recent public moral panics over Indigenous communities that have focused on their violence and dysfunction.

This recharacterization is not necessarily due to a change in the nature or extent of the crime, but a change in the perception of Indigenous law and culture. For example, whereas once Indigenous punishment (which can include hitting and spearing) was regarded as capable of co-existing with Anglo-Australian punishment due to its role in restoring the Indigenous community and offender (*R.* v. *Minor* 1992), it is now seen as contributing to violence in communities (*The Queen* v. *Webb* 2003). In this way, Indigenous culture is treated as a crime problem in itself and out of sync with social norms in the wider Australian community. In addition, the impact of colonization and dispossession that was relevant to reducing an offender's culpability (*Fernando* 1992; *R.* v. *Davey* 1980) has been overshadowed with a focus on the relationship between community dysfunction and offending (*Amagula* v. *White* 1998; *Wurramara* 1999). Indigenous behavioural problems, particularly a lack of self-control, explain offenders' crimes and rationalise harsher sentences in the name of community reform.

On the second reinvention of the terms of Indigeneity, courts have refused to recognize Indigenous offenders from urban communities that they regard as no longer 'Indigenous enough' to be relevant to sentencing (Flynn 2005). The New

South Wales Court of Criminal Appeal from the late 1990s has distinguished these communities from remote 'traditional' communities that fulfil the cultural condition precedent. It draws on *frozen in time and space* notions of culture that are based on a Western sense of authenticity (Cunneen 1992: 11). The court has also called into question the relevance of a part-Indigenous background (*Ceissman* 2001: 540). This judicial limitation rules out a majority of Indigenous people living in non-remote communities who identify as Indigenous and retain cultural links.[11] Indigenous scholars have stressed that urbanization does not obliterate culture and that culture is an experience that cannot be measured as more or less (see Langton 1981; Behrendt 1994; Heiss 2012). The denial of Indigenous identity is contrary to rights to self-determination under international law (see UN Declaration on the Rights of Indigenous Peoples Art. 33(1)). In Australian constitutional and race discrimination law, the High Court and Federal Court have determined that Indigenous identity is based on self-identification, Indigenous community acceptance and Indigenous descent, rather than on geography or skin colour (see *Eatock* v. *Bolt* 2011: 539; *Shaw* v. *Wolf* 1999; *Gibbs* v. *Capewell* 1995). The New South Wales Court of Criminal Appeal's reasoning is based on an 'imaginative geography' which, according to Said (1978), instils a concept of space based on colonizing ideologies.

The Court of Criminal Appeal has instead invoked a form of neo-traditionalism, which is also very much alive in relation to native title determinations. There is a rich literature on the requirement of traditionalism in native title jurisprudence. Claimants in native title cases following the landmark decision of *Mabo* (1992) have been denied native title rights because courts found that their practices were inconsistent with pre-colonial culture. Courts have determined that Indigenous culture had been 'washed away by the tide of history' (*Members of the Yorta Yorta Aboriginal Community* v. *Victoria* 2002: 463 (hereinafter, '*Yorta Yorta*')). They took a narrow view of Indigenous communities' capacities to adapt their laws and cultures to colonial cultures and influences. The High Court in *Yorta Yorta* (2002: 443) drew a rigid line between the traditional and the modern in refusing to give effect to 'rights or interest in land created after [English] sovereignty'. Povinelli (2002: 267) argues that such judicial approaches are based on appropriating 'abstracted anthropological models' to reclaim the authentic Indigenous community.

In criminal sentencing, the imposition of cultural-spatial requirements on defendants who are relying on their Indigenous identity to evidence socio-economic disadvantage rather than the continuation of their culture is incongruous. The new threshold of 'remoteness' applies to Indigenous defendants seeking mitigation based on the 'grave social difficulties' arising from their membership

11 Most Indigenous Australians live in major cities and regional areas. In 2011, an estimated 32 per cent of Indigenous people were living in major cities, 43 per cent in regional areas (21 per cent in inner regional areas and 22 per cent in outer regional areas) and only 25 per cent in remote areas (15 per cent of which were in very remote areas) (Australian Bureau of Statistics 2011c).

of an Indigenous community, including due to dislocation from their culture (*Fernando* 1992: 62). Nicholson (1999: 86) points out that requirements of authenticity and remoteness are irrelevant in relation to mitigating factors based on cultural breakdown, disadvantage and the 'mass post-traumatic stress syndrome' arising from colonization. Further, these cultural requirements misapprehend 'the nature of Indigenous identity in a postcolonial society' (1999: 85–6). Ruling out postcolonial Indigenous factors allows the court to impute white rational choice to Indigenous defendants on the basis that they are the 'same' and punish them for not properly exercising their choice.

The confinement of the class of Indigenous people who can rely on recognition in criminal sentencing has not resulted in the judiciary disavowing the recognition pursuit. To refrain from a recognition agenda would militate against the control that enables the courts to delineate the boundaries of legitimate Indigeneity. Biber (2004: 6) explains that the power to recognize the existence of the Other is also the power 'to refuse to recognize, to exclude from recognition, to dispossess, to disentitle, and to extinguish'. She states that 'this is the seamless violence of the common law, where Indigenous people are "recognized" only when the colonist can always opt not to see them' (2004: 6). Sentencing courts have not ruled out Indigenous considerations, but narrowed the prerequisites of recognition. They have held on to their capacity to recognize Indigenous difference in order to retain their metaphoric licence to govern and, in doing so, to assert the righteousness of Anglo-Australian values against Indigenous laws, cultures and communities.

Vignettes and rationales of analysis

This book conceives the criminalization of Indigenous people as a racializing process with deep historical roots. It therefore is *not* chiefly concerned with the extent of Indigenous offending, the reasons for offending, rates of incarceration or the length of Indigenous sentences. It regards offending as knowable only because hegemonic institutions classify it as such (see Cunneen 2011: 258). Clearly in this analysis, the cultural, economic and political influences on the defendant come into play as they inform the defendant's argument for a reduced moral culpability. But these factors – which place stress on the offender or inform his or her beliefs – are distinct from the reasons for offending that amount to a defence. The inquiry pursued in *Indigenous People, Crime and Punishment* is how the postcolonial criminal justice system controls Indigenous people through epistemic processes. In this respect, sentencing is conceived as a metaphor for the relationship between the postcolonial state and the Indigene. This book analyzes representations of Indigeneity by sentencing courts and contends that higher courts have handed down longer prison sentences based on a reconceptualization of the Indigenous community in the past decade. It contributes to postcolonial criminology that historicizes and contextualizes criminalizing processes and their role in subjugating Indigenous legal systems and societies. Also in the spirit of postcolonial criminology, this book highlights how Indigenous law systems coexist with Anglo-Australian criminal justice and resist its monopolizing imperative.

Unlike purely empirical inquiries that mask the colonizing process of criminalization, this book examines sentencing with a view to exposing its role in subjugating Indigenous 'difference' through its qualitative remarks. Chapter 3 critiques these empirical approaches that are wedded to criminogenic understandings of Indigenous offending and make invisible the role of criminalization in dispossessing and inferiorizing Indigenous people. It enunciates the limitations of a debate on statistics that de-historicizes racial relations. Chapter 2 historicizes the role of punishment and explores the multiple manifestations of criminalizing Indigenous Australians since British colonization in 1788. It argues that contemporary punishment has transcended distinct legal frameworks for capturing Indigenous offenders (such as under the Aboriginal Protection regime in the nineteenth and early twentieth centuries) and moved beyond summary punishment by execution (which took place on the frontier). However, the over-criminalization of Indigenous people has continued despite the application of neutral rules.

The substantive chapters of this book are organized thematically according to recognized Indigenous circumstances: cultural practice, Indigenous punishment, socio-economic disadvantage, dispossession and political protest. These recognition typologies are relevant to explaining the offender's culpability. Each chapter contextualizes an individual recognition theme within the histories of particular communities and the moral panics over Indigenous criminality. By drawing on sentencing remarks over several decades in the higher courts of the Northern Territory, New South Wales and Queensland, it identifies a longitudinal commonality in penal discourses. There is a shift away from Indigenous circumstances producing leniency and a re-imagining of the Indigenous community as a site of risk. This book shows that the higher courts' narrative on Indigeneity is more than a response to a particular community, crime problem or jurisdiction. Rather, recognition has been reconstituted to transform Indigenous communities in line with white social norms.

Chapter vignettes

The first substantive chapter, Chapter 4, analyzes the sentencing of Indigenous offenders who commit crime due to a belief that it is in accordance with Indigenous custom. With a focus on the remarks of the Northern Territory Supreme Court, this chapter traces the judicial developments from the 1970s to the early 1990s when culture was treated as a mitigating factor because the court acknowledged the relevance of community membership, cultural practice and community expectations for reducing culpability. The chapter then traces sentencing narratives over the past decade that have sought to deter Indigenous practices in remote communities, especially customary marriages. They are represented as repugnant, outmoded and precluding liberal opportunities for women in an imagined market economy. The court speaks especially for the 'ideal' victim and the wider community in handing down longer prison sentences. The cases discussed in Chapter 4 were met with a moral panic in the media over Indigenous culture and violence, which is explored in the latter part of this chapter. The government echoed judicial representations of harmful Indigenous cultures, while also attacking the courts for not punishing severely enough (see Roberts *et al.* 2003). This culminated in legislation that prohibited customary law and cultural considerations in sentencing, outlawed under-age sex in Indigenous marriage and intensified policing and restrictions on rights to land, governing councils and welfare in Indigenous communities (see, e.g. the NTER Act).

Turning to Indigenous punishment administered by the Indigenous community on the defendant, Chapter 5 analyzes the corpus of Northern Territory Supreme Court cases where community submissions have sought to reduce imprisonment to account for community disciplinary measures. In these instances the punishment includes exile from the community, shaming, supervision by Elders, hitting and spearing in the leg. In the past the infliction of Indigenous punishment has been a significant mitigating factor because it reconciled the Indigenous community and restored the offender. Among these cases, there have also been instances in the 1980s and 1990s where the court has ordered Indigenous punishment to go ahead under 'supervision'. The Indigenous community was represented as possessing functional laws that could provide salvation to offenders who have been caught in the grander scheme of cultural breakdown. In more recent years, the court has been less inclined to reduce a sentence based on Indigenous punishment because it no longer credits such punishment with a restorative role, but casts it as a threat to white standards. The interests of the wider community in imprisonment prevail over the interests of the Indigenous community in their 'traditional' punishment. The Northern Territory is the locus of this chapter because of the Supreme Court's enduring consideration of Indigenous punishment in both sentencing and bail. There is a discussion on the latter to highlight the retreat from granting bail based on the community's and defendant's interest in Indigenous punishment being carried out immediately to repair relations severed by the crime. This chapter also considers media and political representations of Indigenous punishment that have pre-empted the above-mentioned legislative restraints on customary law considerations in bail and sentencing decisions.

Refocusing attention to the problems presented by colonization, Chapter 6 considers the recognition of disadvantaged and dispossessed Indigenous communities where alcohol abuse abounds and fuels criminal offending, according to the courts. In many respects this is a classic stock story of Indigenous crime in postcolonial society. The chapter draws on New South Wales case law because of the New South Wales Supreme Court's seminal sentencing remarks in *Fernando* (1992), which identified the predicament that Indigenous people faced in postcolonial communities. Less than a decade later, however, the Supreme Court and Court of Criminal Appeal renounced the relevance of Indigenous circumstances in urban environments. These offenders were regarded as 'not sufficiently Indigenous' to warrant recognition in sentencing because they were not from remote communities. The chapter also discusses the Northern Territory Court of Criminal Appeal's re-characterization of remote Indigenous communities as not merely disadvantaged, but dysfunctional, which has had the effect of increasing the punishment for offenders from these communities. They have emphasized the seriousness of offences by pointing to the particular harm faced by victims in Indigenous communities and how the wider community seeks imprisonment for serious offenders.

The final substantive chapter, Chapter 7, analyzes the sentencing of Indigenous defendants convicted of riot and assault for protesting against institutional racism. It considers the only High Court sentencing remarks on Indigenous mitigating factors, where the offence of assault, involving spitting at a government official, was provoked by attempts to undermine Indigenous governance of a reserve (*Neal* v. *The Queen* 1982). In that case a number of judges considered the relevance of responses to racial tensions and paternalistic state control as mitigating factors. The chapter then adumbrates recent sentencing remarks for Indigenous 'rioters' responding to deaths in custody in New South Wales and Queensland. The courts have proclaimed that a death in police custody is *not* a relevant sentencing fact where a serious crime has ensued, especially given that the police were targeted. They classed the Indigenous defendants as members of out-of-control communities that require a strong message of deterrence through harsh sentences. The courts and the media valorized the role of the police, and classed them as ideal victims to underscore the harm inflicted by the rioters.

The concluding chapter returns to the idea that recognition is a one-way knowledge stream that affirms the privileged position of the recognizer over the Other. In reflecting on the Indigenous sentencing vignettes, it underscores the weaknesses of recognition gestures that provide an unstable semblance of justice for Indigenous people and reinforce their subordinated position. Fraser (1996) informs us that 'affirmative' acts of recognition are prone to collapse because the affirmation relies on the benevolence of institutional privilege. Courts tap into dominant white truths about the Indigenous community being part of the crime problem rather than part of its solution. The engagement of the Indigenous community in justice strategies challenges the power relations that underpin judicial recognition. On this premise, this chapter looks to transformative concepts of justice that give expression to the Indigenous domain and utilize alternative Indigenous sentencing courts and processes. This involves transforming the underlying 'cultural-valuational' patterns by enabling Indigenous people to participate as 'peers' in socio-legal life and deconstructing structures of white authority (Fraser 2004: 29).

Rationale and limitations of methodology

The authority and discretion of higher courts means that a qualitative analysis of their sentencing remarks provides insights into much more than the severity of the penalty and the application of rules.[12] While their observations on Indigenous 'difference' augment sentencing precedent on relevant 'material facts', such observations have broader social significance. The courts' published remarks on Indigeneity are fodder for the tabloid press and political debate. Sentencing remarks are analyzed in this book as a series of postcolonial institutional metaphors, signifying the state's relationship with the colonized. In analyzing the jurisprudence on sentencing Indigenous offenders in appellate courts over the past 50 years, this study seeks to identify patterns of recognition of the colonized. It draws a delineation between earlier remarks and the narratives that gird harsher penalties over the past decade. This timeline was discerned from an extensive reading of the Australian sentencing archive, rather than the punitive turn that Garland (2001) discerns in the United Kingdom and United States from the 1970s. Indeed, it is questionable whether harsher penalties in courts, along with the annexation of Indigenous communities in the Northern Territory, denote a 'turn' or are merely an acceleration of the intense criminalization and control of Indigenous people since colonization. There are cases where Indigeneity remains grounds for reduced culpability due to the unique factual fabric of the case and emerging areas of recognition in some jurisdictions.[13] However, these exceptions to the penal tide reinforce this book's central claim about the pliability of judicial recognition.

This analysis of sentencing remarks is supplemented with a textual examination of legislation, ministerial comments, media reports and secondary sources. It is no coincidence that the judicial rewriting of the preconditions of Indigeneity overlapped with the ushering in of a conservative government in 1996 that held power until 2008. Although this book's primary endeavour is to expose the changing judicial politics on cultural difference, it touches on the state's characterizations of Northern Territory Indigenous communities in its assertion of a new control agenda and the moral panics over Indigenous crime. The Commonwealth Government has perpetuated the courts' re-imagining of alterity

12 In a few instances in this book, appeals to a New South Wales District Court are discussed to illustrate the sentencing ideology in the absence of higher appeals. These remarks were reported in the media and therefore had political currency beyond their individual decisions.

13 E.g. the Supreme Court of Victoria has accounted for an Indigenous offender's membership of the Stolen Generations (*R.* v. *Fuller-Cust* 2002: 523; *DPP* v. *Wilson* 2002; *R.* v. *Wordie* 2003: [31]; *R.* v. *Taylor* 2005: [14]). The Stolen Generations comprise Indigenous people who, when they were children, were removed by government authorities from their families. It affected several generations of Indigenous peoples until the 1960s. It was part of a concerted policy by Australian governments to assimilate Indigenous people. The Victorian Supreme Court's recognition contrasts the approach by the New South Wales Court of Criminal Appeal that has deemed such membership as irrelevant to sentencing (see *R.* v. *Newman, R.* v. *Simpson* 2004: 385).

by characterizing Indigenous communities as dysfunctional and their customary laws as a threat to victims and communities, while restricting judicial capacities to recognize culture.

In reading judicial and extra-judicial sources I am influenced by my experiences in the Northern Territory, especially in the Warlpiri communities of Lajamanu and Yuendumu in the Tanami Desert. Talking to Warlpiri people and participating in community meetings have shaped my ideas about the justice and governance capacities of remote Indigenous communities. Since 2008 I have observed Northern Territory magistrates' courts and had meetings with Warlpiri people as well as the police, prosecutors, magistrates and lawyers from the North Australian Aboriginal Justice Agency and the Central Australian Aboriginal Legal Aid Service as well as staff from government departments and Indigenous non-government organizations. This was part of research on policing Indigenous space and ceremonies (see Anthony and Chapman 2008), the criminalization of Indigenous drivers under the Northern Territory Intervention (see Anthony and Blagg 2012) and Indigenous stolen wages (see Anthony 2007, 2012). Nonetheless, it gave me insights into the significance of Indigenous laws in Indigenous communities, their ways of doing justice and, relevant to this book, the dynamics of the courtroom in dealing with offenders in remote communities. It left a lasting impression on the strength and cohesiveness of these communities, their deep and intimate concern for the well-being of their members, their great sense of justice and their tireless efforts to acquire respect for their law from white authorities in the face of ongoing attempts to undermine Warlpiri law. This informed my reading of contemporary representations of Indigenous circumstances in sentencing. However, as a non-Indigenous Australian researcher (of Greek and Cypriot heritage), I bring a set of worldviews and methodologies in reading these sources that constrain my capacity to deconstruct their meaning from an Indigenous perspective. I therefore consciously direct my research to acquiring a sense of the evolving judicial ideologies in relation to Indigenous communities and practices rather than speaking for Indigenous people. My concern is to assemble a critical account that acknowledges the weakness of judiciaries to make substantive truth claims in relation to the colonized.

A methodology that attempts to compare cases across time and themes is not without its problems. There are a range of variables that muddy a 'before and after' comparison. For example, the character of offences before the Northern Territory Supreme Court has changed. There are a number of key statutory rape cases that were among the first of their type to go before the court due to the use of police discretion and legislative provisions for under-age sexual relations within Indigenous marriages (see Chapter 4). These are particularly shocking crimes with grave consequences for the victim and it could be argued that their nature attracted harsher penalties. In attempting to show that the judicial reimagining of the Other is more than a response to a particular set of facts, each chapter uses a case profile that is broader than one type of offending. While the exceptionally serious cases most clearly elucidate the court's new narrative on alterity, this narrative has since been applied more broadly. An ancillary methodological limitation of the diverse facts of the cases is that this book's themes overshadow the complexity of Indigenous circumstances and their bearing on offending. Such circumstances cannot be broken down into discrete factors. Each chapter's concern with one aspect of the Indigenous context is in large part due to the recognition focus of the sentencing courts, especially if the matter is on appeal because the particular circumstances were not properly accounted for in sentencing. Lastly, because sentences rely on a range of factors, the focus is on the rhetorical conceptualization of the Indigenous circumstance rather than the sentencing outcome.

By virtue of its case method, this book runs the risk of painting a picture of Indigenous offenders as predominantly violent, or even Indigenous people as violent. The cases discussed in this book are mostly (although not exclusively) dealing with defendants who have committed *serious* violent or sexual crimes against family members (which is also characteristic of the female victims of non-Indigenous offenders) as well as property and riot offences. The serious nature of these offences is a product of this study's focus on higher court sentencing remarks. In the Northern Territory, as with other Australian jurisdictions, only 3 per cent of offences are heard in the higher courts, with the remaining 97 per cent heard in the local courts (Northern Territory Department of Justice 2010: 88–9). Assault cases only come before the higher courts by way of an appeal. Based on data across New South Wales, Queensland, South Australia and the Northern Territory, the highest principal offences for an Indigenous defendant charged by the police are acts intended to cause injury and property offences, with both constituting approximately 30 per cent (Australian Bureau of Statistics 2012: 60). This is followed by public order offences (14 per cent), although the figures exclude public order offences and traffic offences where an infringement notice is issued (2012: 60).

The fact that *serious* violent offences are not the most common Indigenous acts criminalized makes the judicial comments on these crimes, particularly in relation to the offenders' communities and cultures, more powerful as metaphors. This, nonetheless, does not reduce the harm that they create for the victim and the Indigenous community. Family violence is deeply felt by Indigenous community members and has far-reaching ramifications for Indigenous values, laws and relationships. The victim and victim's family experience a profound sense of hurt and betrayal. Its devastating impact cannot be addressed through singling out the offender alone, but requires 'a holistic process of community healing' (Blagg 2002: 191). The facts outlined in some of the cases in the following chapters are extremely disturbing, and this book in no way seeks to justify these acts of violence or come to the aid of the perpetrators. In a similar study on the portrayal of Muslim people in the media, following the gang rapes by Muslim men, Dagistanli (2007a: 181) has explained that research into representations of the 'Other' in criminal sentences 'in no way diminishes the brutality of the crimes and the experiences of the victims, nor does it exculpate the perpetrators'. Its endeavour is 'to point out the ideological dimensions of the representations of the crimes' and 'to show the ways such representations function within a particular social and political context that exceeds the legal dimension of the cases' (2007a: 181). The function of Indigenous representations, this book argues, is to denigrate Indigenous communities and their role in the socio-legal order. Coupled with a comprehension of the seriousness of these crimes for the Indigenous community, deconstructing representations enables a dialogue on how the community may be ascribed a more productive role in healing beyond satisfying the wider community's hunger for retribution and imprisonment.

Conclusion: recognition and the reinvention of the terms of indigeneity

Judicial recognition provides a space for Indigenous engagement in criminal sentencing, but that space is continually constrained by the recognizer's claim to sovereignty. An incident of this constraint is the dark side to recognition that can lead to harsher penalty based on derisive representations of Indigeneity. Hay writes that mercy judgments uphold the sentencer's legitimacy and their capacity to punish. They reinforce 'bonds of obligation on one side and condescension on the other' (1975: 40, 48). The ameliorating effect of mercy is offset by the 'ever-present threat of malice' (1975: 62). The ruse of recognition in sentencing is that it can provide leniency when the Indigenous circumstances are viewed with sympathy and harsh penalties when they are viewed as a threat to social norms. The Janus-face of sentencers shows a face of leniency that basks in its humanity and morality in recognizing a wronged group and its cultural peculiarities *and* a face of penality that glares at difference with condemnation to rationalize its exclusion of a risk group. Rutherford (2000: 26) explains that there is a link between morality and aggression in Australian history, where the fantasized image of a benevolent Australia is inherent in the ability to deprive. Sentencing is a signpost of the morality of postcolonial institutions that is conditional and contingent on control. The tolerant judiciary ensures clemency is granted as easily as it can be denied.

Judicial endeavours to create and constrict the 'knowable truths' about Indigenous identity provides for metaphoric governance over Indigenous communities (Simon 2001–2: 1062). Dysfunctional, irrational or defunct Indigeneity are the latest manifestations of Indigenous recognition in the sentencing courts. These versions of the Other have enabled more severe punishment and symbolically narrowed the terms in which the Indigenous community can exist within the Anglo-Australian legal system. It undermines their claims to legitimate systems of authority and power that can coexist with Anglo-Australian institutions. Simultaneously, the Federal Government has seized control of Indigenous communities: epistemologically by representing them as a failure and their cultural practices and customary law as repugnant to Australian values, and instrumentally by annexing space in the Northern Territory and imposing restrictive controls over Indigenous communities and courts when sentencing Indigenous offenders. The more penal approaches to sentencing Indigenous offenders are therefore a metaphor for the state's punitive governance of Indigenous communities.

With more punitive approaches in higher courts, matters of moral culpability have been overshadowed by normative sentencing principles, including the seriousness of the offence, victimization and deterrence. Community submissions testifying to the reduced seriousness of the offence in the community context, or pointing to the operation of Indigenous punishment, have been overridden by a judicial genuflection to the interests of the wider community in longer prison sentences. Matters of culture, Indigenous punishment, disadvantage and racism continue to be recognized but in the framework of an Indigenous predilection to crime. The risk of the Indigenous offender attracts harsher sentences to deter the Indigenous community. Higher courts send a message that Indigenous culture and circumstances will not be tolerated. Where the Indigenous community is not regarded as dysfunctional, it is viewed as *non-functional*, with courts showing a tendency to deem urban Indigenous offenders as lacking requisite Indigenous characteristics. This tendency also rules out matters of culpability relevant to the Indigenous offender. These postcolonial imaginings of Indigeneity have limited the authorized space for Indigenous 'difference' in sentencing courts. They have placed artificial boundaries around communities and consequently created a more finite class of offenders who can activate mitigating principles (Edney 2006). This lifting of the cultural bar demonstrates how Indigenous status is susceptible to the courts' changing criteria and control agenda in sentencing.

The limitations of recognition should not suggest that benefits are not derived from recognition in sentencing, such as the capacity for promoting Indigenous welfare, facilitating restorative justice through diversion and granting latitudes for the role of Indigenous punishment (Finnane 2001: 308). However, as long as sentencing is the dominion of the recognizer, the recognized will always be at the behest of the recognizer's whims. Anglo-Australian courts determine and perpetuate the boundaries of Indigenous communities, cultures and laws, rendering any concessions at the margins of their criminalizing framework. As Dodson states, 'Indigenous people have been used to affirm the superiority of the colonizers' through a set of binaries:

> By our lack, we provided proof of their abundance and the achievements of 'progress'; by our inferiority we proved their superiority; by our moral and intellectual poverty we proved that they were indeed the paragon of humanity, the product of millennia of development.
>
> (Dodson 1994: 8)

The High Court's confirmation of the antimony between Anglo-Australian and Indigenous laws, where 'white' laws prevail (*Walker* v. *New South Wales* 1994), ensures that recognition is a one-way process based on transitory affirmation of the Indigene. It contrasts legal plurality that acknowledges the existence of multiple systems of authority. Dodson (1994: 8–9) argues that recognition 'translated and sanitised' through postcolonial norms precludes 'genuine difference' and 'independence' that would break down boundaries of 'identity, knowledge and absolute truth which give the subject a sense of power and control'. It denies 'reciprocal recognition and status equality', which can only be realized by transforming the power relations that underlie recognition (Fraser 2004: 29). Instead, it is the sentencing courts that have sought to transform the Indigenous community through greater penality. This has strengthened the introduced law by chiselling away at spaces of Indigenous accommodation.

Chapter 2

Historicizing colonial and postcolonial Indigenous crime and punishment

> [Indigenous practices] are consistent with a state of the grossest darkness & irrational superstition and although in some cases being a show of justice – are founded entirely upon principles particularly in their mode of vindication for personal wrongs upon the wildest most indiscriminatory notions of revenge.
>
> (*R.* v. *Murrell & Bummaree* 1836: 239, Burton J. notes)

Introduction

The criminalization of Indigenous peoples has been a means of control and containment since British colonization of Australia. Punishment of Indigenous peoples in the early colonial period involved violent displays that climaxed in public executions. Although the violence of the early years continues to haunt the criminalization of Indigenous people and criminal justice processes, overall the late nineteenth century saw a transformation of overt violence into 'epistemic violence' through the production of colonial knowledges and laws (Spivak 1988: 76). White claims to Australian land subjected the Other to an inferior and precarious position that could be undermined and obliterated (1988: 76). This book will shed light on the precarious subjectivity of Indigenous Australians in the process of criminal sentencing. Courts create knowledge of Indigenous peoples that fits within the normative postcolonial paradigm. These representations wax and wane between the judicial will to tolerate or exclude alterity.

As a context for the analysis of Indigenous representations in sentencing, this chapter examines the portrayal of Indigenous people on the frontier and in various colonial and state legislation governing Indigenous Australians. It relies on records of Aboriginal Protectors and legislators, media reports and personal accounts by settlers and Indigenous people. These sources reveal that from the late eighteenth century there were persistent attempts to 'eliminate, restructure and reconstitute Aboriginal identity in the interests of the colonizer' (Blagg 2008: 3). Key to this process is the classification of Indigenous people as 'criminal' as well as their instrumental criminalization and punishment. Punishing Indigenous people for colonial transgressions or simply because of their 'race' was intrinsic to 'obliging the native to cathect the space of the Other on his home ground' (Spivak 1985: 253). In other words, it forced the 'natives' to become outsiders and experience their home space as an imperial space.

This chapter does not endeavour to explain criminal offending per se, but to explore the processes for criminalizing Indigenous people, especially in northern Australia, and how they straddled broader control agendas in transforming the 'space of the colony into a colonised space' (Blagg 2008a: 131). On the frontier on the cusp of the nineteenth century, it was expedient to dispossess Indigenous people of their land through the violence of the free settler, military corps or under the governor's prerogative.[1] It was generally the squatters, who included wealthy pastoralists known as the 'squattocracy', who were given free rein to 'disperse' (violently eradicate) Indigenous people from their land (Kowald and Johnston 1992: 60). This was backed by a media campaign that depicted Indigenous resisters as outlaws. Crime was a mode of 'black subjection', but also ascribed the 'Other' with an agency of criminality – being the only form of 'agency recognised by law' (Hartman 1997: 41, 104). In all other facets of life and law Indigenous people were rendered helpless victims who were in need of salvation. Indigenous agents were a threat to the expansion of British colonial capital and the efforts of settlers in quelling this threat were part of the colonial pursuit.

When the colonial legislature and courts were established, they legalized the force inflicted on Indigenous people. Courts that handed down corporal punishment or ordered public executions for Indigenous people served to make an example of those who resisted colonization. For law-makers, like the punishment-administering settlers before them, Indigenous people were regarded as only capable of learning through might, and special provisions were inserted into criminal laws to allow whipping and other corporal punishment as a sentencing option exclusively for Indigenous people. Such countenances of the criminal law confirm Agozino's (2004: 344) suggestion that criminal justice is 'inherently a colonial enterprise' where 'repressive technology' is 'monopolised by imperialist countries'. The criminal justice system not only punishes Indigenous people, but strives to delegitimize Indigenous sovereignty through the practice of jurisdiction and authority (see Ford 2006: 107).

As these violent punishments went into decline, 'epistemic' violence involving the internalization of colonial knowledge became the new weapon of control. Indigenous people were detained in administrative and penal institutions and instruction and hard labour became the means for transforming Indigenous lives.

1 E.g. the 'black line' was instigated by Governor George Arthur in 1830 in Tasmania to remove Indigenous people from white settled areas. This involved a human chain of over 3,000 convicts, free settlers and troops that pushed Indigenous people out of the settled districts over a six-week period (Moses 2000: 99).

In the late nineteenth century and first half of the twentieth century, race-based legislation, known as the Aboriginal Acts, authorized detention on missions and settlements. Later, policies of assimilation placed Indigenous people in the purview of the police, making prisons the new enclave for Indigenous containment. The courts imposed prison sentences with reference to 'neutral' criminal laws, securing the normative colonial framework. Deterrence was a rationalizing, rather than rational, role of the postcolonial criminal justice system (Norrie 2001: 19; Agozino 2004: 345). Criminalization and imprisonment, as will be contended towards the end of this chapter, have ongoing implications for the management of Indigenous spaces and peoples. When the Indigenous legal domain shows resilience in the face of colonization, such as in the Northern Territory, the penal apparatus of the state has intervened to normalize and civilize.

Constructing the Indigenous criminal on the frontier

On the frontier, 40 years before the establishment of the colonial legislature and courts, punishment mostly took the form of summary justice and operated outside of the British rule of law (Bennett 1819: 96). Historian Rolls (1984: 77) wrote that during the colonial period, 'so much of Australia's history took place outside the law [that] there was more attempt to hide it than to record it'. While the heart and soul of frontier culture could be regarded as 'lawless', Ford (2006: 97) informs us that 'lawlessness' is a 'poor caricature'. This is because the unregulated engagement of settlers and Indigenous people had a productive purpose in fulfilling the 'work of empire' (2006: 97). Decentralized governance was an efficient means of seizing land. Initially, most land was acquired by squatters and they violently responded to Indigenous resistance, along with the assistance of the military in serious cases. These were 'governmental authorities' in their own right, but their exercise of 'governmentality' was not an affront to the sovereign state, but the embodiment of its power (Foucault 1979: 79).[2] The acts of free settlers in punishing Indigenous transgressions were a countenance of colonization and condoned by local British authorities. They were a demonstration of the might of the sovereign unleashed as 'cruel, savage, beasts' ready to launch punitive, even preventative or vengeful expeditions (Derrida 2009: 209).

The ramification of the devolution of punishment was that Indigenous people were subject to unrestrained brutality. New South Wales grazier Robert Scott in the 1830s commented that violence embodied 'our power to punish' and 'outrage' is apprehended 'in our first intercourse with the natives' (quoted in Harrison 1978: 22). Indigenous people were punished through harsh, sometimes fatal,

2 See also Agamben's (1998: 59) discussion on sovereignty as 'law beyond the law to which we are abandoned'.

means without trial or due process. In parts of northern Australia, this approach to punishment lasted into the twentieth century, notwithstanding the formation of courts, state police and later the Federal Parliament under the Commonwealth of Australia Constitution Act 1901 (Cth). In 1890 the South Australian Minister responsible for the Northern Territory, John Parsons, declared: 'Leave the native question alone and the natives will be obliterated' (quoted in Donovan 1981: 184). Protector of Aborigines for the Northern Territory, Edward Hamilton, set the tone for European-Indigenous relations in 1880 by arguing that a strict adherence to the letter of the law was unnecessary and the settler-pastoralist should 'not . . . be taught to rely on the Police' in punishing Indigenous people (quoted in Clyne 1987: 183). In safeguarding 'their' land, pastoralists often took matters into their own hands by personally administering punishment for trespass and interference with cattle.

By casting the Indigenous person as a violator of the colonial project, punishment was reasoned as a rational response. In contrast, the Northern Territory Office of the Government Resident (1929: 3) regarded courts and prisons as a blunt tool for deterring Indigenous people. Violent summary punishment was perceived as effective in sending a message to a 'primitive' race who could only understand their wrong by the immediate dispensation of physical force (Harrison 1978: 22). The *Northern Miner* defended settlers' shooting of Indigenous people to avenge crimes on the basis that 'the one argument a blackfellow understands is that delivered from a rifle or a six shooter' (Fitzgerald 1986: 206–7). The manager of an early Queensland pastoral station advocated shooting as the only punishment 'which Northern Queenslanders have never found to fail' (quoted in Kowald and Johnston 1992: 60). Edward Palmer (1903: 213) wrote in his observations on the settlement of Queensland: 'The pioneers cannot be condemned for taking the law into their own hands and defending themselves in the only way open to them, for the blacks own no law themselves but the law of might'. Indigenous laws, in fact, form strict regulatory systems for governing relationships to land, culture, kin and ceremony (Gaykamangu 2012: 238; Loy 2010). While they are not predicated on Western judicial and parliamentary frameworks or embedded in written texts, Indigenous laws have rigorously maintained the cohesiveness of Indigenous communities for tens of thousands of years (Gaymarani 2011: 283). However, the colonizers' denial of Indigenous systems of laws created a fiction of a homogenous order where only whites possessed law-making capacity.

These colonial imaginings of Indigenous lawlessness coincided with contemporary eugenicist understandings of criminals, marked by the emergent criminology of Cesare Lombroso in the nineteenth century. Biological backwardness of the darker races was grounds for inflicting the death sentence because they had no capacity for rehabilitation (Lombroso 1876/2006: 180). Lombroso (1876/2006) studied what he referred to as 'born criminals' by identifying prisoners' physical appearance and brain capacity. He asserted the ape-like atavism of 'born criminals' was evidenced inter alia by their darker skin and smaller brains. These 'racial' features resulted in criminals having 'primitive behaviour' and lacking remorse, moral indifference and indolence (Anthony and Anthony 2008: 44). Agozino (2004: 350) linked the rise of the discipline of criminology to 'a time that colonial administrations imprisoned most parts of the earth'. Colonial locations were regarded as lawless to justify the imposition of British law (2004: 347).

In colonial northern Australia, a central locus of this book, the government and media framed Indigenous people as barbaric due to their destruction of cattle (Anon 1884: 5). The alternative narratives about Indigenous people being deprived of their sustenance by the colonial land takeover and Indigenous views of animals on their land as part of their food chain were subverted. Hysteria over cattle killing and cattle theft fuelled a great deal of the settlers' punitive activity. 'Destructive and murderous blacks' were portrayed by pastoralists as one of the most serious threats to the emerging pastoral industry (Kelsey 1938: 400). This generated a moral panic which created hostility towards Indigenous people and enforced a white consensus on their criminality. Because of the immediate proximity of Indigenous people to pastoralists, the media promoted a view that pastoralists were best positioned to punish Indigenous crimes of 'larceny of beef' and 'killing cattle' (Anon 1899: 4). Constable Willshire (1896: 43) justified shootings by station owners in response to cattle offences on the grounds that they really knew the 'wild natives'. Northern Territory explorer and pastoralist Nat Buchanan remarked:

> Every man was his own policeman; and the letter of the law was often ignored in favour of summary justice . . . [T]he white man far removed from the restraints of formal law sometimes perhaps rivaled his black brother in savage reprisal . . . Imprisonment for cattle killing was quite impracticable: and if no punishment were inflicted it would have been impossible to settle country.
>
> (Nat Buchanan quoted in Buchanan 1933: 117)

Any Indigenous person was a target in the pursuit to punish cattle killers. The killing of one beast could implicate the whole Indigenous group who would be rounded up and dealt with violently (Bolton 1981: 126). Some of these punitive episodes materialized in massacres such as the 'Sandover Massacre' in the Northern Territory in the 1920s that saw more than 100 Alyawarra people killed as the result of a station manager losing cattle (Johannsen 1992: 66; also see Askins 1965: 56; Elder 2003: 181–215; Green 1995). Reverend J. B. Gribble (1884: 206–7) wrote about Queensland settlers who would 'go out in parties fully armed' to pursue Indigenous cattle spearers and sheep stealers. Northern Territory Government Resident and Resident Judge in the late nineteenth century, Charles Dashwood, drew attention to the uncontrollable shooting of 'natives right and left' in response to cattle interferences (Select Committee on The Aborigines Bill 1899: 24). 'Swift retributive justice' continued into the twentieth century, according to Government Resident, C. E. Herbert, who found that it had 'beneficial effect' despite admitting that 'innocent persons have suffered with the [Indigenous] offenders' (Herbert 1907, 1905: 17). The Native Police Forces, consisting of Indigenous troopers under the authority of European officers, were also responsible for some of these unrestrained punitive expeditions in seeking to assist station owners, and were found to be 'completely out of legal control' (Select Committee of the Queensland Legislative Assembly Inquiry into the Native Force 1861, quoted in Rowley 1970: 161; see also Rusden 1883: 232).

By the twentieth century, especially when Indigenous people were employed in large numbers by pastoralists, the pastoralist's domain could be described as micro-jurisdiction in northern and central Australia. Pastoralists wielded power over Indigenous workers and their families on cattle stations. Their jurisdiction eluded governance by colonial and later state and territory administrations.[3] The remoteness of pastoral properties meant that they were often beyond the purview of central authorities. Parliaments generally sanctioned pastoralists' control of Indigenous people and their use of punishment (especially for trespass, cattle killing or where Indigenous people resisted employment) because of the productivity of pastoralism in the north and the civilizing effect of work for Indigenous people. Nonetheless, the pastoralists' domain would deliver some benefits for Indigenous people who were granted latitudes to participate in ceremonies and maintain cultural traditions where they conformed to the rules of the pastoralists by way of work and discipline (discussed below). For pastoralists, they prospered by producing a chiefly loyal and dependent Indigenous workforce by virtue of their connections to their land and kin on cattle stations (McGrath 1987). A legacy of the cattle era when Indigenous people lived together on stations is the continued practice of their laws and ceremonies today.

The authority of the police in the north was insignificant compared with that of the pastoralist. In 1899 there were 14 police in the Northern Territory, which spans 1.5 million square kilometres (Aborigines Select Committee 1899: 22). Much of this land was designated pastoral land. In the absence of police, pastoralists were made to deal with the 'natives' by taking 'the law into their own hands' (station manager quoted in Reid 1990: 119). This was especially so in the process of seizing land and suppressing Indigenous resistance. It has been noted in relation to northern Queensland that, while the police undertook their own punitive expeditions against Indigenous people, pastoralists took a much heavier toll on the Indigenous population, including killing them *en masse* such as at Cullin-la-Ringo in 1861 (Kidd 1997: 10; Palmer 1903: 213). After the land takeover, Indigenous people were initially forced to work for the white manager through violent means. The judicial system did not keep in check these depredations, due to their acquiescence to pastoralists' power, their influence in

3 The Northern Territory was annexed by South Australian administrators in 1863 and was transferred to the Commonwealth under the Northern Territory (Administration) Act 1910 (Cth).

parliament and the fact that courts in the north were not properly constituted until well after colonization (Gunn 1990: 141; Mildren 2011: 35). The Northern Territory Supreme Court was established under the Commonwealth's Supreme Court Ordinance 1911, and even then Justices of the Peace (who were often pastoralists themselves) continued to adjudicate day-to-day matters (Anon 1899a: 6H). Collecting sufficient evidence for a successful prosecution against pastoralists was also treated by the Northern Territory Government Resident as a futile task (Mildren 1994: 21; Austin 1988: 92). Therefore, even when punitive processes became formalized through the courts and the law evinced a semblance of normalization, it rarely intruded on the pastoralists' domains. This lasted well into the twentieth century in northern and central Australia.

Imposing British jurisdiction: land, sovereignty and crime

The codification of British rule in Australia provided a legal dimension to colonization. This took place irrespective of settlers and military officers remaining a law unto themselves. British laws were received in the 1820s in New South Wales, Australia's first colony, and almost 40 years after its colonization in 1788. The New South Wales Supreme Court formalized its exclusive criminal jurisdiction over Indigenous offenders in the mid-1830s. This paved the way for the normalization of colonial punitive authority over Indigenous people – at least outside of remote frontiers where punishment continued to be inflicted informally. The juridification of British domination through statutes, precedent and proclamations presented the appearance of resolution being achieved (or capable of being achieved) between the colonized and colonizer (Bourdieu 1987: 848). Through juridification power comes to operate as a 'self-evident and normal' dimension of everyday *habitus* (the dispositions that inform assumptions, knowledge and values) (1987: 848). The realization of British land takeover of the south-eastern coast in the 1920s was crucial to the normalization of colonial governance through laws rather than violence. It created 'illusions and impressions' about Australian space as universal British space, notwithstanding that most land remained occupied by Indigenous peoples (Hage 1998: 155). Overt violence outside of the law continued in the form of settler retribution for Indigenous resistance to land dispossession, including in northern Australia until the 1920s. However, towards the end of the nineteenth century, there was increasing recourse to the Anglo-Australian law to enforce punishment on Indigenous people. The imposition of the British legal system legitimated the subjugation of Indigenous people and their legal systems (Brogden 1987: 13).

A raft of British legislation introduced the Westminster system of centralized government to Australia. The New South Wales Act 1823 (Imp) established a Legislative Council and Supreme Court in New South Wales and Van Diemen's Land (Tasmania) and thereby replaced military rule in the colonies. The King's appointees would advise the New South Wales Governor in the exercise of his legislative powers and these decisions were subject to veto by the British government. The Chief Justice had oversight of all legislation to ensure it was consistent with English law. Colonial laws were received into British colonies under the Australian Courts Act 1828 (Imp). This was part of the Reception Acts, which implemented British law into the colony of New South Wales. It provided that all laws of England that were applicable to the new colony's circumstances were automatically incorporated into New South Wales and Tasmanian municipal law. It took 150 years later before it was declared that the Reception Acts operated retrospectively from 1788 – under the Imperial Acts Application Act 1969 (NSW) – reinforcing the artificial legal basis of British title against Indigenous possession.

The reception of English law gave the British Crown a supreme legal claim to land based on the doctrine of tenures. It meant all lands of Australia became in law the property of the King of England (*Attorney-General* v. *Brown* 1847: 317–18). Because 'feudal tenure' was 'universal in the law of England', the New South Wales Supreme Court in 1847 held that 'we can see no reason why it shall be said not to be equally in operation here' (1847: 316). Based on this feudal notion, all land holdings had to be traced to the Crown. Brennan J. in *Mabo* v. *Queensland (No. 2)* (1992: 46, hereinafter, '*Mabo*') articulated that 'every parcel of land in England is held either mediately or immediately of the King who is the Lord Paramount'. This meant that settlers required a Crown grant to validate their possession. Claims made otherwise, including where settlers had entered into treaties with Indigenous people (for example, the 1835 Batman Treaty in Victoria with the Kulin people) were invalidated because settlers did not have capacity to confer possessory title (Attwood 2009; Kenny 2008: 38.6). Indigenous rights to land ownership were nullified, although their legal status was not tested in courts until well into the twentieth century (see *Milirrpum* v. *Nabalco* 1971).

Courts dismissed challenges to Crown title brought by squatters, pastoralists and miners who sought to acquire land by means other than Crown grant. The Crown's superior title arose because the colony of New South Wales was held to be 'without settled inhabitants or settled law' when the British first occupied (*Cooper* v. *Stuart* 1889: 291). The Privy Council decision in *Cooper* v. *Stuart* symbolizes the fantasy of European universality that was espoused by colonial courts. Furthermore, the New South Wales Supreme Court in *Attorney-General* v. *Brown* (1847: 316) declared that since settlement the 'waste lands' of the colony were in the 'Sovereign's possession; and that, as his or her property, they have been and may now be effectually granted to subjects of the Crown'. The Crown, as the 'universal occupant', is guaranteed all titles (1847: 317–18). The myth of an uninhabited land arose from a Eurocentric view that Indigenous peoples were 'too primitive to be regarded as the actual owners and sovereigns' of the land (Reynolds 1996: x). It resonates with John Locke's (1924: 141) notion of 'just acquisition', later adopted by English jurist William Blackstone (1979: 104), that cultivation of land would 'first begin a title of property'. The New South Wales Supreme Court quoted Blackstone's commentary that the Crown has rights where colonial lands are 'desart [sic] and uncultivated' and all English laws are 'immediately' in force where lands 'are claimed by right of occupancy only' (see *R.* v. *Murrell & Bummaree* 1836; *Attorney-General* v. *Brown* 1847: 317–18). In these decisions, the court interpreted Crown title to land as arising from Indigenous inhabitants lacking numbers, civilization and proprietary rights sufficient to claim the land (1836: [211]; 1847: 317–18). By eliding Indigenous rights to land, the Crown could assert sovereignty and the 'genocidal dimension of settlement' could be rendered opaque (Havemann 2005: 63).

The repercussion of non-recognition was that Anglo-Australian criminal laws and courts had exclusive authority over Indigenous people. This included the authorization of exceptional types of punishment for Indigenous offenders. The universality of the Crown and its system of punishment ruled out Indigenous disciplinary processes coexisting with Anglo-Australian processes. Unlike in other British settled colonies such as Canada, New Zealand and the United States, where colonial governments entered into treaties with Indigenous people, in Australia the non-recognition of Indigenous people undermined legal pluralism in the formal sense. Officially, crimes could only be adjudicated by colonial courts in accordance with colonial laws rather than through Indigenous law systems. Therefore, for crimes committed by an Indigenous offender against an Indigenous victim ('*inter se* crimes'), they would be punished by the courts notwithstanding Indigenous community claims to authority over their members. Nonetheless, the policing of *inter se* crimes was not common in the colonial era where Indigenous communities functioned beyond the gaze of the police, allowing Indigenous law and punishment to persevere in remote areas (Finnane 2001: 303).

Indigenous defendants who had been accused of *inter se* offences contested the New South Wales Supreme Court's capacity to try and punish them. Their challenge to the court's jurisdiction was on the basis that they sought to be punished by their Indigenous laws. In *R.* v. *Murrell & Bummaree* (1836), the court denied the Indigenous defendants this right. At the trial of Indigenous defendant Jack Congo Murrell for the murder of an Indigenous man named Jabbingee, the defence argued that Murrell was not guilty but nonetheless he should be tried and potentially punished by his customary laws. His people lived in the white settlement of Windsor in north-west Sydney, where their laws continued to be practised. The defence further posited that New South Wales was occupied by Murrell's, and the victim's, people before the King of England and continues to be regulated by customary law. It argued that because New South Wales was not conquered, ceded or occupied exclusively by the British, Indigenous people were not bound by British law. Indigenous law should apply and if Murrell is found guilty, Jabbingee's family and friends should be entitled to punish him by customary spearing.

In establishing that it had jurisdiction to try Murrell and Bummaree, the Supreme Court held that Indigenous peoples are not 'entitled to be recognised' as 'sovereign states' that are governed by their own laws (*R.* v. *Murrell & Bummaree* 1836: [211]). This is because upon colonization they had not reached the 'numbers' and 'civilization' to form their own government and laws (1836: [211]). In the judgment notes, Burton J. juxtaposed the fair and rational common law guided by principles of equality and procedural fairness, against the 'practices' of Murrell's community that are based on notions of retribution. These practices 'are consistent with a state of the grossest darkness and irrational superstition'. They 'are founded entirely upon principles . . . of vindication for personal wrongs' and 'the wildest most indiscriminatory notions of revenge' (1836: 239–40). The court therefore justified the colonial usurping of Australian land by its perception that the land was without a sovereign (which is the only recognized form of Western authority and power) before it was taken into lawful and 'actual possession by the King of England' (1836: [211]–[212]).

Also in its judgment, the Supreme Court adopted a circuitous legal reasoning in relation to its jurisdiction. Burton J. held that the court had a right to try Murrell because 'this Court has repeatedly tried and even executed aboriginal natives of this Colony' (1836: 214). This has resonance with Bourdieu's (1987: 831) notion of 'symbolic violence' whereby categories of doctrine apply because people submit to them. The offender agrees 'to play the game, to accept the law for the resolution of conflict' in lieu of physical violence (1987: 831). As expressed in Murrell's case, jurisdiction was founded on the fact that the courts tried him and other Indigenous people before him. But to regard Indigenous submission to the judicial process as free choice neglects that British jurisdiction was predicated on force. Furthermore, the Supreme Court relied on the 'law of England' as the basis for rendering Murrell 'amenable to the Jurisdiction of His Majesty's Court of Kings Bench' (*R.* v. *Murrell & Bummaree* 1836: 213). This reasoning removed the need for explanation of why the English law prevails over Indigenous law in the first place. The court situated itself as law interpreter rather than law-maker so it could take 'refuge behind the appearance of a simple application of the law' (Bourdieu 1987: 823). This absolved the court and placed the source of British authority beyond challenge.

Legislated exceptionalism: punishment on the body

The introduction of British statutes did not instantaneously replace physical violence with symbolic control. Rather, legislation juridified force against the 'target' body (Foucault 1979: 82), by providing corporal punishment and public executions as sentencing options for Indigenous offenders. The former was specifically set aside for Indigenous offenders, while the latter was available for both Indigenous and non-Indigenous offenders. The British sovereign, its courts and police had a monopoly over legitimate violence by the late nineteenth century. Criminal law justified its ongoing infliction on the Indigenous body through the rational application of rules. Making an example of offenders through severe punishment enforced a 'policy of terror: to make everyone aware through the body of the criminal, of the unrestrained presence of the sovereign' (Foucault 1979: 49). Legalized terror was invoked where symbolic violence and strategies of self-discipline were ineffective in subjugating Indigenous souls. Therefore, unlike Foucault's concept, targeting the body was not mutually exclusive to targeting the soul because the colonizer was wrestling with an uneven colonial project.

The ultimate punishment that the colonial courts served was public executions, including public hangings for Indigenous people. In Western Australia, the Capital Punishment Amendment Act 1871 provided for the public execution of condemned Indigenous peoples. These executions lasted until the late nineteenth century, while they ceased for non-Indigenous people in most colonies by the 1860s. In jurisdictions where public executions were available for both Indigenous and non-Indigenous offenders, courts were more inclined to use these sentences for Indigenous people. Edmonds (2010: 151) notes that 'colonial officials designed these colonial exercises in terror specifically for Aboriginal people'. Public executions were sanctioned by the law and had important performative currency for the maintenance of the colonial state. The affective power of punishment in symbolizing 'the power of the sovereign over the subject' is set into sharp relief with public executions (2010: 151). For Foucault (1979: 48), the public execution is a ceremony that eclipses and restores the power of the sovereign by focusing all eyes on the 'invincible force' with which a rebellious subject is met.

The public nature of executions reinforced the social order, while keeping the Indigenous population in check. In sentencing an Indigenous offender to public execution, Stephen J. of the New South Wales Supreme Court pointed to the 'necessity of making examples' of Indigenous offenders (*Maitland Mercury*, 16 September 1843: 3, quoted in Harman 2008: 202). Stephen J. has been described as the 'hanging judge' and 'condemned all the Aboriginal defendants to judicial execution' (2008: 173, 217). Executions were perceived by the colonizers as 'educating "untutored savages" in the rule of law' (Finnane and McGuire 2001: 281). This led to the judicial execution of over 100 Indigenous men in New South Wales 'because of their ignorance – or deliberate flouting – of the English derived colonial laws' (Harman 2008: 202). In the Northern Territory in 1893, Dashwood J. sentenced to death ten Indigenous people convicted of murder within his first three days. This included a man named Wandi Wandi, who was ordered to be publicly hanged at the scene of his crime and in the presence of members of his tribe (Mildren 2011: 24). By the 1930s the death penalty was no longer mandatory for Indigenous offenders in the Northern Territory, but the Supreme Court under Wells J. continued to order capital punishment (2011: 106). The court's *discretion* to apply the death penalty made the sovereign's ultimate penalty appear fair because it was determined on the merits of the individual case. However, Wells J. would become infamous for his bias in the case of *Tuckiar* v. *The King* (1934). In that case, Wells J. refused to admit cultural evidence and provide a fair trial to an Indigenous defendant who was sentenced to death for murdering a police officer. On appeal, the High Court of Australia unanimously overturned the conviction, reinstating the rationality and fairness of the law.

Legislation conferred courts with discretion to order corporal punishment exclusively for Indigenous offenders. After this sentencing option had been phased out for non-Indigenous people in the 1870s, whipping remained available for Indigenous people in Western Australia (Haebich 2000: 210). Corporal punishment extended to any male Indigenous offender for 'any felony or misdemeanour' under the Summary Trial and Punishment of Native Offenders Ordinance 1849 (WA) and then again in the Aboriginal Offenders Amendment Act 1892 (WA). In 1892, Western Australian Attorney-General, Septimus Burt, justified the whipping of summary offenders in the following terms: 'You can only deal with [Indigenous offenders] like you deal with naughty children – whip them . . . Give them a little stick when they really deserve it, and it does them a power of good' (quoted in Finnane and McGuire 2001: 284). Premier George Leake defended whipping on the grounds that 'Aborigines' should 'realise their responsibilities through their skins' (quoted in Haebich 1992: 73). Local justices of the peace could order whippings for cattle killing and other minor crimes, which legalized the devolved punitive practices on the frontier (Pedersen and Woorunmurra 2000: 31–2, 89; Melbourne Correspondent 1904: 5). Furthermore, Indigenous workers could be whipped and imprisoned for 5 years for leaving their place of servitude, whereas the maximum punishment for non-Indigenous workers was 3 months' imprisonment because they were protected by the Master and Servants Act 1842 (WA) (Haebich 2000: 210). Hard labour on Rottnest Island, a penal island for Aboriginal offenders off Western Australia, was enforced through 'flogging and chaining to a wheelbarrow', which parliamentarians in 1895 believed would 'reduce the incidence of spearing of cattle' (quoted in Finnane and McGuire 2001: 284).

Western Australia's codified punishment on the Indigenous body reverberated in other Australian colonies. The South Australian Government enacted the Breach of Contract Act 1842 with the Aboriginal Native Offenders Act 1849 to regulate Indigenous employment, including by allowing 'whipping of up to two dozen lashes in lieu of or in addition to imprisonment' where an Indigenous worker objected to employment conditions or absconded (Thorpe 1992: 90–1). Under the Breach of Contract Act (SA), which also applied to the Northern Territory, Indigenous workers who objected to employment conditions or absconded were liable to this corporal punishment. Long after the legislation was repealed, Wells J. of the Northern Territory Supreme Court in the 1930s advocated 'a good flogging' for Indigenous offenders due to their inferior intelligence and the fact they were getting 'cheekier' and it was the only punishment they appreciated (quoted in Douglas 2005: 160). Prominent public servant responsible for Indigenous affairs in the Northern Territory, T. G. H. Strehlow, also endorsed whipping to demonstrate authority over Indigenous people (Rowse 1992: 91). Such punitive approaches to Indigenous people undergirded the new Anglo-Australian order.

The enactment of special punishments for Indigenous defendants would transform the punishment inflicted on Indigenous people on the frontier to a juridified exercise of power. Special punishment did not deviate from the rule of the colonial sovereign, but was a mark of its power (Agamben 1998: 17, 36). It allowed the sovereign's authority to respond to colonial demands. Punitive exceptionalism persisted despite the Supreme Court of New South Wales proclaiming that Indigenous and non-Indigenous people were equally subjected to the law and 'equally entitled to the protection of the law' (*R.* v. *Murrell & Bummaree* 1836). Such reasoning merely served to highlight the hegemonic force of Anglo-Australian laws. Zones of racial exceptionalism would be extended under Aboriginal Protection legislation in the early twentieth century. This conferred broad powers to 'protectors' and other government officials to control Indigenous lives. In using these powers, government officials, especially those in institutions, would subject Indigenous people to whipping, chaining and other brutal disciplinary measures (see National Inquiry into the Separation of Aboriginal and Torres Strait Islander Children from their Families 1997: 100, 128, 139–40; Kidd 1997: 35, 211). However, in the main, the brutal expressions of colonial discipline would become increasingly sublimated into channels of self-discipline in the Protectionist era.

From body to soul: 'protective' containment

The legislative drift towards Protectionism signalled an abandonment of the idea that Indigenous Australians would die out. This idea was premised on a Social Darwinist view of Europeans as a superior and out-surviving race. It represented Indigenous people as 'a backward remnant' that is swept under by progress and white refined humanity (Dodson 1994: 7). For colonists it meant that Indigenous extermination was not a criminal act, but the 'expediting of nature' (Dodson 1994: 7). Indigenous people who escaped or survived extermination in the nineteenth century were resettled on unusable land[4] under a policy of 'Segregationism'. It involved the placement of Indigenous people on missions and settlements controlled by the Church or state as a means of 'smoothing the dying pillow' (Bolton 1982: 59). Although the policy of segregationism was meant to provide comfort for Indigenous people in their inevitable demise, the conditions on missions and settlements were dire. A rapid reduction in the Indigenous population in the nineteenth century was facilitated by the spread of diseases in these enclaves as well as ongoing colonial violence (Briscoe 2003: 187).

While the 'dying out' theory lost its veracity by the late nineteenth century, colonial portrayals of the inferiority of Indigenous people remained strong. On the cusp of the twentieth century, Protectionist policies were introduced to mark a new wave of exceptionalism for Indigenous people. They suspended the rule of law for Indigenous people in every facet of their lives. They were 'citizens without rights' through this policy of legal exclusion (Chesterman and Galligan 1997). Nonetheless, Protectionism in its official guise was a more

4 E.g. land designated under the Waste Lands Act 1842 (SA).

subtle form of power, characterized by ideologies of welfare and civilization. This power involved detaining Indigenous people on 'welfare-penal institutions', which mostly included missions and government reserves, but also extended to cattle stations and other private enterprises or homes (Hogg 2001: 357). Indigenous people were made to live and work on these settlements, and became dependent on them as sources of food, clothing and shelter given that they were deprived of their land and its sustenance. On these sites of welfare colonialism, food rations could be used as punishment, where 'tucker' was denied to Indigenous people who failed to wash or work (Rowse 1990: 185). However, Protectionism's defining feature was the instilment of self-discipline through work, instruction and routine. In this respect it replaced 'modes of violent control' that featured heavily in the dispossession process on the frontier (Finnane and Paisley 2010: 144).

Protectionism was prescribed by the Aboriginal Acts,[5] which was a series of statutes across the newly federated Australian states and territories to control Indigenous peoples. It established or strengthened the powers of Aboriginal Protection Boards and Chief Protectors, who oversaw a network of protectors (see Aborigines Protection Act 1909 (NSW) s. 6; Aboriginal Protection Act 1869 (Vic) s. 4; Aborigines Act 1905 (WA) s. 6; Aboriginals Ordinance 1918 (Cth) s. 4; and Aboriginals Protection and Restriction of the Sale of Opium Act 1897 (Qld) s. 6). Protectors sought to control Indigenous lives through placing restrictions on their movements, culture, language, family life and marriage, employment and money. Through this control, the state and its agents would shift from their negative constraints on the target body to more deeply inscribed power on the target 'soul' (Foucault 1979: 82, 101). For example, the Aboriginals Protection and Restriction of the Sale of Opium Act 1897 (Qld) portended protection from the 'worst excesses of white violence' by enabling Indigenous peoples' removal to isolated missions and reserves for close monitoring and alteration of their daily lives (Chesterman and Galligan 1997: 40). In many ways it was an extension of segregationism, but with vast codified powers allocated to governments to manage and provide salvation for the Indigene. Colonial values, ethics, routines and language were enforced through repetitive daily and working rituals, as well as religion and instruction. In this way, moral constraints became internalized and modes of 'self-constraint' replaced modes of 'social constraint' in this 'civilizing process' (Elias 1978: 127). State 'regulatory and corrective mechanisms' sought

5 See, e.g.: Aboriginal Protection Act 1869 (Vic); Aborigines Protection Act 1886 (WA); Aboriginals Protection and Restriction of the Sale of Opium Act 1897 (Qld); Aborigines Protection Act 1909 (NSW); Aborigines Act 1911 (SA); Aboriginals Ordinance 1911 (Cth); and Aboriginals Ordinance 1918 (Cth). Although by the mid 1800s Protection Boards were operating in the south-eastern colonies such as New South Wales and Victoria, they were not established in Australia's north until the turn of the twentieth century. Nonetheless, at this later juncture all of the boards were restructured to reflect contemporary thinking on the far-reaching powers of the Aboriginal protectorates.

to 'qualify, measure, appraise, and hierarchize, rather than display itself in its murderous splendor' (Foucault 1981: 144). This 'finely tuned' authority, as Foucault (1979: 78) describes, is part of a 'more effective spinning of the web of power over everyday life' (Hoy 1986: 136).

There was nothing home-grown about the policy of Protectionism and its institutional architecture. The British Parliament promoted the policy across its colonies in light of the Report of the British House of Commons' Select Committee on Aboriginal Tribes (1837). Its recommendations provided a framework for the administration of Indigenous affairs in the colonies, including in Australia, until the mid twentieth century. As an alternative to 'extermination', the Committee advocated restrictive policies mixed with education and instruction, especially in Christianity, for the attainment of Indigenous civilization (Armitage 1995: 5). It regarded Britain as having a 'higher purpose' in bestowing 'civilization and humanity, peace and good government' to all ends of the earth (quoted in Select Committee 1837: 105). The report explicitly denounced Australian Indigenous peoples as 'barbarous', and 'utterly disregarded' their claims to sovereignty and propriety (Brennan *et al.* 2005: 53). The Select Committee on Aboriginal Tribes (1837: 116–23) recommended:

- British control of Indigenous subjects;
- appointment of 'protectors' (who could provide Indigenous peoples with a restricted status under the law and subject them to summary discipline);
- integration of Indigenous peoples into established institutions of British society (particularly the wage economy);
- special recognition of the situation of Indigenous children, who were considered particularly open to change, education and salvation;
- a recognized place for organized Christianity as an essential element in the process of producing citizens.

The Aboriginal Acts adopted many of these recommendations and were overlaid with an ideological emphasis on civilizing Indigenous people through displacing their culture, language and identities. While this civilizing process depended on transforming Indigenous behaviours and relationships, it was supplemented with punishment for Indigenous transgressions. The Acts made it an offence to leave a designated area (such as a settlement), marry or work without the protector's permission, have sexual relations with non-Indigenous races, spend or receive money from employment without the protector's permission, and practise Indigenous laws, customs or ceremonies (see Aboriginals Protection and Restriction of the Sale of Opium Act 1897 (Qld) ss. 31–2; and Aboriginals Ordinance 1918 (Cth) ss. 5, 45). Protectors had the power to punish offenders for 'breach of the Regulations relating to the maintenance of discipline and good order upon a reserve' (see Aboriginals Protection and Restriction of the Sale of Opium Act 1897 (Qld) s. 31(13)–(14)). The police could also administer punishment under the Aboriginal Acts (see Aboriginals Ordinance 1918 (Cth) ss. 11(3), 17(2), 18(1), 55–6, 63). Many police, however, served as protectors, blurring their punitive and welfare roles. Employers of Indigenous workers could also take on the role of protector, which has been described as akin to 'leaving a hawk to protect a chicken' (Underwood 1906: 2677).

Physical punishment was replaced by a normalizing power focused on life and its 'value and utility' (Foucault 1981: 144). Integral to the value of Indigenous lives was their labour power. Work meant that Indigenous people could be 'subjected, used, transformed and improved' (Foucault 1979: 136). Foucault (1979: 136) maintained that the body only becomes useful for the sovereign if it is both a productive body and a subjected body. In the Northern Territory, Indigenous labour was essential to the profitability of this predominant beef industry in the twentieth century. Indigenous people were widely recruited through processes of terror, although later became dependent on cattle stations for their sustenance (Bleakley 1929: 6; Austin 1988: 92). In south-eastern Australia, Indigenous people were made to work on missions and settlements, although less commonly in private enterprise. Work set in motion daily routines that restructured Indigenous lives. In the Northern Territory, along with northern Western Australia and Queensland, workers lived on cattle stations and brought up their families under the supervision of managers, and spent long days engaged in regulated tasks such as mustering, gardening, fencing, road works and domestic labour on stations (McGrath 1987). Everyone in the Indigenous family worked, including young children and the elderly. Employers provided Indigenous workers with food, clothing and accommodation, often in the form of 'humpies', but rarely cash wages, enforcing a relationship of dependence (Anthony 2007: 7).

The Aboriginal Acts gave protectors broad powers to handle Indigenous workers. This included the power to punish them for refusing employment or disobeying the working conditions that were determined by protectors and employers collectively (see Aboriginals Ordinance 1918 (Cth) s. 29(2); McCaffery 1953; d'Abbs 1994: 2). In the Northern Territory, Western Australia and Queensland, protectors granted employers licences to recruit countless Indigenous workers, including children, and revoke their industrial rights (see, e.g. Aboriginals Ordinance 1918 (Cth) s. 22). The Northern Territory Chief Protector could exempt employers from the payment of wages to Indigenous workers under Regulation 14 of the Northern Territory's Aboriginals Ordinance 1918.[6] Western Australian Indigenous stockworker John Watson (1988: 221) stated that the police, as official protectors, gave managers licences to 'work them as they saw fit' and 'take charge of their welfare'. This in turn meant that on pastoral stations the manager was granted 'the status of "protector"' in which he 'could do pretty

6 In relation to Indigenous people employed by governments across Australia, their wages were paid into a trust fund, which rarely made it into the hands of Indigenous workers. These trust fund monies were used by governments as if they were part of its general revenue. This expropriation is the subject of ongoing 'stolen wages' claims (see Kidd 2003: 13–16; Anthony 2007: 4–5; and Standing Committee on Legal and Constitutional Affairs 2006).

much as he liked' (Lawford 1988: 15). Ruby de Satge, who worked on a Queensland station, described the Aboriginal Act in the following terms: '[T]he Act means that if you are sitting down minding your own business, a station manager can come up to you and say, "I want a couple of blackfellows" . . . Just like picking up a cat or a dog' (quoted in Huggins 1987–8: 7).

Although protectors were charged with supervising Indigenous workers, pastoralists, irrespective of whether or not they were also protectors, performed the day-to-day oversight and management of the lives of up to hundreds of Indigenous workers on their stations. Governments regarded pastoralists' arrangements with Indigenous workers as instrumental to the Protectionist policy. The Chief Protector of Aborigines in the Northern Territory in 1913 declared that working Aborigines on pastoral stations under the care of the manager would fulfil the government's Protectionist objectives (cited in Reid 1990: 195), and the Department of Territories admitted that 'pastoralists in maintaining aboriginal dependents [sic] are doing the job which would otherwise fall to the Government' (Marsh 1954: 1). The process of self-discipline on cattle stations involved techniques of instilling work routines and divisions of labour, hierarchies and respect for white employers (McGrath 1987: 174). Rowse (1987: 82) suggests that relations of trust, loyalty and stability existed between station managers and Indigenous workers. Stations provided not only rations and predictable routines and rituals, but also a refuge from the 'outside' where there was a 'landscape of terror' (1987: 82). Indigenous people were also able to maintain their land, culture and kin because it assured their labour power (Driver 1949; Hasluck 1988: 54). The process of Indigenous recruitment and employment in the cattle industry has nonetheless been likened to slavery (Gray 2007) or feudalism (Anthony 2003).

Violent punishment was not entirely superseded by 'the gentle way in punishment' for Indigenous workers (Foucault 1979: 104). Foucault (1979: 105) informs us that recourse to violence is not excluded after the demise of the sovereign's punitive spectacle. Indigenous stockmen continued to be punished by shootings or 'flogged to death' for wrongdoings such as losing a horse (Gribble 1884: 30–1). Discipline was particularly fierce for those who questioned the authority of the station manager. A musterer at Meda Station in the Kimberley, Jimmy Bird (1988: 98), claimed that 'whitefellas' 'would pull their gun out and kill any Aborigines who stood up to them. And there was none of this taking your time to pull [up] your boots either. No fear!' Corporal punishment was also dispensed on Indigenous children to predispose them to the pastoralist's authority (McGrath 1987: 107–8). Stockworker Barney Barnes remembers 'trouble on the station' resulting in an Indigenous boy being shot in a grotesque display:

> Shot him! He was a good young boy; I don't know why they did that. He didn't do anything wrong. There were a lot of people there at the time who saw it happen. Women and children were there. Right, then they got wood and woodheap and some kerosene. They chucked that boy on top and lit the fire up. They didn't bury him in a grave, they just chucked him on the fire.

> Everybody was watching, but they couldn't do anything. Some of them started crying but the manager pointed the gun at them and told them, 'Shut up before I blow you buggers out!' Some of the fellas started grumbling amongst themselves, but the manager went at them with his gun and made them go back to work.
>
> (Barnes 1988: 268)

The frontier violence was never far away from the implementation of Indigenous policies in successive periods. Even as the epistemic violence of Protectionism took hold, a reversion to overt violence loomed, especially for violations of the Aboriginal Acts. Protectionism sought to rationalize the power that was posited by arbitrary violence. At the same time, the colonizing state could create an 'imperial fantasy that colonial appropriation was a form of paternal recognition and gift bestowal' (Povinelli 2002: 131). It produced a façade of colonization as a 'gradual and peaceful transition from savagery to civilization' (2002: 131). The normalization of the colonizer's governance would continue to gain traction in the successive Indigenous policy era of Assimilationism.

Normalization of Indigenous punishment in the age of assimilation

Assimilationist policies eclipsed the separate legal and administrative apparatus under the Aboriginal Acts. From the mid twentieth century Indigenous people no longer occupied exceptional legal zones. They were governed by mainstream laws and released from institutions into towns, albeit on their periphery, in an attempt to integrate Indigenous people into the white community. In place of discriminatory Aboriginal Acts, generic welfare legislation provided a normalized regime for the control of Indigenous people. Indigenous people came to be defined by their welfare status rather than their race. The Northern Territory Chief Protector of Aboriginals was redesignated as the Director of Welfare who was the guardian of all wards that included most Indigenous people. Northern Territory's Welfare Ordinance 1953 (Cth) did not mention 'race', but referred to the status of 'ward', classified 'by reason of his manner of living, his inability to manage his own affairs, his standard of social habit and behaviour, his personal associations . . .'. Indigenous people as wards of the state under the Welfare Ordinance had their health, housing and education managed by welfare departments rather than Aboriginal Affairs departments. Similarly, in Queensland, the Director of Welfare authorized the removal of Indigenous children with reference to their neglect or abuse rather than their Aboriginality, although such legislative change did not take hold until the 1980s (O'Conner 1993: 13).[7] Under

7 The Aboriginal and Torres Strait Islander Affairs Act 1965 (Qld) explicitly allowed Aboriginal children to be removed from their families until 1984, when the Community Services (Aborigines) Act 1984 (Qld) was introduced with general application.

this legislative framework, the overrepresentation of Indigenous child removals increased, highlighting the culturally destructive nature of this policy under the guise of neutrality (1993: 16).

The Federal Government convened an Australian Conference for Native Welfare in 1951 that adopted the policy of Assimilation as meaning that 'in the course of time, it is expected that all persons of Aboriginal birth or mixed blood in Australia will live like white Australians do' (Hasluck 1953: 16). The official policy of assimilation shared the civilizing language of Protectionism, but was more intent on cultural absorption into non-Aboriginal society (Ellinghaus 2003: 185). The state perceived that Indigenous self-discipline would make it possible for Indigenous people to acquire the status of citizens, once they had overcome their disability that ascribed them ward status. Reflecting this reticence about their capacity, it was not until the late 1960s that Indigenous people attained the full spectrum of formal citizenship rights, including the right to vote in federal elections, access to mainstream institutions and venues, equal access to welfare payments and the right to equal pay in the Northern Territory (Australian Law Reform Commission 1986: [26]). Indeed, the transfer of Indigenous people from missions and government settlements took up to 20 years and was not fully realized in the Northern Territory until they gained land rights under the Aboriginal Land Rights Act 1976 (Cth) or in Queensland until Indigenous reserves became self-managed (Queensland Government 2011).[8]

Assimilationism saw the governments force Indigenous subjects to be free liberal subjects, but without requisite opportunities for achieving self-responsibility (Hindess 1996: 106). Equal pay was not matched with equal access to jobs, in fact it precipitated the lay-off of Indigenous workers in the cattle industry (Anthony 2007a). Freedom of movement was not matched with access to housing, and for most Indigenous Australians, access to their land. Consequently, many Indigenous people were freed from the clutches of Protectionism only to be released into the perils of the towns and cities. Hogg (2001: 358) explains that it was no longer necessary to control Indigenous people with separate administrative measures because they were subjected to the full brunt of market and legal institutions. Consequently, street police were the arbiters of responsibilization in this new order. They did not 'simply impose the law, they imposed the law of an alien culture' (Blagg 2008a: 131).

From the 1960s the policing of Indigenous people primarily took place on the streets rather than on government settlements or missions. Indigenous people were drawn into the general purview of the police through their occupation of public spaces that were 'worlded' by white power. This 'worlding' saw the inscription of colonizing worldviews, systems, rules, regulations and practices (Spivak 1996). The police exercised their general powers with the effect of

8 These provisions are piecemeal and many Indigenous people across Australia continue to seek rights to land and governance.

disproportionately controlling Indigenous people. The application of neutral criminal procedures and laws presented a systemic disadvantage for Indigenous people who fell outside of white norms. Guha (1998) demonstrates that despite global pressures to an inclusive hegemony, colonial power reverts to exclusion and domination in relation to the colonized. Although criminalization of Indigenous Australians from the late twentieth century was a relatively 'gentle' form of punishment, it would retreat to violent expressions (Foucault 1979: 104). This is apparent in a well-documented history of deaths in police and prison custody (Cunneen 2001; Royal Commission into Aboriginal Deaths in Custody 1991 (hereinafter 'RCIADIC')).[9]

With the decline of corporal punishment and the death penalty for Indigenous Australians, by the late 1960s the ultimate and universal form of punishment was imprisonment. Foucault (1979) in *Discipline and Punish* regarded prisons as a reinvented discipline and new technology of power through the deprivation of liberty rather than the public displays of torture and execution. He claimed that imprisonment is not geared towards deterrence, but is simply part of the 'general tactics of subjection' (1979: 272). The tactic of imprisonment was exercised especially on Indigenous people. It became the new site of Indigenous detainment, with Indigenous people 'grossly over-represented' in state prisons and police custody (RCIADIC 1991: [1.3.3]; and see statistics in Chapter 3). A culmination of higher rates of charges and arrests, especially for minor offences, along with higher bail refusals, convictions and sentences, led to the over-representation of Indigenous people in prisons (Eggleston 1976: 176; O'Shane 1992: 5). Broadhurst (1987: 154) comments that the repeal of the Aboriginal Acts fuelled a 'rapid increase' in levels of Indigenous imprisonment. As a strategy of social control for Indigenous people, detention is entrenched in colonial orthodoxy – whether it is for protective or punitive purposes. It was therefore not a radical shift when administrative detention gave way to punitive detention in the 1960s and Indigenous people were transferred from state welfare institutions and into state prisons. Nonetheless, the sentencing of substantial numbers of Indigenous Australians to prison sealed their fate as a criminal underclass.

The spatial field of postcolonial crime

Since the abandonment of distinct punishment regimes for Indigenous peoples, criminalization has continued to inform the management of Indigenous space. Policing is a vehicle for the exclusion of the Other and the inscription of legitimate uses and claims to space. These inscriptions have broadened with a wider set of spaces regarded as 'public space' for the purposes of policing, including those held under Aboriginal land rights legislation. The policing of Indigenous

9 Imprisonment itself has been described as a form of 'white on black institutional violence' that subordinates Indigenous people (Blagg 2008a: 139).

people in public places is a metaphor for the exclusive right of the state to that space. Hage (1998: 38) claims that the postcolonial state governs through 'spatial management' that involves an 'imagined privileged relation' over 'race' and 'national space'. Although policing is an incident of general law enforcement in public, it has distinct implications for Indigenous Australians. The punitive enforcement of colonial strategies and postcolonial policing of public space are part of the same continuum. Cunneen (1999: 8) claims contemporary policing is an extension of 'an exclusionary social order' that can be traced to the Protection period when Indigenous communities were defined as a public order problem requiring strict surveillance, intervention and control.

Spatial management through criminalization of Indigenous people is especially acute because of their visibility in public space (Cunneen 2008: 44). The police's 'preoccupation with public space' and claims to 'on the street experience', including knowledge of people's movements, inform their cavalier exercise of power in that domain (White 1997: 283). The police impose racial boundaries in public spaces by excluding the Other. The removal of Indigenous people from public space, including through move-on orders, is often referred to as 'street sweeping' and 'social cleansing' (Graham 1999: 10). Indigenous presence signifies a threat to white claims to public space. In addition, police 'move-on' powers facilitate Indigenous dispersal from public spaces, including without evidence that they have or will commit an offence (Eggington and Allingham 2006). Indigenous people caught by these powers have described them as making them feel like they are 'less of a citizen' because they are not permitted to 'hang around in [their] own state' (quoted in Walsh and Taylor 2007: 164). The policing of public order offences and the exercise of move-on orders bring to the fore the 'racialized politics of the settler-colonial streetscape' (Edmonds 2010: 149).

In her seminal book, *Fear, Favour or Affection*, Eggleston (1976: 226–34) documented the intense policing of Indigenous people for street offences in the 1960s when assimilation policies had taken hold and Indigenous public presence acquired a new dimension. Policing was facilitated by the enactment of summary offences legislation that provided for crimes such as public order offences, including offensive behaviour, offensive language and public drunkenness. The effect was to target Indigenous behaviours in public. This is augmented by other forms of criminalized public activity including trespass, petty theft, property damage and riot. The policing of offensive language especially took on a greater intensity in the public sphere from the 1960s (Hogg 2001). Where police deemed an Indigenous person's language to be offensive, it would set in motion a series of offences, commonly resulting in charges for offensive language, resist arrest and assault police – known as 'the trifecta' (Office of the Aboriginal and Torres Strait Islander Social Justice Commissioner 1996: [4.5]). Since the 1960s Indigenous people have been significantly overrepresented in police charges and prison sentences for public order offending (Eggleston 1976; Allard 2010: 3). This offence category contributes to the overrepresentation of Indigenous Australians in prisons nationally and impacts on their performance of territoriality in public space.

Criminalization as a technique of spatial management flows onto other areas of governance.[10] The state 'governs through crime' to facilitate wide-ranging social regulation in Indigenous communities (Simon 2001–2). Simon (2007: 5) observes that 'technologies, discourses and metaphors of crime' create new opportunities for intrusive governance. A contemporary expression of this governing modality is the Northern Territory National Emergency Response Act 2007 (Cth) (hereinafter, 'NTER Act') and its related measures[11] (collectively known as 'the Northern Territory Intervention'). Acquiring its justification from a moral panic over sexual crime and Indigenous culture, controls and restrictions have been placed on Indigenous land rights, social security, education and housing in remote communities (see Chapter 4; Anthony 2010). This is matched with 'governing crime' through greater policing on Indigenous land in the Northern Territory (Simon 2007: 35). Public policing in remote Indigenous communities was extended through the deployment of Federal Police and the military, the installation of 18 new police stations in communities, the broadening of police powers and the establishment of crime intelligence taskforces. The government designated all Northern Territory Aboriginal land, which is held as communal and inalienable freehold title under the Aboriginal Land Rights Act 1976 (Cth), as 'prescribed areas' (NTER Act s. 4).[12] In these areas, alcohol is banned and the police can, without a warrant, randomly enter, search, seize or dispose of any 'thing', namely a vehicle, involved in the carriage or consumption of alcohol (Liquor Act (NT) s. 95; NTER Act s. 17). This authorizes the police to use their powers on Aboriginal land, including in Aboriginal homes, as if it were a public place (Pilkington 2009: 55, 174).

In the Northern Territory and elsewhere, discipline in the streetscape has taken on new dimensions as the boundaries of normal policing and criminalization have shifted. A key area has been the policing of minor traffic infringements, such as driving unregistered, uninsured and unlicensed, driving without a seatbelt and not stopping at a 'stop' sign. These are regulatory offences that are generally processed by way of a ticket (infringement notice) and a fine. However, in remote Indigenous communities in the Northern Territory and Western Australia, these offences have fallen within the domains of courts and prisons. Therefore, the spatial extension of normal offending has come to include roads and vehicles. These are not like most crimes that arise from affirmative acts, such as driving dangerously or stealing a vehicle, but omissions such as *not* having a

10 The contemporary management of Indigenous space through criminalization is not without resistance and competing Indigenous spatial claims (see Blagg 2008).

11 See Families, Community Services and Indigenous Affairs and Other Legislation Amendment (Northern Territory National Emergency Response and Other Measures) Act 2007 (Cth) and Social Security and Other Legislation Amendment (Welfare Payment Reform) Act 2007 (Cth). The NTER Act and its related legislation have recently been repealed and reinstated in the Stronger Futures in the Northern Territory Act 2012 (Cth).

12 These are now known as 'alcohol protected areas' under the remodelled NTER Act embodied in the Stronger Futures in the Northern Territory Act 2012 (Cth) s. 27.

licence or a roadworthy vehicle or insurance. The problem is compounded by the inadequate licensing and registration services in remote communities (Anthony and Blagg 2012: 53). Driving offences that present no immediate risk and were informally tolerated are now the staples of law enforcement in remote communities. Since the Northern Territory Intervention, there has been a 250 per cent increase in minor traffic offences and half of all offences in Indigenous communities are driving-related (Anthony 2010: 103; Northern Territory Police, Fire and Emergency Services 2003–10). About 25 per cent of inmates in Northern Territory prisons are driving offenders and 99 per cent of these are Indigenous (McCarthy 2011; Northern Territory Department of Justice 2008: 24).

The punishment of Indigenous drivers straddles an agenda to colonize Indigenous space. Law enforcement of Indigenous driving has an epistemic effect – creating knowledge and truths about Indigenous roads as tantamount to white roads. In reality, roads on Indigenous land bear little resemblance to the urban streetscape in white towns and cities. Bush tracks are the most popular route for traversing Indigenous land and the roads that do exist in communities are unsealed, unguttered and unlined. They lack footpaths, street signs, speed signs, street lights and traffic lights. Nonetheless, there is a zero-tolerance approach to policing unlawful driving that represents the imposition of white rules on Indigenous places (Anthony and Blagg 2012: 37, 39; Pilkington 2009: 63). It fails to take into account that the theory component of licence tests assess driving as it relates to the white urban streetscape rather than the dirt tracks of remote communities. Further, maintaining a roadworthy vehicle is inhibited where unsealed roads and bush tracks damage cars and there is an absence of mechanics to service Indigenous people's cars. Policing is based on a fantasy of the racial neutrality of space in the application of the Traffic Act (NT) and Motor Vehicle Act (NT) to driving in remote Indigenous communities. The Indigenous road interferes with the 'imaginary nation' that presumes a white order (Hage 1998: 47). Policing the Indigenous streetscape normalizes assumptions of the whiteness of this space.

Coupled with this epistemic process of governing Indigenous space, the Northern Territory Government has recently begun instrumental change by gazetting Indigenous community roads, implanting road signs and allocating street names (Northern Territory Government 2011). As Carter (2010) reminds us, colonial possession is performed through the mapping and naming of the colonized's space. Street signs designate white names for the newly gazetted streets in the central Australian desert community of Yuendumu. A new 'stop' sign was also implanted at the main 'junction' between roads at the centre of the community, with police waiting at the sign to charge drivers who disobeyed the sign. In our fieldwork in Yuendumu, Harry Blagg and I found that there was consternation among community members over police charging those who failed to stop (Anthony and Blagg 2012: 41). Further, a group of Warlpiri people expressed concern that this was just another layer of rules that would make

Yuendumu like a 'white-fella' town, with 'no place for *Yapa* [Warlpiri people]' (2012: 41).

Concluding remarks: state criminalization and the legacy of non-recognition of Indigenous laws

The colonization of Australia involved both the criminalization of Indigenous peoples and the undermining of their systems of punishment. Indigenous resistance to the colonial project – where they 'evinced a disposition to live in their own country' – was the basis for deeming Indigenous peoples outlaws and punishing them as though they were 'aggressors' (Select Committee on Aboriginal Tribes 1837: 4). Indigenous people were prohibited from using their laws to regulate crimes either within their communities or against Europeans who transgressed Indigenous laws. The criminal law did not account for Indigenous laws or cultures in determining culpability, such that the recognition of Indigenous laws became confined to the discretion of criminal sentencing courts.

In his article 'The Force of Law', Bourdieu (1987: 816) tells us that the possibilities of the law are constantly constrained by its 'internal logic' and 'power relations'. This logic relegates Indigenous laws to the margins of the dominant Anglo-Australian legal system. It diminishes possibilities for Indigenous laws and justice solutions to coexist with white institutions through legal plurality. The High Court in *Mabo* (1992: 29) elucidated that Indigenous laws cannot coexist with Anglo-Australian laws because it would 'fracture the skeleton of principle which gives the body of our law its shape and internal consistency'. Subsequently, the court in *Wik Peoples* v. *Queensland* (1996: 179) held that legal developments should be based on 'gradual change' and 'continuity rather than rupture' so it can remain true to the common law's historical foundations. Recognition of Indigeneity in sentencing does not threaten the structure of the Anglo-Australian law, but conserves its premise of individualized justice, which Derrida (1989–90: 1009) describes as repeating its 'value of origin'.

In confirming its authority over Indigenous systems of law and punishment, the High Court rationalized that it was constrained by an 'act of state' that established the colony could not be questioned in the domestic courts (*Mabo* 1992: 31–2). Derrida (1989–90: 943) explains that the 'origin of authority' has its foundation in self-proclaimed authority. Such a self-proclamation negates challenges to the 'acquisition of sovereignty' and ensures 'that no parallel system of authority can emerge or allocate rights and interests after the assertion of British sovereignty' (Strelein 2003: 4). The fictitious idea that Australia was *terra nullius* has cast long shadows over Indigenous legal authority, long after its fiction has been displaced. While there was scope within the Anglo-Australian law of tenure to coexist with native title, there was no such possibility for coexisting criminal laws. This is because, as the High Court posited, it would threaten the exclusivity of Anglo-Australian criminal law by encroaching on its 'inherently universal' application (*Walker* v. *New South Wales* 1994: 50).

The effect of the High Court rendering Indigenous criminal laws inert is that the Anglo-Australian legal system has authority in capturing and characterizing Indigenous offenders. Criminalization has spanned central and centrifugal, official and unofficial, administrative and penal modes. The Indigenous offender has been variously instantiated as cattle killer, trespasser, primitive and public disorderly, in order to be caught by the tentacles of state institutions. The contingency of these representations reveals the Indigenous criminal to be a product of a historical relationship between the colonizing state and the colonized. The punishment of Indigenous people acquires legitimacy because of the dominant role of the colonizing state. Criminal law, according to Derrida (1989–90: 943), justifies inflicting harm on the Other in a way that would otherwise represent 'violence without a ground'.

This book's concern with contemporary judicial representations of Indigenous communities, their laws, identities and cultures is a metaphor for the colonizing state's psyche and relationship with the Other. This psyche is not fixed, but, as Rutherford (2000: 188) explains, 'schizophrenic', vacillating between morality and aggression in relation to the Other. Judicial representations of Indigeneity in sentencing meander between lenience delivered with sympathy and severe sentences dispensed with condemnation. These divergent characterizations can be traced to the bivalent colonial ideologies of protection and punishment; salvation and extermination. They are overlaid with a claim to sovereignty that undermines the authority and capacity of Indigenous peoples. The effect is to inferiorize the Indigene and facilitate their disproportionate incarceration.

Chapter 3

Decolonizing Indigenous crime statistics

> Irrespective of how one measures and describes Aboriginal imprisonment, differences between imprisonment rates of Aborigines and others are so profound, so unfathomable, that rates that normally would scandalise mainstream Australian society appear unreal and 'third world'.
>
> (Broadhurst 1987: 180)

Introduction: sentencing, statistics and social relations

The early colonial judicial decisions that denied the recognition of Indigenous laws also portended formal equality between Indigenous and non-Indigenous people in the Anglo-Australian criminal justice system. Nonetheless ever since colonization, Indigenous peoples have experienced levels of criminalization disproportionate to non-Indigenous peoples. Researchers have found Indigenous Australians to be the most punished population in the world (Skyring 2011; Blagg 2001: 227). This chapter moves more squarely into the territory of this book – the criminal sentencing process. It explores the extent to which sentencing feeds into the processes of criminal justice which discriminate against Indigenous offenders; first with reference to statistical studies and then with reference to qualitative measures. While statistics unequivocally speak to the over-representation of Indigenous people in prison (as outlined below), statistical findings on whether sentencing decisions discriminate against Indigenous offenders are less clear. This suggests a need for a longitudinal, contextual and qualitative analysis of sentencing remarks to discern whether the sentencing process unfairly impacts on Indigenous people.

A qualitative analysis of representations of Indigeneity in higher court discourses reveals an increasingly punitive approach as well as the creation of new discourses on Indigeneity that seeks to exclude and condemn with greater severity. The higher courts match their instrumental role of punishing Indigenous offenders with an epistemic role of producing inferiorizing representations of the colonized. The increasing imprisonment of Indigenous people is inexplicable without an analysis of recent judicial portrayals of Indigenous offenders and communities in terms of failure, dysfunction and victimization. This book is concerned with this shift to harsher penalties over the past decade in the context of renewed images of Indigenous alterity. Courts have admitted that whereas in the past the circumstances of the Indigenous offender may have attracted 'sympathy', they now incite reprimand. Indigenous offenders and their communities are classed as falling outside the moral community so as to warrant reprimand and produce the social effect of the superiority of the white community. Hudson (2006: 235) points out that '[w]here justice is, community is also', such that the offender's community will know through punishment the righteous boundaries of cultural expression.

The increasing severity of sentences and the wider criminal net that the state has cast over deviant behaviours has been well documented by law and order theory. As one of the seminal works in this field, Garland's (2001) *The Culture of Control* unravels this punitive turn towards incarceration and away from 'penal-welfarism' that emphasized offender restoration and reintegration. The 'new punitiveness' ended the softly, softly approach which placed criminals in the care of social workers and transferred control to the prison system (Hudson 1987: 39). An historical analysis of Australian sentencing remarks reveals a shift in the past decade away from the judicial idea that Indigenous offenders could be reformed through integration in their communities, and towards a view that long prison sentences are the only disciplinary instrument. This shift occurred alongside emergent law and order themes, especially community deterrence and victimization. Nonetheless, the meta-narrative of law and order does not account for the postcolonial impetus in the criminal justice system towards controlling Indigenous communities and space. 'Postcolonial' used in this sense denotes the continuation of the colonizing process and how it frames white institutions. Accordingly, it cannot be said that the language of the punitive turn – characterized by discourses on risk, harm and victimization – conveys the entire justification for punishing Indigenous people. The greater proclivity of higher courts to imprison Indigenous offenders, along with the judicial reimagining of Indigenous offenders in more condemning terms, can be characterized more accurately as a neo-colonial turn rather than a punitive turn.

Incidence of over-representation

In 1991, the Royal Commission into Aboriginal Deaths in Custody (hereinafter, 'RCIADIC') widely publicized the overrepresentation of Indigenous people in custody. This was regarded as having a direct correlation with the disproportionate number of Indigenous deaths in custody (RCIADIC 1991: [1.3.2]). Yet the Royal Commission's recommendations to reduce Indigenous overrepresentation in prisons did not set governments on a path of decarceration. Consequently, Indigenous prison rates have risen since the Royal Commission and the gap between the proportion of Indigenous to non-Indigenous Australians in prisons

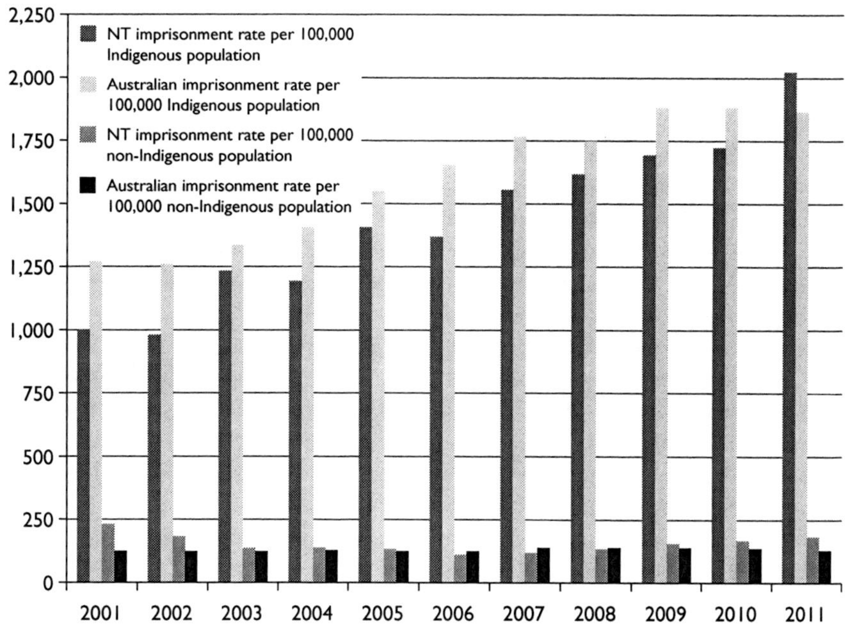

Figure 3.1 Comparison of Australian and Northern Territory (NT) average rates of imprisonment, Indigenous and non-Indigenous populations, 2001–11.

Source: ABS 2011: 56, Table 4.2.

has widened. Indigenous people are over 14 times more likely than non-Indigenous people to be in prison – an increase from 10 times in 2001 (Australian Bureau of Statistics 2011: 50, hereinafter 'ABS').[1] The age-standardized national rate of imprisonment for Indigenous people is 1,868 per 100,000, compared with a rate of 130 per 100,000 adult non-Indigenous people (ABS 2011: 50). In 1992, Indigenous prisoners comprised 14 per cent of the total Australian adult prison population (Bond *et al.* 2011: 273). By 2011, this proportion had increased to 26 per cent, even though Indigenous Australians comprise 2.3 per cent of the total Australian population (ABS 2011: 49, ABS 2011a). Between 2001 and 2008, the Indigenous imprisonment rate rose by 47 per cent, whereas the non-Indigenous prison rate rose by less than 5 per cent (ABS 2011: 50; see Figure 1).

Indigenous people in the Northern Territory – a focal point of this book – have experienced the most dramatic rise in prison rates since 2001 (ABS 2011: 56). It is no coincidence that the Federal and Northern Territory

1 The highest ratio of Indigenous to non-Indigenous imprisonment rates in Australia is in Western Australia, where it is 18:1 (ABS 2011: 50).

governments have pursued a concerted crime control strategy in the Northern Territory since 2006, when prison rates have particularly spiked (Anthony 2010: 94). From 2006, Northern Territory prison rates increased faster than any other state or territory, with a 23 per cent increase – 16 per cent above the national average increase – making the Northern Territory population imprisoned at more than four-and-a-half times the national rate (ABS 2009: 33). For the year 2007/08, Northern Territory prisons were operating at 103 per cent capacity. The following year, 2008/09, this had risen to 120 per cent capacity (Jackson and Hardy 2010: 1). In the Northern Territory, the Indigenous population constitutes 82 per cent of the total prison population – the highest Indigenous prison population of any Australian jurisdiction, and totalling 56 per cent above the Australian average (ABS 2011: 49). This is substantially due to the relatively high Indigenous population in the Northern Territory, amounting to 30 per cent (ABS 2011b). Between 2001 and 2011, the Indigenous imprisonment rate increased by 200 per cent – now constituting 2,028 per 100,000 of the Indigenous population and outstripping the Australian average (ABS 2011: 56, see Figure 1). Australia's Steering Committee for the Review of Government Service Provision (2009: 67) has identified imprisonment as a major problem confronting Indigenous communities in the Northern Territory.

Explaining over-representation and the significance of sentencing

Evidence shows that increasing levels of Indigenous incarceration cannot be attributed solely to the number of Indigenous offenders coming before the courts, nor to the increase in convictions (Fitzgerald 2009). Nonetheless, the issue of Indigenous over-representation in prison divides criminologists between those who implicate the criminal justice system (including sentencing) for its discriminatory processes and those who absolve the criminal justice system by attributing Indigenous over-representation to higher levels of Indigenous criminality. Both schools draw on empirical studies, which point in both directions – that sentencing has discriminated against Indigenous defendants and that sentencing has been fair to these defendants. Conflicting results show the limitations of statistical analysis alone in explaining the treatment of Indigenous people in sentencing.

Statistics have also been used to normalize Indigenous punishment by showing it to be 'reasonable' and 'proportionate' to the seriousness of the offence and other aggravating factors (Hudson 2006: 235). Recent studies pointing to 'fairness in sentencing' have relied on aggravating factors as the only variables in the sentencing process (see Snowball and Weatherburn 2006, 2007; Bond *et al.* 2011), thus undermining other broader considerations in the sentencing mix. In order to paint a fuller picture of how courts treat Indigenous people in sentencing, there is a need for a historical analysis of sentencing that is couched in the individual narratives of the case and the circumstances of the offender, the Indigenous community and broader social relations. Applying this methodology, which eschews a formalist assumption that offenders are all on an equal playing field, there is a clear indication of disproportionate sentences of imprisonment for Indigenous Australians.

For tougher, for lighter, until statistics do us part

Findings of discrimination in sentencing

Early studies on sentencing outcomes found that sentencing courts handed down more severe sentences for Indigenous defendants than non-Indigenous defendants, after accounting for criminal history and the nature of the crime. These findings fuelled contentions that the over-representation of Indigenous people in prison reflects more than a higher rate of offending – namely, the discriminatory nature of the criminal justice system, including at the point of sentencing. As early as the 1970s, the ground-breaking work of Eggleston (1976: 176) identified judicial racism as a causal factor in the over-representation of Indigenous people in custody. Her study of the Western Australian criminal justice system found 'discrimination against Aborigines in sentencing', chiefly 'in the choice of imprisonment as a suitable sentence in a higher proportion of Aboriginal cases' (1976: 176). This difference arose after controlling for offence type and prior criminal record. Despite these findings, research into judicial racism was neglected for many years. Craigie (1992: 15) pointed out that the RCIADIC 'failed to address the whole question of judicial bias'. He stated, '[t]he question was not even raised for discussion, let alone for recommendations' (1992: 15). The only advertence to the matter was Commissioner Elliott Johnston's reference to the fact that 'in certain circumstances Aboriginal people may receive longer sentences for the same offence than non-Aboriginal people' (RCIADIC 1991: 217).

It was not until 1998 that Luke and Cunneen produced results from a comprehensive analysis of Indigenous sentencing. They sought to determine whether Northern Territory's Indigenous people were more likely than non-Indigenous people to receive a custodial sentence after the offender's criminal history and the nature and seriousness of the offence were taken into account. Luke and Cunneen (1998: 80) found that imprisonment was used as a sentencing option twice as often for Indigenous people than non-Indigenous people. Indigenous offenders were also sentenced to prison at an earlier stage of their offending history (1998: 58). Four out of five of all prison sentences in the Northern Territory were imposed on Indigenous people (1998: 9). However, Indigenous people also tended to be handed shorter sentences for most offences, with the exception of a number of serious offences (1998: 60). Therefore, although Northern Territory courts were more likely to imprison Indigenous offenders, the courts were less likely to hand Indigenous offenders long prison sentences. This is not necessarily indicative of more recent trends, particularly over the past decade when the Northern Territory has experienced the highest rate of increase in prisoners in Australia.

Two studies by the New South Wales Bureau of Crime Statistics and Research (hereinafter, 'the Bureau') also found evidence of adverse treatment of Indigenous people in sentencing. Its relatively long-term analysis of sentencing statistics between 1991 and 1999 concluded that Indigenous overrepresentation 'is most problematic' at both 'the point of entry into the court system and the point of sentencing', where 17 per cent of Indigenous offenders received a 'long prison' sentence of 6 months or more (Baker 2001: 3). The Bureau's 2009 report on imprisonment rates between 2001 and 2008 found that the New South Wales Indigenous prison population increased by 56.4 per cent due to an increase in the proportion of Indigenous offenders sentenced to prison and the increase in the length of the prison terms imposed, rather than an increase in the conviction rates (Fitzgerald 2009: 4–5). Furthermore, sentence lengths have increased for the same types of offences. The conclusion drawn was that the increase was due to the way in which Indigenous offenders were processed by courts: 'the substantial increase in the number of Indigenous people in prison is due mainly to changes in the criminal justice system's response to offending', with a 'greater impact on the Indigenous prison population than on the non-Indigenous prison population' (2009: 6). Significant differences also emerge for Indigenous juvenile offenders. An Australian Institute of Criminology report found that in Western Australian children's courts, 25 per cent of Indigenous male offenders and 13 per cent of Indigenous female offenders were sentenced to custody, compared with 9 per cent and 4 per cent for their non-Indigenous counterparts (Richards 2009: 93). This trend was confirmed in Bond and Jeffries' (2012) study that established that Indigenous defendants were more likely than non-Indigenous defendants to be imprisoned in lower courts and children's courts when sentenced under statistically similar conditions to non-Indigenous defendants.

Findings of fairness

A coterie of criminologists have pointed to equality in sentencing based on an identification of sentencing outcomes that are relatively the same for Indigenous and non-Indigenous offenders after specific matters are taken into account. With some qualifications, they conclude that Indigenous people are not disadvantaged at the sentencing stage, or if they are, it is only a marginal disadvantage. Walker (1987) conducted one of the earliest studies which gave an impression of fairness in the sentencing process. He suggested that 'far from being the result of a blatantly biased system', courts were 'particularly lenient' to Indigenous offenders after factoring in their previous offending (1987: 111). This was based on the fact that the average prison sentence was 42.6 months for Indigenous offenders compared to 74.9 months for non-Indigenous offenders, notwithstanding that the former was more likely to attract a prison sentence (1987: 110–11). His finding that Indigenous defendants were imprisoned more than non-Indigenous defendants correlates with Luke and Cunneen's findings. However, Walker (1987: 114) concluded 'that the courts cannot be held to blame for the high rates of Aboriginal imprisonment' because this difference could be attributed to the prior criminal record of Indigenous defendants and the perception created from their greater number of bail refusals. A follow-up study by Walker and McDonald (1995) indicated that Indigenous offenders serve shorter terms of imprisonment than non-Indigenous people for a range of offences.[2] Walker and McDonald (1995: 4) noted that 'courts may have a lenient view of Indigenous offenders, biasing sentence lengths in their favour to avoid accusations of racial biases in sentencing'. However, this finding does not apply to the actual decision to sentence Indigenous offenders to prison.

In a study on the incidence of imprisonment in New South Wales, the Bureau's Snowball and Weatherburn (2006: 1) sought to detect the rate at which Indigenous offenders were imprisoned compared to non-Indigenous offenders. Their study between 2001 and 2004 accounted for the following purported 'important' variables: Indigenous people's higher rate of conviction for violent crime and their higher rate of re-offending, particularly following the imposition of a non-full-time custodial sentence (2006: 5). The 'most important' of these considerations, according to the authors, is 'offence seriousness' (based on maximum penalty established by statute, as well as existence of violence), 'because it is a basic principle of sentencing that sentences must be proportionate to the gravity of the crime' (2006: 5).[3] Hudson (2006: 235) states that 'seriousness' is a means of making harsher sentences appear reasonable and proportionate. Despite its appearance of objectivity, offence seriousness is value-laden and has only taken a prime position in the judicial sentencing discourse in recent years, as this book will demonstrate. Snowball and Weatherburn's (2006: 6) study also took into account whether the offender had been convicted of concurrent offences, whether the offender had previously received a community-based sanction, whether the offender had pleaded guilty and the age and gender of the offender. After these 'legitimate considerations' were removed, they found 'no evidence of racial bias in sentencing' (2006: 1, 3). This finding of parity is consistent with Bond and Jeffries' (2011) analysis of Western Australian higher court statistics. According to these criminologists, Indigenous status has no direct effect on the decision to imprison in Western Australia, after adjusting for other sentencing factors, especially past and current criminality:

> The odds of Indigenous defendants being imprisoned are 1.437 times the odds for non-Indigenous defendants. However, this significant direct effect disappears once we adjust for past and current offending, suggesting that it

2 Luke and Cunneen (1998: 62) note that Walker and McDonald failed to account for the seriousness of the offence when comparing the length of the sentence. This echoes criticisms by O'Shane (1999: 131) of Walker's original 1987 study because it focused on the length of prison sentences at the expense of an analysis of why courts failed to consider non-custodial options for Indigenous offenders.

3 Nonetheless, Snowball and Weatherburn's (2006: 13) research found that Indigenous offenders were slightly less likely to be convicted of a serious violent offence, but more likely to be convicted of '[an]other violent' offence.

is differences in criminal history and the context of the current offence that explains any initial differences between Indigenous and non-Indigenous offenders.

(Bond and Jeffries 2011: 270)

In a follow-up study, Snowball and Weatherburn (2007: 285) sought to develop upon their previous research by accounting for the presence of legal representation, testing for interactions between Indigenous status and other variables, and including offenders who had been previously imprisoned. The new study found that across New South Wales local, district and supreme courts there was in fact 'some residual effect of race on sentencing', which meant that 'racial bias may influence the sentencing process even if its effects are only small' (2007: 286). The risk of imprisonment, after controlling for relevant legal factors, is 4.47 per cent for the median case, and 5.19 per cent if the defendant is Indigenous (2007: 285). The authors concluded nonetheless that 'racial discrimination in sentencing has very little to do with the problem of overrepresentation' of Indigenous people in custody (2007: 286).

Supplementing their analyses on the judicial decision to imprison, Bond, Jeffries and Weatherburn (2011) subsequently sought to identify the *length* of prison sentences imposed on Indigenous versus non-Indigenous defendants in New South Wales. They found 'little evidence to support the claim that Indigeneity directly influences the length of imprisonment orders in the New South Wales courts for comparable offenders' (2011: 286). In the higher courts, Indigenous and non-Indigenous offenders are sentenced to similar prison terms when plea and current and past criminality are taken into account, and in the lower courts Indigenous offenders receive shorter prison terms after adjusting for controls (2011: 286). The authors discerned that courts did not place more weight on aggravating factors that lengthen a sentence when dealing with Indigenous offenders. This contrasts with Jeffries and Bond's (2009) research of sentencing in South Australia from 2005 to 2006, which determined that although Indigenous people were slightly less likely to receive prison sentences, those who were sentenced to prison were more likely to receive *longer* sentences than non-Indigenous people. Jeffries and Bond (2009: 61) were able to include a wider range of sentencing factors, including mental and physical health, substance abuse, familial circumstances and remand, as well as seriousness of offence and criminal history. This clearly demonstrates the inadequacy of sentencing studies predicated on accounting for aggravating factors alone.

Notwithstanding the fact that divergent findings of discrimination and fairness cannot be reconciled, given that they are based on different methods, periods and jurisdictions, one implication is that judicial recognition of Indigeneity has had a negligible effect on reducing the length of prison sentences for Indigenous offenders. If we adopt the criminological plight to take into account aggravating factors of a strictly legal nature (for example, criminal history, seriousness of crime, etc.), then for the sake of balance, mitigating factors relevant to Indigenous people should also be considered in sentencing comparisons. Taking on board aggravating factors alone reflects a formalist methodology that denies the substantive differences among offenders. Furthermore, to conclude that relatively even outcomes amounts to sentencing equality overlooks the discrimination that arises when courts do not take into account Indigeneity to reduce a sentence. The High Court has held that Indigenous background is a 'material fact' that courts are 'bound to take into account' when imposing sentences (*Neal* v. *The Queen* 1982: 326). In this respect, Indigenous people should be receiving lesser sentences if substantive equality is to be realized through recognition of Indigenous circumstances. Indigenous Magistrate Pat O'Shane (1992: 6) maintains that the failure of courts to recognize Indigenous disadvantage and the impact of colonization in mitigation gives rise to substantive inequality in sentencing. Jeffries and Bond claim that there are strong grounds for Indigenous disadvantage leading to a reduced sentence:

> If race/ethnicity can trigger attributions about the causes or reasons for offending, and broader social and policy expectations, then in the context of Australia, the potential for Indigeneity to reduce sentence severity is theoretically strong.
>
> (Jeffries and Bond 2009: 55)

Given that Snowball and Weatherburn (2006, 2007) and Weatherburn *et al.* (2006) have acknowledged that socio-economic disadvantage, membership of the Stolen Generations and alcohol/substance abuse are responsible for higher levels of Indigenous offending, it would follow that these factors should have been taken into account in their analyses of sentencing data. Thus, for the same offence and the same prior criminal history, Indigenous people would receive lesser sentences if courts accounted for Indigenous-specific offending circumstances. Snowball and Weatherburn's (2007) observation that Indigenous and non-Indigenous people receive similar sentences indicates that courts are not properly considering relevant extra-legal factors. Courts are also failing to enforce government attempts, which Snowball and Weatherburn (2006: 5) themselves identify, to promote community service orders and suspended sentences for Indigenous defendants in order to reduce rates of Indigenous imprisonment. It follows, contrary to Snowball and Weatherburn's conclusion on sentencing equality, that Indigenous people are receiving sentences disproportionate to their culpability (see Ashworth 2002: 1079; Hudson 1999: 589). In other words, Indigenous people should be receiving lesser sentences *if* they were to be treated the same.

Implications of sameness in sentencing: difference in criminality

Criminologists who suggest Indigenous offenders are treated fairly in the sentencing process assert that overrepresentation of Indigenous offenders in prison is due to their higher levels of offending or discrimination at other stages in the criminal justice process (Snowball and Weatherburn 2006: 15, 2007: 287; Jeffries and Bond 2009: 49–50; also see Gray *et al.* 2008: 114). Snowball and Weatherburn (2006: 15) adopt an empirical approach in seeking to identify the 'causes' of Indigenous offending based on correlations between factors such as alcohol consumption, lack of education, unemployment or welfare dependence, and crime and imprisonment. Drawing on survey data, they conclude that higher levels of offending are linked to alcohol and illicit substance abuse and economic stress (2006: 16). Further findings by these authors confirmed that the 'strongest correlate' for Indigenous arrests is alcohol consumption (Weatherburn *et al.* 2008: 307), and for Indigenous charges and imprisonment it is drug use (Weatherburn *et al.* 2006: 11).

The contentions of Weatherburn and his collaborators in relation to Indigenous criminality are not new. Their arguments resonate with a stream of orthodox criminological theories of Indigenous criminality that are enmeshed in understandings of destructive colonial influences and Indigenous peoples' lack of self-control in relation to alcohol (see Langton 1993: 205). The implication is that the individual is responsible for succumbing to criminal impulses. This has taken on a more extreme expression recently, when government and media reports of Indigenous family violence and sexual abuse have led certain academics to describe the causes of Indigenous crime in terms of alcoholism and welfare dependence, as well as Indigenous culture. Anthropologist Sutton (2009: 53), for example, regards the welfare state as having indulged Indigenous people – a view picked up in the media and by the former Indigenous Affairs Minister Mal Brough (2007: 2). So-called 'passive welfare' is impugned for providing Indigenous people with a permissive dependency and replacing the coercive restrictions under the Protectionist regime that kept them in line (Sutton 2009: 109). According to this view, welfare policies since the 1970s have precluded Indigenous people's self-responsibility and provided conditions that nurture criminality (see Pearson 2007). Others such as Broadhurst (2002: 262) focus on 'Welfare Colonialism' instituted under the governance of missionaries and protectors that instilled Indigenous dependence (see also Rowse 1998).

Part of the Indigenous crime problem, according to Sutton (2009), is that unrestrained Indigenous culture has a natural tendency towards crime. Constraints in the Protectionist era (until the 1950s) prevented crime by inculcating fear into Indigenous people and controlling their culture (2009: 109). Sutton (2009: 109) states that the 'authoritarian and patriarchal regimes of most of the early Christian missions were, bizarre as this might sound, "culturally appropriate"' because they reined in the excesses of Indigenous culture in a way that has eluded 'liberalized' regimes. This characterization of Indigenous culture has parallels with Lombroso's (1876/2006) ideas of the 'born criminal' where non-European races are intrinsically associated with crime. Indigenous culture is misrepresented as lawless, violent and patriarchal (see Broadhurst 1997: 413).

Sutton provides an indictment of Indigenous culture by pointing to its pre-colonial tendency for violence:

> Some [Indigenous] behaviours such as high levels of interpersonal violence involving both men and women existed well before the impacts of colonisation, both in sanctioned collective forms (as in formal dispute resolution through duelling and warfare) and in forms less subject to such controls (as in the beating of women by their husbands).
>
> (Sutton 2001: 134)

An opposing school of criminology perceives Indigenous criminal behaviour as a socio-historical product of colonizing processes. Indigenous crime is regarded as a reflection of the despair arising from the dispossession of Indigenous land and devastation of Indigenous culture and kinship ties, or as an expression of resistance to these postcolonial conditions. This theoretical approach encompasses the following critical perspectives:

- *Strain theory* – This is one of the most popular frameworks for understanding Indigenous crime, and emerges in the reasoning of sentencing courts. It refers to the limited or 'strained' opportunities and marginalized position of Indigenous Australians who commonly experience poverty and unemployment, and have low levels of education, poor housing and high mortality rates. For Snowball and Weatherburn (2006: 15), these factors give rise to alcohol abuse that is then channelled into crime (see also: Australian Law Reform Commission and New South Wales Law Reform Commission 2010: 11; and Chapter 6 of this book). Others focus on Indigenous anguish as a cause of Indigenous crime. Anguish is a response to disempowerment, loss of culture, law and land and alienation from family and community, especially for the Stolen Generations and those institutionalized on missions and government settlements (see Blagg 2008: 29; Cunneen 2001: 10; Broadhurst 2002: 266–8; Behrendt 2006: 14; Greer 2008; McGlade 2012). Family violence is viewed as a product of 'the injuries inflicted by the founding violence of colonisation', which is 'reproduced within contemporary Aboriginal society' (Blagg 2008a: 132). It arises from colonial oppression and is a manifestation of the offender 'internalizing' colonialism (Aboriginal and Torres Strait Islander Social Justice Commissioner 2011: Ch. 2).
- *Conflict theory* – This posits that crime arises from conflicting Indigenous and Anglo-Australian norms, and competing claims to land, law and governance (see Reynolds 1982; Cunneen 2001). This clash gives rise to legitimate violence by the colonizer and illegitimate (criminal) violence by the colonized. In some instances, Indigenous resistance can be overt, such as Indigenous riots against police (Cowlishaw 2004; Cunneen 1989). But it can also be subtle and in the form of a different understanding of the law, cultural rights and legal evidence (Broadhurst 1997: 414). Indigenous people are caught in

the criminal net because their values, social structures and institutions lack conformity with those of the dominant group (Blagg 2008: 29). Blagg (2008: 16) emphasizes that the loss of (or lack of recognition of) land, culture, sacred sites, skin and moiety systems, and governance structures has '*direct and immediate* relevance to both criminal behaviour and to processes of criminalisation.' This coheres with 'social disorganisation' theory, which proffers that Indigenous people who continue to practise their laws and cultures are classified by dominant institutions as disorganized (see Box 2003: 280–1; Burke 2005: 208–12).

- *Labelling theory* – According to this theory, the dominant classes attach a 'criminal' label to Indigenous people with the effect of increasing surveillance, particularly by police, over Indigenous people (White and Perrone 1997: 36–8). In this way, the label creates the crime by setting in motion the criminalization process, even where the Indigenous person does not engage in criminal activity per se.[4] Alternatively, the label can act as a self-fulfilling prophecy because Indigenous people act out the label, particularly given that it will attach irrespective of their lawfulness (Blagg 2008: 29; Broadhurst 2002: 261). Labelling theory is influenced by symbolic interactionism, which claims that groups appropriate labels to conform to existing stigmatization (Becker 1991). The criminal label is often supplemented with labels of laziness, alcoholism and disregard for property (Broadhurst 2002: 262; Dodson 1994: 8; Blagg 2008a: 133; Morris 1997: 161–2).

Postcolonial perspectives on overrepresentation: contextualizing and critiquing positivism

The inquiry into the '*causes* of crime' relies on assumptions of Indigenous criminality, and focuses on the individual rather than institutional practices. While the above-mentioned theories may provide some insights into offending, at best they provide an incomplete picture of Indigenous crime and punishment and, at worst, they contribute to the colonizing role of criminology as a discipline. 'Positivist criminology'[5] does part of the colonizing job by selectively employing and applying the term 'crime' under the guise of neutrality. Foucault's (1980) account of the power/knowledge relationship challenges the assumption of neutral research and allows us to understand how it is a tool of dominant institutions. In the Australian context, positivist criminology excludes from its inquiry

4 Sanson-Fisher (1978) found that Indigenous Australians were far more likely to be labelled as criminals and punished even where they had not engaged in deviant acts. Criminalization arises from cultural differences in what constitutes a crime and the detector's perception of offensive behaviour.

5 Positivism as a criminological research method seeks to ascertain concrete evidence for explaining criminogenic behaviour and risk factors. It assumes that there are criminogenic variables that are fixed, quantifiable and knowable truths.

the significant criminal nature of colonial wrongs such as land theft and Indigenous dispossession (Cunneen 2011: 253). Its explanations of Indigenous sentencing and overrepresentation in prisons rationalize the punishment of Indigenous people and add to the established wisdom that Indigenous people are more criminal than non-Indigenous people. By engaging statistical methodology in a vacuum, positivist criminology gives the impression of a scientific analysis.[6] This technique normalizes the 'dynamic of difference' of the colonizer over the colonized (Anghie 2004: 4). Derrida (1978) describes this as 'western metaphysics' where substantive truth claims are made in relation to the colonized world to maintain its subordinate position.

Statistics within positivist criminology render opaque the social relations embedded in considerations of race (Cunneen 2011: 253). The historical and social construct of race cannot be understood apart from the colonizing process and its role in criminalization. Positivist criminology deflects attention from the historical facts of Indigenous criminalization and punishment in the colonial project and the ongoing denial of Indigenous systems of law. Indigenous criminality is enmeshed in the Anglo-Australian system's negative imagery of Indigenous people and its decisions over what and whom it criminalizes. The label of Indigenous criminality imposes a boundary between the 'civilized and uncivilized', which according to Anghie (2004: 63) excludes the colonized and their claims to sovereignty.

Reducing Indigeneity to a risk factor presumes a legitimate criminal justice system. The statistical significance of Indigenous risk is measured in a fixed and normal order. Positivists assume that within this order Indigenous offending can be corrected through changes at the margins that alter Indigenous behaviours. This reasoning fails to elucidate the systemic impetuses for Indigenous criminalization or the fact that the Anglo-Australian penal complex exists because of the denial of Indigenous laws. Imprisonment of Indigenous people and under-protection of Indigenous victims are products of introduced colonial laws and the supremacy of Anglo-Australian punishment over Indigenous punishment systems. Punitive imprisonment exists on a continuum with Protective Indigenous segregation and confinement on state settlements, missions and cattle stations (see Chapter 2). According to Hogg (2001: 366), with the dismantling of the Aboriginal Protection Acts, 'administrative segregation' gave way to 'penal incarceration' as the dominant mode of Indigenous regulation. Assimilationism became translated into integration of Indigenous peoples into prisons as Indigenous prisoners soared in this post-Protectionist period beginning in the 1960s.

In reaction to positivism, postcolonial criminology distances itself from identifying causes or measuring the incidence of Indigenous crime as an isolated inquiry. Postcolonial criminologists accuse positivists of complicity in the

6 Stubbs (2008: 13) notes that statistics can be used for critical analysis. Critical criminology – for which postcolonial criminology is a branch – does not eschew statistics altogether, but uses them to provide context or expose the conditions that shape the statistics.

criminalization of Indigenous people by assuming Indigenous crime exists outside of subordinating social structures. For Agozino (2004: 350), the discipline of criminology emerged at a time when 'colonial administrations imprisoned most parts of the earth'. Its function, therefore, was to neutralize incarceration of the Other. He claims that the 'mechanical solidarity between colonialism and criminology', emerging at the height of Europe's empire-building, is signified by the failure of criminology to focus on institutions rather than individual behaviour (2004: 349–50). Postcolonial criminologists seek to break free from serving colonial interests by examining 'the relationship between colonization, state crime and the over-representation of marginalized people' (Cunneen 2011: 258). A postcolonial perspective enables 'an analysis of criminal justice as a set of racializing practices', including the overrepresentation of Indigenous people in penal custody (2011: 257). However, postcolonial studies do not preoccupy themselves solely with the controlling aspects of the colonizer and its criminal justice system. It also identifies the competing governing structures of the colonized. As Blagg (2008: 21) describes, postcolonial studies stress both the 'technologies of control' and 'bifurcated' practices across Indigenous and non-Indigenous domains.

In relation to Indigenous Australians, postcolonial criminologists argue that their overrepresentation in prison is due to criminal justice institutions constructing deviance to capture Indigenous behaviours. This, in part, arises from institutions targeting resilient Indigenous cultures and practices that discord with the introduced law. Blagg (2008) informs us that the operation of the criminal justice system is tantamount to the imposition of an alien legal system. Overrepresentation may also be explained with reference to the very few Indigenous people working as lawyers or judicial officers within the Anglo-Australian legal system (O'Shane 1992). However, it is not necessarily through overt institutional bias that Indigenous people are on the receiving end of higher levels of punishment. Rather, prejudicial outcomes can be attributed to *systemic racism* where the ostensible application of 'fair and universal criteria' in fact entrenches disparities and asymmetrical power relations (Blagg *et al.* 2005: 12). Systemic racism emerges unintentionally by way of adherence to dominant values, systems and procedures that exclude Indigenous people (Gray *et al.* 2008: 119). The endeavour of legal neutrality and objectivity does not merely facilitate systemic racism but is also intrinsic to the 'broader claims of western discourses of dominance' (Cunneen 2011: 8). Systemic racism occurs at each of the criminalizing stages (policing, bail, trial, sentencing, parole), where there is a failure of 'facially neutral laws, policies and practices' to account for cultural factors, leading to outcomes that reinforce inequality (Blagg *et al.* 2005: 12). This is the case where courts apply the same sentencing considerations to Indigenous offenders. In this respect, Shaw (2006: 866) argues that 'whiteness is discursively active regardless of its (in)visibility'.

Viewing crime and crime control as enmeshed in colonizing processes and institutions is key to understanding Indigenous overrepresentation in the criminal justice system. Cunneen (2011: 258) maintains that Indigenous crime and punishment cannot be understood apart from the white 'agencies that identify and process crime'. Criminality reflects dominant relationships, white institutional practices and colonizing legal frameworks. The judiciary's engagement with Indigenous offenders, as articulated in sentencing remarks, is part of the postcolonial institutional and ideological complex that creates asymmetrical relations between the state and Indigenous communities. A critical analysis of these remarks turns attention away from the behaviour of the Indigenous person and towards the subordinating role of the punitive institution. This role is performed not merely by dispensing a lengthy sentence, but where the courts fail to recognize Indigenous circumstances or recognize them within colonizing discourses.

Transcending positivism: towards a postcolonial sentencing paradigm

Criminologists who apply neutral criteria to measure the impact of sentencing on Indigenous defendants do not appreciate how such criteria are unstable and shaped by shifting control agendas. Judicial attempts to control the risk of the Other clouds the application of objective principles or the fair application of subjective considerations. A historical and contextual analysis of sentencing narratives reveals how the Indigenous offender is allocated an inferior and 'precarious subjectivity' (Spivak 1988: 76). Sentencing is part of a subjugating process that maintains the dominance of Anglo-Australian institutions over Indigenous people in instrumental and epistemological ways. However, imputing neutrality to the sentencing process normalizes the authority of these institutions and conceals their violent foundations. A postcolonial sentencing paradigm deconstructs the asymmetrical relationship between the colonizer's law and Indigenous laws. This paradigm, in addition to acknowledging the dominant role of sentencing courts in this asymmetrical relationship, is able to contemplate the active agency of Indigenous participants in sentencing courts and the concerted efforts of Indigenous people to establish Aboriginal legal services across Australia, which provided a channel for the submission of Indigenous community evidence (Faine 1993). However, it also recognizes that such agency does not disrupt the generative colonial framework that gives sentencing courts their authority and inscribes Indigenous people a lesser status (Fraser 1995: 82).

Postcolonial analysis allows us to overcome the debate on whether Indigenous people are sentenced longer and therefore courts act prejudicially, or they are sentenced approximately equally and therefore courts treat Indigenous offenders fairly. It eschews the positivist concern to determine the 'causes' of Indigenous crime and imprisonment. Rather, it interrogates the power relations that predispose sentencing courts to send greater numbers of Indigenous offenders to prison notwithstanding so-called 'legitimate considerations' to rationalize this decision. But at the same time, a postcolonial perspective enables an appreciation of the courts' scope to define mitigating factors and the contingency of these factors. By analyzing *how* courts frame Indigeneity in sentencing reveals the dynamic judicial management of the Other. Jeffries and Bond (2009: 54–5) observe that quantitative research designs cannot 'fully explain the effect of Indigeneity' because of their limited legal focus (2009: 67–8). These designs are unable to convey the textured stories emerging in sentencing that are much more than the quantity of punishment (Daly 1994: 264–5). Empirical studies problematically assume that sentencing involves factors which are immutable, invariant and discrete pieces of information (Tata 2007: 435). They are limited by what they can measure and are ignorant to factors at play, especially social relations, that fall outside of their purview.[7] A qualitative component, including discourse analysis of sentencing remarks, that is interpreted in the postcolonial context of authority paints a fuller picture of the sentencing process.

Hanging from a postcolonial frame, sentencing narratives reveal how courts control the terms of engagement with Indigenous defendants. Sentencing courts may keenly recognize Indigeneity, but generally to assert their superior position in relation to the objectified Other. By 'othering' Indigenous defendants, courts effectively adopt and normalize a position of whiteness. In *Orientalism*, Said (1978) describes 'othering' as an act of constructing the weaknesses of marginalized groups ('others'), as a vehicle for advancing the strength of those in positions of power. Hage (1998) notes that the white fantasy that treats Indigenous people as outsiders emerges from the history of white dominance and colonization. As 'national objects', Indigenous people can be 'moved or removed according to a white national will' – they are 'manageable objects' that sustain the stability and viability of whiteness (1998: 18, 48, 209).

The historical contingency of Indigeneity is revealed by its changing character with emerging penal and racial policies. It ebbs and flows in denoting Indigeneity as a mitigating or aggravating factor. In recognizing Indigenous factors, the judicial pendulum swings between leniency and penality. Rationality *and* repression are synthesized to legitimize the law's existence (Balbus 1973). The judicial pendulum does not swing randomly, but pivots from the law's control imperative. To date, qualitative research has focused on Indigeneity as a mitigating *or* aggravating factor. A number of works by Douglas (2009: 80, 2004, 2002) demonstrate how leniency was first afforded to Indigenous offenders in the Northern Territory to compensate them for the 'disability' of their culture. By the 1980s, the Northern Territory Supreme Court came to see Indigenous cultural factors as vital for Indigenous restoration and invoked mitigation to give rise to a 'soft' form of legal pluralism (Douglas 2005a: 141; see also Finnane 2006: 4). In relation to the traditional punishment, Finnane (2001: 308) notes that Northern Territory sentencing courts in the early 1990s reached 'some greater understanding and recognition of the positive elements of [traditional] payback' under the umbrella of 'restorative justice'. On the other hand, studies have afforded less attention to the judiciary's increasing tendency to regard Indigenous cultural practice as a matter for aggravating a sentence. However, the likes of Edney (2005, 2006),

7 Empirical analysis of sentencing involves selecting a dependent variable (such as sentence length), which is then regressed on a selected legal factor (such as offence type) and an extra-legal factor (such as race). It does not provide a complete representation of how courts identify and construct facts and how this can change over time (Tata 2007: 435).

Flynn (2004, 2005) and Nicholson (1999, 2012) demonstrate how the urban Indigenous offender is less likely to attract mitigation because courts regard his or her culture as having disappeared. Across a range of circumstances the judiciary has shifted in its perception of Indigeneity. Accordingly, whereas Indigenous culture, custom, disadvantage and political resistance were once reference points for lessening a sentence, they are now cited to increase a sentence. Such increases draw on more acute colonizing discourses of the Other.

The punitive turn in sentencing Indigenous offenders

This book demonstrates that the punitive impulse of the courts has manifested in a particularized law and order framework. Emphasis on deterrence, the seriousness of the crime, individual responsibility, the victim and the interests of the wider community in imprisonment pervade sentencing remarks. But in sentencing Indigenous offenders these punitive themes rely on a particular construction of Indigenous communities as *dysfunctional* (because it offends Anglo-Australian norms and is unable to safeguard its members as putative victims) or *non-functional* (because it does not sufficiently operate along cultural lines to be classified as Indigenous and thus requires exclusive attention to the seriousness of the offence). This reasoning, particularly in relation to the dysfunctional community, straddles the government's narrative of Indigenous communities that justifies it 'governing through crime through broad sweeping policy reforms in Indigenous communities' (Simon 2007). The changing guises of the judiciary's imagining of Indigenous factors reveal the importance of couching sentencing in its historical context to highlight the relationship between penality and Indigeneity. This section outlines the characterization of Indigeneity within the punitive turn. This turn is traced to the late 1990s due to landmark decisions of this period in the Northern Territory, particularly *Wurramara* (1999), and in New South Wales, such as *Ceissman* (2001). The late 1990s was also a period of conservative Federal Government in Australia, where Indigenous Affairs policy took a sharp turn from so-called self-determination to practical reconciliation, involving the absorption of Indigenous services into mainstream service providers and departments, alongside the intensified policing of Indigenous communities.

The language of law and order has spread across the Western world since the late twentieth century (Garland 2001), although with uneven manifestations (see Brown 2005: 36; Hogg 2008; Meyer and O'Malley 2005). It justifies longer sentences for offenders on the premise that their criminality is a risk to the broader community. This book suggests that more lenient approaches to Indigenous offenders have been a casualty of the trend towards longer prison sentences and Indigenous representations in sentencing have become more condemning. Nonetheless, the punitive narrative does not account for the long and deep-rooted history of Indigenous control and containment since colonization. The rupture that Garland (2001) refers to between penal-welfarism and the new penal incapacitation has not unsettled the haunting punishment of

Indigenous people. However, it has resulted in a shift in the rhetoric of judicial sentencing, where Indigenous offenders are deemed as threatening social norms and requiring more severe punishment. Classifications of 'dysfunctional' Indigenous communities – equally embraced by the Australian Federal Government – have resulted in more punitive responses to offenders and more coercive measures imposed on communities.

Through analysing sentencing remarks the distinct punitive impact on Indigenous offenders can be understood apart from the general penal wave that has led to increasing imprisonment rates overall (see Figure 1). There is greater capacity to account for the length of prison sentences for Indigenous offenders relative to their culpability, rather than just relative to vertical factors (i.e. time) or horizontal factors (i.e. non-Indigenous offenders). The reduced emphasis on factors relevant to Indigenous culpability, such as cultural circumstances or socio-economic disadvantage, reveals the adverse impact on substantive equality for Indigenous defendants. This is the case even if their prison sentences are no longer in duration than for non-Indigenous people based on seemingly objective criteria such as criminal history. The longer sentences are perpetuated by the judicial will to send a special deterrent message to Indigenous communities by extending prison terms. Since the late 1990s, higher courts have explicitly admitted that punitive considerations prevail over considerations regarding the offender's Indigenous community or background. The following section reflects on the general features of the punitive turn before a discussion on how it has been felt distinctly by Indigenous defendants.

General features of the punitive turn

The sentencing literature on the impact of law and order policies has focused on developments relating to tougher maximum sentences and risk-based guideline sentences (see Tata 2007: 433; O'Malley 2004). Garland (2001: 142) asserted that the punitive turn in the late twentieth century involved a range of state measures which included harsher punishments in the criminal justice arena. It involved a retreat from the 'penal-welfarism' of the preceding era involving rehabilitation and reintegration of offenders.[8] In the post-war 'penal-welfare' era, prisons were considered counterproductive and a last resort, with governmental effort 'expended on the task of creating alternatives to incarceration and encouraging sentencers to use them' (2001: 14). Therefore, for most of the twentieth century a shift away from carceral punishment was evident. Subsequently, the forces of law and order signified a drift from 'reformism, amelioration and benevolent state intervention' to castigation of the offender, accusations of moral corruption and punitive intervention (Cohen 1985: 128–9; Garland 2001: 27; Melossi 2000).

8 This penal policy went into disrepute with the perceived failure of the welfare state in both economic and social terms (Garland 2001: 20).

In his examination of this new penal policy, Garland (2004: 174) applies an idea of 'group projection' in which penal policy represents a series of practices and laws which are designed by high-status social groups for the management and control of low-status groups who are regarded as problematic. This involves:

> ... creating policies to manage the dangerous and the undeserving, [with] dominant social groups necessarily project[ing] certain phantasies and anxieties of their own – images of the dangerous other, self-images of respectability and decency.
>
> Garland (2004: 174)

In Garland's (2001: 195) view, punitiveness is motivated by self-cleansing whereby a 'new structure of controls and exclusions' is directed to those groups most adversely affected by the dynamics of change. Punitiveness also arises amidst a 'wave of anxiety' in relation to social breakdown and disorder where social controls are regarded as inadequate, including welfare controls for the poor and minority communities. The need to re-impose order, according to Garland, gives rise to controls imposed on:

> ... 'dangerous' offenders and 'undeserving' claimants whose conduct leads some to suppose that they are incapable of discharging the responsibilities of the late modern freedom. The most vehement punishments are reserved for those guilty of child abuse, illegal drug use, or sexual violence – precisely the areas in which mainstream social and cultural norms have undergone greatest change and where middle-class ambivalence and guilt are at their most intense.
>
> Garland (2001: 195–6)

In postcolonial society, it is not merely the individual offender who is castigated, but whole Indigenous communities are tarred with the criminal label, particularly men and particularly in relation to sexual abuse. However, as discussed in the previous chapter, it is not merely dangerous and serious crimes that have come under fire. In the ongoing colonizing process, it is crimes relating to the management of space (such as traffic offending and bringing alcohol within Indigenous communities) that have had the greatest impact on criminalizing more Indigenous offenders. Notwithstanding these unique outcomes of the colonizing process, it is worth reflecting on some of the key characterizations of the punitive turn, followed by an assessment of how these themes emerge in sentencing narratives on Indigenous offenders.

From social creatures to individual actors – responsibilization and risk

Penal-welfare deemed offenders products of social relationships and capable of reform, rehabilitation and integration. Since the punitive turn, offenders, both adult and juvenile, have been recast as outsiders without social ties (Cohen 1985: 137, 140). They are ascribed individual responsibility, termed 'responsibilization', which, according to Gray (2005: 938), obscures the 'exclusionary socio-economic constraints' that impede offenders' choices and reinforces moral discipline. Standard sentences, which aim to produce consistency (or 'truth') in sentencing are based on the seriousness of the offence rather than the circumstances of the individual (Cohen 1985: 137). Although responsibilization is generally based on enforcing self-discipline, in an age of law and order it is also predicated on making 'offenders face up to their own responsibilities' through repression (Muncie 2006: 773). This presumes that offenders exercise freedom and choice in committing offences. In the instance of Indigenous offenders, the state and judiciary not only regard offenders as disavowing their responsibility, but also impute irresponsibility to the Indigenous community.

Responsibilization coincides with neo-liberal ideology of risk aversion whereby autonomous individuals are charged with minimizing their risk through responsible behaviours. Punishment is the coercive form of risk 'control' where risk 'self-management' fails (Hudson 2006a). Cunneen (2011a: 318) argues that the development of 'risk' in criminal justice has seen the instigation of risk assessment processes involving the identification, classification and management of groups 'assorted by dangerousness'. Political and sentencing discourses on Indigenous offenders bring into sharp relief the 'ontological insecurity' generated by risk mentalities (Van Marle and Maruna 2010: 9). There is a decline in tolerance and a greater insistence on policing the moral boundaries (2010: 10). The 'demonised other' is managed through offender profiling and risk assessment (Muncie 2006: 774, 778). Such classifications obscure Indigenous identity beyond membership of a risk-defined group. Risk reduction is activated in the punitive sense through incarceration and incapacitation, alongside other interventions and supervision, which purportedly instil feelings of security in the shared moral community.

Protecting the community through deterrent messages

The control aspects of the punitive turn were premised on protecting the community and its 'putative victims' (Hogg 2008: 286). Themes of responsibilization and risk blend with the neoconservative forces of social control in order to cast a broad net over social behaviour (see Muncie 2006: 770). Penal-welfarism was perceived as failing to protect the community from the risks associated with crime (Garland 2001: 141). Cohen (1985: 35–6) claims that in law and order society the state fulfils this role of community protection 'through hard punishment, deterrence [and] incapacitation'. General deterrent messages sent to offenders are a means of averting risk and addressing social insecurity. Deterrence operates on the assumption that harsh punishment precludes criminal activity because it sends a strong message to rationally acting individuals. In relation to Indigenous offenders, courts increasingly refer to protection of the Indigenous community, in handing down harsh sentences. At the same time, higher courts view the Indigenous community as a source of victimization because its dysfunction and cultural practices pose a risk to victims (see, e.g. *The Queen* v. *Bara* 2006: [18]). In this respect, courts consider that the Indigenous community requires a special message of deterrence. Therefore, courts seek to condemn the Indigenous community at the same time that they seek to protect it.

Ideal victims and serious harms

The victim has acquired a new centrality and visibility within law and order discourses (Hogg 2008: 281). This victim is the 'ideal-typical victim'; 'individuals *like us*'; 'or especially our children, wives, elderly parents: respectable, innocent, vulnerable types' (2008: 282; also see Christie 1986). The ideal victim possesses a 'representative character, whose experience is taken to be common and collective' (Garland 2001: 11). Hogg (2008: 282) notes: '*Others* – for example, asylum seekers fleeing torture, disappearances and other human rights abuses – do not necessarily qualify'. Crenshaw (1991: 1278) points out that it is the victim's moral character rather than injury that is the most important issue. These victims are typically female, children and seen as possessing a white morality. Whereas in the past the Indigenous victim had fallen between the moral gaps in white society, the Indigenous victim has increasingly lost the status of the Other. Where their harm touches the moral nerve of Anglo-Australian society, they are embraced as one of 'us'. This is especially so where the harm is purportedly linked to Indigenous culture or the Indigenous community context.

By virtue of the sanctity of the victim, serious harm to the victim has particular significance in sentencing. In law and order society, legislation provides that punishment is proportionate to the degree of harm inflicted on the victim or the seriousness of the threat to the potential victim. The new punitiveness emphasizes the central importance of making punishment commensurate with the crime (Dagistanli 2007: 115). This invokes a notion of retribution or 'just deserts': more harm amounts to more punishment (Lacey 2002: 268). Retribution is distinguished from revenge by proportionality which provides a neutral rationale (Dagistanli 2007: 118). Given that the 'ideal victim' embodies society's moral fabric, proportionality must be seen as a response to the harm done to white social norms. Lacey argues that rankings of offence seriousness are dependent on core social or shared values (see also Hudson 2006: 235). Disproportionately low punishment with an 'expiatory character' is seen as 'subversive of the social order' that attempts to make good the crime inflicted on society (Durkheim 1933: 108). This understanding of proportionality sets into relief the role of punishment as vindication for harm to society as much as harm to the individual victim. Furthermore, the rationale of proportionality not merely pervades sentencing, but also empirical studies on sentencing which seek to measure proportionality in assessing its fairness. Both endeavours mask the social agenda concerning the dangerous Other that overlays decisions of proportionality.

Implications and limitations of the punitive turn framework for sentencing Indigenous offenders

The law and order paradigm provides some insights into the judiciary's practice of imposing harsher punishment on Indigenous offenders and its punitive language of community protection, deterrence and victimization. However, Garland's (2004: 170–1, 174, 2001) observations of more repressive criminal justice techniques overlook the pervasiveness of penal subjugation of Indigenous peoples since colonization. Overrepresentation in prisons can be traced well beyond the punitive turn (see RCIADIC 1991). The recent increase in the rate of Indigenous imprisonment can be better described as intensification of the penal status quo than as a schism. Rehabilitative techniques associated with penal-welfarism, including attempts to reintegrate Indigenous offenders back into their communities, did not temper the mass incarceration of Indigenous people. While the placement of Indigenous people on missions and government settlements, and later in foster and children's homes, may be regarded as penal-welfarist, its mass institutionalization is more consonant with colonizing policies of Protectionism and Assimilation. These placements were just as restrictive as modern manifestations of disciplinary power in the form of prison confinement (Hogg 2001). Clear lines cannot be drawn between penal-welfarism and more recent punitive controls for Indigenous peoples who are relegated to an exceptional zone outside the legal order under the NTER Act. Indigenous criminalization does not simply arise because they are another 'undeserving' or 'dangerous' sub-group of society – or, as Cohen observes (2002: xiv), because they are 'scapegoats for the crisis' of failed reform – but also because Indigenous communities bring into question the authority and normality of white postcolonial society.

Shifts in penal discourses are nonetheless evidenced in sentencing remarks in relation to Indigenous offenders. They expound a penal process beyond, but connected to, state policy. The focus of law and order literature on the state and its institutional apparatus neglects the role of courts, which theoretically operate independently due to the British separation of powers doctrine in Australia. Sentencing courts dispensed more lenient sentences to Indigenous offenders who were deemed uncivilized and unassimilated, as articulated by Kriewaldt J. on the Northern Territory Supreme Court in the 1950s and his successors until the late 1990s. Rehabilitation of the offender, including within the Indigenous community, was viewed as a central consideration. The punitive shift in the last decade saw higher courts resort to harsher penalties in line with a re-characterization of the Indigenous offender and his or her community as either dysfunctional or non-functional. While the state sought to impose its will through longer maximum sentences and guideline or mandatory sentences, the effect was not the totalization of state power over punishment (Tata 2007: 437). The judiciary retained its agency by continuing to account for subjective factors, including the recognition of Indigenous community circumstances, albeit for the purpose of channelling Indigeneity into notions of risk to increase prison sentences.[9]

The value of a law and order analysis is that it enlivens a historical focus on penal institutions, and goes beyond criminogenic understandings of Indigenous crime. As applied to sentencing, it enlightens us on how deterrence, victimization and community protection are construed to engender Indigeneity as a risk factor, and why imprisonment is regarded as the primary means to address this 'Indigenous problem'. Victimization rings especially loud in sentencing Indigenous offenders. After a long period in which the harm inflicted on Indigenous victims was not treated as seriously as that inflicted on non-Indigenous victims (see Finnane 2001; Kimm 2004: 142), courts now embrace ideal Indigenous victims who embody the seriousness of the offence and implicitly seek the imposition of state punishment and Indigenous community denouncement. Where Indigenous victims present submissions supporting Indigenous community sanctions, higher courts rule out their interests and instead impose prison sentences (see Ch. 5). Otherwise the victim's passivity is invoked to contrast and demonize the Indigenous offender's criminality and dysfunctionality. The Indigenous victim is ascribed with 'whiteness' and belonging to a shared moral community (Blagg 2008: 172; Shaw 2007: 4). The Indigenous victim who makes pleas for offender reintegration falls short of this universal ideal. Higher courts instead rely on a stereotype of the passive vulnerability of the Indigenous victim against the cultural agency of the Indigenous offender (see Maddison 2009).

Consistent with a law and order mentality, courts characterize the Indigenous community in terms of its risk – depicting it as a dysfunctional and threatening space for putative victims. They view harsh punishment as a vehicle for teaching obedience and conveying a message of deterrence to the Indigenous community. The courts' justification of 'community protection' to lengthen sentences implies that the Indigenous community needs to be protected from itself. The dysfunction of the community, which is viewed as perpetuating criminality, discounts possibilities for rehabilitation and positive reintegration into that environment. The Indigenous community is on the outside of the 'wider community' and its social norms. This has had an impact on courts not only seeking to impose the interests of the wider community in dispensing lengthy prison sentences on Indigenous offenders, but also denying the legitimacy of Indigenous punishment. Again, the law and order understanding only accounts for the state's impetus to imprison, rather than the content of the relationship between the (post)colonizing state and the colonized. It does not explicate the courts' distinct engagement with Indigenous offenders and how this straddles attempts by the state to impose 'social norms' on Indigenous communities and denounce Indigenous laws and cultural contexts (Brough 2007: 6, 2007a: 15–16).

9 There are some rare cases where judicial discretion has also been used in order to account for Indigenous mitigating circumstances and thereby deviate from legislative restrictions on sentencing Indigenous offenders, e.g. *R.* v. *Wunungmurra* 2009.

In these ways, law and order theorizing provides some signposts for guiding changes in judicial discourses on Indigeneity, but it does not map all the contours. Its framework gives meaning to the language used in sentencing remarks – particularly principles of victimization, community protection and deterrence. However, the recent treatment of Indigenous offenders in sentencing must also be understood in terms of the judicial will to discipline the Indigenous community. Courts attempt to instil the moral constraints of Indigenous law and culture through increased punitive sentences on Indigenous offenders. While Pratt (2005) refers to law and order as a 'decivilising process' (where state controls loosen through neo-liberal political directives and the responsibilization of individuals), judicial reasoning and state policing over the past 10 years has evinced a *civilizing* agenda to control and reform Indigenous communities. The law and order framework does not account for these judicial and governmental modes of discipline over Indigenous communities.

Conclusion: more than mitigation or aggravation

Considerations of Indigeneity in sentencing are more than the sum of mitigating and aggravating factors. Statistical studies of this 'variable' in the context of fixed legal factors neutralize the disproportionate punishment of Indigenous people. As Durkheim (1933: 89) states, punishment requires that we deem fair the vengeful acts that expiate our outrage. Mitigating and aggravating factors are filters for the judiciary's recognition of acceptable forms of Indigenous existence – with those forms that counterpoise white social norms funnelled through aggravating principles. Through this lens, sentencing is not simply an act of punishment (in its lesser or greater degree), but part of an ongoing colonizing process that seeks to apportion blame to Indigenous societies. This can be performed through mitigation where courts sympathize with cultural backwardness, or, in its most recent manifestation, through aggravation where courts blame Indigenous culture and communities for their dysfunctional status and victimizing tendencies, as discussed in the following chapter. The risk of Indigenous culture implores courts, as they proffer, to hand down more severe sentences. These discourses of punishment privilege white cultural norms and undermine the capacities of Indigenous societies.

Chapter 4

Sentencing away culture and customary marriage

> Both Aboriginal and white people are generally speaking subject to the same laws. For years, however, the judges of this Court in dealing with Aborigines have endeavoured to make allowance for ethnic, environmental and cultural matters.
>
> (*R.* v. *Iginiwuni* 1975)

Introduction: culture, custom and culpability

The Indigenous offender in his or her primitive and sexualized state has been the object of fascination for the colonizing world. Courts have not been immune to this captivation. They have injected this cultural construct into their legal reasoning to produce a normative universe (*nomos*) where Indigenous people are backward, criminal and over-sexualized (Cover 1983–4: 4; Watson 2008). This *nomos* reinforces the dominant position of the storyteller. The Northern Territory Supreme Court, where it recognizes Indigenous evidence, conveys alternating stock stories of the noble and ignoble savage to assure its paternalism (Bell 2010: 29). In both its moral and disciplinary guises, the court countenances an anxiety over culture in remote communities. Indigenous culture falls outside the terms prescribed by 'white' spatial management whether lenience or punishment is bestowed (Hage 1998: 202). In the mid twentieth century, accommodation of the Other's culture was provided on the premise that it reflected the backward and uncivilized nature of the offender. Lenience was also extended to offenders who committed offences in cultural contexts in the 1980s and early 1990s because they embodied a romanticized past. By accounting for the reduced culpability of an offender, the court applied the 'same laws' to produce different effects for Indigenous offenders (*R.* v. *Iginiwuni* 1975). Its allowance for culture was not permissiveness or a concession, but an instrument of domination.

However, from the late 1990s moral panics over crime in remote Northern Territory communities impelled the Supreme Court to reimagine culture as a contributor to the 'Indigenous problem'. The panics that implicated Indigenous culture touched a moral fibre in white society and heightened its claims to homogeneity. Over the past decade the court has been concerned to secure the interests of victims, potential victims and the sensibility of the wider community against the risk presented by the Indigenous offender. The Indigenous community too has been recast as perpetuating crimes through maintaining primitive practices and neglecting victims. Culture has been channelled into principles of deterrence and victimization to lengthen criminal sentences and send a disciplinary message to Indigenous communities with respect to their cultural practices. This chapter traces the Supreme Court's shifting representations from culture as an acceptable burden on the Indigenous offender and towards culture as a threat to the Anglo-Australian *nomos*. The court adorns its new narrative with a guarded whiteness, which requires excluding the threat of Indigenous culture through coercive containment.

Continuing, transforming and resisting cultures

In remote parts of the Northern Territory, Indigenous practices, customs and laws are evidence of the resilience of Indigenous communities in the face of colonizing processes. The survival of Indigenous cultures is far from a melancholy footnote to the story of imperialist conquest, but represents the reality of Indigenous human experience (Rowse 2011: 229). Indigenous resistance has tempered the state's attempts to discipline, normalize and assimilate the Indigenous domain (Blagg 2008). There is an ongoing evolution alongside the Anglo-Australian legal system of the laws and cultures that have regulated Indigenous societies for thousands of years and continue to affect the day-to-day lives of Indigenous peoples (Australian Law Reform Commission 1986: [163]; Law Reform Commission of Western Australia 2006: 11). In the Northern Territory this is partly due to Indigenous people's maintenance of connections with country and kinship while they worked on the cattle stations from the late nineteenth century until the 1960s, and then later when a number of communities received formal recognition of their ownership of their land under the Aboriginal Land Rights Act 1976 (Cth).[1] Even where Indigenous communities have not been able to remain on their country, their kinship systems have continued to inform Indigenous social and cultural ontologies to give purpose to their shared experiences (Turner-Walker 2011: 50).

Indigenous cultures across hundreds of communities, however, are subject to varied and dynamic relationships with Anglo-Australian society. Culture is

1 This legislation developed alongside contemporaneous enactments in other Australian jurisdictions, although often granting Indigenous people more limited access to their original land: Aboriginal Lands Act 1970 (Vic); Pitjantjatjara Land Rights Act 1981 (SA); Maralinga Tjarutja Land Rights Act 1984 (SA); and Aboriginal Land Rights Act 1983 (NSW). In the 1990s further legislation was passed allowing grants of land to be made under the: Aboriginal Land Act 1991 (Qld); Torres Strait Islander Land Act 1991 (Qld); and Aboriginal Lands Act 1995 (Tas).

changeable, internally diverse and variously affected by its interactions with introduced cultures (Bhabha 1994; Geertz 1985). Indigenous peoples increasingly move between Indigenous and non-Indigenous domains. For some Australian Indigenous communities, their first contact with non-Indigenous people occurred within current living memory. Where Indigenous people have been able to remain 'on country' it has involved 'enforced sedentarism', especially arising from their enforced dependency on supplies from cattle stations, ration depots or missions (Turner-Walker 2011: 50). This sedentary state is antithetical to Indigenous peoples' vast coverage of country for access to food and kin, and practice of ceremonies in pre-colonial times – although the latter continues to be carried out within more limited confines. Sedentation has also produced ongoing relations with non-Indigenous authorities and peoples and Indigenous cultural practices have been affected by such relationships.

Accordingly, Indigenous people in remote communities live in hybrid or 'liminal' domains where Indigenous and Anglo-Australian cultures and laws overlap, as is true for postcolonial Indigenous communities generally (Blagg 2008). In particular instances, cross-cultural engagement has led younger people away from Indigenous cultures and even fuelled inter-generational conflict. Some Elders believe that young people are becoming 'lawless' with no guiding authority within either Indigenous or Anglo-Australian systems (Anthony and Blagg 2012: 50). This has played out in some of the cases where the older offenders and relatives have sought to bring the victim back into the fold of Indigenous law, especially where the victim has left the community (see *R.* v. *GJ* 2005: 236; Dwyer 2008: 90; O'Connell 2006: 4). These complex experiences are washed over by a judicial alarm over Indigenous cultural practices and 'moral panics' in the public domain that cast a criminal net over all Indigenous communities and cultures (Cohen 2002).

Culture in the courts

Historically the Indigenous offender from remote parts of Australia has appealed to judicial tendencies to engage with 'the primitive' and epitomize its world view. This 'uncivilized' offender reinforces the positivist outlook of the courts and legitimizes their use of power and their jurisdiction over the Other (Anghie 2004: 63). Courts have embraced a paternalistic position in their capacity as sentencers. They act as gate keepers for cultural recognition, in the absence of a cultural defence at the trial stage.[2] They have performed this role by choosing whether to

2 While cultural or customary law evidence cannot be considered as a defence to excuse, justify or authorize criminal behaviour (Law Reform Commission of Western Australia 2006: 7 and 22), the Northern Territory Supreme Court has considered it in relation to provocation (which reduces murder to manslaughter): see *Jabarula* v. *Jambajimba* (1989); *Mungatopi* v. *R.* (1991); and *Lofty* v. *The Queen* (1999). Cultural evidence may also be considered in relation to other criminal procedures including bail (see Ch. 5; and Williams 2003).

accept cultural submissions and, if they choose to do so, how to interpret them. In this way, the courts filter and select which parts of Indigenous culture they deem to be proper and acceptable or repugnant and unacceptable (Motha 2005: 109). Recently they have regarded Indigenous people as having 'too much culture' and requiring normalization through punitive messages. The Northern Territory Supreme Court has advocated cultural change akin to Western norms, such as Indigenous customary marriage should be abandoned to free up Indigenous women to engage in employment and education. This reveals punishment's 'primary datum' to be social effect rather than the 'bodies of individuals', as Foucault (2007: 11) identified in *Sécurité, Territoire, Population*. Its role is to impose 'internal psychic constraints' on the Indigenous community such that the juridical field and social world collide (van Krieken 2004: 18).

Defendant submissions generally evince a *belief* that crimes were committed in the context of cultural practices, rather than arguing that culture actually permitted their actions. Submissions on culture do not excuse the conduct, but provide a context for understanding the beliefs of the offender. Leading cases on statutory rape in customary marriage where these types of submissions are considered involve serious harm (e.g. *Hales* v. *Jamilmira* 2003; *R.* v. *GJ* 2005) but have broader implications in more recent cases where the harm is less apparent (see *The Queen* v. *Redford* 2007; *The Queen* v. *Turner* 2011). The publicity relating to the leading cases creates the impression that they are common and easily made out by the defendant, whereas in fact they are a rarity and must meet special evidential procedures (Mildren 2008: 73). In fact, between 1994 and 2006 less than 1 per cent of Indigenous people sentenced before the Northern Territory Supreme Court submitted that customary law was relevant to their offending (Goldflam 2012: 8).[3] An Inquiry into the Protection of Aboriginal Children from Sexual Abuse stated that it did *not* come across any evidence that children were being regularly abused within customary marriage (Wild and Anderson 2007: 68). Where evidence of Indigenous culture is admitted, it must be presented to the Crown in due time and allowed to be scrutinized in cross-examination to address concerns about the quality of Indigenous evidence and to ensure its 'authenticity' (Sentencing Act 1995 (NT) s. 104A).[4] This measure is, as Watson (2009: 4) informs us, about making Indigenous culture 'knowable' to 'whites'.

From the early twentieth century, the Northern Territory Supreme Court has increasingly interpreted Indigenous cultures as both a damaging and regressive

3 Culture is also occasionally considered in sentencing in other jurisdictions, with the leading authority expounded in: *R.* v. *Daniel* (1998 per Fitzgerald J.) (Queensland); *R.* v. *Williams* (1976), *R.* v. *Shannon* (1991), *R.* v. *Goldsmith* (1995) (South Australia); *R.* v. *Njana* (1998), *R.* v. *Thompson* (2001), *R.* v. *Rictor* (2002) (Western Australia); and *R.* v. *Helmhout & Anor* (2000) (New South Wales).

4 This legislative provision was enacted in 2004 to address claims that cultural and customary law evidence lacked veracity. It was an attempt to tighten the protocol for admitting such evidence. However, the amendment merely formalizes the long-standing common law procedural requirements for the presentation of customary law evidence (Woodroffe 2006: 6).

influence on remote communities. This has seen a punitive turn away from courts affording leniency to offenders whose cultural beliefs have affected their moral culpability (see, e.g. *R.* v. *GJ* 2005: 248–9). The focus on deterrence for Indigenous offenders who submit community evidence crystallizes how Indigenous culture has been directed to aggravating a sentence. The reinterpretation of the role of culture in sentencing decries 'primitive' culture as repugnant to non-Indigenous values due to its criminogenic character. This is a potent metaphor for the illegitimacy of Indigenous culture in Anglo-Australian society. By inferiorizing Indigenous communities, culture has become a canvas for depicting the seriousness of the harm rather than attending to matters of blameworthiness.[5]

Culture, violence and metaphors of state paternalism

The 'legal storytelling'[6] of the Northern Territory Supreme Court has conflated Indigenous culture with violence. The court regards culture as inherently violent or subjugating of its vulnerable members (*R.* v. *Benny Lee* 1974; *R.* v. *GJ* 2005; *R.* v. *Lane, Hunt & Smith* 1980) or distorted by 'postcolonial' influences, such as drunkenness and idleness that give way to violence (Ch. 6; see also Sutton 2001: 135, 152). By cementing a view that Indigenous culture is violent, the Supreme Court justifies bringing Indigenous people under the protection of Anglo-Australian law with its attendant security and rationality. This view burdens everyone in Indigenous communities and confirms the power and privilege of Anglo-Australian culture (Watson 2008: 13). It also undermines the powerful role of Indigenous women in Indigenous law, culture and economies and demonizes Indigenous men (see Behrendt 1993: 28, 2002: 41, 2005: 249–50, 2006: 14; Davis and McGlade 2005; McGlade 2006: 9; Blagg 2008: 173; Atkinson 2006, 2006a: 14; Brown 2007: 14; Fougere 2006).

The presence of family violence in Indigenous communities has provided grounds for the Supreme Court to suggest that this violence is culturally sanctioned (*Amagula* v. *White* 1998: 10). However, it has been strongly asserted that

5 Courts refer to the 'seriousness of the offence' to refer exclusively to its harm, rather than the culpability of the offender. This is contrary to the High Court of Australia's view that Indigenous circumstances as they affect moral culpability are intrinsic to the measure of the seriousness of the offence (*Neal* v. *The Queen* 1982: 325). In the 1980s, the Northern Territory Supreme Court was willing to consider culture in mitigation, because while it did not excuse the crime, it helped explain it. Consideration of moral culpability as a sentencing principle continues to be provided for in legislation (e.g. Sentencing Act 1995 (NT) s. 5(2)(c)). Criminologists have widely recognized that culpability is a 'central dimension of seriousness' (von Hirsch 2004: 361; Ashworth 2002, 2005; Edney and Bagaric 2007: 99; and Easton and Piper 2005: 60).

6 'Legal storytelling' is understood within the critical jurisprudential framework that analyzes the law as a narrative of domination. It is particularly informed by the work of Delgado (2000: 64), who discusses 'stock stories' as the stories that institutions collectively tell about themselves – 'an account that justifies the world as it is' and therefore 'purports to be scrupulously meritocratic and fair'.

Indigenous culture does not permit family violence (Behrendt 2006: 14; Greer 2008; Watson 2008: 3–4; McCausland 2008: 58–9). Indeed, family violence is antithetical to Indigenous cultures and is a product of the violent processes of colonization (Behrendt and Watson 2008: 46; Atkinson 2002: 91–2; McGlade 2012). Criticisms have been particularly levelled at courts for 'culturalizing' rape (Watson 2008: 7, 13–14). Attempts to use culture to justify family violence are products of the 'male-centricity' of Australian law (Watson 2007; McGlade 2006). They amount to 'bullshit law' in their cultural fabrications to suit male interests (Davis and McGlade 2005: 389; Wohlan 2005: 526–8; Kimm 2004: 117; Payne 1990: 10). Such cultural constructs overlook the harmful consequences of violence for the Indigenous community as a whole (Behrendt 1993: 28; Cox *et al.* 2009: 151).[7]

Without wanting to essentialize Indigenous cultures and laws, they play a productive role in sustaining remote Indigenous communities. Judicial representations of culture have increasingly overlooked their functionality and the interest of Indigenous communities to keep culture strong (see Loy 2010; Gaymarani 2011; Gaykamangu 2012). Atkinson (2006b: 20) points out that associating culture with violence contributes to a 'redefinition and recreation' of culture in a 'negative manner' because it 'discounts the contemporary voices of Aboriginal women and men who are working to address the issue of violence'. Although Indigenous laws condemn violence, it cannot be said that Indigenous culture is situated in a chimera of harmony and pacifism, arising from a romantic ideal. Indigenous laws can encapsulate corporal punishment in the form of clubbing or spearing for very serious offenders, although most of their sanctions are non-violent. It is argued that in communities where Indigenous law punishment operates, they have among the lowest levels of violent crime (Loy 2010). Indigenous law punishment is discussed towards the end of this chapter in terms of a cultural practice that informs offending. However, it is dealt with in greater detail in the following chapter on Indigenous offenders who are also subject to Indigenous law punishment and the extent to which the Northern Territory Supreme Court accepts this as a mitigating factor. The courts in these instances have overlooked the positive purposes of Indigenous punishment, instead focusing on its incompatibility with Anglo-Australian norms.

The interpretive contingency of culture is brought to the fore in two key case studies in this chapter: (1) customary marriages where a promised bride is offered by her family to a man once she has reached puberty and the man has undergone initiation, resulting in statutory rape; and (2) assaults arising from contraventions of and stresses on customary relationships, including 'jealousing' (making a partner jealous to test commitment within intimate relationships[8]). It is also

7 Others have emphasized the role of Indigenous women in enforcing the Indigenous law (Dwyer 2008: 90; O'Connell 2006: 4).

8 Turner-Walker (2011: 71) notes that there is no Anglo-Australian equivalent for 'jealousing' because it is embedded in the uniqueness of Indigenous kin relations.

briefly considered in relation to the carrying out of Indigenous law punishment that involves an assault or property damage. The Supreme Court construes these cultural practices as furthering a cultural rite to commit the offence. They explain the offender's beliefs, although do not justify the offence. This includes where the offender has gone beyond the cultural entitlement, for example by committing an act of violence to procure sex by a promised bride. The murky version of culture, nonetheless, attracts the same response as cases where the victim and offender are in a customary marriage and the sexual act does not attach violence. Across all these cases, the Supreme Court is presented with charges of (consensual) statutory rape (to use the generic term for 'sexual intercourse with a child under 16'[9]) rather than (non-consensual) sexual assault, but the court's response of condemning Indigenous culture is consistent. A murky version of cultural rites also emerges in relation to jealousing, which is a product of cultural strain (Blagg 2008: 145) as well as protecting kinship relations because interpersonal capital is 'one of the most highly prized resources in the remote Aboriginal domain' (Turner-Walker 2011: 71).[10] The breakdown of culture inflames stresses and insecurities in Indigenous relationships, but the court has set these issues aside to focus on the role of the Indigenous community in condoning violence.

Despite the problematic and changeable nature of cultural constructs, these case studies are used as a heuristic device to concentrate on judicial interpretations of culture, and demonstrate changes over time based on a reconceptualization of alterity. The focus is on the Northern Territory Supreme Court's concern with crimes that are explicable with reference to Indigenous law or culture, rather than any violent aspect that is not sanctioned by the Indigenous community. Drawing this line shows how the court has reinterpreted Indigenous culture to blame the Indigenous community for the wrongs of its offenders and to set it apart from the morality of Anglo-Australian social norms. Due to its perceived risk, there has been a downplaying of culture in the courts' mitigating repertoire and longer sentences for offenders who are used as an example of the harsh consequences for pursuing cultural practices.

Parliament's privileging of punitiveness above culture

Sentencing remarks on culture are also a product of Federal and Northern Territory parliamentary attempts to confine its relevance in sentencing. In the parliamentary debate on the Northern Territory's Sentencing Bill in 1995, the government refused to list Aboriginal customary law as a consideration (Bell 1995: 4756). Of greater concern than the interests of the Indigenous community

9 Criminal Code Act (NT) s. 127.

10 While 'jealousing' may inform the offender's beliefs, it has been argued that the violent response to this provocative act is not culturally acceptable (Mals *et al.* 2008: 33; and Day *et al.* 2008: 180).

or the defendant's moral culpability, which can contribute to leniency, was the wider community's interest in the imposition of harsh punishment. An emblazoned response to cultural considerations in sentencing was delivered by the Federal Parliament in 2007, which was sparked by moral panics over violent Indigenous cultures and judicial leniency. The Federal Parliament prohibited cultural practice and customary law factors from sentencing and bail considerations in the Northern Territory (Northern Territory National Emergency Response Act 2007 (Cth) ss. 90–1) on the premise that culture was a 'veneer' for Indigenous offending (see Jones 2006).

Before the federal sentencing restrictions, the Northern Territory Supreme Court's sentencing remarks from the late 1990s were watering down the significance of culture, partly in response to sentencing reforms that had promoted longer prison sentences (*Hales* v. *Jamilmira* 2003: 9–10; *R.* v. *GJ* 2005: 238–9). The Northern Territory Legislative Assembly in the mid 1990s challenged the established thinking on the role of culpability in punishment by focusing on the seriousness of the offence. It emphasized 'law-and-order' through longer prison sentences in proposing sentencing amendments (Finch 1995: 3387). The effect of this punitive drift was seen in the Northern Territory Court of Appeal's decision of *Wurramara* (1999) (discussed in Chapter 6), which has made it incumbent on courts to place the seriousness of the offence above considerations of culpability. The Sentencing Act 1995 (NT) provides for higher maximum sentences, the introduction of minimum and mandatory prison penalties and the abolition of suspended sentences for prison terms of more than 2 years (Flynn 1994: 213; Pratt 2008: 269; Zdenkowski 1999). Amendments in 1999 saw mandatory prison sentences for sexual offending and certain violent offences (Sentencing Act 1995 (NT) ss. 78BA–BB). These changes were informed by an ideology of 'truth in sentencing' that endeavoured to have sentences reflect the harm of the offence and respond to public concerns that sentences were too lenient (Flynn 1994: 211).[11] The Northern Territory Government sought to send 'a clear and strong message to offenders' that they 'will not be treated lightly', particularly by imposing mandatory sentences (Burke 1996a: 9689).

The Second Reading Speech for the Northern Territory Sentencing Bill 1995 gave precedence to safeguarding the interests of the victim. The Attorney-General underscored 'the role of the victim of a crime in the criminal justice process' and sought to 'ensure that the victims are not the forgotten people in the sentencing process' (Finch 1995: 3387). Indefinite sentences were proposed to satisfy victims 'that offenders pay their penalty and that society exacts retribution' (Bell 1995: 4756). In a later amendment, Attorney-General Brian Burke (1996: 8080) stated that the government has a 'solemn duty to care for those who have

11 Brown (1989: 161) challenges the assumption behind 'truth in sentencing', arguing that the public are being misled by the politicians and the media who fail to 'explain adequately the mechanics of the existing sentencing structure' (see also Zdenkowski 2000).

become victims of society's outlaws' through imprisoning victimizers and making them 'a secondary consideration'. The victim is an 'ideal victim' who is bereft of culture and through her injury taps into the popular morality (Crenshaw 1991: 1278).

While these law-and-order themes apply to all offenders in the Northern Territory, and operate across Western societies (Garland 2001: 7), they have distinct implications for Indigenous offenders and communities whose crimes occur in cultural settings within colonial states. The blanket focus on the offender's harm or potential for harm downplays a broad understanding of culpability. Where the Supreme Court sees culture, it is through a victimizing lens. This construction of Indigenous culture cements punitive messages of deterrence, delivered through imprisonment, which are directed not only to the offender, but to the Indigenous community more generally. Fleury-Steiner *et al.* (2009: 6) inform us that 'tough sanctions' have been accompanied by a rhetoric that 'creates new forms of knowledge of space, self, and the other'. This knowledge projects Indigenous cultures and spaces as a risk to victims and community members. The court relies on this knowledge to transform Indigenous cultures in accordance with Anglo-Australian norms and to create a *nomos* in which the will of the court prevails over competing cultural norms and mores.

Historical appropriations: cultural exclusion to cultural celebration

Early years of the Northern Territory Supreme Court: disciplining the body

The processes of colonization were still having an immediate impact on Indigenous people in the Northern Territory when the Supreme Court was constituted by a single judge, Wells J., between 1933 and 1952.[12] He was known for variously ignoring Indigenous law, excluding it from evidence or refusing to believe the evidence of Indigenous witnesses (Douglas 2005: 156; Mildren 2011: 119). He shunned government attempts to incorporate anthropological evidence that may have helped explain the offending behaviour in Indigenous cases (Read 2007: 09.5). His stance on Indigenous offenders was that they should have been subject to 'white man's law', its rules and narratives. Wells J.'s exclusion of Indigenous cultural or customary law factors was in line with the contemporary policy of Indigenous exclusion and segregation, which he espoused, including from the Bench (Douglas 2005: 155). He believed that Indigenous people should not be imprisoned with non-Indigenous people, preferring that they 'stayed on their communities away from white people' (Douglas 2009: 153). This explains

12 The Full Supreme Court in its appellate capacity did not commence until 1986. Between 1977 and 1986 appeals were made to the Federal Court of Australia, and before then to at least two judges of the High Court of Australia.

his support for corporal punishment rather than imprisonment, which he advocated exclusively for Indigenous people.

The infamous trial of *Tuckiar* v. *The King* (1934) signified Wells J.'s approach to sentencing Indigenous people in remote Northern Territory communities who were influenced heavily by Indigenous culture and laws. The issue of Indigenous law went to the heart of the trial, where the victim – a non-Indigenous police constable, Albert Stewart McColl – was killed due to reasons premised in Indigenous law. The defendant, Dhakiyarr Wirrpanda, was a Yolŋu Elder who had allegedly speared and killed McColl following his attempted rape of Dhakiyarr's wife (Read 2007: 09.5). Surrounding Dhakiyarr's trial, the media 'demand[ed] vengeance', while omitting reference to McColl's attempted rape (2007: 09.2, 09.5). Wells J.'s remarks reflected the media's sentiment and, following Dhakiyarr's conviction for murder, he refused to take into account matters of Indigenous law when handing down the death penalty.[13] The fact that Dhakiyarr was recognized as a 'completely uncivilised Aboriginal native' with no knowledge of the English language did not sound in leniency (*Tuckiar* v. *The King* 1934: 339). In delivering the sentence on Dhakiyarr, Wells J. focused on the seriousness of a crime and the fact it was inflicted upon a 'white' police officer. He sought especially to vindicate the 'white' officer's reputation. The trial was based on a number of legal errors, including Wells J.'s comment to the jury that Dhakiyarr's failure to give evidence inferred his guilt and his confession was not reliable because of his Indigenous background (1934: 343). Dhakiyarr appealed to the High Court on the grounds that Wells J. had misdirected the jury. The High Court upheld Dhakiyarr's appeal, quashing his conviction[14] and found that Wells J. acted in a way prejudicial to the defendant (1934: 344).

Wells J. would continue to serve a further 15 years on the Northern Territory Supreme Court where he would persistently deny Indigenous sentencing factors. He was vocal in his opposition to 'do-gooders' who sought to recognize Indigenous cultural issues, as well as the 'sloppy sentimentality' of those who believed that Indigenous people should be able to administer their own punishment without interference from the courts (Read 2007: 09.5). Although not generally interested in Indigenous matters, Wells J. still perceived Indigenous offenders as being inherently backward, which required harsh physical punishment to teach them a lesson. His support for corporal punishment was merely hypothetical because at the time it was not available to him as a sentencing option. Therefore, for serious crimes committed by Indigenous defendants, the typical punitive response of Wells J. was to order the death sentence on the grounds that Indigenous people were incapable of integration (Douglas 2009: 153). This is tantamount to

13 The death penalty was not mandated by statute. In sentencing Dhakiyarr, Wells J. refused to mitigate the death penalty as permitted by the Crimes Ordinance 1934 (Cth), as he believed this legislation to be ill conceived in its operation on Aboriginal people (see Douglas 2005: 162).

14 This was largely due to the fact that a retrial could not be fairly conducted in light of the media campaign against Dhakiyarr (*Tuckiar* v. *The King* 1934: 344).

what Foucault (1979: 82) described as inflicting discipline on the body. Power was performed through physical means in order to display the authority of the court.

Justice Kriewaldt's adoption of cultural leniency: disciplining the soul

If Wells J.'s approach to Indigenous offenders was to be understood as disciplining the body, then his successor's approach was one of civilizing the soul through internalizing moral constraints (Elias 1978: 127). This civilizing process of inscribing the 'target soul' (Foucault 1979: 82) sought to integrate Indigenous people into the Anglo-Australian system. During his reign as the sole judge of the Northern Territory Supreme Court, from 1951 to 1960, Kriewaldt J. ordered prison sentences for Indigenous offenders, rather than the death penalty, because it assisted in the integration process. His rationale was that the routine of prison would be beneficial to changing Indigenous habits and drawing them closer to civilization (Douglas 2004: 307). Through prison Indigenous people would also be taught about the superior, more rational punishments of the Anglo-Australian system. At the same time, Kriewaldt J. felt that some leniency should be provided for Indigenous cultural circumstances, given that they were markers of backwardness and disadvantage. In this respect, leniency amounted to a compensatory gesture (Douglas 2005: 174–5). By consistently handing down prison sentences for Indigenous offenders, albeit with mitigatory intonations, Kriewaldt J. demonstrated the authority of the Anglo-Australian law.

Kriewaldt J.'s reasoning was conterminous with the prevailing ideology of assimilation, as Douglas (2002: 204) presents in her vast study of his judgments. It was a break from Wells J.'s segregationist views that dovetailed the contemporaneous protectionist policy of placing Indigenous people on settlements and controlled under different laws known as 'the Aboriginal Acts'. The policy of assimilation was predicated on the view that Indigenous people would come to live like non-Indigenous Australians after sufficient instruction and cultural absorption (Hasluck 1953: 16).[15] Dodson (1994: 8) describes assimilation as based on a view that colonizers would save 'the primitive' from 'a life that is "nasty, brutish and short"'. The implementation of assimilation invoked an increased scrutiny of Indigenous people as the 'objects' of white 'experts'. Kriewaldt J. readily accepted cultural evidence from anthropologists who he regarded as leading authority on Indigenous matters (Douglas 2005: 190). Anthropologists were integral to the assimilationist project by making Indigenous culture and its attendant uncivilized ways knowable to colonizers (Finnane 2006: 11).

15 The assimilation policy was trail blazed in the mid twentieth century in the Northern Territory by the Minister for Territories, Paul Hasluck.

Kriewaldt J. regarded his role on the Bench to inculcate Indigenous people with white norms (Douglas 2002: 211).

In delineating the boundaries for cultural recognition, Kriewaldt J. was inclined to hand down more lenient sentences for Indigenous offenders than non-Indigenous offenders convicted of similar offences due to their Indigenous cultural disadvantage. In *R.* v. *Anderson* (1954: 249), a case of an Indigenous man who attempted to rape a non-Indigenous woman, Kriewaldt J. commented that: 'In general it has been my practice . . . to impose on natives sentences substantially more lenient than the sentence imposed on white offenders for similar offences'. Alternatively, the nearer the offender's 'mode of life and general behaviour' is to a non-Indigenous person, the closer the punishment to that of a non-Indigenous person (1954: 249). Because in this instance the offender was under the influence of alcohol, knew some English and was in contact with 'white civilization', he was regarded as 'sophisticated' and 'substantially civilized' and therefore unable to benefit from mitigation relating to his culture (1954: 249). Therefore, unlike those less 'civilized' in the bush, Indigenous people in 'modern' settings (such as on reserves and where alcohol is accessible) could therefore not rely on their Indigeneity in mitigation because they had the 'benefit' of normalization.

Offenders who were living a 'traditional' lifestyle deserved to have their 'cultural shortcomings' considered in sentencing, according to Kriewaldt J. He perceived these offenders as possessing little knowledge of Anglo-Australian ways, not fluent in English and having little contact with non-Indigenous people or society and therefore cut off from the benefits of Anglo-Australian laws and values. The Supreme Court valorized cultural practices involving Indigenous weapons, such as where spears and boomerangs were used in 'tribal law matters' (see *R.* v. *Aboriginal Charlie Mulparinga* 1953). The weapons spoke to the truly primitive, and much festishized, nature of Indigenous culture in remote communities. In *R.* v. *Aboriginal Charlie Mulparinga* (1953: 220), the defendant, who believed he was acting in accordance with his law, killed an Indigenous man living at Areyonga (west of Alice Springs, Northern Territory) on tribal orders. The victim had breached 'tribal' law by revealing 'tribal secrets' to women and showing blood on his arm from a ceremony. Kriewaldt J. handed down a lenient sentence of 18 months' imprisonment due to what he judged as being the defendant's 'primitive culture', but nonetheless emphasized that a custodial sentence should deter 'other natives who may be minded to exact tribal vengeance' (1953: 223).

In providing mitigation for Indigenous 'backwardness', Kriewaldt J. sowed the seeds for the recognition of Indigenous culture in sentencing. This reveals the fraught beginnings of recognition based on a 'stock story' of Indigenous inferiority that was set on an evolutionary path to civilization (Bell 2010: 29). The court regarded the criminal justice system as a vehicle for facilitating Indigenous advancement. From the Bench, judges could condemn or condone Indigenous actions as fitting within its moral sphere. Indigenous people who did not perform designated 'traditional' roles in the cultural 'script' set for them by the court would be punished more harshly, such as where they consumed alcohol or used weapons of Anglo-Australian society (Goffman 1958). Accordingly, Kriewaldt J. did not hesitate to impose greater penality where culture was insufficiently primitive. In this respect, Hay (1975: 62) informs us that judicial power is assured by giving leniency with one hand and denying it with the other. It places Indigenous community under a cloud of uncertainty in relation to how the court's power will be exercised, and allows the court to present itself as the benevolent paternalist while perpetuating 'bonds of condescension' (1975: 40, 48).

Sentencing from the 1970s: cultural valorization

By the 1980s, no longer satisfied that 'civilization' would cure Indigenous cultural ills, the Northern Territory Supreme Court viewed the 'civilizing' process as a cause of Indigenous disadvantage. To overcome its devastating effect, it encouraged cultural practices to restore Indigenous community harmony, particularly in terms of reintegrating offenders. On this premise, cultural practices and relationships were recognized as critical to Indigenous offenders' world views. Where they were relevant to offending, the court appreciated their role in reducing the offenders' moral culpability and producing shorter sentences. From the late 1970s, culture was not simply construed as a disadvantage or contributing to Indigenous peoples' lack of understanding of Anglo-Australian norms. In line with the abandonment of the official assimilation policy, the court regarded Indigenous societies as capable of coexisting with Anglo-Australian society. The putative government policy of self-determination that gave Indigenous people some control over their affairs, communities and land, including through the Aboriginal Land Rights Act 1976 (Cth), saw the Federal Government recognize the capacities of Indigenous communities to act as self-governing bodies (Mildren 1996: 51–2). From the Bench, judges projected a nostalgic view of Indigenous culture as a product of a romantic past. This, according to Dodson (1994: 8), is the colonizers' recognition of Indigenous people as 'a counterpoint against which the dominant society can critique itself'. The romantic ideal offers Anglo-Australia 'hope of redemption and of recapturing what it feels it has lost in its march forward' (1994: 8).

The Supreme Court conceived culture as a significant mitigating factor because it reduced offenders' culpability and provided options for reformation. It took a keen interest in Indigenous evidence including where the offences were serious (see *R.* v. *Job Warusam* 1993; *R.* v. *Minor* 1992: 192–3). No longer filtering such evidence exclusively through anthropologists, the court accepted it directly from Indigenous people as 'experts' on their culture (Douglas 2009: 181). This tied up Indigenous community members in the work of the court – affording them agency while placing them under intense scrutiny and accountability (Douglas 2005a: 141, 155; Finnane 2006: 11). The Supreme Court's attitude to community submissions on cultural matters is apparent in the case of *R.* v. *Davey* (1980), where a 34-year-old Indigenous person from Borroloola (near the Gulf of Carpentaria,

Northern Territory) was convicted of manslaughter. The Indigenous victim had interfered in an argument between Davey and his wife, and made remarks that Davey's wife was previously promised to him. This provocation led to the offender striking the victim with a large piece of timber. An Elder gave evidence that the remarks were improper under the local Indigenous law. At first instance Gallop J. of the Northern Territory Supreme Court made the following comment to the offender in his sentencing remarks: 'you were forced to take some sort of an action according to your tribal customs and traditions' and the victim 'should not have intervened' (*R.* v. *William Davey* 1980a: 29). The court attached significant weight to the views of the offender's community, stating that it paid 'close regard' to the community's sentiment that the offence was mostly the victim's fault and that the offender 'should come back into the community' (1980a: 29–30).

In *R.* v. *William Davey* (1980a), the Supreme Court imposed a sentence of three years' imprisonment, but suspended it upon Davey entering into a three-year good behaviour bond. Although not challenging the Indigenous evidence, the Crown appealed to the Full Federal Court of Australia on the grounds that too much emphasis was placed on 'tribal customs and traditions' and the sentence was manifestly inadequate. In dismissing the appeal, Muirhead J. noted that the Supreme Court took into account 'relevant considerations' that must be considered when 'dealing with offences which take place within aboriginal communities, and involving only those people' (*R.* v. *Davey* 1980: 257–8). The Federal Court held that it was appropriate to 'inform itself of the attitude of the aboriginal communities involved, not only on questions of payback and community attitudes to the crime, but at times to better inform itself as to the significance of words, gestures or situations which may give rise to sudden violence' (1980: 257).

Muirhead J. further commented that 'association with white people does not necessarily erase deep rooted customary fears or beliefs, nor does it eradicate the sense of what is, or what is not, acceptable or appropriate' (1980: 258). He noted that the defendant's 'past contact with the European community', having spent some years in a leprosarium, and later having worked as a stockman, did not threaten his cultural values. While Muirhead J. stressed the seriousness of the offence, he doubted whether a custodial sentence would have a deterrent effect. Rather, he pointed to the need to promote 'reformation' of offenders as the best form of societal protection and to this end he stated that it was fitting that the sentence be served in the community (1980: 261). This is a far cry from Kriewaldt J.'s position in the 1950s that reformation was not possible where crimes are committed by virtue of Indigenous moral beliefs and only discipline in the prison would advance and deter Indigenous offenders.

For the Federal and Supreme courts during this period, cultural and community influences would play a greater role than imprisonment in restoring the offender. In part this was due to a condescending belief that mainstream rehabilitation programmes outside of the Indigenous community were not tailored to 'the difficulties inherent in [the offender's] lack of so-called sophistication and language' (*R.* v. *Iginiwuni* 1975). In more positive terms, the Supreme Court stated in *Joshua* v. *Thomson* (1994: [39]) that reform could take place in the community on Groote Eylandt in the Gulf of Carpentaria because 'the continued unity and coherence of the group' meant that its own type of community service orders and sentencing regime responded to the significance of the crime. By contrast, long prison terms lack significance for Indigenous people because they 'do not have the same concept of time as do white people' (*R.* v. *Minor* 1992: 191).

Through recognizing cultural and community factors, the Supreme Court presented itself as a rational arbiter providing tailored justice. It sought to make Indigenous peoples appreciate the fairness of its jurisdiction. In *R.* v. *Lane, Hunt & Smith* (1980: 98–9), the court remarked that its duty was to 'encourage the acceptance of the criminal law' by prisoners and by the Indigenous community 'as a step towards a more orderly and unified society'. The court therefore determined that the punishment must be 'seen to be a well-deserved punishment' according to both the non-Indigenous *and* Indigenous community, rather than merely imposing an exemplary deterrent sentence (1980: 99). The seductive nature of individualized justice, according to the court, was matched with a view that the court was taking into account Indigenous circumstances in the same way it sentences any other group. This included recognizing facts relevant to the offender's membership of a particular community and any other relevant circumstances to the offence (*R.* v. *Miyatatawuy* 1996: 579; *Jadurin* v. *The Queen* 1982: 187; *R.* v. *Minor* 1992: 182). The Court of Appeal noted with approval the observations in *R.* v. *Iginiwuni* (1975) that whilst Indigenous peoples are 'subject to the same laws' as 'white people', the court makes 'allowance for ethnic, environmental and cultural matters' (quoted in *R.* v. *Minor* 1992: 191). In this respect, recognition of cultural 'difference' did not threaten the structure or universal application of the criminal law.

These remarks reveal how the court went further than it did under Kriewaldt J. in recognizing the importance of culture as an extenuating factor. While the court from the 1970s retained a discourse of Indigenous peoples' cultural disadvantage, it also acknowledged advantages in the Indigenous community's role in restoring the offender. This has been described as a form of 'soft legal pluralism' based on an acceptance of the capacity of the Indigenous community (Douglas 2005a: 141). It resulted in community-based sentences being offered in lieu of imprisonment for crimes of a cultural nature, which is expounded in the following chapter. This period of judicial accommodation was met with a backlash in the late 1990s due to an outcry over Indigenous crime and the perceived leniency of the judiciary in accounting for cultural circumstances. The Northern Territory Supreme Court and Court of Criminal Appeal after the late 1990s went on to re-imagine culture as harmful to the Indigenous community.

The judicial will to civilize: sentencing contemporary cultural crimes

The late 1990s was a turning point in Indigenous affairs, at which point the Federal Government questioned the policy of self-determination (Watson

2009a: 91–2) and the courts doubted the relevance of Indigenous community submissions. This was accompanied by a proliferation of negative political and media representations of remote Indigenous communities, particularly in terms of crime and dysfunction. Contrary to Indigenous views, the media underscored the relationship between 'customary law and Indigenous violence' and pointed the finger at Indigenous men in particular (Maddison 2009: 186). Commentators portrayed crime as endemic in remote Indigenous communities and claimed that offenders acquired an unfair advantage through cultural submissions (Toohey 2002c: 9, 2007, 2008: 12). O'Connell (2006: 8) claimed that the media and politicians 'love' to place Indigenous crimes under the banner of customary law in order to make a case for its abolition. Prime Minister John Howard (2006) stated that Indigenous offenders use culture as a veneer to avoid punishment by the Anglo-Australian legal system. This was articulated by the Minister for Indigenous Affairs in 2006, Mal Brough, who maintained that Indigenous offenders were 'hiding behind customary law' (O'Brien 2006).

At the same time, the Northern Territory appellate courts were placing less weight on cultural submissions. The courts became sensitized to the problem of violence in Indigenous communities and acted out the outrage of the wider community in relation to the repugnancy of culture. Whereas in the past the appellate courts associated cultural practices with reduced moral culpability and the capacity for offender restoration, in the late 1990s they came to focus on matters such as the interests of the wider community, the seriousness of the offence, the harm to the victim and the need for a deterrent custodial sentence directed to the Indigenous community. For the judiciary, culture was a canvas that created the impression of harm. This exposed the weak undergirding of judicial cultural recognition and how it is bound up with subordinating institutions (Fraser 1997). The courts sought to civilize and normalize Indigenous cultures through its messages of deterrence and longer prison sentences. The courts implied that the Indigenous community, in its will to perpetuate 'traditional cultures' does not appreciate the seriousness of violent offences. Shaw (2003: 329) notes that the courts have created a 'damaging fiction' of culture as 'abhorrent, barbaric and unsuited to the modern world'. This fiction implicates the Indigenous community to which the individual offender belongs.

In sharp contrast to the barbarism and abhorrence of the Indigenous offender is the sanctity of the victim. The victim has risen in status with the punitive shift in the West and the Northern Territory has been no exception (Garland 2001: 11; Pratt 2008: 271–2).[16] The Indigenous victim is classed as the 'ideal victim' who is defined by her moral character, according to Crenshaw (1991: 1278). The victim is devoid of culture and exclusively referred to in terms of her gender and

16 The new primacy placed on the interests of the victim has been facilitated by legislation introduced in 1997 that requires Northern Territory courts to accept Victim's Impact Statements pursuant to the Sentencing Act 1995 (NT) s. 106B. The Northern Territory is the only jurisdiction in Australia where legislation provides for the admission of these statements.

age (e.g. *R.* v. *GJ* 2005: 241). For the Supreme Court the victim embodies non-Indigenous social norms. An attack on the victim is, in the Durkheimian sense, an attack on the 'moral conscience' of society (Durkheim 1933: 70). Blagg (2008a: 138) notes that Indigenous women have traditionally found it hard to achieve victim status because of racist stereotypes, but they are now afforded victim status, 'provided they are positioned within victim discourse as *helpless, hopeless victims of traditional Aboriginal male violence, sanctioned – even encouraged – by Aboriginal law*'. Harm to the victim attests to the seriousness of an offence to legitimize long prison sentences and highlight the danger of culture for the purpose of promoting general deterrence. Where the victim resists Indigenous culture, or where the judiciary construes resistance in the absence of testimony, the victim is embraced (see *The Queen* v. *Redford* 2007). The victim in this sense has a consonance with 'whiteness'.[17] However, where the victim expresses 'cultural' views, such as in favour of the administration of Indigenous law punishment rather than a custodial sentence, the victim is dismissed (see Chapter 5). Through the lens of the victim, cultural factors in sentencing have been dislocated except in so far as they speak to the harm of the crime and justify calls for deterrence.

Sentencing statutory rape in customary marriages: the cultured offender and the culturally devoid victim

The boundaries of cultural recognition were tested in the cases of statutory rape within customary marriage arrangements. Although this type of offence had only been prosecuted once before the case of *Hales* v. *Jamilmira* (2003: 16), the Northern Territory Supreme Court's reasoning reveals a dispensation of the significance of mitigation for cultural circumstances. The defendants in these cases sought to argue that sex with their promised or actual wives in Indigenous law, who were under the age of consent, was allowed under Indigenous law (2003: 17; *R.* v. *GJ* 2005: 237; *The Queen* v. *Redford* 2007: 4). Indeed, until 2004 sex with a minor was decriminalized under legislation where the couple was married under Indigenous law (Criminal Code Act (NT) s. 129[18]). In this way the Northern Territory Legislative Assembly recognized customary marriages to preclude prosecuting these relationships. Nevertheless, since *Hales* v. *Jamilmira*, the court has re-imagined customary marriage as a risk factor in Indigenous communities. The court has sought to strongly deter this practice, which it views as giving rise to serious sexual offending. It is additionally concerned to stop these marriages because they place girls in the hands of older men and have an adverse impact on their employment and education opportunities.

17 Whiteness is a label that is not only attached to white people, but to anyone fulfilling white cultural norms (Brady and Carey 2000: 274).

18 Section 129(1) of the Criminal Code Act (NT), when read with the definition of 'unlawfully' in s. 126 and the definition of 'husband and wife' in s. 1, decriminalized under-age sex in Indigenous customary marriage.

The nature of customary marriage

The practice of customary marriage has taken place in Northern Territory Indigenous communities for thousands of years and continues to operate in a number of remote communities, although the arrangement is generally in decline (Wild and Anderson 2007: 71; Northern Territory Law Reform Committee 2003: 23, 2003a: 26).[19] Customary marriage is based on a highly complex system that involves a myriad of 'strictly regulated' relationships and responsibilities (Haebich 2000: 594; Northern Territory Law Reform Committee 2003a: 24). Where it continues to be practised, customary marriage is regarded as essential to the transmission and continuation of Indigenous law, culture, ceremonies, economies and land custodianship, as well as critical to genetic integrity (Kimm 2004: 62, 66; Gaymarani 2011: 290). The 2007 report of the Northern Territory Board of Inquiry into the Protection of Aboriginal Children from Sexual Abuse, 'Little Children Are Sacred', noted that customary arrangements between appropriate skin groups prevent inter-family marriages that would threaten group survival: 'As traditional "communities" comprised relatively small numbers of people, it was vital for the health of offspring that men only procreated with the "right skin"' (Wild and Anderson 2007: 66). Marriage outside of the right skin relationship is a serious breach of Indigenous law, and can result in harsh punishment under Indigenous law, such as in Arnhem Land where the *Ngarra* law of the Yolŋu people is practised (Gaymarani 2011: 290). Other serious breaches, whether committed by the man or woman, include sexual activity outside of the marriage, sexual assault, sexual relations with a pre-pubescent child, 'stealing a wife', sexual activity with a boyfriend or girlfriend from another clan and domestic violence (2011: 291–2, 294; Gaykamangu 2012: 244).

While arrangements vary among communities, customary marriages generally involve promised brides offered as a reward for male initiates. Very young women from appropriate skin groups are promised to men (around 30 or 40 years old[20]) who have undergone initiation, learnt the Indigenous law and provided food, clothing or payment to the promised wife's family (Gaymarani 2011: 289–90; Gaykamangu 2012: 245; Kimm 2004: 62). Neither the woman nor the man has a choice in the arrangement, which is based on a collective 'marriage contract' between groups (Wild and Anderson 2007: 68). Women enter the marriage once they are post-menarche. In Warlpiri society, the marriage commences when the woman moves in with her husband (Musharbash 2009: 51). However, in Indigenous societies further to the north, such as Yolŋu society, marriage begins from the time of the promise, but the man is forbidden from having sexual contact with the girl until she is a woman (post-pubescent) around 13 or 14 years

19 Customary marriages also exist in Western Australia (see Blagg 2008: 173; and McIntyre 2005: 343).

20 This is a rough figure because the concept of numerical 'age' is distinct to Western cultures (Wild and Anderson 2007: 69).

old (O'Connell 2006: 3; Gaymarani 2011: 289). Justice Mildren (2008: 70) has noted that courts find it difficult to discern when customary marriage has occurred because it is not marked by a symbolic ceremony that is apparent and knowable to outsiders.

Indigenous communities *condone* young women who have reached puberty having sexual relations within a customary marriage. However, sexual assault is *condemned* and punishable by Indigenous law (Gaymarani 2011: 294, 298). As a result, under-age sexual violence in customary marriages is very rare (Wild and Anderson 2007: 68). The cases discussed below are concerned with the charge of statutory rape in a promised marriage context, rather than sexual assault, even though in some cases violence accompanied the sexual act. Dwyer (2008: 90) has argued that the 'issue of promised marriages should be clearly distinguished from sexual abuse, which is part of the breakdown of functioning communities and the cycle of poverty', which can occur in both Indigenous and non-Indigenous communities. The Supreme Court stresses that its sentencing considerations across these cases are in relation to an offence where there is *consensual* sex with a minor within a promised marriage, due to the statutory rape charge brought before it (*R.* v. *GJ* 2005: 237; *Hales* v. *Jamilmira* 2003: 4, 21; *The Queen* v. *Redford* 2007: 6). Whether or not violence is inflicted on the victim, the judiciary's representations of Indigenous culture are consistent.

In the following cases of *Hales* v. *Jamilmira* (2003) and *R.* v. *GJ* (2005), although the promised brides had reached puberty, the offender was not cohabiting with his promised bride. In each case the promise had been made in accordance with local 'traditional Aboriginal law' and the defendants had offered income and goods to the victim's family as consideration for the promise (2003: 4–5; 2005: 235–6). Accordingly, the victim's family sought to have the marriage consummated. These offences 'occurred in communities where the practice of traditional marriage was still relatively strong and the impacts of colonisation [were] reduced due to relative geographical and social isolation' (Wild and Anderson 2007: 69). In *The Queen* v. *Redford* (2007) and *The Queen* v. *Turner* (2011), the offenders were convicted of statutory rape on their wives with whom they were cohabitating. In *The Queen* v. *Redford* (2007: 4), the defendant believed that the statutory rape amounted to an offence under Anglo-Australian law, but chose to follow the Indigenous law nonetheless. Defence submissions stressed that the cultural arrangement reduced the moral culpability of the offender. They pointed to the fact that until 2004 Northern Territory legislation decriminalized sexual relations with minors within customary marriage. This sent an ambivalent message to Indigenous people about the status of their laws in Anglo-Australian law.

Hales v. Jamilmira *(2003): statutory rape on a promised bride*

Within the small corpus of customary marriage cases before Northern Territory's higher courts, *Hales* v. *Jamilmira* (2003) presented the first real opportunity for the

Northern Territory Court of Appeal to consider its significance in sentencing.[21] It arose from the conviction of a 49-year-old Indigenous male, Jamilmira, from Maningrida (in Arnhem Land, on the northern tip of the Northern Territory) for committing statutory rape on his 15-year-old promised wife. The day after the offence, when the victim attempted to leave, Jamilmira fired a shotgun, causing the victim to fear for her friends who were present and for herself (2003: 3). The victim's family had placed stress on Jamilmira to fulfil his responsibilities as a promised husband, which he was seen to have been failing to do because the victim was already sexually active and using 'gunja' (cannabis). Jamilmira was convicted of statutory rape and discharging a firearm likely to endanger others. The offender submitted that his sentence for the statutory rape should be mitigated on the grounds that the relationship had almost reached the status of customary marriage when sex would have been warranted in Indigenous (Burarra) law (2003: 7, 14). He had been providing payment to the 15-year-old's family since she was born in consideration of this marriage and lived according to Burarra laws. A Burarra witness gave evidence that customary marriage was still practised in Maningrida, and the victim's family had arranged for the victim to be sent to her promised husband on his outstation (2003: 15).

Initially, the sentence for statutory rape was 13 months' imprisonment (suspended after 4 months, with an operational period of 18 months) and two months' imprisonment for the firearms offence. On appeal to the Northern Territory Supreme Court, Gallop A.J. reduced it to 24 hours for the statutory rape and 14 days for the firearms offence because the magistrate failed to give due weight to 'traditional law' (*Pascoe* v. *Hales* 2002). The appeal judge also had the benefit of additional anthropological evidence that sexual relations between an older man and his promised wife is not considered deviant in his Burarra society as customary marriage is 'the cultural ideal, sanctioned and underpinned by a complex system of customary law and practice' (2002: [7]). Gallop A.J. stated that he was surprised the appellant had been charged at all, but noted that it was probably his conduct of firing the gun that led to police attention (2002: [5]–[6]).

The Crown then appealed to the Northern Territory Court of Criminal Appeal, where the majority was unwilling to find that the statutory rape was necessitated by customary law and increased the sentence to 12 months, which could be suspended after 1 month (*Hales* v. *Jamilmira* 2003: 11). The court felt that Northern Territory legislation allowing under-age sex within customary marriage constrained it from giving a higher sentence. Notwithstanding the legislative recognition of customary marriage, the court averred to the 'irreconcilable conflict' between Burarra laws of promised marriage and the Anglo-Australian laws (McIntyre 2005: 344). Ultimately, it was determined that 'the law of the Northern Territory must prevail' (*Hales* v. *Jamilmira* 2003: 22). Findlay (2006: 155)

21 The only other previous case was *R.* v. *Mungurala* (1974). This was not analogous to *Hales* v. *Jamilmira* (2003) because it involved an offender who was not aware that the victim was promised to him.

describes this dilemma facing the courts in terms of the need to give universal effect to the protection of young female victims against measuring liability in terms of legitimate customary expectations.

In its remarks, the Court of Criminal Appeal downplayed the significance of cultural context for reducing the offender's culpability. It held that while promised marriage had been part of the law of the Burarra society for thousands of years and sex with a promised female under 16 was not considered aberrant in Maningrida, it could not be regarded as a significant factor given the defendant knew he was not *required* to have sex with his promised bride under Indigenous law (*Hales* v. *Jamilmira* 2003: 15, 9). The court deferred to the wider community which had an interest in protecting women, and sought to deter others in the Burarra community from similar offending (2003: 11, 22). The values of the wider community were placed in opposition to the values of the Burarra community that were constructed as misogynistic. Martin C.J. recognized that for decades the average age of first time mothers at Maningrida was 15 years; however, 'the perspective of the wider Territory community' justifies the operation of the Anglo-Australian law over Burarra law (2003: 7). He noted that 'personal and general deterrence' must feature as significant sentencing factors, otherwise it would send the 'wrong message' to Burarra society that under-age sex in customary marriage is permissible (2003: 9–10).

The majority emphasized the harm to the victim, although the 'victim is rendered mute' in the process (Douglas 2005b: 182, 200). She is quoted as being 'sad and upset' and 'angry with everyone' (*Hales* v. *Jamilmira* 2003: 8). However, the court does not make much of this statement, preferring to rely on an abstract concept of the ideal and passive victim who is defined by her age (2003: 20–1). This allows a binary between the culturally neutral victim, the culturally charged offender and the community who threaten the vulnerable and augments the protective role of the court in relation to victims. Only the dissenting judge, Mildren J., considered that the 'social pressures' on the defendant as a result of Indigenous laws were 'relevant to moral blame and therefore to sentencing' (2003: 15). He was especially mindful of the legislation that allowed under-age sex in customary marriages at the time of the offence (2003: 15). Mildren J. emphasized that this 'was not a case . . . of the respondent using his position as an older person to satisfy his lust' (2003: 14).

The media and politicians devoured *Hales* v. *Jamilmira* as an example of an over-sexualized culture that permitted harm to its children. Such images would later be brought to life by the Federal Government when the Minister for Indigenous Affairs made claims that paedophile rings were operating in remote communities (Jones 2006). In the meantime, Northern Territory parliamentarians claimed that *Hales* v. *Jamilmira* gave the issue of customary marriage a 'high, public profile' and the community reaction demanded that legislators do 'something more to protect young Aboriginal girls' (Braham 2003). The shadow Attorney-General claimed that 'customary law assists violent men and penalises victims who are, for the most part, Aboriginal women and girls' (Carney 2003).

Commentators also criticized the Supreme Court for supporting 'tribal' law and failing to apply Anglo-Australian law and its harsh punishment (Toohey 2008: 12). Toohey (2002a: 10) wrote in *The Australian* that anthropological evidence of custom is 'heavily weighted in favour of the tribal rights of men' and this results in 'lenient and even meaningless sentences for sexual assaults and murders of Aboriginal women'. He described customary marriage as 'barbaric' and contrary to the values of the 'wider Australian community' (Toohey 2002b: 21, 2002: 1). Bolt (2002: 19) in the *Herald Sun* criticized the Supreme Court for applying 'cultural relativism – a fashionable theory that says our culture is no better than more primitive ones'. He called on the government to uphold 'civilised laws' rather than adhere to 'despotic tribal law' (2002: 19). The Northern Territory Legislative Assembly subsequently criminalized underage sex in customary marriage in 2004.[22] The Attorney-General declared: 'This government believes it has a responsibility to protect all Territory children, wherever they live and whatever their circumstances . . . with one law for all' (Aagaard 2004). This enactment paved the way for higher sentences for this category of offence.

R. *v.* GJ *(2005): statutory rape post-criminalization of under-age sex in customary marriage*

The criminalization of under-age sex in customary marriage was tested in the case of *R.* v. *GJ* (2005). It revealed a hardening of judicial views towards statutory rape in customary marriage, especially by Mildren J., who led the majority and departed from his dissenting position in *Hales* v. *Jamilmira.* Three months before GJ's offence on 20 June 2004, the customary marriage immunity for statutory rape was removed and its maximum penalty was increased (2005: 237, 240; Mildren 2008: 71). In *R.* v. *GJ*, a 54-year-old Ngarinaman man had sex with a 14-year-old promised bride from the Yarralin community in central Australia. The defendant lived according to Ngarinaman law and had little contact with Anglo-Australian society and its criminal justice system. English was his fourth language and he had not met a non-Indigenous person until the age of 30. His lawyer described him as a man struggling with change in a colonizing world (O'Connell 2006: 4). The defendant had taken the victim's brother through ceremony and had provided, and continued to provide at the time of the trial, goods to the family of the promised wife as consideration for the customary marriage (2006: 4).

The circumstances of the statutory rape offence were that the victim's grandmother had sent her to be with the defendant on his outstation, as she believed it was her granddaughter's obligation under Ngarinaman law (*R* v. *GJ* 2005: 236).

22 On 17 March 2004, the Criminal Code Act (NT) was amended by the Law Reform (Gender, Sexuality and De Facto Relationships) Act 2003 (NT) to make the criminalization of sexual intercourse with a child under the age of 16 extend to sex within customary marriage. The Act amends s. 127(1)(a) of the Criminal Code Act (NT).

The grandmother and defendant suspected that the victim was having a sexual relationship with a young boy in Darwin and were concerned that she was turning her back on her family and the Ngarinaman way of life (Dwyer 2008: 90). For this, her 70-year-old grandmother struck the victim with a *nulla nulla*[23] and the defendant struck her with a boomerang (*R* v. *GJ* 2005: 236). On the outstation, the defendant threatened the victim with a boomerang and had anal intercourse with her, resulting in a deep laceration (2005: 237). From the outset, GJ asserted that he had acted within his rights, believing it was acceptable to have sex with a 14-year-old who was promised to him, including through force where the promised bride did not comply (2005: 238). It was not argued that forced anal sex was part of Indigenous law, but the defendant believed that the victim must submit to sexual relations to fulfil cultural obligations.

In dealing with the charges of statutory rape and aggravated assault, the Supreme Court imposed a 2-year prison sentence, which could be suspended after serving 1 month. Martin C.J. regarded this as a serious sentence that reflected the objective seriousness of the offence and would send a message of deterrence. The Chief Justice delivered his sentence in Yarralin in front of community members, and had his remarks translated in the local language and distributed in the community (Dwyer 2008: 89). He stated, 'I hope that by the sentence that I am going to impose upon you, that the message will get out not just to your community, but to communities across the Territory' (*The Queen* v. *GJ* 2005a: 3). The victim was of paramount concern and the court sought to remind the defendant 'about how the child felt' (2005a: 4). Nonetheless, the Chief Justice held that the offender's culpability was reduced because he believed that his actions were permissible and justified under the Ngarinaman law. While the Indigenous law did not condone the offence, and nor did the courts condone this law, the defendant's view was 'a factor relevant to sentence' (2005a: 4).

The Yarralin community considered the delivery of sentencing remarks on country, rather than in the far away cities of Darwin or Alice Springs, as a mark of enormous respect (O'Connell 2006: 6). The community embraced the role of the court and sought to heed its remarks. Such respect was subsequently lost when the appellate courts overturned the decision without telling the community. One 'old man' said that 'whitefellas' are 'always doing that – telling us one thing to our face and then changing their minds behind our back' (quoted in 2006: 6). The Court of Appeal's failure to communicate with the Yarralin community nullified the impact of the *GJ* decision, thus failing to shift cultural attitudes about customary marriage (Wild and Anderson 2007: 71). GJ himself was not present at the appeal and had little understanding of the decision when he was picked up 4 months after he was released to be reimprisoned (O'Connell 2006: 6). Consequently, as noted in the 'Little Children Are Sacred Report', 'many Aboriginal people were still confused as to the age of consent and as to

23 A *nulla nulla* is a wooden weapon in the form of a club or hunting stick and approximates a baton.

the general state of the wider Australian law as far as traditional marriage practices were concerned' (Wild and Anderson 2007: 71).

The Northern Territory Court of Criminal Appeal increased the sentence to 3 years and 11 months, which could be suspended after serving 18 months. Mildren J.'s leading judgment proffered that Ngarinaman law carried 'less weight' because the offender was not 'under any pressure' to act in the way he did (*R.* v. *GJ* 2005: 240). Furthermore, the defendant's belief that he was acting in accordance with culture worked against him because he felt vindicated and lacked the mitigating consideration of remorse (2005: 239). The Court of Criminal Appeal found that the Supreme Court failed to adequately account for the objective seriousness of the offence, especially given the youthfulness of the victim (2005: 240–1). The court maintained that the sentence should 'reflect and recognise' the seriousness of the offence 'in the eyes of the wider community' (2005: 239). Mildren J. stated that victims require protection from older male offenders' 'taking advantage of the immaturity of the young in order to *satisfy their lust*' (2005: 241, emphasis added). This is a marked departure from his view in *Hales* v. *Jamilmira* (2003: 14), where he held that the defendant's cultural belief meant that it was not an offence based on lust.

Protecting Ngarinaman people from their laws relating to customary marriage was a significant rationale for a more punitive sentence on the offender. The court held that Martin C.J.'s lighter sentence would not deter 'others who might feel inclined to follow their traditional laws' (*R.* v. *GJ* 2005: 241). Deterrence penalties were required to respond to the threat of violence in Indigenous communities arising from, inter alia, customary law, and to uphold the Northern Territory law. In commenting on s. 127(1)(a) of the Criminal Code Act (NT) that prohibits sex with a minor, including since 2004 in customary marriages, Mildren J. projected a Kriewaldt-like civilizing agenda. He interpreted customary marriage as a threat to 'ideal' victims and claimed that criminalization freed them from customary marriage for their advancement in other spheres. Mildren J. underscored the need to:

> give Aboriginal girls some freedom of choice as to whether or not they want to enter into such a marriage and to thereby empower them to pursue equally with young Aboriginal men employment opportunities or further education rather than be pushed into pregnancy and traditional domesticity prematurely.
>
> (*R.* v. *GJ* 2005: 241)

Although Southwood J. generally agreed with Mildren J.'s conclusions, a few notes of caution were sounded. Against Mildren J.'s emphasis on 'freedom of choice' for women, Southwood J. pointed to the 'beneficial influence' of customary marriage in Indigenous communities (2005: 249). In shying away from Western subjectivities, his dissenting remarks reignited the embers of moral culpability. He maintained that a person acting in accordance with Indigenous law 'may be less morally culpable than someone who has acted in an utterly contumelious way without any justification whatsoever' (2005: 249). Whereas Mildren J. stressed the need to teach Indigenous people in GJ's community to conform to the criminal law (2005: 241), Southwood J. cautioned against the offender shouldering the burden of community education through a particularly harsh sentence (2005: 249).

Nonetheless, these dissenting remarks are the exception that proves the rule: Indigenous law considerations aggravate a sentencing in the name of deterrence, denunciation and protection of victims (Southwood 2007: 12).[24] The Court of Appeal associates culture with harm to victims, including all women whose opportunities are encumbered by the practice of customary marriage. Projecting these values, the mainstream media and Federal Government latched onto *GJ's* case to convey the need for tougher sentences (Toohey 2005; Devine 2006: 1). The Editorial of *The Australian* declared: 'One Law for All: Our legal system must reinforce Australian values' (Editor 2006: 19). The barbarism of Indigenous culture was pitched against the protectiveness of 'white' law. The Federal Justice Minister, Chris Ellison, said he was 'repulsed' by *GJ's* case, which he likened to child trafficking (Young 2005: 16). Citing *R.* v. *GJ*, a senior Federal Government minister asserted that 'Aboriginal culture enshrined exploitation and violence' (Abbott 2006). Toohey (2005) maintained that Martin C.J.'s first instance decision 'succumbed to the charisma of Aboriginal culture' in setting aside the rights of a child 'who should enjoy the protection of the overriding (white) law' (see also Morrell 2005: 18). This strident criticism in the media prompted the Chief Justice to issue a public apology for the light sentence, although not for his consideration of the cultural circumstances (Martin 2005: 12; see also Merritt 2006: 1). The Indigenous Affairs Minister subsequently attacked cultural considerations in sentencing for protecting GJ 'from the full force of law that every other Australian would appropriately have applied to them' (O'Brien 2006).

These anxieties over the misplaced judicial accommodation of customary law in the GJ decision and the threatening nature of Indigenous culture were symptomatic of the 'disturbed state of an unfinished colonialism' (Finnane 2006: 1). They prompted sweeping legislative reforms in relation to sentencing and Northern Territory Indigenous communities broadly. The government's main weapon was the passage of laws that restricted cultural considerations for mitigating or aggravating a sentence in the Commonwealth jurisdiction (where very few crimes are tried) and in the Northern Territory (Crimes Act 1914 (Cth) s. 16A(2A); Northern Territory National Emergency Response Act 2007 (Cth) s. 91).[25] In commending the Commonwealth Bill to Parliament, the Justice

24 The accused unsuccessfully sought leave to appeal the decision to the High Court of Australia (*GJ* v. *The Queen* 2006).

25 Both legislative provisions stated that in 'determining the sentence', 'a court must not take into account any form of customary law or cultural practice as a reason for: (a) excusing, justifying, authorising, requiring or lessening the seriousness of the criminal behaviour to which the offence relates; or (b) aggravating the seriousness of the criminal behaviour to which the offence relates'.

Minister said that it sought to 'remedy those situations in which the consideration of customary law or cultural practice has led or may lead to inappropriately lenient sentences' and to address Indigenous violence against women (Ellison 2006: 15). The editor (2006: 19) of *The Australian* 'applauded' these efforts to 'make sure that the Australian legal system – and not any other system, be it tribal, sharia, or the Napoleonic Code – governs the conduct of all Australians'. Fuelled by this moral panic, the Federal Government also sought to 'crackdown on the practice of young Indigenous girls being subjected to forced marriages under traditional law' through extensive policing and controls of Indigenous communities (Young 2005: 16). This involved the roll out of law enforcement in 2006 and culminated in a military intervention into Northern Territory Indigenous communities in 2007 (see below). In the meantime, the Supreme Court continued to deter customary marriage in consensual relationships when statutory rape cases came before it.

Redford *and* Turner*: statutory rape within customary marriage*

The case of *The Queen* v. *Redford* (2007), involving a defendant who had sex with his under-age bride before and after legislative criminalization, illustrates the problematic intersection between competing expectations, i.e. the expectations of: (1) the Indigenous community; (2) the individual offender; and (3) the expectations established by the legislature. The 25-year-old defendant from Buluhkaduru (south of Maningrida) believed his sexual acts were permitted by his local Indigenous law because he was in a 'tribally arranged marriage' made between the parents several years earlier (2007: 4). The families had placed pressure on the defendant to fulfil his 'cultural responsibilities' and to meet certain expectations in relation to the marriage (2007: 4). However, he was also under the apprehension that he was breaching Anglo-Australian law by having sex with a minor, even though it was legal when the sexual relations commenced in 2003.[26] At the time of the first sexual act, the female from Malnjangarak (near Maningrida) was 14 years old. In 2004, sex with a minor in customary marriage was criminalized. In 2005, the female bore a child to the defendant. A year later, the offender, while intoxicated, struck the complainant 'twice to the forehead' with a 'small tree branch' while she was carrying their baby (2007: 3). The victim subsequently made a complaint to the police and the Northern Territory Supreme Court

Similar restrictions were enacted in relation to bail under the Crimes Act 1914 (Cth) s. 15AB(1)(b) and the Northern Territory National Emergency Response Act 2007 (Cth) s. 90. The bail amendments preclude judges from considering customary law, e.g. traditional punishment when determining a bail application (see Ch. 5). In 2012 the Northern Territory provisions were incorporated into the Crimes Act 1914 (Cth) ss. 15AB (bail) and 16AA (sentencing).

26 Mildren J. stated: 'It seems to me that I cannot hold it against you that you thought you were breaking the law when you were not breaking the law. On the other hand, I can not [sic] take into account that you may have thought that you were not breaking the law' (*The Queen* v. *Redford* 2007: 4).

convicted the defendant of both statutory rape (for the sexual relations after March 2004) and aggravated assault.

At the time of sentencing it was open to the Supreme Court to consider 'customary law', as the legislated sentencing restrictions had not been enacted. The court, presided by Mildren J., reviewed the evidence on customary marriage, stating that it has occurred in the Maningrida area 'for thousands of years' and 'is still a strong tradition' that is linked to 'important cultural ceremonies' and 'responsibilities to the land' (2007: 4). The court noted the expectations placed on the offender to comply with his cultural obligations and the fact that the couple had not been given notice of the changed law and the opportunity to adapt (2007: 4).[27] Nonetheless, the Supreme Court showed the same persuasion as in previous cases towards outlawing customary marriages. It signalled that promised marriages will not exist forever, stating that 'things are changing' in Indigenous communities (2007: 4). The court sought to hasten this change by imposing a 12-month prison sentence on the offender 'to deter others' and 'express the Court's disapproval' of sex with minors in customary marriage (2007: 6). It endeavoured 'to prevent early pregnancies and to give young persons the opportunity to fulfil their educational needs before being pushed into traditional domesticity prematurely' (2007: 6). The court's focus on deterrence is executed in a cultural vacuum that presumes women who enter such marriages live in a liberal market society without the inhibiting unemployment rates and the limited educational opportunities that are a reality in remote Indigenous communities.

Similar sentiments were expressed in *The Queen* v. *Turner* (2011: 2) involving a 23-year-old and 13-year-old who lived in a customary marriage in Lake Nash on the Northern Territory and Queensland border. They were found to be having a sexual relationship when the female gave birth. This led to a prosecution and the Supreme Court imposed a nine-month prison sentence. Although legislation forbade customary law considerations in mitigating or aggravating the sentence, the court did note that the couple was married 'in an Aboriginal sense' and continued to be living together at the time of the trial, 4 years later. It focused on the interests of the 'ideal victim' who needed the court's protection. As no impact statement was received, the court made general comments about young victims in customary marriages. It stated that the criminalization of sex with minors in customary marriage is 'designed to protect young girls' who will be

27 Stewart O'Connell (2006: 2), a long term Northern Territory Aboriginal Legal Services lawyer, comments in relation to this issue of notice in GJ's case: 'Many in Australian society now recognise certain "human rights" that in some instances are at odds with traditional ways. If the dominant culture has decided that traditional ways must be superseded by these "human rights" then the way to do it is through culturally appropriate education, a plan for adaptation and support through that process. That has rarely been done. The biggest complaint from the old people of GJ's region was that they had never been informed that the age of 16 was the magical age below which sex was illegal. Once properly educated they were happy to adapt and conform'.

'deprived of educational, employment and other opportunities' by entering motherhood at a young age (2011: 3). Again the court presumes that opportunities in remote Indigenous communities are on a level playing field with 'white' communities in towns and cities. They act as 'spatial managers' defining the terms of the space in an imagined field of whiteness (Hage 1998: 202).

Sentencing 'jealousing' and decontextualization

The Northern Territory Supreme Court's disavowal of cultural practices in the late 1990s also emerged in relation to the sentencing of cases involving instances of 'jealousing'. This involves testing intimate relationships through making a partner jealous. It can also arise where a third party attempts to make a partner jealous and can be particularly offensive when the third party is not of the right 'skin' to be lawfully connected to the partner. In these cases the court showed a tendency to devalue the community submissions on the jealousy circumstances that would warrant a shorter sentence. The court parted from its approach in the aforementioned case of *R.* v. *Davey* (1980: 257–8) where community considerations and pleas for shorter sentences were relevant because the matter concerned interference with relationships that breached Indigenous laws. In more recent cases the Supreme Court has applied a punitive agenda by focusing on the seriousness of the offence to the 'ideal' victim who is defined by her fragility and helplessness. In the case of *The Queen* v. *Bara* (2006), the offender and victim lived together in Angurugu on Groote Eylandt in the Gulf of Carpentaria, north-eastern Northern Territory. The offender attacked the victim with a knife, causing serious wounding, after she had made him jealous. The victim, who subsequently reconciled with the offender, made a statement to the court that she did not want the offender to go to prison. The Angurugu Elders told the court they would discuss the offence as part of 'men's business' and this would involve a period of isolation in a male-only environment (2006: [11]).

The Northern Territory Court of Criminal Appeal noted that the victim's and Elders' wishes for a non-custodial sentence were not a significant consideration (2006: [12]). It emphasized the need to send a 'message' to 'men in Aboriginal communities that the wishes of a victim, be they freely given or given under some form of duress, will not prevail in the face of serious criminal conduct' (2006: [19]). The court did not advert to the Indigenous community's interests in disciplining and rehabilitating the offender (2006: [16]–[17]). It focused on the 'objective circumstances' of the crime and the need for a harsh punishment to deter offences in Indigenous communities that arose from the 'common motivation' of jealousy (2006: [17]). It emphasized the vulnerability of victims in remote communities who 'lack the support mechanisms that are available in many other sections of our community' (2006: [18]). Thus, the Indigenous context was treated as an aggravating circumstance due to the helplessness of victims and the prevalence of jealousy. This cohered with the court's approach in *R.* v. *Dylan Jagamarra Charles* (2004), where the victim of an assault had been 'jealousing' the offender about her sister. Martin C.J. acknowledged that imprisonment was required because 'the court must send a message to men in the community' that women will be protected by the courts (2004: 3). This sweeping statement implicates all Indigenous men while positioning the court as the protector of Indigenous women.

In an alternative incident where a female perpetrator killed her husband in response to jealousing, the court more willingly genuflected to the victim's community in justifying a severe sentence. The case of *The Queen* v. *Linda Nabarula Wilson* (2006) involved a Warlpiri woman in Alice Springs who stabbed her husband after a verbal argument where he was 'jealousing' her (2006: 3). The Supreme Court focused on the need to 'assuage the anger of the community at Lajamanu' where the victim's family resided (2006: 4).[28] It referred to 'deep trouble within the Aboriginal community' arising from the manslaughter (2006: 4). The victim's family had made threats to the defendant and the court anticipated 'further trouble' in terms of 'revenge' for the killing (2006: 3–4). The court stated that the sentence 'must stress the need for denunciation, retribution and deterrence both general and personal in this case' (2006: 4). However, this view oversimplifies the response of the Warlpiri community. As will be shown in the following chapter, appeasing the Warlpiri community's anger requires Indigenous law punishment, which can be derailed by imprisoning the offender and making her unable to face the punishment. Nonetheless, in the case of *Wilson* the court mobilized the interests of the victim's community in alignment with its punitive response, and dismissed the defendant's claims to reduced moral culpability in handing down a six-year prison sentence.

Conclusion: legislative implications of the punitive turn for Indigenous communities

The Northern Territory Supreme Court's recognition of Indigenous culture sways between valorization of the functional role of culture and condemnation of its criminal tendencies. Both proclivities evince a claim to the Other through essentialist discourses (Dodson 1994). Recognition of the Other's culture secures the dominant order and compounds institutionalized knowledges by assuring stigmatization (Fraser 2000: 114). It is an unstable gesture that is prone to revert to the dominant punitive ideologies that deny the relevance of Indigenous culture in reducing moral culpability. Without a stable undergirding in the form of legal pluralism, judicial recognition of Indigenous cultures can operate as much to incorporate Indigenous community views as to subordinate and sideline them.

The Supreme Court's shift away from relying on Indigenous culture to reduce culpability since the late 1990s has arisen from a reprioritization of sentencing principles and reimagining of Indigenous communities. Culpability is

28 In a similar case, Riley J. disregarded 'jealousing' (*Jones* v. *Hales & Rigby* 2003).

overshadowed by the sentencing principles of the seriousness of the offence, deterrence, and the concomitant interests of the victim and the wider community in long prison terms. Epitomizing its paternalism, the court simultaneously endeavours to *protect* and *condemn* the Indigenous community for giving rise to a crime problem through cultural practice (see *Hales* v. *Jamilmira* 2003: 11, 22; *R.* v. *GJ* 2005: 241; *The Queen* v. *Turner* 2011: 3). In other words, it seeks to protect the community from both itself and its own culture. The reimagining of culture coheres with dominant ideologies on the risk that the Other poses to victims and the need to manage this class (Garland 2004: 174). Accordingly, culture has become a lens to magnify the vulnerability of victims and the interests of the wider community and to justify longer prison terms for Indigenous offenders. In recent customary marriage and jealousing cases, the Supreme Court seeks to deter and eradicate these cultures by referring to their harmfulness and the superiority of non-Indigenous ways (*R.* v. *GJ* 2005: 238, 241; *The Queen* v. *Bara* 2006: [18]). This tarnishes the productive elements of Indigenous laws and cultures, including maintaining peace in Indigenous communities (Shaw 2003: 329).

The moral panic over the leading cases relating to under-age sex in customary marriage cascaded into coercive interventions into Northern Territory Indigenous communities (see, e.g. Northern Territory National Emergency Response Act (Cth) 2007 ss. 4, 31, 26, 126 (hereinafter, 'NTER Act')). These measures are collectively known as 'the Northern Territory Intervention', and include a raft of restrictions placed on Indigenous community governance, welfare entitlements, land rights, housing, computer access, alcohol possession, Indigenous night patrols and bail rights. In the words of Simon (2001–2), perceptions of offending in Indigenous communities allowed the Federal Government to 'govern through crime'. The Federal and Northern Territory governments tapped into an anxiety about unfinished colonialism in Indigenous communities to take control of these communities by installing Government Business Managers and replacing community councils with Northern Territory Government Shires (Altman 2007: 8; Porter 2009: iii). This was sparked by a national television programme on sexual abuse in Mutitjulu, where the Alice Springs Crown Prosecutor, Nanette Rogers, criticized the cultural practice of 'promising wives' for contributing to the 'depraved and dysfunctional' status of Indigenous communities and criticized the courts for allowing sexual offenders in these circumstances to get off lightly (Jones 2006a; Smith 2006).[29] The Indigenous Affairs Minister also stated on the programme that Indigenous offenders were hiding behind a veil of customary law (Jones 2006). The effect of the moral panic was escalated in June 2007 when the 'Little Children Are Sacred Report' by the Board of Inquiry into Aboriginal Sexual Abuse was released. It identified strategies for protecting Indigenous

29 The Mutitjulu community subsequently brought a defamation claim against the Australian Broadcasting Corporation for the negative reporting of its community.

children from sexual abuse and violence, focusing on community-based justice responses and genuine consultation with Indigenous people (Wild and Anderson 2007: 21). The nature of the report, nonetheless, created a heightened state of crisis over Indigenous sexual abuse that legitimated top-down interventions into Indigenous communities. Despite claims in the report that Indigenous women and men 'felt deeply offended' by the way the media and politicians had spoken about culture in negative terms (2007: 58), the Federal Government used the report to blame Indigenous culture for the violence and sexual abuse in Indigenous communities.

The response to the report was expedient: within days the Federal Government declared a *state of national emergency* across Northern Territory Indigenous communities and mobilized the military. By August 2007, 2 months after the report was released, the Federal Government passed the NTER Act and wide-scale control measures were implemented across Indigenous communities to reinforce 'social norms' (Brough 2007: 6). Cohen (1985: 1) has pointed out that moral panics place crime issues *suddenly* in the 'limelight' to allow expedient and exceptional action.[30] Federal police were deployed to the Northern Territory and given new powers, and intelligence taskforces were established to collect and analyze crime data (Pilkington 2009). Although the government claimed that it was addressing the purported problem of sexual abuse of children in cultural circumstances, policing and intelligence taskforces did not uncover culturally condoned violence or widespread sexual assaults of minors in Indigenous communities (Central Australian Legal Aid Service and North Australian Aboriginal Justice Agency 2010; Liston 2010; Murdoch 2009: 8; Northern Territory Emergency Response Review Board 2008: 116).

Rather, the upshot has been the prosecution of teenage relationships. The North Australian Aboriginal Justice Agency (2008: 5 (hereinafter, 'NAAJA')) has reported that there has been an increase in prosecutions of consensual relationships involving teenagers and young adults, and not an increase in prosecutions of sexual abuse of pre-pubescent children (see *The Queen* v. *Aiden Kelly* 2010; *A* v. *The Queen* 2010; *The Queen* v. *Tewedy Maxwell* 2011). Such prosecutions have also resulted from the introduction of compulsory medical checks and mandatory reporting by health professionals of suspected under-age sexual relations (Care and Protection of Children Act 2007 (NT) s. 5). In one case, *The Queen* v. *MC* (2012), where the child was about 14-years-old and the defendant was about 17-years-old, the offender was prosecuted when his girlfriend had a baby. The court admitted that the case presented 'no element of older male predatory conduct', but nonetheless stressed that such prosecutions are necessary to protect 'ideal' victims by ensuring that older men do not take advantage of the young 'to satisfy their lust' (2012: 3). NAAJA (2008: 11) has reported that these

30 In fact there had been reports on sexual abuse in Indigenous communities for decades. The 'Little Children Are Sacred Report' acknowledged that there was 'nothing new or extraordinary about the allegation of sexual abuse of Aboriginal children' (Wild and Anderson 2007: 5).

prosecutions have resulted in harsh penalties and characterizations of young Indigenous defendants as 'sexual predators'.

The reforms that most directly responded to criticisms of sentencing leniency were those that prohibited cultural considerations in sentencing in the Northern Territory (NTER Act s. 91). This sounded the death knell for cultural considerations to mitigate a sentence and suspended ordinary judicial discretion to account for cultural facts (see *Neal* v. *The Queen* 1982: 326).[31] For the Federal Government, these reforms meant that 'all Australians' would be treated *equally* in sentencing (MacDonald 2006: 12).[32] The Law Council of Australia (2006: 4–5) phrased this differently when it stated that Indigenous offenders would be treated 'as if they did not belong to a particular Indigenous or ethnic group'. The government claimed that removing cultural factors would allow the courts to focus on the 'seriousness' of the crime (House of Representatives 2006: 1, 3; MacDonald 2006: 12; Brough 2007a: 15–16). These sentencing restrictions climaxed the Northern Territory Supreme Court's tendency to set aside Indigenous cultural contexts. Mildren J. (2008: 73) foreshadowed that the amendments would have a 'negligible effect' on sentencing outcomes.[33] Symbolically, however, singling out 'culture' enforced the idea that non-Indigenous Australian cultures are normal and non-violent. The Human Rights and Equal Opportunities Commission (2006: 5) pointed out that the Federal Government's sentencing amendments were 'premised on a false assumption that only some (other) people have "culture" whereas the cultural practices of non-Indigenous Australians would in practice continue to receive the benefit of sentencing consideration'. This is the 'majoritarian privilege of never noticing oneself' (Williams 1997, quoted in Hunyor 2007: 9).

The fact that the amendments remove culture as a mitigating *and* aggravating circumstance demonstrates the Federal Government's will to annul 'difference' irrespective of whether or not it extends a punitive agenda.[34] In order to enact these and broader policies in relation to Indigenous communities, the government had to suspend the Racial Discrimination Act 1975 (Cth) that protects racial

31 The legislation does not affect judicial discretion in sentencing in states and territories other than the Northern Territory, despite Commonwealth Government attempts to have states insert the provision (Brough 2007a: 16).

32 This claim to 'equality' is an avowal to the dominant norm. It reflects the colonial sentiment in *R.* v. *Murrell & Bummaree* (1836), where the New South Wales Supreme Court denied the Indigenous community from exercising jurisdiction over its offender on the premise that all Australians are to be treated equally under the jurisdiction of the New South Wales Supreme Court.

33 This in part is because not many offences of this type are tried in the courts. Mildren (2008a: 24) nonetheless has praised the NTER Act as an attempt to reduce crime in Northern Territory communities.

34 Indigenous culture and law may otherwise result in an increased sentence where the Indigenous community submits to the court that the matter particularly offends the community or its laws. This includes where non-Indigenous people act inappropriately on Indigenous land, an issue which arose in *Aboriginal Areas Protection Authority* v. *S & R Building & Construction Pty Ltd* (2011).

minorities and enforces the UN Convention on the Elimination of all forms of Racial Discrimination.[35] The reforms resonate with Valverde's (1996: 360) notion of 'liberal despotism' in which governments brutally enforce liberal norms on groups requiring civilization. She reiterates John Stuart Mill's charge that: 'Despotism is a legitimate mode of government in dealing with barbarians, provided the end be their improvement' (Valverde 1996: 360). To achieve liberal freedoms, in this version, entails taming those who are different before they too can enjoy the freedom of the majority. Legal philosopher Agamben (1998: 15–16) describes how separate legal provisions create states of exception to normalize the dominant culture. The exception, for Agamben (1998: 289), is not simply outside the social order, but crucial to its existence. The punitive suspension of rights is another phase in the recognition of the criminal Other. It signifies ongoing attempts by postcolonial institutions to establish legitimacy and universality over space, especially where the Other's cultural practices pose a risk to the normative order.

Intersection of cultural considerations and 'traditional' punishment: segue to the next chapter

While this chapter was concerned with the judicial re-imagining of Indigenous culture that has been the basis for an offence, the following chapter addresses the re-evaluation of Indigenous law punishment where it is administered on an offender *following* an offence. There are nonetheless some recent cases where offenders have claimed that their crime was committed in the *process* of Indigenous law punishment to reduce their culpability. In those cases, the Supreme Court has also discounted their cultural context. For example, in *Amagula* v. *Chambers* (2007), a young offender who was described as pursuing 'payback' against members of the Untunga clan on Groote Eylandt was sentenced to prison for damaging five cars and carrying a wooden pole. This harsh penalty for a young offender with no previous convictions was ordered on the grounds that a strong deterrence message needed to be sent to the community that such 'mayhem and anarchy' will not be accepted (2007: [15], [18]–[19]). The court emphasized the seriousness of the vehicle damage and the risk of harm to local residents (2007: [22]–[23]). It quoted the magistrate who stated that 'this kind of behaviour' existed in the 1940s and 1950s and has no place in contemporary society where the 'rule of law is entrenched' (2007: [18]). In sentencing his young co-offender, Mamarika, the Supreme Court stated that the payback, which arose out of family pressure and 'cultural imperatives' and did in fact result in the families resuming on good terms, has no place in Anglo-Australian society (*Mamarika* v. *Murphy & Anor* 2007: [26], [30]). The court upheld the magistrate's comments

35 There are a number of UN committee decisions criticizing the Northern Territory National Emergency Response Act 2007 (Cth). See: UN Human Rights Committee 2009; and Committee on the Elimination of Racial Discrimination 2010: 4–5.

that the criminal justice system will intervene to uphold the view of the 'wider community' that 'such activity is not to be tolerated' (2007: [33]).

Chapter 5 discusses the fact that a similar re-conceptualization has taken place by the judiciary that no longer regards 'traditional' Indigenous punishment as a legitimate mitigating factor. Reflecting the themes in this chapter, the Northern Territory Supreme Court now regards Indigenous law punishment as a repugnant expression of culture. It also perceives communities as too dysfunctional to have a disciplinary effect on their offenders. Sentencing courts seek to punish irrespective of the Indigenous community's or victim's desires for Indigenous law punishment to be imposed in lieu of imprisonment. A prevailing concern for courts is to impose the will of the wider community for a lengthy prison sentence. Tougher penalties are justified with reference to the legitimacy of the judicial punitive apparatus over Indigenous forms of punishment. As with attempts to militate against culture underpinning an offence, the judicial attitude towards Indigenous law punishment post-offence reveals a politics of recognition that seeks to repress difference.

Chapter 5

Traditional punishment in the new punitiveness

> Payback is not vendetta. There must be clear evidence of the difference. As I understand it, payback, in certain cases, which must be carefully delineated and clearly understood, can be a healing process; vendetta never. It would be a serious and impermissible abrogation of the court's duty to reduce a sentence on any person of whatever race or creed because of assurances that friends or relatives of the victim were preparing their own vengeance for the assailant. If payback is no more than this it is nothing to the sentencing process. If, however, it transcends vengeance and can be shown to be of positive benefit to the peace and welfare of a particular community, it may be taken into account.
>
> (*R.* v. *Minor* 1992: 181)

Re-imagining Indigenous community punishment

The counterpart to the prevailing legal narrative on the 'traditional' sexual offender is the 'barbaric' violent offender. Indigenous culture is portrayed as violent and vengeful, especially in terms of the infliction of punishment. In the popular and legal parlance, punishment dispensed on the Indigenous offender by his or her community is labelled 'payback' to denote retribution – an eye for an eye. However, this term misapprehends the nature of Indigenous punishment, which does not replicate the offence or merely seek retribution, but endeavours to restore community relations, denounce the crime and uphold the local Indigenous law (Loy 2010). The most common forms of Indigenous punishment comprise public shaming, exile from the community, compensation or restitution, community work, public denunciation and public apology. However, it can also include corporal punishment such as spearing and clubbing where the offence is serious, including for murder, sexual assault and interferences with ceremonies or land custodianship (see Gaykamangu 2012: 247; Gaymarani 2011: 298–9; Loy 2010). Indigenous punishment is dispensed after meetings between the families of the offender and victim reach a collective resolution.

Along with 'payback', the courts and other Anglo-Australian institutions also use the problematic term 'traditional punishment'. This term could be said to insinuate backwardness. It may also overshadow the fact that Indigenous and contemporary Anglo-Australian punishment have common purposes, including deterrence, condemnation, rehabilitation and reparation – notwithstanding that Indigenous punishment has the further objective of reconciling and restoring Indigenous relationships (Finnane 2001: 293; Spielmann 1994). Given that the terms 'payback' and 'traditional punishment' delegitimize the regulatory function of Indigenous forms of punishment, this chapter uses the term 'Indigenous law punishment' to indicate its legal validity in Indigenous communities and to distinguish it from 'Anglo-Australian law punishment' inflicted on Indigenous people. For simplicity, the term is often abbreviated to 'Indigenous punishment' or 'collective punishment'. Nonetheless, there is the occasional slippage of the label 'traditional punishment' where it is in accordance with the Northern Territory Supreme Court's use or for effect.

This chapter considers the dispensation of Indigenous law punishment *after* the commission of a violent offence within an Indigenous community, whereas the previous chapter was concerned with the role of culture in the commission of a criminal offence. This chapter primarily addresses how the Northern Territory Supreme Court and Federal Court of Australia's sentencing remarks accommodate Indigenous law punishment. To further illustrate the judicial imagining, it also refers to the Supreme Court's consideration of bail applications where the defendant seeks to undergo Indigenous punishment while on bail. The Indigenous offenders who are sentenced tend to have been subject to Indigenous punishment before the trial. However, in some instances, namely where bail has been refused, the offender has told the court that he or she will undergo Indigenous collective punishment once released from prison. The cases illustrate the tension that arises from the disjuncture between Anglo-Australian law and Indigenous law, where both assert jurisdiction over the offender. This is notwithstanding that some Indigenous people have expressed a willingness for the courts to imprison serious Indigenous offenders in addition to having Indigenous punishment administered (Loy 2010).[1] In general, those exerting authority in Anglo-Australian legal and political institutions have condemned the practice of Indigenous law punishment, claiming that it has no place in the Anglo-Australian system. Dorsett (2002: 35) points out that the Anglo-Australian concept of legal uniformity constrains the 'threat of legal pluralism'. The genesis of this legal constraint can be traced to *R.* v. *Murrell & Bummaree* (1836: 211), where the New South Wales Supreme Court held that Indigenous offenders are subject to the court's jurisdiction and are *not* 'entitled to be recognised as . . . sovereign states governed by laws of their own'.

1 In the documentary *Bush Law*, Jungarrayi stated that after the Warlpiri offender has 'been through our punishment, our tribal punishment . . . they can be taken away and dealt by the whitefellas' law . . . I don't care how long they go to gaol for, so long as they've cleared the family name and cleared the problem according to our eyes' (Loy 2010).

Resilience of Indigenous punishment systems

Despite Anglo-Australian claims to punitive exclusivity, Indigenous people have shown resilience in the practice of their laws and have resisted the monopolizing force of the introduced criminal justice system. They continue to adhere to the Indigenous laws that have guided Indigenous societies for thousands of years (Gondarra 2011: 24). Yolŋu people in Arnhem Land, on the northern tip of the Northern Territory, describe their *Ngarra* customary law as playing a crucial role in their economy, community well-being and safety, cultural obedience, marriage, ritual, ceremony, moiety systems, environmental and land law, treason, leadership and sentencing (Gaymarani 2011: 283). This is also the case for Warlpiri people from the central Australian desert whose laws are intimately tied to their 'skin' relationships, connections to land, ceremony and languages (Loy 2010). The administration of Indigenous punishment maintains these pillars of Indigenous society. Through promoting discipline, respect and community cohesion, Indigenous laws support everyday rituals in community life (Gaykamangu 2012: 245).

With the ongoing practice of Indigenous law punishment, there exists a 'complex and interactive relationship' between the introduced and pre-existing methods of dispute resolution and social control, according to Smandych and Linden (1995: 4). Therefore, despite limited common law or constitutional recognition of Indigenous systems of punishment and dispute resolution in Australia, legal pluralism arises from the social practice of Indigenous laws in the social arenas of remote communities in the Northern Territory (Tamanaha 2000: 315; Blagg 2012). Cornell (2012) describes this as Indigenous governance by 'stealth'. It offsets the ubiquity of the colonizing state by operating as an extra-state 'governmentality' with separate political subjects (Foucault 1991). A Yolŋu Elder,[2] Gondarra (2006: 43), reflects on how Indigenous law continues to apply to Indigenous people: 'Our Traditional Law is still here and it is keeping the peace on hundreds of Aboriginal communities'. Up until the last few years, Indigenous law punishment (including corporal punishment) had been under-policed, under-prosecuted and thus under-punished by the Western legal system. Anglo-Australian authorities perceived it to be impractical or economically and politically necessary to reach into remote Indigenous domains, thereby allowing for coexisting jurisdictions to endure (Tamanaha 2008: 382–3).

Judicial engagement with Indigenous law punishment: chapter overview

The recognition of Indigenous punishment had a delayed gestation, with the Northern Territory Supreme Court denying the relevance of Indigenous punishment to the court's exclusive jurisdiction throughout the 1950s. However, from

2 From Galiwin'ku, Elcho Island, Northern Territory.

the 1970s until the early 1990s, the court accepted the positive role of Indigenous punishment. As will be explored in the earlier part of this chapter, the court afforded substantial leniency on account of the significance of Indigenous punishment for disciplining and rehabilitating the offender and for restoring his or her Indigenous community to its natural order. During this period the Supreme Court and its appellate courts skated a fine line between *embracing* Indigenous punishment's disciplinary and restorative functions – particularly where they were seen as fulfilling the purposes of the Anglo-Australian criminal law – and *constraining* the authority of Indigenous punishment. This situation has been variously described as 'weak' legal pluralism (Douglas 2005a: 141; Finnane 2006: 4) and as a reflection of the 'vibrancy of white Australian law' through the engagement of different legal systems (Woodroffe 2006: 1). The dialectic in sentencing recognition involves giving Indigenous norms a voice while subjecting Indigenous practices to rules and conditions (see Dorsett 2002: 35). Conditions on Indigenous punishment included oversight by corrections officers of spearing, and including in the terms of a good behaviour bond that the offender participate in Indigenous law ceremonies. This allowed the courts to maintain control of the Indigenous law process. Symbolically, the judicial portrayal of Indigenous punishment captured a romantic savagery, which rekindled the harmony of a past lost to the colonizer while affirming the colonizer's progress and civilization (Dodson 1994: 8). Such imagery was invoked to both offer and deny recognition in sentencing and bail decisions.

From the late 1990s, judicial tolerance for Indigenous punishment gave way to condemnation and exclusion. The Northern Territory Supreme Court represented the postcolonial Indigenous community as dysfunctional, and the Indigenous community's punitive processes as threatening dominant norms, which is addressed in the later part of this chapter. It winnowed the restorative and disciplinary aspects of Indigenous punishment, leaving only a portrayal of its violent features. The court characterized Indigenous punishment as mere retribution and suggested that Indigenous punishment contributed to the perceived problem of Indigenous disorder. It downplayed Indigenous community views that the defendant should receive a reduced prison sentence because the Indigenous law had dealt sufficiently with the matter. Rather, the court emphasized the seriousness of the offences and determined that the interests of the wider community in subjecting Indigenous offenders to long prison sentences should prevail. The same approach has been applied to bail decisions, where the court has refused bail conditions which would allow Indigenous punishment. This is because in the court's view the welfare and protection of the wider community take precedence over that of the Indigenous community.

The eruption of a moral panic over Indigenous violence in remote communities underpinned these new legal narratives. Indigenous punishment was treated as a danger to Indigenous people themselves and non-Indigenous 'societal values and interests' (Cohen 2002: 1). The public alarm produced a 'collective wave of righteous condemnation' directed at Indigenous communities

(Durkheim 1982: 18), reinforcing images of barbaric and uncivilized Indigenes. Public intellectual Sutton (2009: 91) recently referred to 'limited forms of warfare, blood feuding, aggressive wife-raiding expeditions and incidental homicides' in 'classical Aboriginal life'. He contended that punitive dispute resolution is indicative of the 'high levels of interpersonal violence' that exists within Indigenous communities and extends to 'the beating of women by their husbands' (Sutton 2001: 134; see also Nowra 2007: 28). Franklin (2008: 24) also maintained that Indigenous communities are unable to manage disputes without escalating these disputes into out-of-control violence with 'combatants hitting one another'. This chapter depicts how these moral panics reverberate in judicial perceptions of Indigenous justice processes and the decision of the Federal Government to restrict customary law considerations in sentencing and bail determinations.

Purposes and processes of Indigenous law punishment

There is a false perception that Indigenous punishment is a matter of revenge that incites 'mob violence' (Woodroffe 2006: 3). However, Indigenous punishment is in fact strictly regulated and, like any system of punishment, operates to enforce the moral and legal order in Indigenous communities (Durkheim 1973: 167; Finnane 2001: 293). Indigenous punishment operates through consensual community processes and involves voluntary submission by the offender. This is far from the characterizations of mob rule or revenge attacks.[3] The objectives of Indigenous punishment – deterrence, denunciation, rehabilitation, restitution and reparation for the victim and community – cement social ties within Indigenous society. Despite Durkheim's (1933: 93) portrayal of Indigenous 'primitive' justice as based on 'private punishments', the objectives of Indigenous punishment imbricate with the goals of Western punishment in its law and order and restorative justice guises. Although some academics have pointed to the retributive aspects of Indigenous punishment (Cunneen 2008a: 298), and others have emphasized its restorative functions (Finnane 2001: 308), the purposes of Indigenous punishment can be seen to cut across the polarity of retribution and restoration that exists in Western concepts of justice.[4] This does not diminish the possibility that violence may be dressed up as Indigenous punishment. However, community members widely attribute Indigenous punishment to reconciling relationships and denouncing crimes, which evidence its lawful role. Indigenous

3 Offenders voluntarily submit to this punishment so they can be accepted back into the community and prevent violence that would otherwise be inflicted on their families (Squires 2005a: 4).

4 Indigenous punishment may alternatively be regarded as a form of 'reintegrative shaming' that brings the offender back into the fold of the community, while also providing community resolution and allowing the stories of the victims and the families to be told (Braithwaite 1989: 14; and Kimm 2004: 144–5).

people claim that ultimately Indigenous punishment is 'used for the safety and wellbeing' of their communities (Gaymarani 2011: 299).

The nature of the Indigenous punishment process is collective, which reflects how the offence has ramifications that ripple through the whole Indigenous community. Responsibility for the crime is attributed to the offender's family and skin group as much as it is attributed to the offender. A criminal matter is dealt with through a formal agreement between the families of the victim and the offender. After the crime, meetings take place to decide the form of punishment and to confront the offender about his or her actions. This process helps to heal relationships, allows the victim's story to be told and restores the peace in the Indigenous community (Gaymarani 2011: 295; Kimm 2004: 144–5). If the punishment involves force, it is dispensed by Elders in the presence of the families of the victim and offender (Loy 2010). This communal approach to punishment contrasts with the approach of the Western criminal justice system where its court process, incarceration and control orders isolate the individual offender (symbolically and physically) from his or her family, the victim, the victim's family and the local community.

The Indigenous law process follows 'clear codes of practice' for dispute settlement within each Indigenous community (Calma 2007: 78; Australian Law Reform Commission 1986: [499]). In *Ngarra* law in Arnhem Land, punishment is negotiated between the families, and generally 'the offender will, after going through negotiations, agree to the punishment' (Gaymarani 2011: 285). There is an informal 'court' procedure where 'people of different clans come to hear the verdict' that is delivered openly by a chief Yolŋu Elder, the *jungay*. If the families are not satisfied, the decision can be appealed 'for further investigation and possibly additional law enforcement' (2011: 285). Gaymarani (2011: 286) explains that 'observance of *Ngarra* law accomplishes *magaya* – a state of people living in peace with each other and their environment'. In Warlpiri society, punishment is focused on achieving a resolution among skin groups, and there is every effort to ensure that corporal punishment is not fatal, by spearing being aimed at the leg. Japanangka explained that the spearing is concluded with an apology and a hug or shaking of hands among the skin groups: 'Then it's finished – not to be carried on. We're back to square one again' (Loy 2010).

Affirming the regulatory function of Indigenous law, Warlpiri Elders in Lajamanu attribute very low levels of violence to the 'strength of Aboriginal law and our people's respect for it' (Loy 2010). Punishment is integral to the Warlpiri system of law that shapes 'everything we do', as Japanangka articulated (Loy 2010). He went on to state: 'It is with us, forming the guideline for our life from when we're born to when we die . . . It is our history, it is our story, our ceremony and our court system' (Loy 2010). Inversely, if rituals and ceremonies are lost, Jampijinpa said, 'we will forget what it is trying to say and we will disappear as Warlpiri people'. When *Yawaru manu* (punishment) is imposed 'by the lawful Elders in a lawful manner', the community is 'happy and satisfied' (Loy 2010). Alternatively, as Jungarrayi expressed, when Indigenous law punishment does not take place, violence occurs throughout the community, particularly when imprisonment precludes its operation for many years (Loy 2010). Because of these consequences, it is important that the punishment is decided and conducted 'straight away' so that justice has been seen 'in the eyes of the people' and '*Yawaru manu* business is finished' (Loy 2010). Indigenous punishment settles the matter and prevents ongoing feuds and retaliations being directed to the offender's family or skin group (Fryer-Smith 2002: 8:5).

Early judicial exclusions of Indigenous law punishment

Under the reign of single judge Wells J., the Supreme Court upheld the exclusivity of the Anglo-Australian jurisdiction in criminal matters. The court criticized Indigenous law for being uncivilized. It is not without irony that Wells J. advocated state-administered corporal punishment for Indigenous people (Mildren 2011: 121–2). For serious offending, Wells J. handed down the death penalty routinely on Indigenous defendants, especially where the victim was European (Read 2007: 09.5).[5] In imposing the death penalty on eight Indigenous people who killed two European prospectors, Wells J. stated, 'retributive justice was all the savage could understand' (Anon 1934: 11). In the case of *Tuckiar* v. *The King* (1934), Wells J. ordered the death penalty for an Indigenous person convicted of murder.[6] He deemed Indigenous evidence that the European victim (a police officer) committed a cultural wrong by raping the offender's wife to be irrelevant, and held that there was a need for condign punishment that would give effect to general deterrence (Mildren 2011: 111). But while Wells J. had the opportunity to take a hard line on crimes where Europeans were victims, he was not able to deliberate on the significance of Indigenous punishment in sentencing. This was because Indigenous offenders seldom came before the court for *inter se* offences;[7] a product of the infrequent policing and prosecuting of these offences during Wells J.'s time on the Bench (Finnane 2001: 303).

Wells J.'s successor in the 1950s, Kriewaldt J., accepted submissions on Indigenous punishment. However, he did *not* provide additional mitigation for its dispensation beyond recognizing it as evidence of the offender's 'traditional' background (Douglas 2009: 160). His strong support for the prison system as an effective form of disciplining, and ultimately assimilating Indigenous offenders, correlated with his perception of the illegitimacy of non-Western modes

5 This was particularly the case before the High Court upheld the appeal in *Tuckiar* v. *The King* (1934) against the trial conducted by Wells J. and his decision to sentence Dhakiyarr to death. Wells J. exercised more restraint in handing down the death penalty after the High Court's decision (Mildren 2011: 149).

6 On the High Court appeal in *Tuckiar* v. *The King* (1934), see Ch. 4.

7 The exception was a number of sexual offences involving young Indigenous female victims, where the issue of Indigenous punishment did not come before the Supreme Court (Mildren 2011: 122).

of punishment for serious offenders (Douglas 2005: 185–7, 2002: 208). This contrasted with Wells J.'s opposition to imprisonment because he felt it would attract Indigenous people to towns (Mildren 2011: 123). Kriewaldt J.'s stance was that long terms of imprisonment played a positive role in so far as it would 'de-tribalise them' (Mildren 2011: 161). Due to the benefits of incarceration, Kriewaldt J. would not allow Indigenous punishment to encroach on Anglo-Australian penality. He also reasoned that accommodating Indigenous punishment was inimical to the assimilation and civilization of Indigenous people. The authority of the courts and corrections would teach Indigenous people to live by Anglo-Australian law (2011: 160). During the 1950s there was an increased policing of *inter se* offences and Indigenous law practices, giving the Supreme Court a greater opportunity to adjudicate on the relevance of Indigenous punishment in sentencing (Finnane 2006: 3). The level of scrutiny continued to rise in the late twentieth century with more of these types of cases coming before the Supreme Court. But even then policing would be patchy and consideration of the legitimacy of Indigenous punishment remained a rarity for the Supreme Court (Zdenkowski 1994).

During Kriewaldt J.'s time on the Bench, Indigenous people who administered punishment through corporal punishment were subjected to judicial punishment. Kriewaldt J. held that Indigenous people had no authority to impose punishment, especially where violence resulted. In *R.* v. *Wheeler* (1959a: 276), an unintended fatal spearing in the course of Indigenous punishment prompted Kriewaldt J. to comment: 'Laws are part of assimilation; prosecution of Aborigines who break the law must be an integral part of any assimilation policy' (1959a: 276). He handed down a heavy sentence, which he regarded as 'an aid in the process of the assimilation of the Australian Aboriginal into the integrated community' (1959a: 276). He sought to send a message of deterrence through being seen to punish – thus upholding the legitimacy of the Anglo-Australian punisher against the illegitimacy of Indigenous punishment (*R* v. *Wheeler* 1959: 240). It is anomalous that Kriewaldt J. provided mitigation for offenders who came from 'traditional' cultures and yet dispensed harsh punishment for those engaged in 'traditional' Indigenous punishment. This approach to Indigenous recognition, which seeks to maintain the privileged legal status of the judicial recognizer, indicates its precarious foundation. It is a product of recognition reflecting dominant socio-cultural norms (Fraser 1996: 7). For Kriewaldt J., culture was capable of recognition as long as it did not challenge Anglo-Australian claims to exclusive legal authority.

Paternal and paradoxical attempts to harness Indigenous law punishment from the 1970s

By the late 1970s, and up until the early 1990s, the Northern Territory Supreme Court and the Federal Court of Australia embraced Indigenous law punishment as a means of doing the disciplinary work of the courts and restoring communities. This was an era where the ideology of self-determination was being touted in federal policy and measures such as land rights legislation and wide-scale funding for Indigenous organizations were introduced. Indigenous citizenship came to represent more than incorporation of Indigenous people into mainstream institutions. It represented the provision of unique rights for Indigenous people that reflected their distinct history and identity. This rights-based approach to Indigenous issues permeated judicial reasoning on the recognition of Indigenous law punishment. The Northern Territory Supreme Court took an intimate interest in Indigenous law and routinely accepted sentencing submissions on the practice and outcomes of Indigenous punishment. It was interested to see how it could address the adverse impact of colonization on remote communities, including increased crime rates. The court regarded the disciplinary role of Indigenous communities as effective in doing the court's work in the Indigenous domain (Finnane 2001: 307). Through support for Indigenous laws, the Supreme Court perceived that it was returning the Indigenous community to its traditional peace and harmony.

The Northern Territory's higher courts perceived that Indigenous law punishment supported 'an authentically Aboriginal way of life' that was otherwise being destroyed by the encroachment of 'white' society (Douglas 2009: 7). The recognition of Indigenous punishment could help restore Indigenous communities to their 'orderly and peaceful' ways and discipline offenders (2009: 196). The community was regarded as an effective medium for fulfilling the sentencing objectives of the courts – including denunciation, deterrence, reintegration and rehabilitation – by bringing offenders back into the fold of the Indigenous community. Indeed, the courts viewed the reintegrative role of Indigenous law punishment as more effective than the exclusionary prison system (*Jabaltjari* v. *Hammersley* 1977: 101). It also served the victim's interests, atoned the outrage of the Indigenous community and helped reconcile relations in the Indigenous community, thereby precluding further violence which might otherwise have emerged from the crime. Due to the restorative and disciplinary capacities of Indigenous punishment, higher courts considered the offender's subjection to Indigenous law as a significant factor in reducing a sentence, including by commuting a prison sentence for homicide (*R.* v. *Charlie Limbiari Jagamara* 1984). The Northern Territory Supreme Court and Federal Court have been willing to recognize violent and non-violent forms of Indigenous law punishment, including banishment, spearing and shaming (*Jadurin* v. *The Queen* 1982: 185; *The Queen* v. *Berida* 1990: [21]; *R.* v. *Mamarika* 1982: 358). Their reasoning was that Indigenous punishment could complement the criminal justice system's punitive role.

However, in all key cases, the Supreme and Federal Courts have been at pains to state that they do not condone Indigenous law punishment, but merely recognize it as a fact of the offender's Indigenous community membership (e.g. *R.* v. *Minor* 1992: 193). In doing so, they retain the exclusive legitimacy of the Anglo-Australian punitive system. Consequently, the courts do not enliven the principle of double jeopardy, or at least not to any significant degree, when sentencing offenders who have undergone Indigenous law punishment (see *R.* v. *Gorey* 1978). The principle protects against being tried or punished twice for the same offence. In the leading cases where the Indigenous community has submitted that double jeopardy is grounds for commuting a prison sentence, the courts have failed to aver to its significance (see *Jadurin* v. *The Queen* 1982: 186; *R.* v. *Miyatatawuy* 1996: 577). This is arguably due to courts being ill-at-ease with placing Indigenous law punishment on the same plane as the courts' punishment. The courts contrast the violence of Indigenous punishment with the civilized nature of the Anglo-Australian punitive system that condemns violence. This is notwithstanding the fact that the Anglo-Australian legal system condones a wide range of violent activities, including boxing, tattooing and surgical procedures (Bielefeld 2003: 144). Unlike those activities, consent to Indigenous law (corporal) punishment does not provide a criminal defence (Law Reform Commission of Western Australia 2006: 147).

The courts' recognition *and* refusal of Indigenous punishment pervades the cases discussed below. This paradox is at its boldest when the Federal Court has provided substantial leniency for the harshest types of Indigenous law punishment. Indeed, the more severe the violence attached to the Indigenous punishment, the greater the concession to the offender. In *R.* v. *Charlie Limbiari Jagamara* (1984), the 75-year-old Warlpiri defendant was banished from his community, speared, cut, stabbed, beat with a *nulla nulla* and hit with a tomahawk. The Federal Court reduced the defendant's sentence to the rising of the court (a matter of moments) because the 'accused has already suffered punishments far more severe than any that I would be authorised to inflict'. The Supreme Court has also endeavoured to oversee its occurrence where the Indigenous punishment has not yet been administered on the defendant (*The Queen* v. *Walker* 1994: 10). Notwithstanding its violent consequences, Indigenous law punishment has been identified as warranting a non-custodial sentence where its disciplinary 'rationality [is] visible to the criminal law' (Finnane 2001: 308).

Judicial alacrity for the restorative qualities of Indigenous law punishment

Restoration of Indigenous community relations was at the forefront of the judicial concern to recognize Indigenous punishment from the 1970s. The Supreme and Federal Courts perceived that Indigenous communities possessed the requisite functionality to restore community peace and protect victims. They appreciated the strain that offences caused to community relations that were otherwise harmonious, and realized that this strain would continue until Indigenous law punishment took place. In *Munungurr* v. *The Queen* (1994), the Supreme Court valued the Yolŋu defendant's desire to be returned to his community to be dealt with by way of collective punishment in order to promote community reconciliation. The court also regarded imprisonment as futile in sending a message to the Indigenous community about the crime because at the completion of Indigenous law punishment 'the community regard the matter as at an end'

(*Police* v. *Bernard Wurramurra* 1977: 9). In *R.* v. *Poulson* (2001), the defendant who had killed a man at Yuendumu (a Warlpiri community in central Australia, Northern Territory) received collective punishment by being hit with *nulla nullas* and spears. The Supreme Court in handing down a prison sentence of four months accepted that the punishment 'has been effective in resolving the enmity between the families' (2001: 392). Thomas J. noted that the ritual was 'important in avoiding further conflict' and the defendant's 'participation in the walolokarri [agreement] has gone a long way toward making reparation for his offence' (2001: 392).

In the landmark case of *Jadurin* v. *The Queen* (1982), the Federal Court provided an authoritative determination on how Indigenous law punishment is considered in sentencing mitigation. This case involved a manslaughter offence by a Ngaringman man against his wife. The collective punishment involved the Ngaringman community, in north-west Northern Territory, letting 'fly boomerangs and *nulla nullas* and spears' towards the defendant (1982: 185).[8] Evidence was presented to the court that Indigenous punishment would prevent the defendant's family getting 'into trouble' and it carried 'considerable shame'. It was submitted that afterwards 'the whole issue will be forgotten by the community' (1982: 185). According to the court, the gravity of the evidence allowed it 'to recognise certain facts which exist only by reason of that offender's membership of a particular group' in accounting for Indigenous punishment (1982: 187). It stressed that the mitigatory effect of Indigenous punishment should not signal that the court sanctioned the community's 'retribution'.

The Northern Territory Court of Criminal Appeal went a step further in *R.* v. *Minor* (1992) by considering Indigenous punishment where it had not yet been administered by the Hermannsburg community in central Australia for the crime of manslaughter. The court unanimously held that Indigenous punishment reduces the severity of the sentence where it 'can be shown to be of positive benefit to the peace and welfare of a particular community' (1992: 181). It emphasized the role of Indigenous punishment in wiping out 'all feuds arising from the defendant's actions' and allowing the community to 'put the whole episode behind them and get on with the more positive aspects of their lives' (1992: 181). These remarks convey the virtues of Indigenous punishment and the 'positive aspects' of life in communities where Indigenous law is pursued. *Minor's* case revealed Mildren J. as a force in promoting recognition principles on the Northern Territory Supreme Court in the 1990s. As a public proponent of Indigenous rights (see Mildren 2003), he sought to contextualize the offender within his or her community and its historical, political and legal milieu. In doing so he underlined the interests of the defendant's Indigenous community in having its relationships reconciled. Although the previous chapter traced his more recent

8 There was also evidence of possible punishment through banishment for a number of years and hidings and burnings at a men's ceremony (*Jadurin* v. *The Queen* 1982: 185). Some but not all of the punishment had been carried out before the trial (1982: 184).

inclination to give precedent to the seriousness of the offence and downplay matters of culpability, in *R.* v. *Minor* (1992: 191) Mildren J. forcefully remarked that past or prospective Indigenous punishment is relevant in sentencing Indigenous offenders due to 'considerations of fairness and justice'.[9] In an oft-cited quote, he stated:

> In my opinion, a sentencing judge is entitled to have regard not only to the interests of the wider community, but also to the special interests of the community of which the respondent is a member.
>
> (*R.* v. *Minor* 1992: 193)

Recognition of Indigenous disciplinary and rehabilitative roles

Over the course of the 1980s and into the 1990s, the Supreme Court focused on the disciplinary capacity of Indigenous punishment. There was a loss of faith in the prison system's ability to 'control' Indigenous people. Indeed, the 'white' ways and civilizing endeavours were considered part of the crime problem in Indigenous communities. In *R.* v. *Charlie Limbiari Jagamara* (1984), the Supreme Court refrained from handing down a prison sentence because it was likely to exacerbate the 'problems of the Aboriginal' and increase difficulties through 'his withdrawal from Aboriginal society' (quoted in Fisher 1985: 11). The court noted that the matter was adequately dealt with through spearing, cutting, stabbing, beating with a *nulla nulla* and hitting the offender with a tomahawk. Muirhead J. believed that the offence of manslaughter by spearing in response to the victim's unlawful association with the offender's wife was 'truly a cultural matter, which has been tackled energetically by the people' (quoted in Fisher 1985: 11). In other cases where banishment was imposed as part of a collective punishment, the Supreme Court noted its role in 'preserving peace in the community' and symbolizing the 'community's disapproval' (*Atkinson & Anor* v. *Walkely* 1984: 35–6). Therefore, the court achieved its disciplinary objectives by appropriating the Indigenous domain and operating as a tenuous *liminal space* of Indigenous and non-Indigenous punishment (Blagg 2008).

During the late twentieth century, offender rehabilitation also featured in the Supreme Court's punitive objectives and the court capitalized on the rehabilitative role of Indigenous law punishment, as in *R.* v. *Miyatatawuy* (1996). That case, iterated in this book's epigram, involved an intoxicated Indigenous woman who had stabbed her husband in the chest, resulting in a puncture to his lung. The assault was in breach of a recognizance to be of good behaviour, which had been imposed for an earlier conviction of assaulting her husband. The victim sought to have the matter availed from the Anglo-Australian legal system because his

9 However, in recent years Mildren J. has increasingly downplayed Indigenous mitigating factors and focused on the seriousness of the offence. See the latter part of Ch. 2 and his joint judgment in *Wurramara* (1999).

wife had already been dealt with under Yolŋu law and he feared that it would destroy the marriage in the eyes of the Indigenous community. The victim said in a statement that 'the issue is finished' and proceeding with the prosecution would 'discredit our decision to deal with our own problems according to our cultural law' and result in the defendant being 'tried twice' (1996: 577). In addition, the court received a statement, signed by 140 community members, which expressed support for Miyatatawuy and claimed that the matter has been 'settled in the traditional way' (1996: 578). Several meetings between groups from Milingimbi, Ramingining and Gatji in Arnhem Land discussed the circumstances of the crime. The offender had to face the 'clans and families' at these meetings 'under distressing conditions' (1996: 577). The Chief Justice felt that the offender had been rehabilitated while in exile from her community (1996: 577). In deciding to release the offender on a good behaviour bond, he noted that 'the wishes of the relevant community' are a relevant mitigating factor (1996: 578). Martin C.J. was confident in the community's role in settling the dispute and rehabilitating the offender:

> A most significant circumstance bearing upon the sentence was that concerning the resolution or settlement of matters within the relevant aboriginal community and the *integral rehabilitation of the offender.*
>
> (*R.* v. *Miyatatawuy* 1996: 575, emphasis added)

The Supreme Court also acknowledged the rehabilitative quality of initiation – an important ceremony for teaching initiates Indigenous law once they have reached puberty, which can involve circumcision and other wounding for young males (Gaymarani 2011: 293). The court was willing to assent to community submissions that initiation was a means of reintegrating the offender into the community, and preventing the perpetuation of a criminal cycle. In *Jabaltjari* v. *Hammersley* (1977), Muirhead J. ordered that initiation take place as a condition of a juvenile offender's bond in Papunya, central Australia. He stated that the juvenile 'undergo such discipline or training for his rehabilitation, of a traditional aboriginal nature or otherwise, as the Papunya Council may from time to time direct' (1977: 101). He determined that prison is ineffective for young offenders because it is often a rite of passage, and in some instances a means of escaping initiation ceremonies (1977: 97).[10] Participation in ceremony, by contrast, would lead to the offender developing a sense of responsibility necessary for deterring future participation in crime (1977: 97; see also *R.* v. *Williams* 1976). The court in *Jabaltjari* v. *Hammersley* (1977: 97) refused to hand down a prison sentence because of its lack of disciplinary effect on the young offender.

10 Similarly, in *R.* v. *Wilson* (1995: 276), the Northern Territory Supreme Court was dubious as to whether the defendant surrendered himself to the police to avoid traditional punishment involving 'harm at the hands of the vengeful kinsman of a deceased'.

Paternalist attempts to supervise Indigenous law punishment

Embracing their self-assigned role as the gatekeepers of Indigenous punishment, the Federal and Supreme courts occasionally took it upon themselves to manage Indigenous law processes. In this invasive move they delegated supervision of the collective punishment to corrections officers and required that they report back to the court. Their reasoning was to ensure that the offender was disciplined through Indigenous punishment if he or she was to receive the ensuing benefit of mitigation. The courts have also ordered for the Indigenous community to carry out banishment, spearing and participation in ceremony as a condition of clemency or of a good behaviour bond. Requiring these forms of punishment is a magnificent leap away from the historical approach of excluding evidence of Indigenous law punishment and condemning its performance. While it creates a space for the conjunction of Indigenous and non-Indigenous laws, it also reflects an invigorated paternalism over Indigenous rituals and dovetails the courts' intimate inquiry into the laws of Indigenous communities. More cynically, it indicates the courts' distrust of Indigenous community testimony that Indigenous punishment will take place. Through judicial oversight of the process, Indigenous punishment became accountable (Finnane 2001: 308).

Making Indigenous law punishment a condition of a good behaviour bond reconciled the imperatives of the criminal justice system with the interests of the Indigenous community. This accommodation furthered, rather than compromised, the ends of the criminal justice system. The courts could hand responsibility for the offender's behaviour and rehabilitation to the Indigenous community in fulfilment of their duties. This was the case for an offender convicted of raping a two-year-old girl in *R.* v. *Iginiwuni* (1975). The Supreme Court imposed a sentence of five years and eight months' imprisonment, to be released after five months on a good behaviour bond that required the Indigenous community to assure his good behaviour and restoration. Muirhead J. stated that the community has inflicted its corporal punishment and will continue to bring shame to the offender, but will eventually accept him back into the community and 'exercise some influence over [him] in the future' (1975: 24). In relation to an offender convicted of manslaughter from Umbakumba, Groote Eylandt in the Gulf of Carpentaria, the Full Federal Court ordered the accused to be banished from the community as part of his bond (*R.* v. *Mamarika* 1982). The President of the Umbakumba Community Council submitted a letter to the court, countersigned by 20 community members, which read: 'We would like him [the offender] to be set free if possible, but not to come to Groote Eylandt. He would have to stay on an out-station on the mainland for three years or more' (1982: 357). Mamarika's lawyers drew parallels between Indigenous punishment and Anglo-Australian punishment, arguing that community banishment was 'an effective form of restraint' that accorded with the terms of a good behaviour bond (1982: 358). The court agreed to exclude him from his community for a period of three years (1982: 359).

The orders for banishment in Mamarika's case came with the requirement of supervision by a state corrections officer. 'In all the circumstances', the Full Federal Court stated, banishment is an 'appropriate' penalty for manslaughter where properly enforced (1982: 358–9). This is because it essentially fulfilled the objectives of the court's punishment. The court made it clear that *it* was the one determining the banishment on the *advice* of the community. It sought a surety from the Umbakumba community that the 'traditional punishment' had been administered in order to 'give the community an opportunity to demonstrate its support for the course which *we* are taking' (1982: 359, emphasis added). In this way, the court characterized the process as the Umbakumba community acceding to *its* punishment. The court also stated that the Correctional Services Division should not have its hands tied, but should be provided with 'some flexibility in dealing with the appellant' (1982: 359). Ultimately the Director of the Division could vary the Indigenous law punishment condition at any time (1982: 359–60). Similar conditions, and flexibility for the director, were conferred in *Mununguurr* v. *The Queen* (1994). The Northern Territory Court of Criminal Appeal ordered as part of a bond that the defendant attend a tribal reconciliation meeting between the 'Djapu and Mungalilli clans for the purpose of sealing the peace in the traditional aboriginal way' (1994: 77). The court requested that the Director of Correctional Services report to it on the outcomes of this meeting and permitted the Director to change the terms of the recognisance in the event 'that the meeting does not take place within a reasonable time' (1994: 77).

Where the Indigenous community has ordered indefinite banishment, as occurred in *The Queen* v. *Berida* (1990: [24]), a case involving an offender convicted of manslaughter from Port Keats (now known as Wadeye in the north-west of the Northern Territory), the Supreme Court has ordered that supervision by the Department of Correctional Services be supplemented with the supervision by the Indigenous community so that banishment can remain effective. The court's paternalism extended to surveillance of physical forms of Indigenous punishment, where the community had made submissions that it would occur at the conclusion of the court-imposed sentence. The court sought assurances from corrections officers that it took place within the scriptures of Indigenous law. This was a prerequisite for the offender being afforded leniency. In *The Queen* v. *Walker* (1994), the court made the punishment of spearing a precondition for releasing Walker on a 2-year good behaviour bond for the crime of manslaughter. The court requested the Department of Correctional Services to supervise the spearing at Yuendumu and to report back to the court within 6 months confirming its occurrence (1994: 10). Martin C.J. stated that 'the first thing the court has to do in this case, and maybe others, is to try and work out a regime whereby it can be informed as to whether what is expected has happened or not' (1994: 9). Zdenkowski (1994: 27) commented that in *Walker's* case 'the court appears to pay lipservice to "autonomy", yet is very interested in the outcome'.

Supervision of Indigenous law punishment is part of a process in which Indigenous culture must be 'knowable' to 'whites' (Watson 2009: 4). Colonial discourse ascribes a 'fixed reality' to the colonized, which is 'knowable and visible' (Bhabha 1990: 371). Douglas (2005a: 152) argues that the requirements set down for Indigenous punishment make the defendant's community 'a disciplinary space' that is 'connected to the white legal system'.[11] The alternative authority of the Indigenous domain is only allowed to operate according to the checks and balances imposed by the white legal system. Courts maintain that they have the greatest interest in Indigenous law punishment being carried out and are able to assess whether it meets the requirements of 'tradition'. This continued to ring true when the Supreme Court rejected the operation of Indigenous punishment in more recent times, which the following section examines. One example of the contemporary court's need to know the form of traditional punishment is the case of *Parmbuk* v. *Garner* (1999: [7]). There, the offender submitted that he would receive 'traditional punishment' from his family and members of his community for damaging a motor vehicle and dangerous driving. The Supreme Court rejected this submission because evidence was not adduced on 'the form of traditional punishment' (1999: [20]). The invisibility of Indigenous punishment evaded the court's disciplinary control and was therefore incapable of recognition in sentencing.

Indigenous law punishment in the current era: from tool of discipline to requiring discipline

The highpoint of recognition of Indigenous punishment in the 1980s and early 1990s was met with a judicial backlash at the end of the twentieth century. Before cultural practices and customary laws were prohibited from sentencing and bail under sections 90 and 91 of the Northern Territory National Emergency Response Act 2007 (Cth), the Supreme Court had departed from affording significant mitigation where the offender was subjected to Indigenous punishment. From the late 1990s, the court no longer viewed Indigenous punishment as rehabilitating or disciplining the offender or restoring community relations. It reasoned that Indigenous community dysfunction undermined the capacity of Indigenous punishment to restore community relations and punish and deter crime. At the same time, the court has more vividly underscored its disapproval of the practice – aligning it with notions of revenge rather than restoration. It questioned whether Indigenous punishment was simply an act of out-of-control retribution. Its violent nature signified to the court the disorder and breakdown of Indigenous society. This re-imagining of Indigenous punishment is set against the rational manner and form of Anglo-Australian punishment (see Buchan 2008).

Judicial disapprovals and doubts over Indigenous punishment have been echoed in parliamentary proclamations and sensational media coverage (Toohey

11 Another subtle but insidious implication of the surveillance of traditional punishment is that it is used as evidence of the guilt of the accused. The criminal justice system, including courts, has sought to ascertain whether traditional punishment has been meted out as part of its investigation (see *R.* v. *Daniel* 1998).

2001: 3). In 1997, the Northern Territory's Chief Minister and Attorney-General, Shane Stone, stated: 'I consider customary law barbaric and unacceptable. There is no way we will have two laws up here' (Zinn 1997: 19). In response to the 'unprecedented level of outrage and anger' over Indigenous punishment, the Chief Minister sought to introduce legislation to ensure that it has no legal standing (although in fact it had no separate legal standing) (1997: 19). A number of years later when Indigenous people sought to have Indigenous punishment recognized, the *Daily Telegraph* criticized the 'right to mete out harsh tribal justice free from the constraints of the courts' (Squires 2005: 13). The newspaper commented that customary laws 'were suppressed by the British' 200 years ago, perpetuating an idea that Indigenous punishment is outmoded (2005: 13). The moral panic over Indigenous punishment reflects an anxiety in Anglo-Australian society about the operation of a system that challenges the whiteness of Australian sovereignty (Hage 1998). The competing Indigenous order sets into sharp relief that the Anglo-Australian jurisdiction is contingent on an unfounded notion of *terra nullius*. To buttress jurisdictional claims, Indigenous laws are derided and the courts' rational authority and monopoly over legitimate coercion is asserted.[12] Both the courts and parliaments have sounded a warning that anyone caught administering physical forms of collective punishment will be criminalized by the Anglo-Australian law (*R.* v. *Wilson* 1995: 276; *Police* v. *Dickenson & Ors* 2010; Johnson 2010).

The paramount concern for the contemporary Northern Territory Supreme Court is not recognition, restoration or rehabilitation, but rather sentences that are proportionate to the seriousness of the offence and that respond to the wider community's demands for lengthy prison sentences (*Wurramara* 1999). The court now regards Indigenous law punishment as contrary to the policy of 'truth in sentencing', which demands longer prison sentences (Flynn 1994: 211). This coincides with punitive reforms in the Sentencing Act 1995 (NT), including higher maximum sentences, the introduction of minimum and mandatory penalties and an abolition of suspended sentences for prison terms of more than 2 years. These considerations have overshadowed concerns for reconciling relations in Indigenous communities. If the courts have retained a scintilla of optimism about the capacity of Indigenous law punishment to rehabilitate the offender through reintegration, they have suppressed this urge in favour of denouncing the offender through imprisonment (see *The Queen* v. *Webb* 2003: 8). In this respect the courts have latched on to the broader punitive trend of condemning offenders and seeking to dissociate them from their communities based on notions of individual responsibility (Cohen 1985: 137; Muncie 2006: 773). These approaches have culminated in harsher penalties that have reinforced the common law's supremacy over Indigenous laws and its monopoly over penality.

12 This is reminiscent of the colonial reasoning in *R.* v. *Murrell & Bummaree* (1836).

Sentencing away Indigenous law punishment

The tide against Indigenous punishment came on the cusp of the twenty-first century when the higher courts refuted its role in a disciplinary system predicated on imprisonment. Misgivings over community submissions in relation to Indigenous punishment came to the fore in *The Queen* v. *Webb* (2003). In that case, a 21-year-old defendant was convicted of manslaughter of an Indigenous man and two counts of aggravated assault of Indigenous females in Alice Springs. In a victim's impact statement, the deceased's sister referred to the offender as having visited Nyirrpi (central Australia) to receive Indigenous law punishment while being released on bail for six days. The punishment involved spearing the offender three times in one leg and twice in the other, as well as receiving stab wounds to the arm and back and having his head split open with a blunt instrument. The deceased's sister, on behalf of the deceased's family, expressed satisfaction with the Indigenous punishment and felt that the matter was 'now settled' and the offender should not be further imprisoned (2003: 4). A cousin of the deceased also gave evidence 'to the effect that the deceased's family feels that the prisoner has suffered enough, that justice has been done, and the deceased's family will not seek further retribution against members of the prisoner's family' (2003: 4). The victim's family and community did not believe that the offender should also serve time in prison (2003: 8).

In sentencing the offender, the Supreme Court questioned the disciplinary role of Indigenous law punishment. For the court, it was tantamount to a private retribution process between families (*The Queen* v. *Webb* 2003: 6). Accordingly, it could not be considered in lieu of a prison sentence. It also disputed the evidence of the Indigenous community in relation to Indigenous punishment and dismissed the views of the victim's family that the matter had been settled. Bailey J. stated: 'I am not satisfied that the wishes of a victim of an offence in relation to the sentencing of an offender can usually be relevant. The criminal law is related to public wrongs, not issues which can be settled privately' (2003: 6–7, quoting *R.* v. *Miyatatawuy* 1996: 580). The victim's views are only incorporated where they comply with the court's sensibility. In the case of *Webb*, because the victim's impact statement did not voice the concerns of the 'ideal' victim – whose moral character resonates with the universal white victim (Crenshaw 1991: 1252) – its relevance to the sentencing outcome was dismissed.

The Supreme Court expressed misgivings over the testimony of the victim in *The Queen* v. *Webb* (2003: 5). It queried the evidence of the victim as to whether the defendant did attend 'customary or traditional punishment' while on bail, since there was only 'oblique reference' to 'traditional ceremonies' in the bail application. The implication was that the violence meted out was mere revenge rather than a lawfully administered process. A critical view of Indigenous community claims of Indigenous punishment also emerged in *R.* v. *Wilson* (1995). There, the court questioned whether the offender would be speared in the thigh after a lengthy sentence, given that such punishment required, in its view, immediate reconciliation between the 'two groups of people involved with the dead person and the prisoner' (1995: 276). It went further to warn Indigenous people at Imanpa (central Australia) that 'anyone who is caught engaging in such lawless behaviour [as collective punishment], is [to be] dealt with, with the full rigour of the law' (1995: 276). The court not only sought to deter the Indigenous community from carrying out Indigenous punishment, but also sought to send a direct message to the police or prosecution about how they should use their discretion in relation to those engaged in administering Indigenous punishment.

Similarly, in *The Queen* v. *Webb* (2003), the Supreme Court questioned the disciplinary impact of Indigenous punishment on the offender. It emphasized that the purpose of Indigenous punishment was not to punish the offender (2003: 5). The court sought to characterize the Indigenous law punishment as solely retribution. Bailey J. regarded the only suitable disciplinary avenue to be the prison. The judge referred to the need for a 'strong element of both general and personal deterrence in the prisoner's sentence', which would be realized through a lengthy prison sentence (2003: 8). He also stated that any social benefit to the Indigenous community from Indigenous law punishment should not 'override the discharge of a judge's duty to the wider community' (2003: 6). In other words, while 'the deceased's family may regard this episode as closed', 'the interests of the wider community demand the prisoner be punished by the loss of his liberty' and the judge would be failing in his duty if he did not order the offender to serve 'a considerable period behind bars' (2003: 8). To this extent he dismissed the relevance of the wishes of the Indigenous community for a non-custodial sentence (2003: 7) and handed down a head sentence of 9 years' imprisonment with a non-parole period of 4 years and 6 months.[13]

The normative effect of this shift is that Indigenous society is characterized as unreasonably violent, which in turn produces longer prison sentences to deter Indigenous punishment. The Supreme Court states that it 'strongly deprecates such acts of physical violence' involved in Indigenous punishment (*R.* v. *Wilson* 1995: 276). The reasonable standpoint of wider society is adopted because 'society generally is concerned about human life' (*The Queen* v. *Webb* 2003: 8). Motha (2005: 119) explains how recognition of 'proper tradition' only holds up where it is compatible with 'natural justice, equity and good conscience', otherwise the recognition framework falls apart. The court's criticism of Indigenous punishment has translated in bail refusals where the applicant has sought bail to

13 Interestingly, Bailey J. refers to the doctrinal ground of double jeopardy as potentially 'lessen[ing] the severity of a sentence' where Indigenous law punishment occurred (*The Queen* v. *Webb* 2003: 6). On this basis there was a very minor reduction of the prison sentence (at most 5 per cent) in recognition of the fact that the defendant would have been punished twice. This figure is deduced from the fact that there was an overall reduction of the defendant's sentence by 30 per cent, which included the prisoner's plea (worth 25 per cent) and other mitigating circumstances (2003: 8; *Bellas* v. *The Queen* 2006; *Sargeant* v. *Verity* 2009). Significantly less weight is afforded to mitigatory considerations than when the higher courts acknowledged the restorative function of Indigenous law punishment between the 1970s and the 1990s.

undergo Indigenous punishment immediately after the crime. It has determined that Indigenous punishment is not in the best interests of the accused, notwithstanding the accused's assent to collective punishment in order to prevent harm to community and family members or to cure any curses associated with the offence.

Refusing bail to prevent Indigenous law punishment

Indigenous people have voiced that of greater concern than being punished twice is the denial of the opportunity to administer Indigenous law punishment straightaway (Loy 2010). If the offender is not available, because they have been detained, the lawful process cannot be carried out immediately and violence can break out against the family of the offender, which is referred to as 'payback'. On this premise, Indigenous community members have conveyed to the Northern Territory Supreme Court that they wish the accused be released on bail for Indigenous punishment to be carried out so peaceful relations in the community can be resumed. The Northern Territory's Bail Act 1982 section 24 sets out the main considerations for determining bail, including, as relevant to this discussion: the accused's 'background and community ties' (s. 24(1)(a)(i)); 'the needs of the [accused] to be free for any lawful purpose' (s. 24(1)(b)(iii)); whether the accused will be 'in danger of physical injury or in need of physical protection' (s. 24(1)(b)(iv)), and the 'protection and welfare of the community' (s. 24(1)(c)).[14] In the 1980s there was a presumption in favour of bail for murder.

Applying these provisions, the Northern Territory Supreme Court in the 1980s granted bail so Indigenous punishment could be carried out (Australian Law Reform Commission 1986: [505]–[506]). For example, in *R.* v. *Jungarai* (1981), the court granted bail to an applicant who was accused of murdering another Indigenous man and who was 'willing, indeed anxious, to undergo [traditional] punishment' in his Warrabri community (now Ali Curung, 350 kilometres north of Alice Springs, Northern Territory). Forster C.J.'s reasoning was that 'once the ritual spearing has taken place, peace will be restored between the families and in the community' (1981: 31). He noted that it is exceptional to allow a person charged with murder to be released on bail (1981: 32). However, without the ceremonial spearing, 'the matter of retribution or pay back in Aboriginal terms will be unresolved and the community will be ill at ease and serious trouble may flare up at any time' (1981: 32). Forster C.J.'s view that 'ordinary harmony which prevails in the Warrabri community will be disrupted' without Indigenous punishment, revealed a perception of a *generally* harmonious community (1981: 31). The court appreciated the capacity of Indigenous law punishment to prevent 'serious violence' erupting and did not feel the need to send a

14 Section 24 has since been amended to remove the term 'protection and welfare of the community'.

message of deterrence in relation to the criminality of 'customary spearing' (1981: 31). In dealing with the bail application, Forster C.J. expressed 'neither approval nor disapproval of the course proposed to be taken by the family of the deceased, endorsed as it is by the community' (1981: 32). He continued:

> Whether or not the proposed action constitutes an offence under the law of the land seems to me, for present purposes, to be irrelevant. The order for release on bail should not be interpreted as necessarily involving approval of what will happen nor, of course, should my failure to approve it be interpreted as disapproval. What will almost certainly happen is simply, for present purposes, an important fact to be considered.
>
> (*R.* v. *Jungarai* 1981: 32)

More recently, however, the Northern Territory Supreme Court has stated that bail will not be granted where the accused returns to his or her community to receive corporal Indigenous punishment, because it cannot condone serious assault. Its decisions have dovetailed amendments to the Bail Act 1982 (NT) section 7A that created a presumption against bail in cases of murder. The principal solicitor of the Northern Australian Justice Agency, Glen Dooley, stated that 'barriers' have been placed by judges and parliamentarians to 'virtually ensure that people who are charged with murder don't actually get out to participate in these ceremonies' (Bullock 2010). The changed judicial mindset has seen bail refusals where the defendant, who is not a flight risk, seeks to return to the Indigenous community to be dealt with by collective punishment. A major turning point was the case of *Barnes* (1997), where the applicant was charged with the murder of his nephew. Warlpiri law in that instance required that the offender be speared repeatedly, hit with boomerangs and punched. The applicant was willing to undergo the Indigenous punishment for the peace and well-being of the Lajamanu community and for his own benefit (1997: 595). Bailey J., who also decided the sentence in *The Queen* v. *Webb*, refused to grant bail to Barnes. The court held that the presumption against bail for the charge of murder had not been rebutted (*Barnes* 1997: 593).

In his reasoning, Bailey J. noted that there were grounds for rebutting the presumption against bail – namely, the Bail Act 1982 (NT) section 24 allowed the judge to take into account the applicant's interests and the interests of the community. However, he concluded that 'the interests of the applicant (s 24(1)(b)) would *not* be served by facilitating his release to be unlawfully stabbed and bashed' (*Barnes* 1997: 597, emphasis added). He held that the court should prioritize the 'applicant's need for physical protection' by continuing his detention in custody (1997: 593, 598). Therefore, the court regarded Indigenous punishment as operating against the interests of the Warlpiri applicant. Furthermore, in considering section 24(1)(c), which provided for the protection and welfare of the community, the court held that this did not concern 'a particular community's "harmony" or any general beneficial effects which might flow to a community from the imposition of traditional punishment' (1997: 597). The court interpreted 'the community' exclusively in terms of the wider (non-Indigenous) community and not the applicant's particular Warlpiri community. Ultimately, the court in *Barnes* (1997: 593) dismissed what it called 'tribal retribution' and refused bail.

In the bail hearing in *Barnes*, the Warlpiri community made a strong case for the recognition of Indigenous punishment. It used the case to test the boundaries of legal pluralism. In presenting evidence on the importance of Indigenous punishment, the Lajamanu Council President asserted that the community had altered Indigenous law punishment out of respect for Anglo-Australian laws, such that it no longer involved fatal spearing. Due to these concessions the president sought to have the same latitudes reciprocated (*Barnes* 1997: 594). The carrying out of a modified form of collective punishment, by spearing in the leg and below vital organs, was a means to ensure that the 'justice system is balanced between the white and the black' (1997: 594). It was submitted that to disregard this compromise position would demonstrate the court's contempt for Indigenous laws and pose serious spiritual and health risks to the applicant (1997: 594). In refusing to countenance these submissions, Bailey J. attempted to present himself as a humanist who was nonetheless bound to uphold the Anglo-Australian law. He stated that he was not being 'paternalistic or lacking in sensitivity to the increasing calls for reconciliation between the Aboriginal society and that of the wider Australian community', but believed that 'the Court cannot facilitate what would amount to a crime' (1997: 597–8).

A subsequent bail decision in *Anthony* (2004: 442) saw the Supreme Court disallow the applicant's return to his community of Lajamanu to undergo Indigenous punishment because the court 'cannot condone' such 'unlawful act[s]' under the Anglo-Australian law. The applicant who was accused of manslaughter submitted that he needed to be freed 'for cultural purposes, namely, undergoing lawful traditional punishment' (2004: 442). His family, the family of the deceased victim and the Elders of Lajamanu had 'agreed upon the form of traditional punishment to be administered' (2004: 442). Without Indigenous punishment taking place, the family feared reprisals, and the applicant, who believed he was 'cursed by Aboriginal magic', feared that a curse might kill him (2004: 442). A letter submitted by the Warlpiri Elders sought for the matter to be 'dealt with according to customary practice' in order to avoid ongoing 'violence between families concerned' (2004: 444).

The Supreme Court did not accept the Lajamanu community's evidence on the effects of its Indigenous punishment. The community members submitted that its collective punishment had not in their living memory resulted in 'death or permanent injury' and full recovery was often achieved within a matter of weeks (*Anthony* 2004: 445). The court dismissed the claim of an Elder that if the 'applicant starts to get weaker the Elders will intervene and bring the punishment to a halt' (2004: 445). Rather, the court highlighted that there was 'a significant risk that the applicant will suffer grievous harm' and it was the role of the court to adjudicate on all forms of violence (2004: 445). Martin C.J. held that the Bail Act (NT) did not provide for the interests of the Indigenous community, but merely the wider community's interests. Therefore, the wishes of the Indigenous community, and ensuing detriment facing the Warlpiri community and the offender in the absence of Indigenous punishment, were not relevant bail considerations (2004: 446). Martin C.J. stated, 'the applicant and his community's wish that he be free to undergo traditional punishment in respect of the death of the deceased is not a proper basis for the grant of bail' (2004: 447). Given that the nature of the offence and the accused would ordinarily give rise to bail, Martin C.J. granted bail on the condition that the accused lives with his sister at Ngukurr and did not enter Lajamanu, which was several hundred kilometres away. Therefore, his bail conditions explicitly forbade Indigenous punishment. Ultimately, Anthony breached these conditions by returning to his community to undergo collective punishment, and accordingly faced further punishment by the courts (Gray 2005a: 45).

The lack of recognition of Indigenous punishment in bail decisions came to a head when the Federal Government removed the courts' capacity to consider cultural and customary law in determining bail applications under section 90 of the Northern Territory National Emergency Response Act 2007 (Cth).[15] This measure, as discussed in the previous chapter, was part of a raft of measures to restrict the rights of Indigenous people in remote Northern Territory communities. It was the counterpart to the legislative provision removing these considerations in sentencing and arose from the moral panic in relation to violence and dysfunction in Indigenous communities that was attributed to Indigenous culture. Denying the consideration of Indigenous punishment in bail both precludes collective punishment going ahead expeditiously and extends troubles in remote communities that emerge from criminal conduct. It is also a metaphor for the monopoly of Anglo-Australian criminal justice processes to the exclusion of Indigenous laws.

Payback for lack of recognition

The troubles arising from an inability to dispense Indigenous law punishment were crystallized in late 2010 when fighting broke out in the Warlpiri community of Yuendumu in central Australia. It followed the killing of a 21-year-old Warlpiri community member by another one of its members. The deceased's family was unsettled because Indigenous punishment, *mala mala*, could not go ahead in the form of spearing (Gosford 2010; Anon 2010). This resulted in feuding among families, with vehicles and houses being damaged and up to 100 community members fleeing to Adelaide for protection. Ultimately, tactical

15 This provision has since been transferred to the Crimes Act 1914 (Cth) s. 15AB(1)(b). The restrictions also apply to the Commonwealth jurisdiction, but do not apply to other individual states and territories.

response officers were sent to the Yuendumu to quell the fighting, but Warlpiri people regarded this as an 'overreaction' and inappropriate for addressing a Warlpiri issue (Everingham 2010).

The mainstream media criticized Warlpiri calls for Indigenous punishment as having no place in Australian society (Mills 2011; Anon 2010a). It portrayed the Warlpiri involved in the dispute as savage 'warring tribes' (Mills 2011). The Australian Broadcasting Corporation described Indigenous punishment as embedded in 'beliefs in sorcery' and a product of 'a dearth of education' (Bullock 2010a). Similarly, the *Northern Territory News* stated that it was 'barbaric' and reflected a lack of 'sophistication' (Anon 2010b: 12). Alternatively, *The Australian* reported that the punishment is 'an excuse for random and destructive violence' (Anon 2010a: 15). In amplifying a moral panic, the media referred to the situation at Yuendumu as a 'clan war' (Murdoch 2010: 3) that 'could go on 20 years' (Neill and Schliebs 2010: 9) and proclaimed that the violence was 'out of control in Central Australia' (Bullock 2010b). These representations add to the judicial perception of the illegitimacy of Indigenous punishment in order to retain the exclusivity of the non-Indigenous criminal domain.

Arising from the Yuendumu dispute, 11 family members of the murder victim were convicted of riot-related offences. Their defence lawyer submitted that the threats were made as part of 'payback'. The mother of the deceased also told the Magistrates' Court that she no longer had any feelings of 'anger' against Sims' mother because it was dealt with under Warlpiri law through hitting her with a *nulla nulla* and this allowed for positive restoration of the relationship (Goldflam 2012: 10). Magistrate Bamber stated that Indigenous punishment should be discarded and that consensual violence is 'nonsense' (*Police* v. *Dickenson & Ors* 2010). Indigenous Member of Parliament Marian Scrymgour asserted that consensual violence is common in the Northern Territory: it is 'called "boxing"' (Murdoch 2010a: 4). The magistrate went on to assert that the Elders 'should be concerned with changing their law' and 'the days of payback with violence must end' (*Police* v. *Dickenson & Ors* 2010). In ordering prison sentences for the deceased's family, the magistrate said, 'the message, if it is not clear, needs to be made clear' that 'whitefella law' applies and 'old punishments' are prohibited (*Police* v. *Dickenson & Ors* 2010). This was echoed by Attorney-General Delia Lawrie, who asserted that the same laws apply to all Territorians 'regardless of their race' (Johnson 2010).

Furthermore, in sentencing the defendant who was charged with the manslaughter that precipitated the feud at Yuendumu, the Supreme Court warned that anyone dispensing Indigenous punishment upon the release of the offender would be breaking the Anglo-Australian law. It stated: 'The court has dealt with the matter and the business has to finish now' (*The Queen* v. *Sims & Walker* 2012: 8). However, more than two years later the conflict continues. Anger was also renewed by the imprisonment of the deceased's family for riot-related offences. Some of the family members felt that the magistrate's interference with the Indigenous law process undid the restoration achieved prior to their imprisonment (Spiers-Williams 2011: 16).

Concluding remarks

The recognition of Indigenous punishment at the sentencing stage gives accommodation with one hand and takes authority with the other. Zdenkowski (1994: 27) described the recognition of Indigenous punishment as a 'version of cultural relativism which accepts that the general legal system is presumptively applicable but will make concessions to specific cultural arguments'. In the interplay of jurisdictions, Indigenous offenders are ultimately subject to Anglo-Australian punishment. The legitimacy and universality of Anglo-Australian punishment is self-assigned and emerges through mainstream praxis, notwithstanding the continuation of collective punishment in Indigenous societies. When the courts have recognized Indigenous punishment, they have also mandated its supervision where the punishment had not yet been carried out – signifying how judicial recognition opened a Pandora's Box for Indigenous law processes. This imposition of Western standards is part of a process of 'spatial management' which essentially entails exclusive 'white' claims to Indigenous spaces (Hage 1998).

More recently, however, the Northern Territory Supreme Court subverted Indigenous punishment and Indigenous community views. Since the late 1990s, 'white' claims to Indigenous spaces have culminated in the exclusion of Indigenous law practices. This shows that recognition of a 'different' penality is contingent on maintaining Anglo-Australian authority. The judiciary's tolerant countenance is eclipsed when its domain comes under threat. So-called weak legal plurality (Douglas 2005a: 141), where judicial recognition of Indigenous punishment could mitigate a sentence, has given way to judicial claims of legal antinomy where Indigenous and non-Indigenous laws are incapable of coexisting. This results in longer prison sentences, refusal of bail (which precludes Indigenous punishment) and the criminalization of those who administer Indigenous punishment. A defining tenet of contemporary sentencing remarks is that the interests of the wider community prevail over the interests of the Indigenous community. For the judiciary, this means favouring imprisonment over the administration of Indigenous law punishment. As Warlpiri Elder Jampijinpa stated: 'One law is up, one law is down. Our law is down . . . They think what is the best for the community or for Aboriginal people is from the white men law' (Loy 2010).

Undermining the practice of Indigenous laws are judicial and popular portrayals of Indigenous communities as dysfunctional. Courts, governments and media classify Indigenous punishment as tribal revenge (Murray 2010: 20; Squires 2005: 13). The supposed customary excesses of Indigenous punishment are regarded as offensive to Anglo-Australian norms and lacking the *proper* elements of culture sufficient for judicial recognition (Motha 2007: 88). The desires of the community in sentencing submissions are disregarded in what has been described as the 'triumph of anti-relativism' (Goldflam 2012: 12). This situation reflects a historical denigration of the justice traditions of the Other who is seen as barbaric (Adjin-Tettey 2007: 188). Significantly, this narrative casts doubt on the capacity of Indigenous communities to discipline and reform their offenders. It coincides with a contention in Federal Government that Indigenous communities are 'failed states' that are unable to achieve 'order and good governance' (Dillon and Westbury 2007: 39). According to a senior policy adviser, endemic social dysfunction in Indigenous communities manifests in 'ad hoc and opportunistic violence' and emerging 'zones of violence and disorder' (Dillon 2007: 5–6). Through this lens, Indigenous punishment operates as a catalyst rather than a cure for the breakdown of Indigenous society. This view runs against that of the Northern Territory Board of Inquiry into the Protection of Aboriginal Children from Sexual Abuse, which recommended that Indigenous law be 'utilised and incorporated as an integral part of the solution' to problems in Indigenous communities (Wild and Anderson 2007: 176).

The narrative of dysfunctionality extends to circumstances of socio-economic disadvantage in Indigenous communities. In sentencing offenders who submit that their impoverished background warrants mitigation, higher courts have underlined the perceived hopelessness of their Indigenous communities. They have made a rhetorical shift from referring to these communities as 'disadvantaged' to 'dysfunctional'. The following chapter considers these representations in relation to urban Indigenous communities in cities and regional towns of New South Wales and remote communities of the Northern Territory that are beset with poverty. Higher courts in these jurisdictions have swayed between reimagining Indigenous communities as not *properly* Indigenous (because they are dysfunctional) and as not Indigenous *enough* (because they are not functioning in a traditional Indigenous manner). These reimaginings of Indigeneity converge with those in Indigenous law punishment cases. Both convey an idea that Indigenous communities have failed due to their breakdown in governance, laws and cultural identity. They have therefore become risk sites for victims who require protection exclusively by white authority structures. But despite courts shifting the recognition goalposts away from accounting for Indigeneity in mitigation, the judiciary has retained its capacity to recognize the Other to send a message to the Indigenous community that its practices are not condoned.

Chapter 6

Sentencing anxieties over 'degenerates, drunks and criminals'

> It is proper for the court to recognise that the problems of alcohol abuse and violence which to a very significant degree go hand in hand within Aboriginal communities are very real ones and their cure requires more subtle remedies than the criminal law can provide by way of imprisonment.
>
> (*Fernando* 1992: 62)

Denying and deriding Indigeneity in disadvantaged contexts

In the postcolonial mindset, images of Indigenous communities tend to be situated in the bush or backwoods (Edmonds 2010: 5). They lie far beyond the urban streetscape that is shrouded in a fantasy of homogenous whiteness. Where the national imagination contemplates Indigenous alterity, it is associated with pre-colonial practices, ceremonies and rituals. There may be outrage expressed in relation to Indigenous law punishment and cultural marriages, but mainstream institutions nonetheless consider such practices to be 'Indigenous'. The same cannot be said about urban Indigenous experiences.[1] Postcolonial 'white' society has struggled to characterize Indigenous people in cities and regional towns as anything more than 'degenerates, drunks and criminals' (Dodson 1994a: 11). This is due to a nationalist anxiety about the Other (Hage 2003). The colonial encroachment of Indigenous space produced a 'stock story' of the inferiority of Indigenous communities beset with cultural breakdown (due to evolutionary forces) and socio-economic disadvantage (due to their lack of assimilation and integration into the mainstream economy) (Bell 2010; Tingle 2007: 87). These stereotypes are as essentialist as the ones of the 'traditional' Indigenous offender but without attracting the same level of sympathy or idealization.

The supreme courts in New South Wales and the Northern Territory have embraced the narrative of the disadvantaged Indigenous offender with varying

1 Most Indigenous Australians live in major cities and regional areas (Australian Bureau of Statistics 2011c).

intonations and intensities. This chapter elucidates shifting judicial notions of Indigenous socio-economic disadvantage in urban cities and regional towns and more remote contexts over the past 40 years. It is a companion to the following chapter on the Indigenous experience of resistance through riots which similarly defies 'traditional' imaginings of Indigeneity. In both instances the judiciary conveyed the helplessness and *pathos* of Indigenous offenders and their communities. This chapter explores how courts associate Indigenous disadvantage with poverty,[2] alcoholism and inter-generational crime, initially to afford sympathy and mitigation and later to extend antipathy and penality.[3] Recognition at the behest of dominating institutions associates Indigenous people's disadvantage with moribund communities that lack control over their members and circumstances, rather than with colonizing and capitalist processes (Fraser 1996: 18). This judicial mode of recognition further entrenches rather than emancipates Indigenous people's disadvantaged position, including in the criminal justice system.

In accepting sentencing submissions that the Indigenous offender's disadvantaged background reduced their moral culpability, the courts have acquiesced to a body of criminological and political thought that attributes crime to socio-economic stress (*Fernando* 1992: 63; Broadhurst 1997: 413–14; Weatherburn *et al.* 2006: 2–3). Criminologists argue that disadvantage reduces people's choice over their actions (Tonry 1995: 125; Hudson 1999: 589–90) and proportionate sentencing requires consideration of its effect on culpability (Ashworth 2002: 1079; Hudson 1999: 584). These arguments were increasingly put to the courts after Aboriginal legal services were established in Redfern, New South Wales in 1970 and in Alice Springs, Northern Territory in 1973 (Foley 2001; Faine 1993). In more radical instances, courts sought to reintegrate Indigenous offenders back into their communities by providing non-custodial sentences and resisting penal pressures to imprisonment (*R.* v. *Smith* 2003). Criminologist McCoy (1997: 611–12) argues that prisons are a means to exclude the underclass from the moral community. In addition, some criminologists regard lenience for the oppressed as redistributing the burdens of socio-economic disadvantage (Hudson 1999: 583; Tonry 1995; Ashworth 2002, 2005: 86). It helps redress the imposition of punishments 'upon those already unfairly low on the scale of benefits and burdens' (Goldman quoted in Sadurski 1985: 58). By contrast, imprisoning

2 Poverty in Indigenous communities is marked by low levels of income, unemployment, education, quality housing, basic infrastructure and healthcare (Thomson *et al.* 2012: 5–6).

3 This approach in sentencing Indigenous offenders reverberated in sentencing courts across Australia. For remarks in Western Australia, see *Juli* v. *R.* (1990), *Rogers & Murray* v. *R.* (1989): 307; in Queensland, see *R.* v. *Friday* 1985, *R.* v. *Bulmer* 1987, *Yougie* (1987: 304); in New South Wales, see *Fernando* 1992, *R.* v. *Stone* (1995: 224); in South Australia, see *Ingomar* v. *Police* 1998, *Police* v. *Abdulla* 1999, *R.* v. *Tjami* 2000, *R.* v. *Smith* (2003: [60]); in the Northern Territory, see *R.* v. *Benny Lee* 1974, *R.* v. *Davey* 1980, *R.* v. *Herbert & Ors* 1983, *Robertson* v. *Flood* 1992; in Victoria, see *DPP* v. *Terrick* (2009: [50]), *R.* v. *Mustey* (2001: [13]), *R.* v. *Fuller-Cust* (2002: 520); in the Australian Capital Territory, see *Crawford* v. *Laverty* 2008.

Indigenous offenders compounds their disadvantage by perpetuating their cycle of poverty and their postcolonial subordination (Nicholson 2012).

While disadvantaged circumstances have provided the preconditions for mitigation, as espoused by the Northern Territory Supreme Court from the 1970s and the New South Wales Supreme Court in the early 1990s, generally they have not carried the same weight as the cultural circumstances of the 'traditional' offender. This demarcation was originally set by Kriewaldt J. of the Northern Territory Supreme Court in the 1950s. He regarded Indigenous offenders exposed to white ways, and therefore having experienced the benefits of 'civilization' through cultural breakdown, as not deserving the same degree of mitigation as the 'uncivilized' offender (*R.* v. *Anderson* 1954). According to the court, civilization was seen as providing opportunities for the Indigenous person and also carrying obligations of proper behaviour. Offenders of this class could not claim that they did not know better. Furthermore, 'tribal' offenders, unlike their civilized counterparts, were not affected by messages of deterrence (Douglas 2005: 174). The court after Kriewaldt J.'s reign held that romantic notions of Indigenous savages resolute in their 'traditional' culture and collective punishment had more appeal than Indigenous offenders who had a weakness for modern vices such as alcohol. In *R.* v. *Minor* (1992: 190), for example, the Supreme Court endorsed Kriewaldt J.'s practice of providing greater lenience to Indigenous people in 'traditional' circumstances.

Nonetheless, from the 1970s, sympathy was increasingly bestowed on Indigenous offenders suffering from the detrimental impact of colonization. The Northern Territory Supreme Court perceived the withering of Indigenous society and traditional authority structures as threatening their peaceful ways and the loss of traditional land and sustenance as generating impoverishment. Disadvantage was intimately connected to colonial oppression and dispossession, and it followed that colonialism and non-Indigenous influences were implicated in criminality. Both in the Northern Territory and New South Wales, offenders represented the problem of modernization and deserved reductions in their criminal sentences, albeit not as much as for the 'traditional' offender. Alcohol in particular signified the problem of introduced cultures. The court assumed a position of benefactor in granting lenience as compensation for Indigenous loss and subordination (Douglas 2009: 80). Through more lenient sentences, colonialism and its legacy could be held to account. Therefore, unlike the earlier remarks of Kriewaldt J., succeeding courts perceived cultural breakdown as a problem rather than a blessing for the Indigene. They regarded their role as softening the burden of 'civilization' through a lighter sentence. Clemency for 'drunken Aborigines' encodes the Australian version of the white man's burden where the colonizer is obliged to care for inferior races. As Langton (1993: 205) argues, the 'drunken Aborigine' is representative of 'living a fantasy of wanting to become like the white man, but unable to do so'. The courts came to the aid of offenders who succumbed to these vices.

Leniency was also granted for Indigenous people in this earlier period due to the courts' recognition that prison was an ineffective deterrent where offending arose from disadvantage (*R.* v. *Davey* 1980: 258). In addition, the New South Wales Supreme Court held that imprisonment had an unduly harsh impact on Indigenous offenders because it is 'served in an environment which is foreign' and 'dominated by inmates and prison officers of European background' (*Fernando* 1992: 63). This encouraged courts to order alternatives to prison sentences, especially rehabilitative, community-based programmes to further their opportunities and their reformation, which was perhaps the clearest expression of 'penal welfarism' across sentencing discourses on Indigenous offenders (Garland 2001: 49). The courts believed that the 'problems' of Indigenous people could only be 'solved' through broader social policy and institutions other than prisons.

Since the late 1990s, the higher courts in New South Wales and the Northern Territory have recast Indigenous circumstances of disadvantage as markers of Indigenous community 'non-functionality' or 'dysfunctionality'. In New South Wales, they posit that disadvantage has become so defining that it has faded the 'Indigenous' character of their communities. These communities are 'non-functional' in the courts' eyes and do not warrant mitigation. In the Northern Territory, the courts express a sentiment that the inability of Indigenous communities to govern their members results in dysfunction and violence. This dysfunction poses a particular risk to its members, which justifies longer prison sentences for Indigenous offenders. Whereas the earlier judicial perception of Indigenous helplessness opened up possibilities for mitigation (see *R.* v. *Friday* 1985: 472), the reimagining of non-functional or dysfunctional communities has downplayed factors of moral culpability. This reasoning rekindled notions of the unviability of Indigenous communities in the mid twentieth century, and has spawned strong messages of deterrence and denunciation. The courts regard the reintegration and rehabilitation of Indigenous offenders as a futile task given their community hopelessness.

The seesaw approach to the recognition of Indigenous disadvantage over the late twentieth century rings true to Fraser's (1997: 25) concept that recognition provides piecemeal justice and lends itself to *misrecognition* (where the identity of the Other is 'routinely maligned' or disparagingly stereotyped) and *non-recognition* (where the identity of the Other is 'rendered invisible' by falsifying the universality of dominant groups). In terms of non-recognition, a corpus of New South Wales Court of Criminal Appeal sentencing remarks demonstrates how the courts have imposed a notion of 'authentic' Indigenous identity to elide the recognition of urban or 'part' Indigenous offenders (see *Ceissman* 2001).[4] Alternatively, the Northern Territory Court of Appeal's reimagining of remote communities as

4 However, in exceptional cases where the offender has been 'particularly disadvantaged as a result of his upbringing', the New South Wales Supreme Court has applied the *Fernando* principles to provide mitigation, such as in *R.* v. *F.A.P.* (2007): [39]. See also: *R.* v. *Bashford* (2007): [45]–[46]; and *Waters* v. *R.* (2007): [39].

'dysfunctional' – because they are seen as breeding grounds for criminals – misrecognizes the complexity of Indigenous circumstances, including the various functional aspects of their cultures and law systems and their capacity for self-determination (see *Wurramara* 1999).

Recognition contingencies: authenticity and appropriateness

Highlighting the recognition of Indigenous disadvantage across two jurisdictions illustrates the judiciary's divergent responses to urban and remote settings as well as their convergent punitive impulses. Accordingly, it enables harsher sentences to be understood as more than simply a response to a localized crime problem. Rather, it shows that they are part of a broader shift in sentencing principles and conceptions of Indigenous alterity. The focus on two jurisdictions and their sentencing of offenders from a range of communities also indicates that there is not one homogenous Indigenous community, but there are hundreds of Indigenous societies that have diverse geographies and experiences. In New South Wales, the Supreme Court's jurisprudence is mostly in relation to urban offenders who have struggled with socio-economic hardships and alcoholism, whereas the Northern Territory Supreme Court has a greater interface with the remote offender who is regarded as experiencing cultural breakdown, alcoholism and poverty as a relatively new phenomenon. In both jurisdictions in the late 1990s, mitigation was wound back as the seriousness of offending took precedent over the relevance of community circumstances. In this respect, culpability took a back seat to the gravity of the harm and the need for deterrence. This, according to Hudson (1999: 584), reduces the crime to its *actus reus* by removing the mental element. Harm supervenes because the judicial denial of Indigeneity ('not Indigenous enough') or refusal of Indigeneity ('not appropriately Indigenous') undermines the relevance of Indigenous community facts related to culpability (O'Malley 1996: 319). By focusing on harm, courts are justified in increasing sentences and reimagining the Indigenous community solely in terms of its risk.

The New South Wales Court of Criminal Appeal has applied a prerequisite of authenticity for Indigenous community membership that has barred a significant class of Indigenous people from acquiring leniency in sentencing. According to current jurisprudence, Indigenous offenders living outside of remote areas are not considered to be a part of a recognizable Indigenous community. This is analogous to native title cases where the judiciary has defined Indigenous culture according to an essentialized notion of tradition. Indigenous culture is considered as frozen in time and thus prone to being washed away by the tide of colonization (*Members of the Yorta Yorta Aboriginal Community* v. *Victoria* 2002). It reflects a colonial representation of the Indigenous community, culture and identity in accordance with its defining features of primitive, pre-colonial and uncivilized. In failing to recognize the dynamic and amorphous nature of Indigeneity, the courts produce an 'absolute truth' which gives the 'subject a sense of power and control' (Dodson 1994: 9). At the same time it brings the Other 'back into check' (1994: 9). The modern/primitive and remote/urban dichotomies are a means of excluding those who do not meet requirements of tradition, and oversimplify the complex realities of postcolonial Indigenous experiences. They conceal the diversity of Indigenous communities as 'a network of people and organisations linked together by a web of personal relationships, cultural and political connections and identities, networks of support, traditions and institutions, shared socioeconomic conditions, or common understandings and interests' (Hunt and Smith 2007: 4).

While Indigenous communities are geographically dispersed, the New South Wales Court of Appeal's 'imagined community' places non-Indigenous people in urban spaces and Indigenous people in peripheral spaces (Anderson 1983). The spatial parameters set by the court align with Said's (1978) notion of 'imaginative geography', which is produced by colonial knowledges of space and governance. A corollary of this reasoning is that only offenders with 'full' Indigenous heritage meet the physiological prerequisites designated by the court to Indigenous peoples. This is reminiscent of colonial classifications of Indigenous people who are graded according to skin colour.

In the Northern Territory, the membership of an offender to an Indigenous community has not been challenged, but the courts have reassessed the nature of those communities as dysfunctional. The story of endemic socio-economic failures (such as in housing, education and employment) and prevalent criminal offending pervades the reimagining of remote Indigenous communities over the past decade. Rather than focus on the capacity of the community or the reduced culpability of the offender who was affected by community disadvantage, courts now focus on victims and potential victims in dysfunctional settings. These judicial characterizations are part of a larger narrative of 'failed Indigenous states' in Australia that laments their disorder and disconnection from the mainstream (Dillon and Westbury 2007; Steketee 2008: 16). It is augmented by a moral panic that has stirred the collective conscience about Indigenous dysfunction. It has led to calls for tougher approaches to Indigenous people across institutional settings, and has reverberated in the courts' genuflection to the demands of the 'wider community' for harsher punishment (*The Queen* v. *Webb* 2003: 8; *R.* v. *Riley* 2006: 425). The Australian Government additionally justified coercive intervention into remote Northern Territory Indigenous communities since 2007 due to their lack of social norms, neglectful parenting and criminal tendencies. Cohen (1985) and Garland (2001) have identified notions of the failed states as triggers for law and order politics in the West because they drive governments to rethink their control agenda.

In Federal Parliament the Minister for Indigenous Affairs, Mal Brough (2007: 6), articulated that 'normal community standards' and 'social norms' have 'broken down' and Indigenous communities 'are trapped in an intergenerational cycle of dependency'. He spoke of the need to 'normalise' and 'stabilise' these remote communities (Brough 2007b). In the Northern Territory Legislative Assembly, John Ah Kit (2002), the Assisting Chief Minister on Indigenous Affairs, claimed that it was 'almost impossible to find a functional Aboriginal community anywhere in the Northern Territory'. The mainstream media, leading commentators and government figures associated the dysfunctional status of Indigenous communities with 'rivers of grog' and crime (Toohey 2007; Murdoch and Skelton 2011: 8; Kelly 2011). One headline in the *Sydney Morning Herald* read: 'Shame in [the] nation's dead heart' (Skelton 2006: 26). The dominant narrative of Indigenous communities' hopelessness downplays their strengths (Blagg 2008: 170; Gray *et al.* 2008: 123). As evidenced in the sentencing remarks on Indigenous law punishment, the Northern Territory Supreme Court has discounted Indigenous community capacity to discipline their offenders and restore peaceful relations. These notions of Indigenous social dysfunction reinforce the normative order of Anglo-Australian society.

The pliability of judicial recognition means that compensatory gestures of leniency can rapidly give way to heavier sentences to send disciplinary messages to Indigenous communities. Sympathy has given way to outrage over the seriousness of crimes and the fact that sentences in the past have not reflected the interests of the 'wider community' in long prison terms for Indigenous offenders. The focus on seriousness has been made possible by the courts' reimagining of Indigenous communities as either not functioning properly or not functioning at all. It imputes crime to Indigenous individuals and communities rather than Australia's colonial legacy and proclivity to criminalize Indigenous people. The story of dysfunctionality reinforces stereotypes of Indigenous inferiority and bolsters the superiority of the dominant society (see Cowlishaw 1991: 107).

Recognition of Indigenous hardship: the early cases

From the 1970s until the late 1990s, supreme courts in New South Wales and the Northern Territory recognized contemporary Indigenous communities as sites of disadvantage. They received sentencing submissions from Aboriginal legal services evidencing the defendant's membership of deprived Indigenous communities beset by poverty, unemployment, lack of education, alcohol abuse, isolation, racism and loss of customary law, land and family ties through colonial dispossession (Omeri 2006: 78). The New South Wales jurisprudence enunciated in *Fernando* (1992) recognized poverty and alcoholism as grounds for mitigation. In the Northern Territory, the Supreme Court regarded the Indigenous offender who was dislocated from his or her community as the victim of 'social devastation' (Douglas 2005: 187). Alcohol became a signpost for 'Aboriginal cultural breakdown, social devastation and disadvantage' (Douglas 2009: 170). From the 1970s, the Northern Territory Supreme Court provided leniency to Indigenous offenders to compensate for this disadvantage.

New South Wales: 'grave social difficulties' of urban Indigenous offenders

The principles set out in the seminal case of *Fernando* (1992) did not emerge in a vacuum. This New South Wales case drew on a body of sentencing remarks across Australia that endorsed leniency for Indigenous defendants who experienced disadvantage (1992: 62). This included the Queensland Court of Criminal Appeal case of *R.* v. *Friday* (1985: 472), where it was held that the defendant was 'a victim of the circumstances in which her life had placed her'. A subsequent case by that court, *Yougie* (1987), also cited in *Fernando* (1992: 62), supported this view of helplessness. In *Yougie* (1987: 304), the court held that 'it would be wrong to fail to acknowledge the social difficulties faced by Aboriginals' that have 'placed heavy stresses on them leading to alcohol abuse and consequential violence'. The Western Australian Court of Criminal Appeal, in *Rogers & Murray* v. *R.* (1989), recognized the 'notorious fact' that the 'use of alcohol by Aboriginal persons in relatively recent times has caused grave social problems, including problems of violence', which should 'provide circumstances of mitigation'. In *Juli* v. *R.* (1990: 36), the same court maintained that the 'abuse of alcohol reflects the socio-economic circumstances and the environment in which [the Indigenous offender] has grown up and should be taken into account as a mitigating factor'. Also bearing down on the New South Wales Supreme Court in *Fernando* were the findings of the Royal Commission into Aboriginal Deaths in Custody (1991), which had just been handed down when the case was heard. The Royal Commission's Final Report fuelled concerns about the over-imprisonment of Indigenous people and made a case for only imposing imprisonment as a 'sanction of last resort' (1991: Recommendation 92). This report was referred to in *Fernando* (1992: 62) as evidence of the unique conditions for Indigenous people in the criminal justice system, although the New South Wales Supreme Court did not aver to its significance.

While Wood J.'s remarks in *Fernando* were not unique, they synthesized the Indigenous considerations to be taken into account and formulated them within a paradigm that balanced competing sentencing considerations, such as the seriousness of the crime and the harm to the victim. Consequently, the eight *Fernando* principles for sentencing Indigenous offenders from disadvantaged communities have been influential across Australia (Omeri 2006: 76). Fernando's circumstances of disadvantage were mentioned in the epigram to this book as an illustration of an Indigenous stock story. To reiterate, Fernando stabbed his friend and onetime de facto partner, causing serious wounds to her neck and leg. Fernando's background was marked by low levels of education and forcible removal from his family by the Welfare Department. He was sent to an isolated property and thereafter lived in Walgett, a racially divided community in north-western New South Wales, where Indigenous people, including Fernando, were beleaguered with socio-economic hardship (Zagar 1990: xi; Ross and Taylor 2000: vii–viii). He had drunk large amounts of alcohol just before the stabbing and had a criminal history that was linked to his excessive alcohol consumption. When his matter went before the New South Wales Supreme Court, the appalling nature of this crime and the impact on the victim were not in dispute.

Wood J. of the Supreme Court had to contend with the significance of the defendant's Indigenous circumstances. Should his economic disadvantage and ensuing alcoholism mitigate the criminal sentence? Do these factors weigh particularly heavily on Indigenous offenders? What bearing would a lighter sentence have on social justice for Indigenous people? Is sentencing a means of compensation or restoration? The New South Wales Supreme Court's answers to these questions framed the *Fernando* principles that provide lighter sentences for offenders whose Indigeneity, alcoholism and disadvantage reduce their moral culpability. Non-custodial penalties also sought to redress the disproportionate impact of imprisonment on Indigenous offenders. The court handed down what it considered to be a mitigated sentence of four years' imprisonment with a nine-month non-parole period. In his remarks, Wood J. meandered between recognizing Fernando's disadvantaged Indigenous community and invoking normative sentencing principles, which are paraphrased as follows:

1. Facts relevant to the offender's membership of a group should be accounted for, but 'the same sentencing principles are to be applied in every case'.
2. Aboriginality does not necessarily 'mitigate punishment', but may 'throw light on the particular offence and the circumstances of the offender'.
3. Alcohol abuse and violence 'go hand in hand within Aboriginal communities', feeding into 'grave social difficulties' of unemployment, low education, stress and so on.
4. Mitigation should be provided where alcohol abuse reflects the offender's 'socio-economic circumstances and environment'.
5. Courts should provide punishment to protect Indigenous victims and reflect the seriousness of 'violence by drunken persons', particularly domestic violence.
6. A long prison term is particularly alienating and 'unduly harsh' for Indigenous people who come from a 'deprived background' or have 'little experience of European ways'.
7. The relationship between violence and alcohol abuse in Indigenous communities requires 'more subtle remedies' than imprisonment.
8. The public interest in 'rehabilitation of the offender and the avoidance of recidivism on his part' should be given full weight (*Fernando* 1992: 62–3).

In the aftermath of *Fernando* (1992), the New South Wales Court of Criminal Appeal and higher courts in other states adopted and expounded its principles and observations. In *R.* v. *Hickey* (1994: 4), the court referred to the 'tragic truth' of the 'litany of disadvantage' that frequently accompanies Indigeneity and should be taken into account in sentencing where relevant. In *R.* v. *Stone* (1995), the court allowed an appeal against the trial judge's finding that the *Fernando* principles had been eroded due to the defendant committing similar serious offences in the past. The Court of Criminal Appeal held that subjective mitigating factors should be accounted for notwithstanding the objective circumstances (*R.* v. *Stone* 1995: 224). The *Fernando* principles have also had a significant influence on sentencing in South Australia, which was relatively late in developing its Indigenous sentencing jurisprudence for Indigenous urban offenders. In 1999, the South Australian Supreme Court held that the *Fernando* principles have broad application to Indigenous offending from remote and urban communities and cannot be offset by 'tariff' (minimum) sentences (*Police* v. *Abdulla* 1999: 343–4). Also commenting that the *Fernando* principles were 'not restricted to traditional aboriginals', the South Australian Court of Criminal Appeal found that heritage, rather than geography, contributes to the offender's circumstances: 'no distinction is to be drawn between an Aboriginal person to whom European culture is foreign' because of lack of exposure to 'white' culture and 'an Aboriginal person to whom European culture is foreign . . . simply as a result of that person's identity as an Aboriginal person' (*R.* v. *Smith* 2003: [60]–[61]).

Unlike other recognition instances, which attend to the nature of the Indigenous community, South Australia's higher courts recognized the impact of Indigenous over-representation in the prison system. This has implications for structuring sentences to provide leniency on a consistent basis. It creates an opportunity for recognition to redress institutional paradigms that subordinate Indigenous people. South Australia's judiciary has shifted the focus from 'the problem' of the Indigenous community and circumstances, to 'the problem' of punishment and imprisonment for Indigenous people. It points the finger at prisons rather than the Indigenous community for disadvantaging Indigenous people. The South Australian Supreme Court highlighted the 'debilitating effect' that imprisonment has on Indigenous people, and referred to the Indigenous and Tribal Peoples Convention (1989) as endorsing penalties 'other than confinement in prison' (*Police* v. *Abdulla* 1999: 344). In *R.* v. *Smith* (2003: [61]), the South Australian Court of Criminal Appeal noted that the 'cultural milieu' of the prison is foreign to remote and urban Indigenous offenders. By contrast, New South Wales higher courts have been concerned to afford Indigenous offenders the same treatment in sentencing as all other offenders in accounting for the material facts of offending and the offender, including the offender's community (*Fernando* 1992: 62; *R.* v. *Ah-See* 2004: [15]; *R.* v. *Kelly* 2005: [52]). These courts do not refer to the detrimental impact of imprisonment on Indigenous communities in justifying mitigation. Consequently, their characterizations of material facts of the Indigenous community have been prone to judicial reassessment and invalidation. The reasoning of the New South Wales higher courts lacks what Hudson (1999: 583) describes as a 'principled' approach to lighter punishment that redresses the disadvantage borne out of the over-incarceration of Indigenous people.

Northern Territory's mitigation for cultural breakdown

The effects of colonization in Northern Territory Indigenous communities were still relatively new well into the latter twentieth century – long after the south-eastern regions of Australia were colonized. The despair attendant to 'social devastation' arising from 'cultural breakdown' was embraced by the Northern Territory's higher courts in the 1970s as a basis for leniency (Douglas 2009: 170).[5] In the same manner as the New South Wales Supreme Court, the Northern Territory Supreme Court channelled considerations of disadvantage and cultural breakdown to alcohol abuse. Unlike Kriewaldt J., who presided on the Northern Territory Supreme Court between 1951 and 1960 and punished harshly offenders who committed crimes where alcohol was involved in order to reflect their level of (misused) civilization, the court from the 1970s regarded alcohol as one of the greatest vices delivered to Indigenous people by colonialism. It implicated Anglo-Australian society in the social problems of Indigenous communities and determined that alcohol consumption relating to a crime warranted lenience. In *R.* v. *Long* (1995: 26), the Northern Territory Supreme Court remarked that Indigenous problems arise out of 'things introduced by white Australians', which create a 'familiar pattern' of alcohol consumption and offending and provide for mitigating circumstances. To account for these circumstances, the court developed a sentencing jurisprudence independent of the *Fernando* principles, which distinctly accounted for the contemporaneity of cultural breakdown and the alienation derived from the imposition of a foreign culture and society.[6] The court's representations of Indigeneity conveyed a narrative of hopelessness in the face of an all-encompassing colonial culture in which 'absolute sovereignty' had completely undermined Indigenous cultures, notwithstanding their profound continuing influences (Cunneen 2011: 258).

Recognition of the concomitance between cultural despair, alcoholism and poverty was noted by the Northern Territory Supreme Court in *R.* v. *Benny Lee* (1974). The court regarded alcohol dependence as a 'much more' mitigating circumstance 'in the case of Aboriginal people' than non-Aboriginal people because the former were often led to drinking out of 'despair' (*R.* v. *Benny Lee* 1974). The court adopted a similar approach in *R.* v. *Herbert & Ors* (1983), in which three Indigenous women were convicted of murdering a 'handicapped man' by striking him to the head with an iron bar at least eight times. The mitigating factors included that the defendants were 'reared in a traditional Aboriginal environment' and had 'abandoned their traditional lifestyles and set out to take up a city lifestyle, finally in Darwin' (1983: 29). This was described as

5 The term 'cultural breakdown' is problematic given that many Indigenous communities in the Northern Territory continue to practise their culture. It is used by the courts to describe the unsettling impact of colonization on pre-colonial Indigenous practices.

6 The Northern Territory Supreme Court has noted that the *Fernando* principles 'have been adopted in appropriate cases': *The Queen* v. *Booth* (2005: 4). Northern Territory cases that refer to the *Fernando* principles include: *Leering* v. *Nayda* (1997); and *Cook* v. *Chute* (1997).

'a way of life that [Indigenous people] are ill-equipped to handle' because they cannot draw on 'traditional' relationships 'that not only protect them from undue physical violence but also that censor their moral conduct' (1983: 29). Instead, they find themselves in a 'limbo', in which they 'belong nowhere', due to the 'trans-cultural dimension of their condition' (1983: 29). Consequently, 'they soon fall prey to the destructive influences of alcohol' and 'become fringe-dwellers, or perhaps town campers in the city' (1983: 29). Rounding out this account of cultural despair, the court remarked that the transition to city life:

> . . . is psychologically, and often physically, a brutalizing experience for [Aboriginal women], giving rise to tension and acute emotional distress. Their plight is a desperate one from which they cannot escape. *They have a feeling of helplessness, hopelessness and purposelessness.* Their whole sense of themselves becomes so abused that they lose that natural dignity that Aboriginal women have. As it was put to me, they feel 'they are no longer clean . . . they feel dirty and sullied but they are caught'.
>
> (*R.* v. *Herbert & Ors* 1983: 29, emphasis added)

Supreme Court sentencing remarks in the 1980s and 1990s focused on the poverty and economic difficulties facing Indigenous communities and their members. These factors, along with their bedfellow, alcohol abuse, gave rise to the dispensation of 'special leniency' (*Gadatjiya* v. *Lethbridge* 1992: 273). In *Robertson* v. *Flood* (1992: 187), the court regarded alcohol abuse as reducing the offender's 'chances in life', and being a symptom of deprivation. The offender's community of Ali Curung (north of Alice Springs) was viewed as having 'a particularly serious problem with alcohol' (1992: 179). In this context, the court held that there must be 'regard to the general policy of leniency towards those Aboriginal offenders who are disadvantaged socially, economically and in other ways because of their membership of a deprived section of the community' (1992: 187). In addition, the Full Federal Court, hearing an appeal from the Northern Territory Supreme Court in *R.* v. *Davey* (1980), emphasized the bluntness of the deterrent effect of imprisonment where the offence was alcohol-related. The court noted that sentences should instead be directed towards the reformation of Indigenous offenders to provide the 'greatest protection to society' (1980: 261). In that case, the offender, from Borroloola near the Gulf of Carpentaria, was intoxicated when he struck another man with a large piece of timber, resulting in the man's death. In upholding a suspended sentence of three years' imprisonment, the court stated that:

> The devastating effects of liquor, especially upon Aboriginal society, are daily demonstrated in our courts. I am afraid in this area sentencing policies are unlikely to prove an effective deterrent. A man crazed with alcohol seldom takes stock. The concept that imprisonment must be regarded as an effective deterrent is now enshrined in our law despite the fact that modern

> research throws some doubts upon its validity. It is perhaps accurate to say that it is because of awareness of the difficulties of the Aboriginal and with knowledge that the source of practically all Aboriginal crime is alcohol, that lenient penalties are frequently imposed.
>
> (*R.* v. *Davey* 1980: 258)

The Northern Territory judiciary regarded Indigenous problems of alcoholism, poverty and violence as intrinsically connected to colonization, dispossession and displacement. The imposition of Anglo-Australian social norms was conceived as having a deleterious impact on Indigenous cultures, and in light of this, imprisonment was a blunt instrument. Compensatory measures in sentencing were, nonetheless, provisional on the will of the courts to recognize such 'difference'. This is set in sharp relief where higher courts have withdrawn from discourses of Indigenous disadvantage that provide latitudes to Indigenous offenders. The emergent judicial view in the Northern Territory and New South Wales sets aside the relevance of the offender's Indigenous community due to its geographic location, its failure to meet thresholds of disadvantage or its level of dysfunctionality.

Reimaginings of hardship in the late twentieth century

In the late 1990s there was a retreat from subjective Indigenous circumstances in New South Wales and Northern Territory sentencing considerations. Judicial narratives of Indigeneity have been rewritten to produce new types of knowledge about the circumstances of Indigenous communities. They signal a diminution of the significance of Indigenous factors in sentencing and a punitive turn for Indigenous offenders. The reconstructed identity of the Indigenous offender in New South Wales relies on fixed and arbitrary concepts of what constitutes Indigeneity for the purpose of leniency. Fraser (2000: 110, 113) claims that recognition encourages the 'reification of group identities', placing pressure on groups to display an 'authentic' and rigid collective identity and culture. The Supreme Court has confined the recognition of Indigenous identity to reflect membership of a geographically remote *and* especially disadvantaged and alcohol-prone community. The requirement of remoteness has the effect of bolstering colonial binaries between traditional and civilized Indigenous communities (Rolls 2001: 9).

In the Northern Territory, the Indigenous community to which the offender belongs has been reclassified as 'dysfunctional' rather than 'disadvantaged'. This reclassification implicates the Indigenous community (rather than colonizing processes) in the crime and undermines the community's functionality. In both jurisdictions, subjective factors relevant to Indigeneity have been overshadowed, first by objective circumstances, the seriousness of the offence and victimization, and second by normative principles such as deterrence. These narratives produce, as Fraser (1996: 7) would term it, a non-recognition and misrecognition problem. Motha (2005: 119) argues that just as Indigeneity is prone to disappearance, it is also prone to a view that the Indigenous community is too 'repugnant' to be recognized. These changing representations serve 'the various and changing interests and aspirations' of the colonizer by constantly inventing new categories to undermine the Other and thus rendering Indigenous people 'objects' of a continual flow of commentary and classification (Dodson 1994: 3, 7).[7]

In a formative lecture on Indigenous identities, Dodson (1994: 8) despaired fixed notions of identity that are determined according to a colonial 'relation' rather than 'on our own terms'. He claimed that they neglect the heterogeneous nature of Indigenous identities, which are formed across and within Indigenous communities and are subject to change and variation. To adopt Dodson's tone, sentencing courts have reimagined Indigenous alterity as fixed in time. They enforce an idea that the remnants of Indigeneity are fading in Australian post-colonial society. Channelling Indigeneity into traditionalism is conterminous with the abandonment of urban Indigenous identities. But even where communities are regarded as sufficiently Indigenous, sentencing courts have provided other layers of recognition requirements. On the one hand the offender must belong to a 'functional' Indigenous community, which is an impossible threshold to meet because the Supreme Court deems that the crime speaks to the dysfunction of the community. On the other hand, the Indigenous offender must display the requisite attributes of disadvantaged offenders, including alcohol abuse and an extreme form of disadvantage. These requirements constitute a 'cunning of recognition' that make the just recognition of Indigeneity in sentencing an impossible dream.[8]

New South Wales: non-recognition and Indigenous stock stories

Stock story of the remote, full-blooded Indigenous person

The New South Wales Court of Criminal Appeal, since the late 1990s, has restricted who can be classed as Indigenous for the purposes of applying the *Fernando* principles. It increasingly regards Indigenous identity and community connections as having been washed away by colonialism and urbanization. Offenders from remote Indigenous communities are more likely to activate the principles. In this way, offenders from urban communities in New South Wales are perceived as not 'Aboriginal enough' to activate the *Fernando* principles

7 Since colonization, Europeans have attempted to categorize Indigenous Australians according to the darkness of their skin colour and the alleged size of their brains.

8 Critical legal theorists argue that judicial recognition of Indigeneity gives rise to a 'cunning of recognition' – requiring both traditionalism and modernism: see Povinelli (2002: 267); Dorsett (2002: 26); and Amankwah (1994: 32).

(Flynn 2005: 18).[9] In adopting a neo-traditionalist stance, the court has tended to only recognize 'authentic' types of Indigenous people. Through authenticity, Borrows (2002: 60) argues, Indigeneity becomes a 'once upon a time' concept based on a retrospective rather than contemporary experience. One of the first New South Wales Court of Criminal Appeal cases of this genre, *Ceissman* (2001: 541), downplayed the significance of Indigenous circumstances because the offender resided in an urban environment. In upholding a Crown appeal against the lenience of his sentence, the court held that Indigenous factors did not apply to the defendant.

Ceissman, who was convicted of trafficking cocaine, 'grew up in extreme poverty', received little education, had parents who were drug addicts with criminal histories, witnessed serious physical violence between them, and was orphaned when he was 11 years old (*Ceissman* 2001: 543). His circumstances did not enliven the *Fernando* principles because Ceissman was not 'from a remote community for whom imprisonment would be unduly harsh' (2001: 540). Chief Justice Wood, the judge who set down the *Fernando* principles, remarked that *Fernando* does not justify 'special leniency, merely because of the Aboriginality of the offender' (2001: 540). In this case 'the fact that the respondent's grandfather was part aboriginal' was regarded as lacking relevance to sentencing (2001: 540).[10] This reference to 'part' Aboriginality is contrary to Indigenous concepts of identity as well as the current three-part legal definition of Indigenous identity based on: (i) self-identity; (ii) community acceptance; and (iii) genealogical descent (see *Shaw* v. *Wolf* 1999; *Eatock* v. *Bolt* 2011: 304). The line drawn between 'full' and 'part' Indigeneity is reminiscent of colonial classifications of 'half-castes' or 'hybrids' that are based on biological taxonomies. Ultimately the court in *Ceissman* (2001: 541) privileged the guideline sentence that is predicated on the seriousness of the crime of drug importation over subjective Indigenous considerations.

Following *Ceissman*, the New South Wales Court of Criminal Appeal, in *R.* v. *Morgan* (2003: 535), applied its reasoning to an offender who committed robbery, breaking and entering and assault. The defendant was brought up in a town in central Victoria and had an 'intimidating, violent and alcohol dependent' father. The offender was found *not* to be 'particularly disadvantaged', despite having to regularly flee his home to avoid his abusive father and spending 'a good part of his early life in boys homes or correctional centres' (2003: 535). Because the 'offences were not alcohol-related and the appellant did not come from a *remote* community, nor was he unfamiliar with the justice system', the *Fernando* principles were not enlivened (2003: 539). Remoteness here appears to be a matter of degree, given that he lived near Shepparton – a town 200 kilometres out of Melbourne with less than 40,000 residents and on the traditional land of the

9 Criminal sentencing courts have long relied on claims to authenticity. In the 1930s, the sole judge of the Northern Territory Supreme Court, Wells J., perceived that Indigenous cultures had broken down to such a degree that they were irrelevant to sentencing (Kimm 2004: 145).

10 For applications of *Ceissman*, see: *Andrews* v. *The Queen* (2007); and *Carr* v. *The Queen* (2009).

Yorta Yorta people. These factors, as far as they related to the *Fernando* principles, 'added little to the . . . sentencing exercise beyond those matters which would otherwise have been taken into account, for any offender', according to the court (2003: 539). The court also upheld the distinction between modern and traditional racial circumstances of Indigenous offenders in *Andrews* v. *The Queen* (2007). There, the offender's removal to a 'white family' as a child and ensuing 'feelings of abandonment, frustration, loss and hopelessness' as well as alcohol abuse were not relevant to the offender's 'racial background' and could apply to any offender (2007: [22]).

The narrow application of the *Fernando* principles were crystallized by the Court of Criminal Appeal in *R.* v. *Newman, R.* v. *Simpson* (2004). It held that the regional town of Griffith in central New South Wales was not sufficiently remote for the *Fernando* principles to apply. The court distinguished these Indigenous defendants from Indigenous defendants in 'a remote community', who would be more likely to enliven the *Fernando* principles (2004: 376, 378). One defendant, Newman, was forcibly removed from his family at a young age to an isolated mission property (2004: 385). He had an early introduction to alcohol in communities where this conduct was 'not only the norm but positively encouraged by peer group pressure', and his criminal record was 'exclusively, if not entirely' alcohol-related (2004: 386). Submissions were also made that the 'defendant had endured childhood taunts and gotten into fights because of his colour' (Flynn 2005: 16). The court questioned whether Aboriginality was an issue at all, observing that the offenders' 'lamentable' background of disadvantage and alcohol and drug abuse 'is not in any way unique nor is it restricted to any particular community group' (*R.* v. *Newman, R.* v. *Simpson* 2004: 378–9). It regarded alcohol and drug abuse as arising from a common type of 'deprivation or abuse early in life' that does not give rise to special consideration, 'notwithstanding [the offender's] Aboriginality' (2004: 379). The seriousness of the offence – aggravated entering dwelling with intent to commit a serious offence – made it legitimate to 'give little weight to the applicant's subjective circumstances' (2004: 379).[11] However, in the Minority, Shaw J. regarded the defendants' disadvantage as being 'associated with growing up as an indigenous citizen of this country' and therefore the 'aboriginality of the applicants and the social and economic difficulties flowing from that fact' were 'relevant consideration[s]' (2004: 384, 388). Commenting on this case, Flynn states that the majority's failure to apply the *Fernando* principles overlooked important factors relevant to the offender's Indigenous background, which 'ought, consistently with the substantial equality principle, [to have been] considered' (Flynn 2005: 16).[12]

11 This reasoning that privileged the seriousness of the offence above the subjective considerations in the *Fernando* principles was applied in: *Gillon* v. *R.* (2009: [30]); *R.* v. *Blow* (2010: [55]); and *Russell* v. *The Queen* (2010: [50]–[51]).

12 See applications of *R.* v. *Newman, R.* v. *Simpson* (2004) in: *R.* v. *Kelly* (2005: [20], [57]–[59]); and *R.* v. *Knight* (2005: [81]).

The remarks of the New South Wales Court of Criminal Appeal misapprehend the nature of postcolonial Indigenous identity and communities in order to 'confine the reach of *Fernando*' (Edney 2006: 8). It misconstrues Indigeneity by assessing it in terms of geography and colour. Nicholson (1999: 86), who represented the defendant in *Fernando*, expresses that it is nonsensical that the *Fernando* principles, which rest on the breakdown of Indigenous culture, would require proof of the retention of culture in a remote community. He states that requirements of authenticity and remoteness are irrelevant to mitigating factors based on cultural *breakdown*, disadvantage and the 'mass post-traumatic stress syndrome' arising from colonization (1999: 86). The diversity of Indigenous experiences in postcolonial society includes the predicament of negotiating the demands of Anglo-Australian society, which involves identity permeations between 'black and white' (Rolls 2001: 9, 16; Cowlishaw 2009). These experiences extend to urban communities that exhibit 'complex rules of kinship' that determine an individual's role in their Indigenous society (*R.* v. *Smith* 2003: [54]). The courts create this dichotomy between urban and remote offenders for the 'spatial management' of postcolonial space, metaphorically securing white urban space to the exclusion of Indigenous people (Hage 1998: 32). The 'imaginative geography' is determined by colonial demarcations and a nationalist sense of 'white' homogeneity that excludes those on the outside (Said 1978: 55; Anderson 1983: 7).

Stock story of the 'drunken' Indigenous person

Alternating with the stock story of the remote Indigene is the stock story of the drunken Indigene. As mentioned, the New South Wales Supreme Court in *Fernando* pointed to the nexus between violence and alcohol abuse. Courts have regarded alcohol as an endemic problem in Indigenous communities and thus a material fact in sentencing – despite evidence that alcohol consumption is lower than in the general population (Thomson *et al.* 2012: 47).[13] Langton (1993: 205) asserts that the image of 'the drunken Aborigine' portrays the incapacity of Indigenous people to 'adopt the genteel constraints of civilisation'. It is an image that has attained judicial sympathy and clemency in the past. However, the rigidity of the drunkenness requirement was made apparent in recent cases that denied mitigation where the offenders were under the influence of other substances. These offenders were more likely to receive an aggravated rather than mitigated sentence (*R.* v. *Ah-See* 2004: [18]). Similarly, the New South Wales Court of Criminal Appeal has refrained from applying the *Fernando* principles to offenders who were not drunk at the time of the offence (*R.* v. *Morgan* 2003). In *R.* v. *Trindall* (2005: [27]), an Indigenous offender, convicted of stealing and common assault, who was raised in a remote community and had been abused

13 Nonetheless, the veracity of measurements of alcohol consumption are methodologically problematic as they are based on surveys and self-perception (see Thomson *et al.* 2012: 47).

by her relatives with whom she was placed, did not activate the *Fernando* principles because she had not experienced problems 'referable to the applicant's membership of the Aboriginal society'. Rather, the court described the offender's problems as 'more generally associated with the destructive effects of drug addiction' (2005: [27]). These offenders fell short of iconic images of drunken Indigenous persons. They were comparable to the broader criminal population rather than the Indigenous cohort and their Indigenous identity was deemed irrelevant. The judiciary's refusal to recognize the urban, non-alcoholic Indigenous offender reveals how recognition does not provide a stable means of addressing Indigenous difficulties in the criminal justice system.

Stock story of the hopelessly destitute and idle Indigenous person

In order to satisfy the recognition standard set by New South Wales higher courts, the remote Indigenous offender must also experience the worst kinds of disadvantage to activate recognition of his or her subjective circumstances in mitigation. An ordinary type of disadvantage is insufficient because it is subsumed into the 'normal' experience of Indigenous people (see *Anderson* v. *The Queen* 2008: [24]–[25]; *Croaker* v. *The Queen* 2008: [6]–[7]; *R.* v. *Knight* 2004: [14]). Allowing an ordinary degree of disadvantage would challenge the courts' concept of virtually all Indigenous offenders. In *Gillon* v. *R.* (2009: [9]), the New South Wales Court of Criminal Appeal dismissed the 'subjective matters' related to Indigeneity, which included an upbringing on an Aboriginal mission reserve, early exposure to violence, alcohol abuse from the time he was 16 or 17 years of age and extending up until the time of the offence. The offender was guilty of recklessly causing grievous bodily harm on his sister's de facto partner who regularly hit the offender's sister. The court found that the offender's Indigenous background did not constitute 'special circumstances' that warranted mitigation: 'it is not every case of deprivation and disadvantage suffered by an offender of Aboriginal race or ancestry that calls for the special approach adopted in *Fernando*' (*Gillon* v. *R.* 2009: [30]).

The New South Wales Court of Criminal Appeal posited the requirement for a greater degree of disadvantage in *R.* v. *Pitt* (2001). In that case, the appellant, who had pleaded guilty to malicious damage by fire, claimed that the trial judge had not given sufficient weight to his deprived background and intoxication as required by *Fernando*. The defendant was raised on a mission in the remote community of Moree, and was subject to abuse by a drunken and violent father. He had limited education and employment history, and was susceptible to self-harm. However, the Court of Criminal Appeal held that these circumstances were not sufficient to activate the *Fernando* principles, stating that 'there was nothing of an exceptional kind, in the aboriginality or upbringing of the applicant, that called for any particular mitigation of sentence' (*R.* v. *Pitt* 2001: [18]). According to the court, the defendant's 'childhood experiences [had] been shared by many persons across a wide range of ethnic, social and racial backgrounds' (2001: [18]). Also, references to his occasional employment countered the judiciary's stock story of the idle Indigene (2001: [15]). The court is normalizing Indigenous disadvantage by requiring something more, which is unspecified by the court, and subjecting the Indigenous defendant to the judiciary's whim. The ability to acquire a job operates to the Indigenous defendant's disadvantage because he is not able to rely on Indigenous mitigating factors.

The requirement for 'something more' also arose in *R.* v. *Walter & Thompson* (2004: [37], [57]), a case involving two Indigenous defendants. The New South Wales Court of Criminal Appeal held that the *Fernando* principles should not apply to mitigate the sentence of one defendant, who was adopted into a 'white' family in northern New South Wales at the age of 3 months and physically and emotionally abused by his step-mother, who called him 'little black bastard'. The other defendant was not deemed by the court to come within the *Fernando* principles because his situation was simply 'in common with other members of the community, [he] had resorted to alcohol as a comfort from his troubles' (2004: [58]). There was also no regard given for the fact that the offences of robbery and assault were provoked by an act of racism (Flynn 2005: 17). Edney (2006: 9) has commented in relation to the court's reasoning that 'Aboriginality is rendered invisible as this disadvantage is assumed to be the same as all other ethnic groups'. This is a 'classic type of liberalism' that divorces Indigenous people from 'the operation of historical forces' such as dispossession and institutional control, and assumes that they commence life on an equal footing to other groups (2006: 10).

Recognition of difference in the Northern Territory: maligned dysfunction

The renewed representations of disadvantaged Indigenous alterity by the Northern Territory's higher courts has shown a different disposition from that in New South Wales. In the Northern Territory, there has not been a challenge to the Indigeneity of the offender or the requirement of an additional exceptional factor for the purposes of Indigenous recognition. Rather, the Northern Territory Supreme Court and Court of Appeal have condemned the offender's Indigenous community for presenting a crime risk, which has attracted increased penalties to manage this danger. To facilitate this reimagining of the Indigenous community, there has been a change in language, from the 'disadvantaged' to the 'dysfunctional' Indigenous community. The word 'disadvantage' imputes Indigenous offending to colonizing processes and the postcolonial system, whereas the term 'dysfunction' attributes responsibility to the Indigenous community itself. The court hones in on this dysfunction to emphasize the seriousness of crimes in Indigenous communities, especially for victims in these hopeless conditions. This change of terminology – from disadvantaged to dysfunctional – implies that the Indigenous community lacks the functionality or will to be involved in the processes of justice. The attribution of dysfunction justifies punishment being confined to the prisons of the Anglo-Australian system, and undermines the capacity of Indigenous communities to prevent or respond to crime, or to be involved in the structuring of punishment.

The idea of a dysfunctional or failed alterity secures the homogenous white order (Hage 1998). The broad brushstrokes with which the Supreme Court paints the criminality of the offender also taint the image of the Indigenous community as a whole. On this canvas, the court depicts the contrasting image of the Indigenous victim as an 'ideal victim', one who is characterized by a vulnerability to harm and the dangers presented by the Indigenous community (Christie 1986: 18). According to the court, the victim does not have a stake in the Indigenous community and is not of concern to it. The victim is one of 'us' in the 'wider community', and the Indigenous offender, along with the Indigenous community, is one of 'them' (Hogg 2008: 282). In law and order regimes, the victim is invoked 'in support of measures of punitive segregation' (Garland 2001: 11). Judicial reasoning that positions the victim as particularly vulnerable in Indigenous communities undermines their active efforts to protect victims (Atkinson 2006b: 20). The venerated victim in these cases is distinct from the victim who seeks Indigenous law punishment for the offender. The interests of the latter victim are cast aside where they contradict with the court's interest in imposing a custodial sentence (see previous chapter; *The Queen* v. *Webb* 2003: 6–7; *R.* v. *Miyatatawuy* 1996: 580).

For offenders subjected to disadvantaged circumstances, their sentences are aggravated to send a special message of deterrence to the Indigenous community, and to uphold the wider community's interest in lengthy imprisonment. Deterrence is directed to the community because the Supreme Court conceives it as condoning violence and failing to protect victims, and juxtaposes this with the court's own role in protecting victims. In a speech to the Law Council of Australia, Southwood J., well known for his dissenting judgments on the Bench, cautioned against dysfunction being used to justify harsher punishments for Indigenous offenders:

> In view of the recent media coverage of the violence and dysfunction in some Aboriginal communities, it must also be noted that each Aboriginal offender is not to be punished as if he or she were responsible for all of the violence and dysfunction in Aboriginal communities. Often Aboriginal offenders are also victims.
>
> (Southwood 2007: 3)

Sentencing remarks on dysfunction and deterrence

In *Amagula* v. *White* (1998), the Northern Territory Supreme Court described the prevalence of assaults as a key marker for dysfunction in the Angurugu community on Groote Eylandt in the Gulf of Carpentaria. Although counsel for the defendant submitted that assaults on Anindilyakwa women in Angurugu had reduced in recent years, Kearney J. said that he preferred to rely upon '[his] own general experience over the years' (1998: 9). The court held that 'the prevalence of an offence is a matter to be taken into account in determining the appropriate sentence' (1998: 9). This included the 'fairly widespread belief that it is acceptable for men to bash their wives in some circumstances' (1998: 10). The offender in *Amagula* v. *White* had pleaded guilty to aggravated assault in which he punched his wife in public, resulting in bruising and scrapes to the skin. The court's punishment sought to 'erase' the community's belief that violence is acceptable, and to 'send the correct message' to the Angurugu community (1998: 10). This conveyed that the court stood above the community, which had failed to care for its own members, and that punishment was needed in order to provide 'general deterrence' to the community (1998: 3–4). The court's endeavour to deter crime through imprisonment permeates cases since the late 1990s, including in *Wynbyne* v. *Marshall* (1997: 15), in which Martin C.J. remarked that imprisonment 'is undoubtedly an instrument for the maintenance of law and order' and operates 'so as to deter' the Indigenous community. The Court of Criminal Appeal also pointed to 'general deterrence' as being of 'particular importance' in the context of violence in Indigenous communities in *R.* v. *Riley* (2006: 419).[14] Because of community dysfunction, victims are regarded as especially vulnerable because they lack 'significant support' (2006: 419). This channelling of Indigeneity into the risk of violence is embodied in the discussion of the 'significance of Aboriginality' in *Amagula* v. *White* (1998: 10), in which the court referred to it in terms of what the court can do to deter crime rather than in terms of moral culpability.[15]

Justice Kearney in *Amagula* v. *White* (1998: 4) also spoke for the Angurugu community when he stated that 'the Groote Eylandt community acting through the court does not approve of what you [the defendant] did'. This indicates the Supreme Court's paternalism where it simultaneously disciplines *and* speaks for the Indigenous community. In *Amagula* v. *White* (1998: 5), reference to the victim also operates on this dual level – protection through imprisoning the offender *and* denunciation of the victim's request for the offender (her husband) not to be imprisoned. The Supreme Court rejected the victim's submission that a custodial sentence would bring hardship for her and her family, stating that hardship to a third party is only considered where it is 'highly exceptional' (1998: 7). This fulfils the court's paternal role of caring for, but not listening to, the victim.

14 Because of the focus on general deterrence, the Northern Territory Court of Criminal Appeal ruled against the significance of the 'deprived and dysfunctional circumstances' of the offender in mitigating the sentence (*R.* v. *Riley* 2006: 425). This position that 'general deterrence is a matter of particular importance' in punishing the Indigenous offender was upheld in: *Mununggurr* v. *The Queen* (2006: [22]); and *The Queen* v. *Walker* (2007: 7).

15 This approach is echoed in: *R.* v. *Riley* (2006: 419); and *R.* v. *Rindjarra* (2008).

Both in New South Wales and the Northern Territory, courts have emphasized the seriousness of the crime, eclipsing subjective Indigenous factors and allaying mitigation. The high watermark for the Northern Territory Court of Criminal Appeal's disregard for the recognition of 'difference' was embodied in *Wurramara* (1999). In this seminal decision, the court stressed the *seriousness of the offence* above all other sentencing considerations. Although 'seriousness' has been held by the High Court to encompass a range of factors, including the subjective circumstances of the offender (*Neal* v. *The Queen* 1982: 325), the Northern Territory judiciary now tends to measure seriousness chiefly in terms of the harm of the offence to the victim (*Wurramara* 1999: 521; Southwood 2007: 6; Martin 2006).[16] The defendant in *Wurramara* (1999) was also from Groote Eylandt, and had stabbed his wife and his neighbour. In pointing to the seriousness of the offence, the court held that harsh punishment for offenders from dysfunctional Indigenous communities was needed to protect vulnerable victims in those communities (1999: 520). The court noted that the 'dysfunctional' status of the Groote Eylandt community, with its prevalence of alcohol abuse and violence, was 'by no means' justification for 'a lower sentence' (1999: 522). Rather, the dysfunctional community illuminated the difficulties faced by the Indigenous victim, warranting harsh punishments for offenders within it. The court stated that vulnerable victims – 'Aboriginal women, children and the weak' – are entitled to look to the courts to send 'the correct message' that they will be protected (1999: 520). The offender's membership of a disadvantaged Indigenous community did not sound in mitigation, and *Fernando* was cited only for the proposition that 'Aboriginal offenders are not to be treated differently' such that 'offences of serious violence call for condign punishment' (1999: 512). In fact, it was taken to signal the need for a strong deterrence message, notwithstanding the court's recognition that imprisonment has limited impact on the 'dysfunction or deprivation' that lie at the root of violence (1999: 521).[17] According to the Principal Solicitor of the North Australian Aboriginal Justice Agency, Glen Dooley, *Wurramara* (1999) has contributed to the rapid increase in the Northern Territory's prison population (Bullock 2010). Between 1999 and 2009, the number of Northern Territory prisoners almost doubled in absolute and per capita terms (Northern Territory Department of Justice 2009: 3; Australian Bureau of Statistics 2009: 26).[18]

The emphasis on 'seriousness' in *Wurramara* (1999) has been applied consistently to increase sentences for Northern Territory Indigenous offenders (see *R.* v. *Jinjair* 2003: 4–5). In *Bryce Jabaltjari Spencer* v. *The Queen* (2005: [23]), the Court of

16 See also New South Wales cases projecting a judicial focus on the seriousness of the harm of the offence: *R.* v. *Fernando* (2002: [68]); and *R.* v. *Kelly* (2005: [56]).

17 See also *R.* v. *Downes* (2001: 8), where the Northern Territory Supreme Court stated that '[i]mprisonment is a very blunt instrument to protect Aboriginal women from drunken and violent men'. Also in *R.* v. *Wanambi* (2001: 6), the court stated that although prison may not be the ideal environment for the Indigenous offender, 'no-one has suggested any better environment for him'.

18 In the Northern Territory 82 per cent of prisoners are Indigenous (Australian Bureau of Statistics 2011: 49).

Criminal Appeal stated that *Wurramara* displaced the *Fernando* principles and its Northern Territory iteration in *R.* v. *Benny Lee* (1974). Therefore, membership of a 'deprived or dysfunctional' community 'does not mean that lower sentences should prevail' where there is a serious offence. For this reason, the offender – a 'traditional Warlpiri man who was alcohol-dependent and living in a fringe bush camp' – did not receive leniency for the manslaughter of his wife (*Bryce Jabaltjari Spencer* v. *The Queen* 2005: [23], [31]). The Court of Appeal has also favoured a standard sentencing approach for serious offenders, based on a scale of seriousness (see *Inkamala* v. *R.* 2005; *R.* v. *Rindjarra* 2008: [52]).[19] Standard sentences generally rule out considerations of offender circumstances and reinforce a homogenous legal order. Reminiscent of Bentham's (1962: 579–80) position that punishment should be imposed through sanctions that are infinitely gradable to match seriousness, the Court of Appeal seeks to impose consistent sentences where there is comparable harm. For example, in *The Queen* v. *Inkamala* (2006: [19]–[20]), where an 18-year-old defendant from the Hermannsburg community in central Australia committed statutory rape by digital penetration on a seven-month-old child, the court handed down a sentence of nine years' imprisonment to make it commensurate with the sentence in *R.* v. *Riley* (2006). In doing so, it ruled out the relevance of the offender's psychological disorders, attempted self-harm in custody, domestic violence in early childhood and petrol sniffing and alcohol and drug use from a young age because 'punishment and general deterrence must take precedence over rehabilitation' (*The Queen* v. *Inkamala* 2006: [7], [9]–[10]). This not merely conceals disadvantaged contexts in offending, but results in harsher sentences relative to non-Indigenous offenders, because the court is concerned to send a deterrence message to Indigenous communities that fail to protect their vulnerable members (see *The Queen* v. *Inkamala* 2006: [10], [19]; *R.* v. *Rindjarra* 2008).

Even where offences are at the 'lower end' of assaults, with no serious injuries, *Wurramara* has been relied on to hand down a harsh penalty to deter and protect others in the community from violence. The Indigenous community as a whole is a site of risk for its members. For example, in *Alderson* v. *The Queen* (2002: [14]), the defendant unsuccessfully appealed that 'too much weight' was placed on these considerations when the trial judge handed down a three-year prison sentence (with two years and six months' non-parole) for striking his de facto partner with a stick, causing swelling and a headache. The trial judge, Riley J., found that it was at the lower end of assaults with no serious injuries, but that a long prison sentence was needed to reflect the seriousness of such offending for victims in Indigenous communities (cited in *Alderson* v. *The Queen* 2002: 3). The defendant argued on appeal that Riley J.'s approach 'offended the basic principle that all people should stand equally before the law and that criminal sanctions

19 However, the Court of Appeal has distinguished standard sentences from tariffs that completely remove judicial discretion to consider offender circumstances (*The Queen* v. *Inkamala* 2006: [30]; *R.* v. *Rindjarra* 2008: [30], [52]; see also: *Mununggurr* v. *The Queen* 2006; *Green* v. *The Queen* 2006).

should be applied uniformly' (*Alderson* v. *The Queen* 2002: [14]). In other words, the defendant argued that he had received a harsher sentence because of his membership of an Indigenous community. The Court of Appeal stated that it was legitimate for Riley J. to bear in mind the precedent set in *Wurramara* for dealing with violent offenders from Indigenous communities (*Alderson* v. *The Queen* 2002: [14]).

The Supreme Court has stressed that Indigenous offending attracts longer prison sentences because it is what the 'wider community' demands. In *The Queen* v. *Webb* (2003: 8), it was stated that due to the seriousness of the crime, 'the interests of the wider community demand the prisoner be punished by the loss of his liberty'. This reasoning, following *Wurramara*, sets the wider (non-Indigenous) community apart from the callous Indigenous community. It implies that the Indigenous community is not concerned with the delivery of justice, while the wider community understands the need for serious penal consequences. In *R.* v. *Rindjarra* (2008: [28]), a case of statutory rape by digital penetration on a 10-year-old girl, it was noted that the initial sentence of six years' imprisonment was 'so disproportionate' to the serious gravity of the crime that it would 'shock the public conscience'. The Court of Criminal Appeal in *R.* v. *Riley* (2006: 425) pointed to the fact that the defendant's crime of digital penetration on a two-year-old girl was 'particularly abhorrent to right thinking members of our community', based on 'widespread concern about crimes of violence'. Violent and sexual offending, however, is deeply felt by Indigenous community members, and has far-reaching ramifications for Indigenous values, laws and relationships. These crimes are also severely punished by Indigenous law (Gaykamangu 2012: 247). Additionally, there is also a sentiment among members of Indigenous communities that they can only effectively address family violence and sexual offending through community-based programmes that promote community healing (Wild and Anderson 2007: 175–92). Northern Territory's higher courts, rather, seek to reinforce their own legitimate and legitimizing role of promoting the interests of the wider community in imprisoning Indigenous offenders.

Concluding observations

Recognition of Indigenous disadvantage in New South Wales and the Northern Territory sentencing remarks arose from a stock story of Indigenous helplessness, which has more recently been narrated as a story of dysfunction. Community dysfunctionality signifies the need to send a message of deterrence by imposing the white penality and whitewashing the effect of disadvantage on moral culpability. The alternate view is that the community has become so hopeless that it has lost any semblance of culture and identity to warrant its Indigenous status. Motha (2005: 119) has argued that the 'essential' idea of 'tradition and custom' is prone to disappearance, because it is based on unattainable neo-colonial ideals. The judicial imaginings of Indigenous disappearance and dysfunction are powerful metaphors for the exclusive rule of postcolonial institutions.

Even at the height of sentencing leniency in the early 1990s, with the *Fernando* principles, the higher courts reinforced a view of the hopeless and drunken nature of Indigenous peoples and their communities. Although sentencing leniency benefits some Indigenous people and may help redress the over-representation of Indigenous people in prison, it is based on an unstable recognition gesture that is constantly tested and often found wanting (Fraser 1996: 45–6). The *Fernando* principles have proven to be an insufficient premise for addressing the disadvantage of Indigenous people in the criminal justice system. They have had negligible impact on prison rates with continual rises in prison populations in New South Wales, the Northern Territory and across Australia since the Royal Commission into Aboriginal Deaths in Custody reported on the problem of Indigenous overrepresentation in 1991 (Cunneen 2010: 44). Rather, recognition of Indigeneity has provided a tenuous premise for reduced sentences, while reinforcing a white racial fantasy of tolerance and accommodation (Hage 1998: 155).

While *Fernando* lurks in the background, Indigenous ameliorating principles in New South Wales have been prone to disintegration in the face of judicial claims to formal equality and protection of victims. Courts have fallen back on a position that Indigenous offenders are to be treated equally to all other offenders, allowing the courts to deny leniency and refuse to recognize offenders' Indigeneity. The New South Wales judiciary has reconceived Indigenous communities in urban areas as not sufficiently Indigenous to receive clemency. The judiciary has attempted to 'white out' the Indigeneity of urban offenders who do not subscribe to the remote full-blood stereotype, or do not meet the requisite level of destitution, idleness or drunkenness.

In the Northern Territory the higher courts have highlighted Indigenous dysfunction to condemn the community and aggravate sentences. The victim has become a symbol of community dysfunction and represents the hopelessness of communities and their lack of will to reduce crime. Unlike the courts' preceding perception of disadvantage, which was tied to the impact of colonization, the Bench blames offenders and their complicit communities for the dysfunction. Consequently, sentencing remarks over the last decade have stressed the need to send a message of deterrence to Indigenous communities and have focused on the seriousness of crime. Roach (2009: 473) has noted a similar trend in Canada, where despite legislation allowing Aboriginal considerations in sentencing and promoting non-custodial sentences for Aboriginal peoples, courts have not relied on these provisions for serious offenders. This has militated against leniency for Indigenous offenders and contributed to their increase in imprisonment in Canada.[20]

20 However, the Supreme Court of Canada in its recent decision of *R.* v. *Ipeelee* (2012: [37]) has stressed the need for that recognition of Aboriginal offenders in sentencing to involve consideration of the unique 'systemic or background factors which may have played a part in bringing the particular Aboriginal offender before the courts' and appropriate sanctions given the offender's Aboriginal heritage and connection to community. This may see Canadian Courts retreat from

These themes of seriousness, victimization and dysfunction also arise in the cases on Indigenous 'riots', discussed in the following chapter. Those cases also give rise to another stock story: the Indigene lacking self-control and reason. Recently, courts sentencing riot offenders have nullified the police violence and institutional racism that has underpinned the riot. These courts in New South Wales and Queensland have privileged a narrative of the seriousness of the crime for the police victims of the riot who have been threatened by its perceived disorder. This has neutralized the racist acts of Anglo-Australian society and cathected to the image of the irrational Indigene.

an emphasis on the seriousness of the harm in favour of mitigating considerations of Aboriginal background.

Chapter 7

Sentencing Indigenous rioters as if the racism never occurred

> Many of the great religious and political figures of history have been agitators, and human progress owes much to the efforts of these and the many who are unknown. As Wilde aptly pointed out in *The Soul of Man under Socialism*, '. . . agitators are so absolutely necessary. Without them, in our incomplete state, there would be no advance towards civilisation'.
>
> (*Neal* v. *The Queen* 1982: 318)

Introduction: racism, riots and the righteous

Colonialism has cast long shadows over spatial contestations in Australia. Non-Indigenous attempts to exclude alterity did not subdue Indigenous claims to land and self-governance, which continue to the present day. It did nonetheless produce a narrative of Indigenous inferiority that delegitimizes Indigenous struggles and portrays Indigenous participants as lacking self-control and reason. Indigenous protesters on the streets especially create a moral panic over their out-of-control nature that is brought to the fore in media and government responses (Cohen 2002). Both reflecting and projecting these narratives, criminal courts in New South Wales and Queensland share an anxiety about the lack of containment of Indigenous claims to space and challenges to white authority. This is especially true in the last decade, during which rioters were regarded as unjustified in their claims and requiring a severe sentence. However, even when higher courts conceived these claims as reducing rioters' moral culpability, the courts have consistently pointed to the need for Indigenous people to provide a more measured response that sustains the 'white' social order.

Higher sentencing courts over the past decade have reimagined Indigenous riots[1] as embodying Indigenous disorder. They juxtapose this with the harmonious

1 The term 'riot' or 'rioters' problematically implies that the protesters are out-of-control and lacking reason. It negates the legitimate frustrations of the protesters. Where it is employed, it is to accord with popular use and to be consistent with the gravamen for which the Indigenous protesters are charged, rather than to reflect the nature of the protest.

order of the non-Indigenous 'white' community. Gore and Pratten (2003: 212) argue that discourses of 'instrumentalized disorder' delegitimize the Other. Anglo-Australian institutions, especially the police, are constructed as 'bastions of order' – they protect 'social order and stability against the threat of "Aboriginal hordes"' (Gargett 2005: 10). This dichotomy silences the causes of the riot while cementing 'police neutrality' (2005: 10). It precipitates a law and *order* response with ever tougher criminalization of Indigenous people. Mickler (1992: 324–5) argues that riots and protests provide 'sumptuous spectacles for the front-page imaging of disorder' as 'the major threat to the order of white society'. The bipolarity between Indigenous disorder and non-Indigenous order – the tribal and the modern, the irrational and the rational – adds to the sense of unpredictable Indigenous danger to Anglo-Australian society. Narratives of disorderly Indigenous communities imbricate with narratives of 'dysfunctional' Indigenous communities – both portray Indigenous people as lacking purpose, internal-regulation and rational motivation.

However, the riot also puts on display Indigenous claims to space and authority. Through their public assertion of power, the rioters provide a counter-narrative to state rule (Gore and Pratten 2003: 212). In the media, Indigenous people involved in protests are 'increasingly active performers, pressing all the time for better roles, lines and scripts' (Mickler 1992: 324). The protesters in the cases discussed in this chapter are challenging white control and expressing broader grievances about systemic and institutional injustices against Indigenous people (Funnell 2005; Cunneen 2007). The riots are an open show of resistance to white institutional control, especially impugning police discrimination, the lack of police accountability and state officials' undermining of Indigenous self-determination. However, this challenge to state authority is marginalized in the production of mainstream knowledge on Indigenous disorder.

This chapter analyzes sentencing remarks for Indigenous offenders who were convicted of assault or riot for violently protesting against police or government officials for their racist acts or involvement in a death in custody or police chase. A number of higher courts, particularly in the 1980s and early 1990s, pointed to the stress caused by racism that provoked the riot. However, recent sentencing remarks have tended to privilege aggravating circumstances, especially the seriousness of the riot, the harm or potential harm to the victims and its threat to the wider community. In doing so, courts in New South Wales and Queensland have elided the context in which the riot occurred and emphasized Indigenous criminality and irrationality. The removal of any justifiable reason for the riot has meant that courts have ruled out reductions in moral culpability. In handing down severe penalties, these courts point to the need for a proportionate response to the seriousness of the offence and the need to deter the Indigenous community from such offending. They assume that rioters exist in a vacuum and make rational calculations about the ensuing punishment. This shift in sentencing dovetails a reimagining of the Indigenous offender and their community as lacking reason or legitimacy in the contest for space. The media also crystallizes this view in their creation of moral panics and construction of Indigenous people as deviant 'folk devils' (Cohen 2002). The panics create new modes of regulating Indigenous behaviour and reclaiming what has been placed under threat through the acts of resistance (Goode and Ben-Yehuda 1994: 159, 169).

In drawing the battle lines in favour of a homogenous moral community, the courts have responded to Indigenous rioters with varying moral responses for offenders who protested through assaulting (spitting on) a government officer on Yarrabah Reserve (north Queensland) in 1981 (*Neal* v. *The Queen* 1982); rioting against the death in police custody of an Indigenous man at Brewarrina (western New South Wales) in 1987 (*R.* v. *Murray, R.* v. *Bates* 1992; *R.* v. *Boney* 1991); rioting in 2004 against the death on a police chase in Redfern, Sydney (*R.* v. *Cargill* 2005), and rioting (including with destruction to property) against the death in custody on Palm Island, Queensland in 2004 (*R.* v. *Poynter, Norman & Parker* 2006; *The Queen* v. *Wotton* 2008). With few exceptions, across their sentences, the courts have condemned the violent actions of the protestors, but in the earlier sentencing remarks in relation to Yarrabah and Brewarrina, the appellate courts demonstrated an appreciation of the personal stress the offenders were under during the offences due to discrimination, paternalism and over-policing (*Neal* v. *The Queen* 1982: 325; *R.* v. *Boney* 1991: 6). They took into account the circumstances to reduce the offenders' culpability, and in turn the seriousness of their offence and the sentence.

Seriousness would later be divorced from the offenders' circumstances and individual culpability. It would be linked exclusively to harm or potential harm in justifying harsher sentences for the Redfern and Palm Island rioters. The emphasis on victimization focused on the threats to the vulnerable and 'ideal' police victims (Christie 1986: 18; see *R.* v. *Poynter, Norman & Parker* 2006: [5], [29], [33]). In doing so, the courts mute the wrongdoing of the police in deaths in custody, and attempt to create a fantasy of racial neutrality in the management of space.

Moral panics of the self-righteous

Cohen (2002: 1) writes that moral panics are directed to those who 'become defined as a threat to societal values and interests' and are presented 'in a stylized stereotypical fashion in the media'. This is no clearer than in relation to a perceived 'riot', which generates an image of 'a besieged town from which the innocent' are made to escape a 'marauding mob' (2002: 20). Social anxieties about difference peak to create a mass euphoria in relation to this crime problem (Cohen 2002: 8). Hogg (2005: 341) asserts that behind the 'perception of crime' are real or imagined threats by 'alien cultures' and social anxieties. Hall *et al.* (1978) point out that a specific group of deviants is singled out for 'folk devil' status because it possesses characteristics that make it a suitable screen for social anxieties. These anxieties are quelled through punishing the Other. Punishment reinforces the authority of the dominant culture and creates a collective wave of righteous condemnation (Durkheim 1933: 90; Durkheim 1982: 50–2).

Judicial imaginings of Indigenous community members involved in rioting project a moral panic about the threat of this community to the social order and their lack of cause. In the Palm Island case, the Queensland Court of Appeal regarded the Indigenous offenders as being out-of-control and not reasonably responding to an injustice (*R.* v. *Poynter, Norman & Parker* 2006: [36], [39]). They are presented as having the same set of choices as everyone else but failing to exercise them reasonably (2006: [71]). In sentencing the Redfern and Palm Island rioters, the courts did not advert to the antagonistic relationship between the police and Indigenous people. This is also apparent in the media reporting on the riots, which erased the narrative of Indigenous 'desperation and frustration' in relation to police injustices against their community members (Gargett 2005: 9; Little 2010: 51). The rioters at Palm Island, Redfern and Brewarrina were generally presented as irrational deviants and outsiders who were placing Australian society 'under imminent threat' (see Royal Commission into Aboriginal Deaths in Custody 1991: 186).

During all the trials and sentencing of Indigenous rioters examined in this chapter, the mainstream media sought to undercut the rationality of the riot and vindicate the police victims. Assigning deviance denies 'rioters' their role in creating their own political space through their resistance. The media concealed the power relations underlying the deaths in custody and presented the rioters as 'backward, ignorant and irrational' (Morris 2001: 261; Morris 2005: 69). The characterization of 'riots' ignores questions of why they occurred and produces a story of 'blind, lawless purposelessness' and 'chaotic spontaneity' (Cunneen 2007: 23; Scraton 2007: 25). By criminalizing rioters and presenting them as disorganized 'rabble' ensures their illegitimacy and reinforces the legitimate response of the police (Silver 1976: 15). It undermines the rioters' deep grievances over the Indigenous death in custody and its historical legacy. In contrast to these popular representations, historical and anthropological analyses suggest that riots are 'articulate protests against genuine grievances', and have varying levels of organization, restraint and impulsiveness (Fogelson 1968: 37; Cowlishaw 2004: 75, 236). Rationality, imbued with cultural, spatial and historical meaning, is among a riot's 'most crucial features' (Fogelson 1968: 37; Cowlishaw 2004: 242).

Spatial aspects of the riots

The Indigenous riot unsettles non-Indigenous claims to Australian space that are based on illegal dispossession (Moreton-Robinson 2003: 32). The media's response is a reassertion of white dominance. For Hage (1998: 17), the 'whiteness' of space has critical significance for settler societies that arise out of an 'imagined community' and '*internal* orientalism'. Nationalism is based on 'spatial management', involving the preservation of an 'imagined privileged relation' over 'race' and 'national space' (Hage 1998: 38). Ang (1999: 191) also notes that 'white racism in the Australian context has peculiarities which have to do with the spatial dimensions of this settler colonial project' (1999: 191). The distance of the 'mother country' produced 'a particularly antipodean sense of place' that perceived an empty distant land (1999: 191). She explains that the

> totalising nature of British annexation and control paved the way . . . for the creation of 'one Australia' . . . imagined in terms of a transplanted British homogeneity. In other words, what was produced here was the collapsing into one of physical and human geography, which had a powerful imaginative effect on the white settlers. It provided the fledgling settler society with a singular sense of spatial identity.
>
> (Ang 1999: 192)

The riot brings to the fore this contest over territory. As a collective act, the riot seeks to 'force political matters into view', and to construct a political challenge (Cowlishaw 2004: 244–5, 75). In the words of Cowlishaw (2004: 195), the Indigenous riot is 'ordered around a conversation with whitefellas'. It creates 'a productive space where racialized bodies carry powerful messages' and 'police stand accused of interfering in others' domestic spaces' (2004: 245). It creates an electrifying space for those involved, with a release through recognition and a 'carnivalesque' thrill at disrupting the symbolic order and imposing desires (Presdee 2000: 29). Cowlishaw (2004: 245) notes that 'violent actions are needed to shatter the complacency and moral superiority [over Indigenous people] that accompany and naturalize the state power'. The destruction of property is an attack on the economic control of towns by whites, and sends a message about the 'clumsy limit of police power' (2004: 75). However, the rioters' claims to space do not receive the same national attention as the deniers of their space. Although the riot can be regarded as a spatial contest, it is the 'spatial managers', including the courts and mainstream media, who have a dominant position in the publicity of their opinions about those who do not belong and should be excluded from the space (Hage 1998: 42–6). By contrast, the 'spatially managed' have opinions expressed about them in the mainstream media (1998: 42–6). This constructs the managed not only as inferior, but 'as an object of spatial exclusion' (1998: 48). Media and court representations of Indigenous rioters as uncontained rabble are a legacy of the colonial mentality that allowed Indigenous people to be segregated and their places to be claimed and named by whites (see Rutherford 2000: 31–2; Curthoys 1999: 281).

Situating riots in historical geographies of contested space

Spatial encounters defined the organization of 'settler' space in the places discussed in this chapter – Yarrabah, Brewarrina, Redfern and Palm Island.

These places, although divergent in their experiences of colonization, have the common thread of being occupied by missions and government reserves. These settlements brought in Indigenous peoples forcibly removed from other lands as well as local Indigenous people. The exception is Redfern, where work opportunities were a significant impetus for Indigenous peoples from other places initially coming to Redfern. Displacement, however, did not result in placelessness – with Indigenous people establishing a new sense of belonging and community on the lands to which they were relocated. It did nonetheless inform ongoing Indigenous grievances about the white control. In New South Wales, Brewarrina was the site of the first and longest running Aboriginal mission and the first institution to officially segregate Indigenous from non-Indigenous people (Barker 2006: 1–2). The mission, established by the Aboriginal Protection Board in 1886, brought together Indigenous peoples from surrounding Indigenous communities by removing them from their lands. There were a range of strategies and civilizing ideologies used, including the forcible removal of young girls from their families at the age of 13 or 14 to be educated in domestic work at the dormitory (Brewarrina Aboriginal Health Service 2010). This institutional community lasted until 1966 when many of its residents moved to the town of Brewarrina where they settled in impoverished conditions. For Indigenous people who were moved to the town earlier in the twentieth century, their lives were tightly controlled by the Aborigines Protection Board and heavily policed; by 1904 there were five police officers for approximately 1,000 inhabitants (Brewarrina Aboriginal Health Service 2010). This set the tone for penal surveillance over its Indigenous people and has continued into the twenty-first century. It has spread across the borders to the 'Far North-West' towns of Brewarrina, Walgett and Bourke, where collectively there is the highest police to population ratio in New South Wales (Morris 2001: 244; Morris 2005: 76; Lucas 1995: 47).

Yarrabah mission, like many Indigenous settlements in Queensland, was a product of government relocations of Indigenous peoples from vast lands and communities to create a melting pot. Beginning in 1892, Yarrabah housed a dormitory, a school, a hospital and five churches for Indigenous people. Its superintendent controlled Indigenous peoples' marriage, work and daily routines. Yarrabah mission was founded by Reverend John Brown Gribble, 'an Anglican minister intent upon bringing the word of God to Aborigines' (Hume 1991: 4). Although Yarrabah was well known as a 'model mission', its conditions could be cruel and destitute for its 800 Indigenous 'inmates', resulting in conflict between the Indigenous population and the mission management and, after 1960, government management when state control replaced church control (Hume 1991: 22–3; Loos 1991: 73, 81). In the mid 1970s, movements for self-determination culminated in the passage of the Aboriginal and Torres Strait Islanders (Queensland Reserves and Communities Self-Management) Act 1978 (Cth), which enabled Aboriginal councils to govern reserves. Despite this legislation, the Yarrabah council remained accountable to government officials and the community continued to be under the strict control of the Department of Aboriginal and

Torres Strait Islander Advancement and 'white' economic interests (Chesterman and Villaflor 2000–1: 92). Indigenous people at Yarrabah harboured grievances about the lack of application of the legislation and the fact that while the Commonwealth had legislated in 1976 for Aboriginal land rights, there were no comparable developments in Queensland (2000–1: 92). In Yarrabah this spurned contests over control and management of the land that came to the fore in the facts of *Neal* v. *The Queen* (1982). This situation lasted at least until 1986 when, after a long struggle, the Yarrabah Council received the Deeds of Grant in Trust for their land from the Queensland government (Thomson 1989: iv).

Redfern is an 'embattled' place that Indigenous people have long-struggled to retain, including in the early nineteenth century through guerrilla warfare led by the heroic Pemulwuy (Shaw 2000: 291). Such struggles have been constantly met with aggressive policing. From the late nineteenth century, local Indigenous people who had been driven out by the warfare returned to Redfern to take up employment on the railway and reclaim a pocket of their land (Redfern Residents for Reconciliation 2012). This was matched with displaced Indigenous people from other areas relocating to Redfern. By 1965 the Indigenous population was 12,000, and Redfern became a home for the Indigenous rights movement (Redfern Residents for Reconciliation 2012). Anderson (1993: 81) notes that 'Redfern became a sphere of [I]ndigenous protest, an heroic site of resistance to European culture and colonialist control'. In 1973, the Aboriginal Housing Company bought housing in an area of Redfern that would come to be known as 'The Block' (Spark 2003: 34–5).[2] This purchase was regarded as 'part of the process of self-determination and reconciliation' (McAuliffe 2009: 627). It has since been owned by the local Indigenous community and 'remains the symbolic heart of (post)colonial political struggle' (Forbes-Boyte 2009: 153; Shaw 2000: 298). It is also the site of the establishment of the Aboriginal Legal Service in New South Wales (Foley 2001).

Since its beginnings, The Block has been challenged by high-level policing and criticized by the media and state government as 'imploding in a sea of drugs, crime and cultural inferiority' and as an example of 'failed (urban) Aboriginal self-determination' (Shaw 2000: 291). Narratives of the out-of-'placeness' of urban Indigenous people help to justify white claims to The Block (Shaw 2007). Indigenous struggles and achievements at Redfern are constructed as inferior to the progress of 'colonial capitalism' and urban gentrification (Anderson 1999: 215; Spark 2003: 36). In the late 1990s, the gentrification of inner-city Sydney emerged as 'the latest phase of capitalism's re-colonization of inner city residential space' (Shaw 2000: 296). In 2004, the Redfern Riot, which brought the spatial contest over Redfern into sharp relief, sparked calls from the New South Wales Opposition leader for 'bulldozers' to 'flatten the area known as the Block' (Anon 2004).

2 The Block is bounded by four streets: Eveleigh, Caroline, Louis and Vine Streets.

If Redfern grew up as a place of resistance, Palm Island was a place to suppress resisters. The island and its mission was organized along penal lines from 1918. The purpose of the penal settlement, as stated by Queensland's Chief Protector of Aboriginals in the early twentieth century, was to isolate and punish Indigenous 'troublesome cases' and assure colonial expansion on the mainland (Watson 2010: 18). Indigenous peoples from at least 57 language groups on the mainland were detained on the island and subjected to strict discipline (McDougall 2006: 27). They were sent to Palm Island for a range of crimes, but especially violating Queensland's Aboriginal protection legislation (Watson 2010). Their crimes included speaking in language, associating with another Indigenous person or dissenting against white authorities. Indigenous behaviours were also dressed up as crimes to justify transportation to what became Australia's largest Aboriginal settlement (Watson 1993: 176). Detention on Palm Island was an indefinite punishment, but transgressions on the island would attract additional penalties, including incarceration in the watch-house for novel reasons such as laughing (Watson 2010: 104).

The spatial boundaries were fiercely enforced by whites on the island, and Indigenous people were unable to visit 'white zones' (Watson 2010: 110). They also could not walk into shops, but had to queue for rations, and had to 'salute any white person they passed' (2010: 82). Despite Palm Island being inhabited by its own Indigenous population, Indigenous residents could not escape the criminal label and the ensuing policing and white control (Wilson 1982). Nonetheless, Indigenous peoples on the island resisted white policy and management, extending the opposition to the protection legislation that brought many to the island. Such resistance materialized in a 1957 strike against the non-payment of wages and violent rule by white authorities (Watson 1995). There were also protests in the white zones against the racism on the island and the establishment of the Palm Island Aboriginal Community Council (Watson 2010: 110). In 2004, the Palm Island riot exposed ongoing Indigenous grievances with white policing. The following sections will consider how sentencing courts conceived Indigenous protesters across the communities of Yarrabah and Brewarrina in the 1980s and 1990s and then Redfern and Palm Island in the twenty-first century.

Early judicial concepts of Indigenous rioters: entitled to be agitators

The terms set by white 'spatial management' that are imposed on the Other are not delivered through a singular message (Hage 1998: 38). They ebb and flow between romanticization and condemnation of Indigenous people on that space. To be solely aggressive would undermine the imagined social harmony within national borders. Therefore, colonizers match moments of lawlessness with lawfulness 'through the elaboration of a new fantasised form of social harmony', according to Rutherford (2000: 57). In criminal sentencing, both goodwill and reprimand are variously imposed on the Indigenous offender to create an image of a social order in control. Oscillating between moderation and malevolence, the courts retain a quality of mysterious authority. Some judges have embraced the Indigenous protest as an indicator of human progress that fulfils white society's aspirations for the Other. Alternatively, courts have romanticized the paternalism and segregation policy of white society to contrast with the uncontrolled rioter and deviant Indigenous subject (Carins Magistrate Court, quoted in *Neal* v. *The Queen* 1982: 325; Bathurst District Court sentencing remarks for Brewarrina rioters, quoted in Lewis 1991: 6). This romanticization is symptomatic of Australian nationalism where the 'power to do good' through social engineering has 'deprived Aboriginal Australians at every turn' (Rutherford 2000: 27). The Frankfurt School suggests that the state acts out a paternal role in which its caring nature becomes disciplinarian when the relationship between the nation and the subject deteriorates (Fromm 1963; Adorno *et al.* 1950). For Hage (1998: 79), this is signified in the swing of Australian nationalism between 'evil white' and 'good white' nationalism (see also Hage 2003: 39).

Projecting the good white nationalism, Australian courts in the 1980s and early 1990s exhibited a sympathetic paternalism towards Indigenous protesters and their grief from the racist circumstances. This was an era in which self-determination, land rights and the Royal Commission into Aboriginal Deaths in Custody set the tone for the relationship with the Indigenous Other. In *Neal* v. *The Queen* (1982) – the High Court of Australia's most significant exposition on the relevance of Indigenous circumstances to sentencing – a number of judges self-consciously embraced their role as benefactors to a people disavowed of their sovereignty. The High Court found that it could reduce the sentence because Indigenous background was relevant to the moral culpability of the offender and the seriousness of the offence, thus ameliorating the sentence (1982: 325).

Neal v. *The Queen* (1982) involved an Indigenous offender who committed a violent offence after being provoked by racism. The circumstances of the offence were a confrontation on the Yarrabah Aboriginal Reserve between Mr Collins, a non-Indigenous officer of the Department of Aboriginal and Torres Strait Islander Advancement and store manager on the reserve, and the accused, Percy Conrad Neal, the elected chairman of the Yarrabah Community Council on the reserve. Neal had campaigned against the paternalistic treatment of Indigenous people on the reserve by white authorities, and sought to institute Aboriginal self-management – a political cause of Indigenous communities across Australia (Chesterman and Villaflor 2000–1: 91). The deep-seated grievances over the paternalist environment at Yarrabah found expression when Collins, the store manager, sold rotten meat to the Indigenous residents living on the reserve. With 12 other Indigenous people, Neal approached Collins at his home. While the others waited on the street, Neal had an argument about reserve management on Collins' front porch. Neal swore at Collins, telling him that he was racist and that he and all other whites should get off Yarrabah reserve. He then spat in Collins' face. For this, Neal was convicted of unlawful entry and assault (*Neal* v. *The Queen* 1982: 311, 321).

At first instance, a Cairns magistrate sentenced Neal to imprisonment for two months. The magistrate criticized the political statement behind the act of resistance: 'Your actions in taking unto yourself the task of removing all whites from Yarrabah cannot be condoned from any angle' (quoted in *Neal* v. *The Queen* 1982: 325). He blamed Neal for the racial tensions between black and white society: 'Violence is something in recent times which has crept into Aboriginal communities: I blame your type for this growing hatred of black against white' (quoted in 1982: 325). Neal was regarded as upsetting 'the harmonious running of these communities' (quoted in 1982: 325). This reflects, as Hage (1998) suggests, a fantasy of the invisible yet racialized European hegemony. Hage (1998: 155) points to Goffman's idea that 'illusions and impressions' about space are 'necessary for the construction of the self'. It is the judicial 'presentation of the self' as tolerant that is superimposed on white Australia's treatment of Others (1998: 155). Equally, the image of harmony is threatened when the Other fails to acquiesce to the hegemony.

The Queensland Court of Appeal, upon hearing Neal's appeal, increased the sentence to six months' imprisonment on the basis that two months was manifestly *inadequate* for such an offence that involved 'a mob' (quoted in *Neal* v. *The Queen* 1982: 313). Neal successfully appealed to the High Court, which reinstated the magistrate's two-month sentence. Two of the four judges, Gibbs C.J. and Wilson J., allowed Neal's appeal on the technical basis that the Court of Appeal was acting *ultra vires* by extending the sentence (1982: 307–8, 320). All judges accepted that racial tensions on reserves were legitimate sentencing considerations. Wilson J. held that the magistrate's sentence appropriately took into account the 'frustration and emotional concern engendered in [Neal] by the manner in which the reserves were administered and his endeavour to obtain self-management' (1982: 320). Like Wilson J., Brennan J. personalized the act by focusing on the 'emotional stress' created by the 'paternalistic system' of the reserve, which affected Neal (1982: 325). Nonetheless, Brennan J. appreciated that it did not arise from 'any ill-feeling between Messrs Collins and Neal personally', but was a 'dramatic and emotional confrontation' produced 'by a deeply-felt objection to departmental control of the reserve' (1982: 324). The objection was a 'material factor' that went to 'the reason why Mr Neal engaged in that conduct' and reduced the 'gravity for the offence' (1982: 323–4). Brennan J. explained that the facts of the case 'point to some "special problems" which may explain — though they cannot justify or excuse — Mr. Neal's conduct' (1982: 324–5). In accepting these problems as relevant to mitigation, Brennan J. nonetheless noted that the conduct was 'an unlawful and an unacceptable means of seeking political or administrative changes' (1982: 325). In an oft-quoted statement, Brennan J. pointed to the importance of Indigenous circumstances in sentencing considerations:

> In imposing sentences courts are bound to take into account, in accordance with those principles, all material facts including those facts which exist only

> by reason of the offender's membership of an ethnic or other group. So much is essential to the even administration of criminal justice.
>
> (*Neal* v. *The Queen* 1982: 326)

The treatment of Indigenous people on the reserve and Neal's grievances were relevant to moral culpability and a reduced sentence. Brennan J. noted that Neal was 'entitled lawfully to advocate political or administrative changes without penalty' (1982: 325). Murphy J. went further in tracing the 'Aboriginal sense of grievance' that 'developed over the two hundred years of white settlement in Australia', with its 'arrogant superiority' and 'considerable brutality' (1982: 317). This resonates with Cowlishaw's (2004: 195) observations that Indigenous riots emerge from a 'colonial rage'. Murphy J. recognized that 'Aborigines have a right to participate in and direct their own policies' and protest against the 'reserve conditions and race relations', which are to be treated as special mitigating factors in a sentence (*Neal* v. *The Queen* 1982: 318). He cited US experience where 'persons frustrated by powerlessness through the exercise of racist policies and practices . . . sometimes express [grievances] in the only way possible – by protest or violence' (1982: 318). Murphy J. further stated that Neal as an agitator was 'in good company' and 'agitators are so absolutely necessary' for 'human progress' and 'advance towards civilisation' (1982: 318). Brennan and Murphy JJ.'s comments remind us that the space of the reserve is not fixed, but 'emerges relationally' through contestation (Carter 2007: 440). Carter (2007: 430) reflects on the formation of public space not as governed by the law, but as a 'mobile and self-constituting' set of exchanges between Indigenous and non-Indigenous systems.

Ultimately, Murphy J. treated sentencing mitigation as a vehicle for reconciliation between Indigenous and non-Indigenous Australians. He gave meaning to Hudson's (1999: 590) theory that sentencing should involve 'society acknowledg[ing] responsibility' for the circumstances that lead to the offending. Murphy J. was in favour of imposing a non-custodial sentence, as a prison sentence would 'not improve race relations but will tend to embitter them' (*Neal* v. *The Queen* 1982: 318). For Murphy J., the inferior status of Indigenous people *vis-à-vis* the white victim in a position of authority was a special mitigating consideration:

> Taking into account the racial relations aspect of this case, the fact that Mr Neal was placed in a position of inferiority to the whites managing the Reserve should have been a special mitigating factor in determining sentence.
>
> (*Neal* v. *The Queen* 1982: 318)

All judges of the High Court enunciated that the personal stress of racism on the offender reduced the seriousness of the offence.[3] However, with the exception

3 The position in *Neal* (1982: 326) that sentencing courts are bound to account for material facts of ethnic group membership has been applied to Indigenous offenders who receive Indigenous law punishment (*Jadurin* v. *The Queen* 1982: 187; *R.* v. *Minor* 1992: 191; *R.* v. *Miyatatawuy* 1996:

of Murphy J., who treated sentencing as a metaphor for reconciliation, the court regarded the space of Yarrabah Reserve as fixed by white law, with tolerance for difference in this space seen as something bestowed by the white system on Indigenous people. As Hage (1998: 140) notes, white notions of cultural diversity hinge on whites possessing the terms of its existence, rather than cultural diversity undercutting whiteness. Similar social fantasies of tolerance to 'difference' are created in the sentencing of the Brewarrina rioters.

Sentencing Brewarrina 'rioters' in the aftermath of Boney's death in custody

The catalyst for the Brewarrina riot of 1987 was the death in custody of a local Indigenous man and the perceived failure of the justice system to bring the police responsible to account. Brewarrina, like its surrounding towns in north-west New South Wales, is beset by ongoing spatial contests between the Indigenous and non-Indigenous residents (Cowlishaw 2004). The backdrop to the riot was anger at the forthcoming celebrations for Australia's Bicentenary of European occupation, the over-policing of Indigenous people at Brewarrina and a growing movement against a spate of Aboriginal deaths in custody across Australia. A number of rioters would stand trial and their sentencing submissions would highlight the death in custody as the precursor to the riot. In 1991, the New South Wales Court of Criminal Appeal reviewed the sentences of a number of the rioters. It regarded the death in custody of Lloyd James Boney, which fuelled the riot, as well as the high-level policing at the time as mitigating factors. This is because they explained the reasons for the riot and reduced the offenders' moral culpability (*R.* v. *Murray, R.* v. *Bates* 1992: 9; *R.* v. *Boney* 1991: 1–2).

The death in custody and moral panics

Leading up to the riot, policing had intensified in Brewarrina in anticipation of protests against Australia's Bicentennial commemoration of colonial settlement. The Tactical Response Group was mobilized to Brewarrina due to police fears about an Indigenous insurrection in response to the celebrations (Wootten 1991: 95). There was also a 'law and order' campaign among the New South Wales Government and opposition in the lead-up to the 1988 election that 'positioned non-Aborigines as victims of "Aboriginal criminality"' and called for more policing of Indigenous people in places like Brewarrina (Morris 2001: 248). However, these developments merely confirmed to the Indigenous community at Brewarrina the police mistreatment over many years (Cunneen and Robb 1987: 263, quoting a Brewarrina protester).

579); those who come from low socio-economic backgrounds (*Rogers & Murray* v. *R.* 1989: 307); and those who belong to communities inflicted with alcohol abuse (*Fernando* 1992: 62; *R.* v. *Churchill* 2000: [25]).

During the police descent on Brewarrina in August 1987, Lloyd James Boney, a 28-year-old Indigenous man, died in police custody. Boney was found hanging by a football sock in a police cell one-and-a-half hours after he was arrested for breaching bail conditions (Hope 1991: 2). The Indigenous community was suspicious of the police involvement in the death, and demanded a proper inquiry and justice to be served against the police. The community took the view that it was physically impossible for Boney to kill himself by hanging, given his heavily intoxicated state (Wootten 1991: 2, 97–8; Williams and Cordell 1987: 1; Williams and Cordell 1987a: 8). Also, as a 'happy-go-lucky guy', Boney was seen as lacking the disposition for suicide (Wootten 1991; Williams and Cordell 1987: 1). At the same time, Boney had expressed fear that the police would kill him (Williams 1988: 7). There was growing publicity across Australia about both Indigenous deaths in custody and police mistreatment of Indigenous people. The Committee to Defend Black Rights had been monitoring Indigenous deaths in custody in 1987 and found an average of one death every 11 days, which had led to calls for a Royal Commission into Aboriginal Deaths in Custody (Williams and Cordell 1987: 1). Boney was the sixteenth Aboriginal death and the final straw that would lead to the Federal Government forming a Royal Commission (Tatz 1996: 11). The Commission later found that there was a 'widespread view' among Indigenous people that Boney's death was part of a pattern of Indigenous deaths in custody (Wootten 1991: 1).

The Indigenous community at Brewarrina was outraged by the police removing Boney's body to Bourke before notifying his family of his death and also at what they saw as police lies about attempting to organize bail for Boney (Wootten 1991: 17, 55–62). These events 'aroused suspicion of a cover-up of a killing' (1991: 17). There was an overnight internal investigation into the death, involving only one interview conducted by the Internal Security Unit with a police officer. The findings were that Boney had committed suicide with 'no suggestion at all of foul play in any sense' on the part of the police (1991: 124). Consequently, there was a strong view in the community that justice would not be served through lawful channels. Ultimately, no charges were ever laid for Boney's death.

In the week following Boney's death, a series of protests took place outside the police station. When riot-clad police with shields and batons turned up to Boney's wake, and in doing so flouted an agreement between the Western Aboriginal Legal Service and the police, the 'Brewarrina riot' materialized (Pitty 1994: 10). In response to the police hostility, about 20 mourners armed themselves with iron bars and fence posts and shouted: 'Black people have been killed by white people for more than 200 years' (Lewis 1991b: 3). The riot lasted for about 40 minutes, during which rioters broke windows at the local hotel (Duboudin 1987). Two police officers were taken to hospital, with one sustaining a broken leg (Hewett 1987: 1). There was one report in the mainstream media of an Indigenous man who was taken to hospital. Most injuries sustained by Indigenous people, including by those sentenced for the riot, went unreported (Fife-Yeomans 1988: 8; Pitty 1994: 9).

Seventeen Indigenous people – labelled the 'Brewarrina 17' – were arrested for riot and riot-related offences. The inspector who investigated Lloyd Boney's death in custody also investigated the rioters, creating a perception of bias among the Indigenous community members (Wootten 1991: 125). The most serious charges and convictions for riotous assembly and assaulting police were laid against 'ringleaders' Arthur Murray (an Aboriginal Elder who was a campaigner for the Royal Commission into Aboriginal Deaths in Custody and whose son had died in police custody in 1981), Soney Bates (Lloyd Boney's brother-in-law) and Glen Boney (Lloyd Boney's cousin) (*R.* v. *Murray, R.* v. *Bates* 1992: 13; *R.* v. *Boney* 1991). The ensuing moral panic in the mainstream media highlighted the violence of the riot and the role of its protagonists. Televised and print media focused on the uncontrollable and intoxicated behaviour of the rioters – an approach shared by the coroner appointed to inquire into the death of Lloyd Boney (Carter 1987: 18). The Australian Broadcasting Corporation was also accused of 'staging the riot' by supplying the mourners with alcohol (Morris 2005: 70). The *Sydney Morning Herald* described how Indigenous people stacked beer bottles in the park as weapons and ammunition (Lewis 1991: 6). Headlines read 'Blood on the Street: the Night a Town Exploded' (Hewett 1987a: 1) and 'Police Hurt in Clash with Aborigines' (Anon 1987). The Australian Associated Press reported that 'a mob of aborigines attacked police in an outback town' (Anon 1987). Coinciding with the media's depictions of irrational Indigenous offenders was the illustration of the reasoned and legitimate police response. The front page story in the *Sydney Morning Herald* used matter-of-fact terms when describing the para-military's involvement in the riot: 'Officers from the Tactical Response Group are providing assistance to local police in the wake of the rioting' (Hewett 1987a: 1).

However, some media reports were balanced with a portrayal of the death in custody and the police provocation as underlying the protest. The *Sydney Morning Herald* described the riot as an act of resistance to the death in custody, poor living conditions and 200 years of Aboriginal abuse (Anon 1987a: 16). The article stated that the violence was that 'practised by oppressed groups at "the end of their tether"' to beg 'the dominant group to take notice of their inhuman plight' (1987a: 16). A journalist questioned official reports of the numbers of Indigenous rioters, claiming it was closer to 30 than the 150 alleged by the police (1987a: 16). In its front page story, the *Sydney Morning Herald* canvassed the narrative of the death in custody and police abuse as the riot's precursor and quoted James Boney, Lloyd's brother, who alleged that the police had been harassing his family and that Aboriginal people were looked upon as 'less than human' (Hewett 1987a: 1). Therefore, there were two trajectories in the media reporting on the Brewarrina 'riot' – one on the uncontrollable and intoxicated state of the rioters, and the other on the death in custody and police racism provoking the 'riot'. Both narratives were taken up in the judicial imaginings of the Brewarrina Indigenous community when sentencing the 'ringleaders' of the riot. This nuanced narrative would later manifest in the sentencing remarks for

Murray, Bates and Boney. Reports identified the death in custody and police racism as precursors to the riot (Anon 1987a: 16; Hewett 1987a: 1).

Court of Criminal Appeal's latitude for context of death in custody

The Bathurst District Court's first instance sentence for rioters Bates and Murray emphasized the violent, unpredictable and unstable nature of the Brewarrina Indigenous community. The court, whose remarks were directly quoted in the media, focused on the seriousness of the riot and defended the police during the trial (Morris 2001: 246). It did not portray the riot as a reasoned response to the death in custody, despite the contemporaneous handing down of the Royal Commission's report on Boney's death, recommending disciplinary action against the police officers (Hope 1991: 2). Indeed, the court directed the jury to ignore the death in custody as a causal factor and the commission's findings (Lewis 1991: 6). The court depicted Murray and Bates as responsible for disturbing community harmony by promoting hatred of police. The court reflected on the harmonious Aboriginal–white relations in the 'old days' of the 1950s and 1960s, when whites controlled Indigenous lives and 'whites and blacks' lived 'happily together' (Nash J. quoted in Lewis 1991a: 3). The worsening of race relations was evidenced by Indigenous people attacking police in what 'could only be described as a completely *unprovoked* and violent riot' (Nash J. in 1991a: 3). In handing down 18-month prison sentences for riotous assembly, the court concluded that the rioters had been affected by alcohol in carrying out their 'half-hour of madness' (Nash J. in 1991a: 3). This reasoning reveals the District Court's capacity for fantasy creation about harmonious racial relations alongside a narrative of Indigenous deviance (Hage 1998: 78–9).

The appeal to the New South Wales Court of Criminal Appeal against the convictions and sentences of Bates and Murray, and the sentence of Glen Boney, focused on District Court judge Nash J.'s alleged biased interventions and his failure to consider the death in custody as a mitigating sentencing consideration (*R.* v. *Murray, R.* v. *Bates* 1992: 22).[4] The Court of Criminal Appeal found that Nash J. gave an 'unhelpful review of the evidence' that 'weighed unfairly against the accused' and gave the 'impression that World War III was taking place in Brewarrina that night' (1992: 22). The appellate court was critical of the District Court's idealizing of the 'virtuous' past of racial discrimination and its blaming of Indigenous people for the problems relating to the tense relations with non-Indigenous people. For the appellate court, the problems confronting the Indigenous community could be explained with reference to its harsh treatment by non-Indigenous society, including by the police. It put the death in custody at

4 The Court of Criminal Appeal held that Nash J. of the District Court played a prejudicial role in cross-examination and 'actually helped a police officer' give answers that were favourable to the prosecution's case (*R.* v. *Murray, R.* v. *Bates* 1992: 22).

the forefront of assessing the offenders' conduct (1992: 2). In the final analysis, the convictions were quashed due to the bias of the District Court and the insufficient numbers to constitute a riot (1992: 6). Nonetheless, the Court of Criminal Appeal accepted that the death in custody should have been a relevant factor:

> It would have been quite unrealistic for the jury to have considered the specific blows alleged to have been inflicted by each of the accused upon which the riot charge was based without knowledge of the initial reason for which the crowd had gathered (following the funeral of the Aboriginal man who died in police custody).
>
> (*R.* v. *Murray, R.* v. *Bates* 1992: 9)

The other defendant, Glen Boney, appealed against his six-month prison sentence on the basis that the Bathurst District Court gave him a disproportionate sentence compared with the other rioters, and failed to account for the death in custody in mitigation.[5] The New South Wales Court of Criminal Appeal described the death in custody as a mitigating factor for Boney's offence of assaulting police. It noted the 'close emotional relationship between the applicant and the deceased [Lloyd Boney] in that they had been raised, effectively, as brothers' (*R.* v. *Boney* 1991: 1). Accordingly, the death had a significant personal impact on the defendant, which should have been considered in the sentence. The appellate court thus resisted the District Court's exclusive focus on the seriousness of the offence and the need for general deterrence, instead identifying the police's involvement in the death in custody as spurring the protesters. Grove J. of the Court of Criminal Appeal recognized that 'a number of people had acquired a notion that the death of Lloyd Boney had, in some fashion, been facilitated or even brought about by acts of police officers' (1991: 1–2). Grove J. held that many of the 'adherents to the[se] beliefs' were part of the 'large crowd of mourners' at the funeral (1991: 2). Boney was released, having served 75 days, because the 'subjective consideration of the applicant's close relationship to the person believed to have died unnecessarily must have borne some weight' (1991: 6).

The contrast between the District Court's reasoning and that of the Court of Criminal Appeal reveals how new fantasies of social harmony vacillate, as Rutherford (2000: 57) suggests, between moments of lawlessness and lawfulness in the law's narratives about Indigenous offenders. Invoking Lacan's psychoanalysis, Rutherford (2000: 57) explains that the nation seeks to transgress the 'pleasure principle' through morality *and* aggression to the Other.[6] In its sentencing

5 There was no reporting of the lower court's reasons for Glen Boney's initial sentence.

6 Lacan posits that the 'pleasure principle' is a limit to enjoyment (*jouissance*). It is a 'law that commands the subject to "enjoy as little as possible"' (cf. Freud who regards the pleasure principle as the exclusive desire of the id – a personality trait that produces urges and impulses). Accordingly,

considerations, the Court of Criminal Appeal acknowledged the fraught relations between the police and Indigenous communities that placed considerable stress on offenders as relevant to reducing the culpability of the offender and the seriousness of the offence. The court regarded the Indigenous community as having legitimate grievances in relation to the death in custody. It displayed sympathy for the circumstances of the community and the offenders, while denouncing the District Court's view that Indigenous people and their 'liberal rights' should be blamed for their hardship. For the Court of Criminal Appeal, the moral cause of the Brewarrina rioters due to their personal loss and political grievances was a means to lessen their culpability.

The remainder of this chapter addresses how courts sentencing riot offenders over the past decade have focused on the seriousness of the riot offence rather than culpability. They have reimagined the Indigenous community grievances over the death in custody, which culminated in the riot, as an illegitimate ground for mitigation. It reveals the foreboding aspect of the Australian psyche where the fantasy of a universal white culture denies the validity of specific Indigenous concerns and deems them irrational. It is the realization of the swing from 'good white' nationalism to 'evil white' nationalism (Hage 1998: 79).

Punitive approaches to sentencing Redfern 'rioters' after the death of 'TJ' Hickey

In more recent years, sentencing courts have regarded Indigenous violent offenders who have been provoked by racism as out-of-control. They are perceived as products of dysfunctional Indigenous communities that are incapable of reasoned responses. This view enabled courts to construe Indigeneity as grounds for sentencing aggravation in relation to the riot offence. This is exemplified in the sentencing of Indigenous people who were part of a protest at Redfern after the death of a young Indigenous boy during a police chase and on Palm Island after the death of a well-respected Indigenous man in police custody.

Redfern 'riot' and media portrayals

At least since the late 1960s, the Redfern Indigenous community has been subject to over-policing and police aggression, and has responded with resistance (Cunneen 1990). The over-policing of Redfern, including police raids throughout the 1990s, sparked public protests and widespread policy debates (Cunneen 2001: 99–100). The 'Redfern riot' that took place on the night of 15 February 2004 was the culmination of these tense Indigenous–police relations (Funnell 2005). The high-level policing of Redfern perpetuated 'notions of risk and

the subject constantly attempts to transgress the prohibitions set by the pleasure principle: see Žižek (2007).

ever-present danger' and 'enabled a widespread expectation and acceptance that The Block must go' (Shaw 2009: 432; Shaw 2000: 298–9). Indigenous people's resistance to white claims to The Block and over-policing often manifests in 'quiet persistence' to hold on to their space (Ormesher 1995: 21). However, it can also erupt in contestation, as occurred after Thomas 'TJ' Hickey's death.

Hickey was a 17-year-old Indigenous boy who lived at Redfern and was impaled on a fence as a result of a police chase that was observed by Indigenous community members. There was a widely held belief within the Indigenous community that the police were responsible for the death.[7] Within a few hours of Hickey's death, posters were put around Redfern stating 'WANTED Child Murderers' and featuring pictures of the police (Kennedy *et al.* 2004: 1). Wilkinson, an Aboriginal community liaison officer, claimed that 'the police actually rammed the young kid' (quoted in Jackson 2004: 5). Hickey's mother was quoted as saying, 'these dogs [the police] . . . kill[ed] my son' (Anon 2004c). Hickey's friends and family maintained that he was terrified of the police as a result of being beaten by the police a few weeks earlier (Moon and Munckton 2004).

The Redfern 'riot' lasted approximately 6 hours (Strike Force Coburn 2004: 52–4). The Police Minister stated that the police were never 'overwhelmed' by the rioters (Totaro *et al.* 2004: 1), although eight required hospital treatment (Corder 2004: 31). The pre-emptive mobilization of riot police to Redfern on the day of TJ's death has been regarded as provoking the riot (Gargett 2005: 10). According to one commentary, witnesses said 'the police had not only incited the initial confrontation but had themselves acted violently' (Birch 2004: 18). The mainstream media focused on the blameworthiness of the Indigenous 'rioters' and neglected the grievances of the rioters. It brought to the fore long-term white anxieties about the Indigenous Other occupying space at Redfern. The moral panic pervaded the *Daily Telegraph*'s reporting, which stressed the unjustified violence by an 'uncontrollable mob' and vehemently defended the police against suggestions that they were to blame for TJ's death (Penberthy and Kamper 2004: 1; Miranda 2004: 2). This was also the view put in *The Australian*, which claimed that suspicion of a police chase of TJ 'was based more on rumour than reason' (Chulov *et al.* 2004: 1; Anon 2004a: 12). Coined as a 'race riot' (Corder 2004: 31), the media framed the violence as a racial outburst rather than the expression of frustration towards institutional injustices.

The media represented the police's role in the riot purely in terms of victimization from 'hordes of Aborigines' (Barrett 2004: 5; Atherfold 2006: 43). Police were championed as sacrificing 'their well-being to return order to the streets' (Gargett 2005: 10). In defence of the police, the *Daily Telegraph* made a call for the '[Indigenous] participants of this outrageous incident . . . [to] be identified and prosecuted' (Anon 2004b: 26). These sentiments in the media were echoed

7 Indicating this ongoing belief among members of the Indigenous community at Redfern, hundreds of people rallied at the place TJ Hickey was impaled by the police on 14 February 2012 to commemorate 8 years since his death and protest against black deaths in custody: Bassi 2012.

in the report of Strike Force Coburn (2004: 7), which the police instigated to investigate the 'civil disobedience at Redfern'. It emphasized the out-of-control and drunken mob mentality of the Indigenous rioters. Funnell (2005: 6) claims that the report revealed a 'complete neglect of the underlying causes of the riot'. In the mainstream media, the only 'cause' countenanced was the sense of helplessness among the Redfern Indigenous community due to 'depression, drug and alcohol addiction, and a life of petty criminality' (Gargett 2005: 9, citing Priest 2004: 13). Carlton (2004: 26) wrote in the *Sydney Morning Herald* that the community was 'lashed by scourges of alcohol, heroin, prostitution, crime, illiteracy, innumeracy and ignorance'. Signifying the lack of control that Indigenous people have over alcohol, the media focused on Indigenous protesters using beer bottles as weapons (Eastley 2004). A report in *The Australian News Commentary* blamed so-called 'liberal rights', which have been afforded to Indigenous people since the 1970s, for their problems. In this report, Marshall (2004) suggests that rights have not been exercised responsibly, but have nurtured an unfounded sense of historical self-entitlement among Indigenous people, which surfaced in the Redfern 'riot':

> Years of pandering to Aboriginals with massive welfare payments and special privileges while simultaneously fuelling their resentment by dwelling on past grievances, blew up in the faces of the social engineers, do-gooders and the politically correct elites on a hot February night in the Aboriginal ghetto of Redfern when a horde of rampaging, rioting Aboriginals torched the Redfern railway station and then set about assaulting police with bricks, bottles and fire-bombs.
>
> (Marshall 2004)

This imagery of an out-of-control community with irrational despair prevented understandings of the 'riot' as a reasoned response to police involvement in TJ's death. It also enforced a narrative that The Block had spiralled into 'uncontrollable lawlessness and incivility' to justify plans for its closure (Shaw 2009: 431). Shaw (2009: 431) argues that '"Whiteness" was threatened during the riot as [its] control was lost'. Accordingly, new fantasies emerged about the need for police to be defended.

Trials and sentencing of the Redfern 'rioters'

Fourteen people were charged following the Redfern riot, with the offences of riot, affray, violent disorder, throwing a missile and assaulting police. The two cases that were reported in the media were those of Marilyn Cargill, who was TJ's aunt, and Raymond Carr, TJ's cousin. The audio recording of the review of Cargill's sentence was accessed from the New South Wales District Court; all other sentencing remarks were quoted in mainstream newspapers. Initially, the Redfern Local Court refused Cargill bail due to the seriousness of the offence arising from the threats made against police. This was in spite of Cargill's plea for permission to attend TJ's funeral and her grief from the loss of her nephew, TJ Hickey (Corder 2004: 31). Despite 'vague and unspecific' evidence, based on police testimony, linking Cargill to the riot, she was convicted and imprisoned for one year based on the seriousness of the offence (New South Wales District Court quoted in Levett and Kennedy 2004: 6). The District Court held that her anger at the death was not relevant. When her sentence was reviewed after three months, following a parole and probation report recommendation, the District Court released Cargill from prison citing mental health problems and the fact that Cargill 'regarded the young person TJ Hickey as a son and was most distressed in regards to his death' (*R.* v. *Cargill* 2005). In this forum alone, the court was willing to concede that TJ's death caused personal despair to Cargill.

The deemed ringleader of the riot, Raymond Carr, was also charged with riot, affray, throwing bottles at police and maliciously damaging a police car (Colman 2004: 7). Carr told the Central Local Court in Sydney that he threw bottles at police and cars because 'he was angry at the death of Thomas Hickey' (quoted in Colman 2004: 7). Magistrate Moore refused bail, saying that the defendant played 'a significant role' in the Redfern riot and the seriousness of the offence was to prevail over the reasons that explained his culpability (Central Local Court (Sydney) quoted in Colman 2004: 7). His prison sentence of 12 months reflected the objective seriousness of the offence (quoted in 2004: 7). On appeal, the District Court refused to consider mitigating evidence of TJ's death during the police chase. The court focused on the harm caused by Carr, stating that the sentence 'was about as low' as he could hand down, given that he smashed a vehicle window and brandished pavers at police (District Court (NSW) quoted in Lamont 2005: 5). Although the quotes from the judgments are mostly based on selective media reporting and one audio recording of court proceedings, it appears from the Cargill and Carr cases that the courts were mindful foremost of the seriousness of the offence. For the courts, the defining feature of the riot was the threat it posed to the police. The riot was isolated from the spatial contest and provocative policing in Redfern. In this way, the court was playing the role of the 'spatial manager', who constructs the Other as 'standing between them and their imaginary nation' (Hage 1998: 47). Hage (1998: 47) describes spatial managers as seeking to remove 'undesirable' Others from 'national [non-Indigenous] space'. Courts not only have the discursive power to manage space, but also the punitive capacity for enforcement, which was used unhesitatingly with the Redfern rioters. This power would be taken a step further in sentencing the protesters to Mulrunji's death in custody on Palm Island.

The Palm Island protest and the sentencers' denial of the death in custody

In the sentencing of the Palm Island riot offenders of 2004, the Queensland Court of Appeal and Townsville District Court ruled that the death in custody of Mulrunji was not a relevant consideration. This position converged with a moral panic about the riot and its unruly Indigenous participants who were without a legitimate cause. The judicial remarks and media reports reflected a broader social misgiving about the riot and the dysfunctional status of the Indigenous community on Palm Island. However, the media and sentencing process did not identify its tumultuous history as a matter of context and mitigation, but focused on the irrationality and uncivilized nature of the rioters and the serious harm caused by the riot. In reality, the riot merely brought into the limelight the historical problems on Palm Island, including punitive policing, which are a legacy of the Island's formation as a penal colony for Indigenous people in the 1920s (Hooper 2008: 11).

Background to the Palm Island riot and media indignation

On the eve of 19 November 2004, Senior Sergeant Chris Hurley arrested and detained Mulrunji Doomadgee. Mulrunji was a widely-respected 36-year-old Palm Islander who had virtually no criminal record, and was arrested for offensive language (Watson 2010: 2; Glowczewski and Wotton 2008: 63). Forty minutes later he was dead in the island's police station. A coronial inquiry found that Sergeant Hurley was also responsible for Mulrunji's death, which resulted from a range of injuries, including a ruptured liver and portal vein, four broken ribs and a black eye (*Inquest into the Death of Mulrunji* 2006: 27). Following the death, Sergeant Hurley's 'mates' who had been connected with his police command, investigated the death and Hurley's role (*The Queen* v. *Wotton* 2008: 2–3). The 'relationships between the investigating police officers and the police officer under investigation' sent a message to the Indigenous community that injustice would prevail (*R.* v. *Wotton* 2007: [4]). Both the arrest and the investigation were contrary to the recommendations of the Royal Commission into Aboriginal Deaths in Custody (1991), which sought to prevent such deaths from occurring.[8] Anger within the community intensified when Indigenous people were told that Mulrunji's death occurred accidentally when he slipped on a step (*The Queen* v. *Wotton* 2008: 3).

Public meetings were held in the following week to discuss the death and prejudicial investigation. This culminated in a protest on 26 November 2004 in which approximately 300 people (one-eighth of the Palm Island population) assembled at the police station demanding that the police leave. The Queensland Government sent 80 Tactical Response Group commandos to the island

8 The Royal Commission into Aboriginal Deaths in Custody (1991) recommended refraining from arresting Indigenous people for offensive language (Recommendation 86(a)) and that arrest should be the sanction of 'last resort' (Recommendation 87). It also recommended that an investigation into a death in custody should be conducted independently from the responsible officers and not be connected with the police command in which the death occurred (Recommendations 27 and 33).

(Hunter 2005: 16). The gathering threw stones and mangoes at the police building and yelled abuse at the police. The police officers were armed, pointed rifles on the crowd and were prepared to fire (*R.* v. *Wotton* 2007: [6]–[7]). The officers ultimately retreated to the hospital. Over the next three hours, the barracks, police station and courthouse, 'which were all part of a fairly modest complex of prefabricated buildings', burned down (Carrick 2008). Some officers sustained minor injuries, but there were no serious injuries. Nonetheless, the Queensland Police Union, Queensland Police Commissioner and Queensland Government ran a concerted campaign to highlight the sacrificial police role in the riot. This went hand in hand with their campaign to absolve Hurley of any wrongdoing associated with Mulrunji's death and to undermine the prosecution against him (Queensland Police Union 2005: 26; Eastley 2004a; Willoughby 2007: 4).[9] Newspapers reported 'Police Lost Everything in Island Riots, Says Union' (Anon 2004d) and '[Premier] Beattie Defends Police Tactics in Island Riot' (Pavey 2004).

The protest on Palm Island flooded the national media. In the mainstream media, it was portrayed as an impulsive event that was incited by a 'mob' of rioters. No reference was made to the compromised investigation into Mulrunji's death in custody and generally there was scant reference to the death in custody that precipitated the riot (Little 2010: 51). Headlines such as 'Palm Island Erupts' (Mancuso and Connolly 2004) and 'Palm Island Explodes: Anarchy on Palm Island on Knife's Edge Overnight' (Lineham and Seeney 2004: 1) cast the rioters as uncontrollable and irrational, without cause or reason. The media constructed the riot as spontaneous and excessive, rather than as arising from legitimate grievances in relation to the police. The pathos of the community and its deplorable living conditions were also highlighted (Cunneen 2007). As with the Redfern riot, the police were depicted as being terrorized by the Palm Islander mob (Ketchell *et al.* 2004: 30). Newspaper headlines that reflected this included: 'How Rioters Set Trap for Police – Unarmed Officers Feared They Would Die as 300 Rampaged Trap for Police' (Ketchell *et al.* 2004a: 4) and 'Police Tell of Terror' (Ketchell 2004: 6). These reports resonated with the judicial focus on the seriousness of the harm for the police.

Grievances of Palm Island rioters nullified and police victimization magnified in sentencing

The Palm Island protest resulted in a number of participants being charged with offences, including assaulting police, riotous assembly and rioting causing

9 It was only after an independent review of the coronial evidence and a prosecution outside the office of the Director of Public Prosecutions that the responsible officer, Senior Sergeant Hurley, was prosecuted for the death of Mulrunji. Hurley was acquitted of manslaughter in June 2007. Hurley was the first police officer prosecuted for an Aboriginal death in custody: see Mackenzie *et al.* (2007).

destruction. Lex Wotton was the most widely publicized protester, and would ultimately receive the harshest penalty (discussed below), but it was not his sentence that provided the precedent. The main appeal to the Queensland Court of Appeal was brought by the Attorney-General against the sentences of Jason Poynter, Alissa Norman and Russell Parker on the grounds that the sentence of the Townsville District Court failed 'to reflect the seriousness of the offence' (*R.* v. *Poynter, Norman & Parker* 2006: [15], [21], [28]). At first instance, Townsville District Court had accounted for the death in custody as a relevant sentencing factor. For instance, in relation to Norman, the court noted that she attended the meeting that led to the 'riot' 'out of a genuine interest in how the death had occurred'. It noted that 'she shared the crowd's frustration . . . that their concerns really had not been dealt with, that they really had not been fully informed' of the issues surrounding the death in custody (Townsville District Court quoted in 2006: [20]).

The Queensland Court of Appeal upheld the Attorney-General's appeal to the sentences and provided a clear statement that that death in custody was not a relevant sentencing consideration, given the seriousness of the riot offence and police victimization. The court denounced the rioters for targeting 'members of the police service, the very agency charged to maintain the security of persons and their property' (*R.* v. *Poynter, Norman & Parker* 2006: [30]). It failed to recognize the gathering's grievance that such protection had not been afforded to Mulrunji. The victimization of police rendered the riot 'distinctly grave' (2006: [35]). At the same time, the court accepted that there were no serious injuries (the worst being a fractured rib), and the greatest threat was to the rioters themselves (2006: [29]). De Jersey C.J. was particularly evocative in his description of the protest: 'The crowd descended on the police barracks, where the police were bunkered inside. Threats were shouted at the police officers' (2006: [5]). The court quoted a victim's impact statement by a police officer that recalled that he had 'made a cold, logical decision to fire into a large crowd if necessary' (2006: [29]). However, it was the threat presented by the riot to the police that was the significant consideration in sentencing (2006: [5]). The court referred to the 60 pages of victim impact statements provided by police officers that described 'the terror they experienced' and how they 'feared for their lives, with some telephoning family members to say goodbye' (2006: [5]). Illustrating the righteousness of the police force, the court referred to 'one officer [who] feels his Catholic faith and ability to live up to the precepts of it have faced a challenge which he may not be able to overcome' (2006: [29]).

The Court of Appeal noted repeatedly the need to deter riot offenders and the Indigenous community generally from committing such offences (2006: [30], [38]). McMurdo P. described riots as 'terrifying and destructive' and said the Palm Island riot was a 'notorious event in Queensland's history' that could not be allowed to occur again (2006: [60], [71]). The Chief Justice quoted *R.* v. *McCormack* (1981: 109) on the necessity of a custodial sentence for riot offenders to promote deterrence: 'courts have commonly regarded an attack on the police in the execution of their duty as calling for custodial sentence with a deterrent component' (*R.* v. *Poynter, Norman & Parker* 2006: [33]). The Court of Appeal's approach to deterrence assumed that the rioters were acting with free and individual agency and overlooked the context that impelled the protest. The court viewed the offenders as acting according to a rational calculation of punishment rather than a deep-seated grievance.

Ultimately, the court decided that the death in custody was not a relevant sentencing consideration. It stated that the fact that 'one police officer is *perceived* – whether or not with justification – to have done a terribly bad thing, does not justify the wholesale, violent, condemnation of the contingent of which he forms part' (2006: [35], emphasis added). McMurdo P. remarked that 'Mulrunji's death . . . and its subsequent investigation . . . does not excuse the rioters' resort to lawlessness in pursuit of their cause' (2006: [71]). He went on to note that the 'rioters could have expressed their concerns through lawful channels' (2006: [71]). After all, they had been told that 'an inquiry was underway and the matter was to be referred to the Crime and Misconduct Commission' (2006: [71]). De Jersey C.J. stated unequivocally that the death in custody lacked significance:

> Mr Devereaux SC, who appeared for the respondent Parker, submitted that 'the riot in this case was not directed at police as a result of their carrying out their lawful duty, but was a response to perceived unlawful fatal violence by a police officer on a community member'. *That may be, but for sentencing purposes, the point lacks significance.*
>
> (*R.* v. *Poynter, Norman & Parker* 2006: [31], emphasis added)

The court stressed that 'mob conduct at the police station was a reaction which could not be tolerated in a civilized community' (2006: [36]). It pointed to 'recent and not so recent world history [that] illustrates the immense danger wrought by riots' and their potential to lead to 'anarchy' (2006: [37], [39]). This is a bold departure from Murphy J.'s sentiment in *Neal* v. *The Queen* (1982: 318) that 'agitators' facilitate the 'advance towards civilisation'. In *R.* v. *Poynter, Norman & Parker* (2006), the Indigenous community was imagined not only as lacking a cause, but also as lacking civilization. The Queensland Court of Appeal's imagery of an uncivilized anarchical mob terrorizing defenceless police reflects the media's representation of the Indigenous community as uncontrollable. This message was carried through in the sentencing of Lex Wotton.

Application of decontextualized sentencing approach to Lex Wotton

Lex Wotton was regarded as the ringleader of the Palm Island riot, although the courts did not establish whether he was an instigator or conciliator between the rioters and police.[10] He was charged with partaking in a riot in which a building was destroyed. Of the Palm Islanders involved in the protest, Wotton was charged with the most severe offence. The 37-year-old was a long-term Indigenous activist and community leader who was involved in rehabilitation and healing programmes (*The Queen* v. *Wotton* 2008: 13). These facts were taken into account in relation to Wotton's character, but not in relation to understanding Wotton's culpability in the riot itself.[11] The police described him as a serious offender and the office of the Director of Public Prosecutions sought to make an example of him by pressing the most severe charges. Indeed, police identified Wotton 'as the person that they would shoot first' if the riot turned sour (*The Queen* v. *Wotton* 2008: 11). Ultimately, Wotton would receive the longest sentence of all the rioters.

In December 2008, four years after the protest, the Townsville District Court sentenced Wotton to six years' imprisonment, eligible for parole after two years. In the meantime, Wotton had faced a trial by media, adverse police publicity and criticisms by courts hearing preliminary matters that he was 'morally wrong' (*R.* v. *Wotton* 2007: [8]). The District Court followed the Queensland Court of Appeal's reasoning in *R.* v. *Poynter, Norman & Parker* (2006) by disavowing the circumstances of the death in custody and the mishandled investigation, and focusing instead on deterrence and the seriousness of the offence, especially as police officers were victims. District Court Judge Shanahan noted:

> . . . the Court of Appeal has indicated that *the background to this matter* [ie the death in custody] *is not particularly relevant* for the purpose of the sentence. The reason for that, in my view, is the serious nature of the offence itself, rioting with destruction.
>
> (*The Queen* v. *Wotton* 2008: 2)

The District Court recognized that the 'history and disadvantages of Palm Island' – which include widespread poverty, unemployment and illness – '[are] not something for which successive administrations of this State and the Commonwealth could in any way be proud' (2008: 2). This acknowledgement did not result in sentencing mitigation, but merely recognition of the hopelessness of the Indigenous population. Shanahan J. concluded that 'it is a community that faces a number of serious problems and has for a number of years' (2008: 2). The riot was viewed as part of these problems (2008: 2) rather than caused by the problem of failed white control. The District Court's reasoning contrasts with

10 The Townsville District Court heard evidence that Wotton attempted to assist the police to get off the island in order to prevent their harm: *The Queen v. Wotton* (2008: 8–9).

11 These submissions were accepted per the Penalties and Sentences Act 1992 (Qld) s. 9(2)(p), which allows 'any submissions made by a representative of the community justice group in the [Indigenous] offender's community'. This provision coexists with s. 9(2)(g), which provides that the court 'must have regard to the presence of any aggravating or mitigating factor concerning the offender'.

that of the High Court's in *Neal* v. *The Queen* (1982: 318), in which Indigenous dissent was treated as a product of, and a valid response to, white authority. The District Court and the Queensland Court of Appeal primarily considered the serious danger presented by the riot to 'ideal' police victims and the uncivilized nature of the Palm Island community (*R.* v. *Poynter, Norman & Parker* 2006: [36], [39]). This judicial mindset underpins punitive sentences that seek to teach the offender and the Indigenous community a lesson through a lengthy prison sentence.

Concluding remarks: sentencing in a spatial fantasy

Sentencing leniency based on fantasies of the benevolent judicial-self swings to punitive responses when spatial contests threaten the dominant order. This is based on the Janus-faced Australian nationalism that portrays 'good nationalism' through tolerance of the Indigenous Other and 'evil nationalism' through coercive integration of the Other (Rutherford 2000: 27; Hage 1998: 79). Recent sentencing remarks dealing with Indigenous protesters have privileged considerations of the seriousness of the offence with reference to the harm to police victims over considerations of the racist circumstances provoking the riot, including deaths in custody for which Indigenous people have long been over-represented. These courts in New South Wales and Queensland have referred to the 2004 Redfern and Palm Island rioters as out-of-control and uncivilized. They have retreated from attributing the rioters with a legitimate political grievance as the High Court did in *Neal* v. *The Queen* and the New South Wales Court of Criminal Appeal did in the Brewarrina cases in the 1980s. The Indigenous community is cast as presenting a serious danger to society due to its impulsive violence directed at the police.

In reimagining Indigenous communities in order to lengthen prison sentences, courts set up a number of culturally contingent binaries. The danger of the offence committed by the Indigenous person is contrasted with the innocence of police victims. The disorder of the Indigenous community is contrasted with the law and order provided by the police. The uncivilized anarchy of the Indigenous community is contrasted with the civilization of white society. Pervading these binaries is the enforcement of neutral sentencing principles of serious harm and victimization that ostensibly remove considerations of Indigenous difference. However, when applied, they give rise to longer sentences for Indigenous offenders by ignoring factors that may reduce their culpability, including the death in custody and the over-policing of Indigenous spaces. Cowlishaw (2004: 237) comments that the legal arena provides 'no moment when the rioters' rage [can] be attended to, and no possibility of any respect being paid to [the riot's] genesis or its justification'. This is because courts have come to focus on the violence alone and thereby reinforce the threat of the Indigenous Other. Judicial responses and media moral panics in relation to Indigenous riots bring into the limelight the underlying nationalist impulse to assert a non-Indigenous order over the

Indigenous Other (Hage 1998: 17). As with narratives of dysfunction, narratives of anarchy preclude a recognition of Indigenous communities as functional entities capable of determining their own paths, structuring their own authority and responding to deep-seated grievances – thus diminishing their position in the spatial contest.

Chapter 8

Conclusion: transforming Indigenous recognition

> Escape from self-enclosure depends on continuing resistance, on the resurgence of the other, that which transgresses existing limits, introduces the new and unexpected, and reopens the dialogue through which social forms are renewed and revitalised.
>
> (Falzon 1998: 59)

The sentencer's recognition of Indigeneity is a problematic premise for legal plurality in the Australian criminal justice system. At best, the sentencer's use of discretion can instrumentally structure sentences to soften the devastating effect of incarceration on Indigenous Australians. Epistemologically, it creates knowledges of Indigenous cultures, laws and experiences through channelling Indigenous viewpoints. At worst, recognition in sentencing can produce harsher penalties to deter the practice of Indigenous cultures and customary laws. It can never foster Indigenous laws because the source of recognition presides in dominant Anglo-Australian institutions that exist due to the subordination of Indigenous societies.

Through the sentencing vignettes of each chapter, this book showed how the recognizer appropriates stock stories of Indigenous 'difference': the barbaric and over-sexualized Indigenous offender who exhibits too much culture; the 'traditional' Indigene who executes retribution through violence; the drunken and idle offender living on the urban periphery, and the out-of-control Indigene who is unable to reasonably respond to grievances. These stories increasingly converge on a notion of Indigeneity as a crime risk. This concluding chapter argues that for recognition to provide a semblance of legal plurality, the dispensation of lighter prison sentences alone is insufficient. Indigenous people need to be involved in the recognition process. This means, to adopt Fraser's (1996: 54) theory, recognition must be deconstructed so the recognized becomes the recognizer.

Indigenous peoples' involvement in punishment and dispute resolution processes would enable the Indigenous community to impose and manage sentences that restore their communities. Within this alternative imagining, the Indigenous defendant's community would also regulate the entry points to the Anglo-Australian criminal justice system for the offender. Moving away from the affirmation of stereotyped identities and towards deconstructed identities can give Indigenous communities a stake in the justice process. Following a review of the weaknesses of judicial recognition of Indigeneity, this chapter discusses mechanisms for empowering communities in criminal justice processes.

Weaknesses of affirmative acts of recognition

Judicial interpretations of Indigenous 'difference' in each of the sentencing vignettes bring to life the contingent nature of recognition. Courts make or deny surface gestures again and again in order to assert their privileged position (Fraser 1996: 45–6). These are referred to as 'affirmative acts' because they affirm the superior status of institutions in relation to the inferior Other (Fraser 2000: 114). As a pliable instrument, recognition provides no guarantee for Indigenous justice and is prone to non-recognition and misrecognition (Fraser 2004: 29). Courts vacillate between lenient and harsh punishment; between accommodation and discrimination, based on their ever-changing characterization of the place of Indigenous alterity in postcolonial society. However, the weakness of recognition is more than its susceptibility to change, but rather its inherent subordination to dominant discourses. This subordination arises from the Anglo-Australian institutional framework that is based on the unlawful displacement of Indigenous law systems. It is reinforced through recognition where the Other is marked as 'deficient and insatiable, as always needing more and more' recognition (Fraser 1997: 29). This stigmatizes Indigenous people by setting 'them' up as dependent on the benevolence of Anglo-Australian institutions. Recognition can never de-criminalize Indigenous people because the judicial recognizer is part of the criminalizing process. Its tendency to penality is no more evident than where piecemeal offerings of leniency are washed away by the punitive tide and the judicial will to incapacitate and exclude.

The misrecognition and non-recognition of Indigeneity in criminal sentencing cohere with colonizing ideologies. Dodson (1994: 9) points out that Indigenous identity is constantly subject to the whim of the colonizer without genuine negotiation with Indigenous peoples. Courts engage in myth creation about Indigenous people in remote, urban and contested spaces. This is predicated on notions of 'white' spatial ownership and the capacity of the recognizer to tolerate or exclude the Other (Hage 1998: 58–9). Harris (1995: 283) affirms that whiteness and white spaces exist because of racial subjugation. Labelling Indigenous Australians, their cultures and laws as deviant assures their position as 'outsiders' and their exclusion from space and shared community values (Becker 1991: 9; Anderson 1983; Said 1978). A nationalist anxiety about the Other cements the 'white' community and solidifies its affective bonds. Indigenous exclusion over the past decade has been informed by discourses of Indigenous dysfunctionality and non-functionality. This corresponds with a view that Indigenous communities are increasingly part of the crime problem rather than part of the solution. The relocation of the recognition goalposts in sentencing in the Northern Territory, New South Wales and Queensland has coincided with moral panics over Indigenous communities, unearthing social anxieties over the deviant Other (Hogg 2005: 341; Hall *et al.* 1978; Durkheim 1982: 50–2).

Legal representations of Indigenous offenders and their communities have much broader currency than in law alone. Legal narratives in sentencing reproduce a normative universe (*nomos*) that subordinates Indigenous people (Cover 1983–4: 4). Cover (1983–4: 5) explains that laws are intrinsic to their narratives, such that law becomes 'not merely a system of rules to be observed, but a world in which we live'. The hermeneutic devise of 'legal storytelling' reveals law as a bridge between real and imagined Indigeneity. Narratives that cross this bridge are tied to dominant epistemologies that operate throughout postcolonial institutions. The multiple contexts of judicial shifts in Indigenous sentencing exhibit a broad misgiving about Indigenous communities. The media and politicians have been strident in representing Indigenous communities and their members as culturally backward and dysfunctional. As discussed in Chapter 4, the Federal Government and commentators have focused on the failure of Indigenous communities in remote parts of Australia; those least affected by colonization and those heavily guided by their laws and cultures. Senior government advisers have described remote Indigenous communities as presenting a 'security risk'; that their 'endemic social dysfunction' will flow into larger centres to create 'zones of violence and disorder' (Dillon 2007: 5–6; Dillon and Westbury 2007: 30). Mainstream commentators have alternatively criticized Indigenous peoples in urban areas who overstate their Indigenous identity to get benefits from the (white) system (Bolt 2009: 22; Sutton 2009: 57–8). Both strands resonate with legal portrayals of Indigenous offenders as personifying the failure of the Indigenous community.

While there is a body of law that affords leniency on the basis of Indigeneity, especially in the 1980s and early 1990s, the common law does not provide an assured inlet for the engagement of Indigenous perspectives in sentencing. Consequently, courts can recognize, misrecognize or not recognize Indigenous identities and circumstances. The sentencing remarks traced in this book demonstrate the weakness of an affirmative approach to recognition that reinforces the laws of the postcolonial order. The apparent justice of recognition can rapidly turn into an injustice when its dark side emerges to exclude and condemn alterity. The peril of recognition is particularly powerful in the criminal justice system because of its attendant images of Indigenous barbarism. The higher courts in the Northern Territory, New South Wales and Queensland have drawn moral boundaries around Indigenous communities to demonstrate their threat to mainstream legal norms. Whether over-cultured, under-cultured or pursuing an improper culture, Indigenous communities are presented as a threat to mainstream legal norms.

Reflecting on the sentencing vignettes

This book has shown how in relation to a number of sentencing vignettes, Indigeneity has become framed as a threat. The courts have endeavoured to send *special* messages of deterrence through lengthy prison terms. Because of the risk of Indigenous communities and the vulnerability of their members, the crimes of Indigenous offenders are regarded as *particularly* serious. This mode of representation, like those of the past, is moulded to dominant social policies pertaining to Indigenous people. The contemporary era of policy-making is variously expressed as coercive intervention targeted at difference or liberal assimilationism through mainstreaming services and imposing formal equality (Howard-Wagner 2010). In sentencing, longer prison sentences have been justified for Indigenous defendants by, on the one hand, highlighting their dangerous 'difference', and on the other hand, emphasizing universal sentencing principles of deterrence, seriousness of the harm and interests of the wider community.

In all the sentencing vignettes – Indigenous culture, punishment, disadvantage and political protest – the legal justification for Indigenous recognition is judicial discretion to consider relevant 'material facts' (*Neal* v. *The Queen* 1982: 326). Indigenous defendants do not attract special leniency merely by virtue of being Indigenous (*Fernando* 1992: 62). Rather, they receive the same consideration as all other offenders, in the interests of an 'even' administration of justice (*Neal* v. *The Queen* 1982: 326; *Rogers & Murray* v. *R.* 1989: 307). The choice to mitigate or aggravate a sentence depends on how the courts conceive the Indigenous community and its circumstances, as well as how they seek to transform Indigenous communities. Further, the discretion to account for Indigenous difference is also the discretion to deny it. The judicial imagining of the Indigenous community as exercising legitimate cultures, or otherwise beset by legitimate problems of postcolonial society, reduces the culpability of the offender. By contrast, notions of Indigenous communities as exercising inappropriate cultures, or suffering from their own pathos and dysfunction, results in aggravated sentences to deter others in the community.

The slippery slope of recognition comes to the fore in sentencing considerations where cultural practice and customary law explain the commission of the crime. The Northern Territory Supreme Court regards offenders who have committed offences in circumstances of customary marriage, jealousing and involvement in Indigenous law punishment as defying non-Indigenous social norms. Chapter 4 showed how these practices have been grounds for lengthy prison sentences in the name of deterrence. In addition, the Northern Territory's higher courts have encouraged the abandonment of cultural practices such as customary marriage. For these courts, Indigenous law marriage offends non-Indigenous morality, and defendants who rely on these circumstances are classified as lustful old men (*R.* v. *GJ* 2005: 241). Blagg (2008: 172) wrote in relation to promised marriages that 'Aboriginal women's bodies have acted as a palimpsest for the inscription of white fears of unrestrained native sexuality, as represented particularly by the tribal Aboriginal male'. Anxieties over Indigenous sexuality are not only channelled into notions of Indigenous victimization, but also affirmations of the beneficence and protectiveness of Anglo-Australian culture and law. Chapter 4 detailed how customary marriage, following the case of *Hales* v. *Jamilmira* (2003), spurned on a moral panic over Indigenous statutory rape and resulted in the criminalization of underage sex in customary marriage by the Northern Territory Legislative Assembly. While this arises from a legitimate concern for the needs of victims and the interests of the child, criminalization is a weak instrument for change. Rather, the 'Little Children are Sacred Report' of the Northern Territory's Board of Inquiry into the Protection of Aboriginal Children from Sexual Abuse found that protecting Indigenous victims and children requires engaging Indigenous communities (Wild and Anderson 2007: 71).

The alarm over Indigenous cultural practices also flowed into the Federal policy arena. Chapter 4 showed how the cultural offender has been a poignant subject for politicians and the mainstream media. This representation of the uncivilized Indigenous offender, who is let off lightly by the courts, galvanized support for punitive measures in order to protect helpless victims in Indigenous communities (Toohey 2002b: 21; Haebich 2000: 593–4). The Minister for Indigenous Affairs, Mal Brough, expressed gratitude that media reports on customary marriage have shocked the sensitivities of the Australian public to the core (Jones 2006). This highlights how crime and criminalization is normal and healthy for 'social life' (Durkheim 1933: 73). A moral panic over Indigenous cultural crimes since 2006 has endorsed the morality of non-Indigenous norms and the universality of non-Indigenous space. It resulted in coercive government policy in Northern Territory Indigenous communities and the suspension of the Racial Discrimination Act 1975 (Cth)[1] to sequestrate Indigenous spaces.

The moral panic over Indigenous cultural crimes unleashed the animalistic side of the state. As Derrida (2009) shows us, where the state disavows the law because of the perceived threat of the 'animal', the state displays its own animalistic tendency. In 2006, the Federal Police were deployed to Indigenous communities and intelligence taskforces were established with special powers in communities. There were also prohibitions placed on judicial discretion to consider cultural and customary law factors in sentencing (Crimes Act 1914 (Cth) s. 16A(2A)). A year later when the Report of the Inquiry into the Protection of Aboriginal Children from Sexual Abuse (Wild and Anderson 2007) was released, the army was sent to Northern Territory communities and a raft of controls over Indigenous peoples in remote communities was enacted (see Northern Territory National Emergency Response Act 2007 (Cth), hereinafter 'NTER Act').[2] This

1 This statute gives effect to Australia's ratification of the United Nations Convention on the Elimination of All Forms of Racial Discrimination (1965).

2 Controls over, e.g. welfare, computers, houses, Aboriginal land and alcohol consumption have translated into higher levels of formal and informal policing, including by government and health professionals (Anthony and Blagg 2012: 16).

legislation has been described as an aggressive annexation of Indigenous space, governance and land rights (Howard-Wagner 2008: 58), and has given non-Indigenous people 'permission to . . . unequivocally, unashamedly and unsentimentally' pursue a punitive agenda over Indigenous people (Goldflam 2012: 11). Unprecedented levels of Indigenous imprisonment in the Northern Territory have ensued. This is not due to the alleged sexual offending that fuelled the moral panic, but from minor offences such as driving without a licence or vehicle registration (Anthony 2010: 90; Anthony and Blagg 2012).

Misgivings about cultural practices underpinning the offenders' beliefs in committing crimes extend to misgivings over Indigenous forms of punishment that succeed crimes. Indigenous law punishment has attracted the same punitive response and judicial messages of deterrence. Chapter 5 considered the Northern Territory Supreme Court's re-evaluation of Indigenous punishment where it was physically inflicted on the offender, such as spearing. It also traced the reconceptualization of other forms of Indigenous punishment, including participation in ceremony, supervision by Elders and exile from the community. Over the past decade the court has placed less emphasis on community submissions in relation to its punishment, favouring the wider community's interest in imprisonment. The court has sent a strong message that anyone caught administering Indigenous law punishment will be subject to the full brunt of the Anglo-Australian law (*R.* v. *Wilson* 1995: 276; *The Queen* v. *Webb* 2003: 8; *The Queen* v. *Sims & Walker* 2012: 8). As such, it has positioned Anglo-Australian law as constituting the exclusive punitive domain. This reflects a disregard for the role of Indigenous punishment in quelling tensions in the Indigenous community that arise from the crime, restoring the victim and disciplining and rehabilitating the offender.

The Northern Territory Supreme Court's refusal to accommodate Indigenous punishment has given rise to longer prison sentences for defendants who have or will undergo Indigenous punishment. It has also resulted in bail being denied to defendants who will submit to Indigenous punishment while awaiting their trial. This is now reinforced by section 90 of the Federal Government's NTER Act, which precludes cultural and customary law considerations in bail determinations, and supplements section 91 of the same Act that precludes these considerations in sentencing mitigation and aggravation. Notwithstanding these legislative restrictions, the court has continued to signal to Indigenous communities its contempt for punishment outside of its judicial system (*The Queen* v. *Sims & Walker* 2012: 8). Government and judicial restrictions on Indigenous law punishment represent governance through cultural suppression. Indigenous laws are presented as a law and order problem that contributes to Indigenous risk, rather than a law and order solution that enables Indigenous rights.

The idea in sentencing that Indigenous communities and their laws lack functionality, and that their punishment systems are 'lawless' (*R.* v. *Wilson* 1995: 276; *The Queen* v. *Webb* 2003: 8), also arises in public outcries over Indigenous violence. According to the mainstream media and Federal Governments since the mid 1990s, violence in Indigenous communities is evidence of the failure of communities to self-govern following the so-called policy of 'self-determination' from the 1970s (Anthony 2009: 38–9).[3] Senior Federal Government advisers, Westbury and Dillon (2007), labelled the Indigenous community as a 'failed state', prone to erupt in violence at any time.[4] This discourse on Indigenous failure, dysfunction and violence allowed for 'new disciplining, prohibitive and corrective practices' directed exclusively at Indigenous people (Howard-Wagner 2010a: 218). It also provided a metaphor for the exclusivity of the postcolonial state, which helped to sustain a 'fanatical dream' of a monist legal order based on 'whiteness' (Motha 2005: 125).

The notion of the failed Indigenous community in need of reshaping is also espoused from the bench in relation to communities beset by alcoholism, socio-economic disadvantage and crime. In these instances, it is disadvantage rather than culture that is attributed to the offending. In recent years, as elaborated in Chapter 6, the Northern Territory Supreme Court aligned Indigenous disadvantage with community dysfunction to endorse harsh prison sentences. It reasoned that vulnerable victims require the protection of the courts in these abject and hopeless community circumstances.

This judicial dream of legal monism also arises in sentencing disadvantaged Indigenous offenders in New South Wales. There the Supreme Court and the Court of Criminal Appeal have perceived disadvantaged Indigenous communities as non-functional for the purpose of recognition. Chapter 6 discusses how these courts regard urban communities as insufficiently authentic to warrant Indigenous mitigation through the application of the *Fernando* principles. Also, Indigenous identity has been deemed irrelevant to sentencing where the offender is 'part' Aboriginal, with the New South Wales Court of Appeal drawing an artificial line between full and part Indigenous people (*Ceissman* 2001: 540). These distinctions assume a postcolonial erasure of Indigenous culture due to the imposition of white space and white genetic lineage. Once again, the courts create a chimera of an exclusively white legal order. In place of accommodations for Indigenous community disadvantage, the supreme courts in the Northern Territory and New South Wales have focused on the seriousness of the crime (*Wurramara* 1999: 521; *Ceissman* 2001: 541; *R.* v. *Newman, R.* v. *Simpson* 2004: 379).

Finally, Chapter 7 unpacked the judicial characterization of Indigenous communities where Indigenous claims to space and justice manifested in 'riots'. Higher courts in Queensland and New South Wales sentenced Indigenous protesters who were challenging state authority and resisting the policing of their space. Their grievances over racism, deaths in custody and over-policing, which once sounded in mitigation and reflected their reduced culpability, are no longer

3 These were very limited attempts to support Indigenous self-governance, which involved measures such as funding for Indigenous organizations and enacting land rights legislation that has thus far resulted in land being granted to a small portion of Australian Indigenous communities.

4 Westbury and Dillon (2007) latch on to the 'nothing works' mentality that arises in the contemporary response to the crisis of the welfare state and rising crime levels in the West (see Garland 2001).

regarded as legitimate sentencing considerations. Rather, these higher courts condemn the plight of Indigenous protesters, focusing on the seriousness of the threat to the police and the Anglo-Australian legal order through their acts of 'anarchy' (*R.* v. *Poynter, Norman & Parker* 2006: [37], [39]). The courts portray the Indigenous community in these circumstances as so hopelessly dysfunctional and lawless to possess any rationality in their protests (2006: [36], [39]; *The Queen* v. *Wotton* 2008: 4–5). The riot, as an irrational and unreasoned act, attracts harsh penalties. By underscoring the harm of the rioters, the courts figuratively exculpate the Anglo-Australian system for its wrongs inflicted on Indigenous communities that provoke the protesters. For the mainstream media, the Indigenous riot conveys the violent threat of the Other. Violence against the state is also depicted as inherent in 'their' lawless culture. Dillon (2007: 5–6) writes that Indigenous communities present security problems for Australian society where their 'ad hoc and opportunistic violence' lends itself to 'increased communal violence' and 'in the longer term opportunistic subversion and violence directed against government institutions'.

A historical analysis of sentencing across the vignettes of each chapter demonstrates a broad shift in judicial attitudes on the significance of Indigenous 'difference'. From the 1970s to approximately the mid 1990s, higher courts in the Northern Territory and New South Wales have regarded Indigenous circumstances as mitigating a sentence based on the cultural or economic disadvantage or injustice suffered by the offender. This approach was replaced with a judicial view that Indigenous difference was more of an aggravating than a mitigating factor due to the need to promote deterrence. This latter approach, developed over the last decade, is based on a perception of Indigenous communities as dysfunctional and plagued by endemic problems of alcoholism and physical and sexual abuse of its vulnerable members. In this respect, sentencing remarks resonate with policy views on the failures of Indigenous communities and the latitudes that they were granted from the 1970s, especially in relation to equal access to welfare, land rights and some provisions for self-determination (see Howard 2007; Hughes 2007; Sutton 2009; Johns 2011). Sentencing remarks on Indigeneity provide insights into how Indigenous alterity is imagined and managed in a postcolonial order.

The case for transformative justice

Overcoming the postcoloniality of recognition

Recognition can be regarded as a form of 'coloniality', which Tully (2008: 244–5) describes as imposing alien practices and knowledges over the Other. It manages a dialogue between the imposing self and the encountered other while always ensuring that the Other remains other, partially welcomed into the arrangement, but necessarily in a subordinate position, subjugated, inscribed as other by self, so as to further secure the legitimacy of self. Judicial recognition arises because of the imposing will of the court on the Indigene, which has endured in the criminal jurisdiction at least since the 1836 case of *Murrell*. The act of recognition creates a powerful metaphor for state legitimacy and control over the illegitimate Indigenous Other. It conceals the unlawful nature of the state's authority that is based on a fiction that prior to its sovereignty the land belonged to no one (*terra nullius*). It also erases the violent dispossession from the national memory (Watson 2011: 43). The content of recognition reinforces the order of Anglo-Australian society by focusing on the disorder of Indigenous societies and their proclivity for violence. This ultimately underlines the exclusivity of Anglo-Australian governance and undermines coexistence with Indigenous governance structures.

Any concessions provided through recognition, namely lenience in sentencing, are subject to constant scrutiny, and require ongoing surface gestures to maintain their relevance. This assures the institutional superiority of the recognizer (Fraser 1996: 46). While some offenders benefit from a lighter sentence because their Indigenous circumstances reduce their culpability, the results are piecemeal. Accordingly, recognition has not reduced the overrepresentation of Indigenous people in prisons, which has steadily risen since the 1991 Royal Commission into Aboriginal Deaths in Custody (Cunneen 2010: 44). Ad hoc dispensation of lighter prison sentences alone is insufficient for Indigenous justice because it does not threaten the position of the Anglo-Australian legal order over Indigenous peoples and laws. Leniency props up the sentencing mantle by enabling it to rest on claims to 'individualized justice'. Accordingly, sentencing considerations of Indigeneity feed the white racial fantasy of tolerance (Hage 1998: 17). On its flipside, the reasoning of 'individualized justice' also grants courts the discretion to deny consideration of Indigenous factors where the courts disparage or denounce their existence. Ultimately, recognition is provided on the terms and at the times that the courts so choose. Consequently, even where the legislature has sought to prohibit the recognition of Indigenous culture (NTER Act ss. 90–1), the Northern Territory Supreme Court has found spaces in the legislation to use its discretion to recognize Indigeneity, such as in relation to the character of the offender (see *R.* v. *Wunungmurra* 2009). Recognition is jealously guarded by the courts because it provides its only tool to govern Indigeneity and to transform their social norms.

As this book has shown, the institutional dominance of the courts allows recognition to be a gesture to condemn, exclude and punish as much as to valorize, include and accommodate. It tends to lead to misrecognition of Indigenous culture as violent in the Northern Territory and non-recognition of Indigeneity due to a perception of cultural assimilation in New South Wales. Maligning Indigenous communities or rendering invisible their Indigenous identity has resulted in harsh penalties for Indigenous peoples since the late 1990s and higher levels of incarceration. This has had the uncanny effect of Indigenous defendants now arguing for *formal* equality and the uniform application of criminal sanctions, because the recognition of their Indigeneity is a disadvantage to them as it produces longer sentences (see *Alderson* v. *The Queen* 2002: [14]). However, legislative prohibitions on judicial considerations of Indigenous culture and laws in sentencing have also focused attention on the need for substantive equality (Law Council of Australia 2006: 5; Aboriginal Legal Rights Movement 2006: [14]; Australian Law Reform Commission 2006: [8]).[5] Both criticisms highlight how recognition is a tenuous premise for Indigenous justice.

Empowering Indigenous communities and deconstructing recognition

For recognition to provide Indigenous justice, it must transform the generative framework of the dominant Anglo-Australian legal system over Indigenous peoples. In this respect, recognition must be deconstructed rather than bestowed in a one-way process from the colonizer to the colonized. 'Deconstructivist'[6] approaches to recognition involve breaking down differentiated identities by engaging marginalized groups as 'peers' in institutional processes, such that the recognition of identity is a two-way process (Fraser 2004: 29). This deconstructs the identities of the recognizer *and* the recognized and universalizes 'difference' by re-ordering social patterns (Fraser 1996: 7, 54, 2004: 29). At one end, the Indigenous community would be given authority to practise their laws and punishment and the Anglo-Australian courts would constitute only one punitive or dispute resolution route available to the community. At the other end, the state and courts would adopt Indigenous collective and relationship-based legal concepts. In other words, there would be a two-way approach to deconstructing recognition to engage Indigenous people as peers in the legal system. This is put eloquently by Gaykamangu (2012: 236), a Yolŋu Elder, who states that justice is about bringing Indigenous and non-Indigenous law together 'to recognise each other'. Jampijinpa, a Warlpiri Elder, also tells us that there needs to be a two-way understanding between Indigenous and non-Indigenous laws so one does not prevail over the other (Loy 2010).

Fraser (1995: 82) coins the term 'transformative justice' to explain the structural shifts that are required to engage the 'recognized' as peers in legal norm creation and dispensation.[7] 'Transformative' speaks to the need to deinstitutionalize patterns of cultural value that 'impede parity of participation' and replace them with patterns that foster participation of low-status groups as peers

5 The Australian Law Reform Commission (1986: [517]) and the Law Reform Commission of Western Australia (2006: 183) have recommended the enactment of a legislative requirement that sentencing courts consider Indigenous customary laws and community views in order to respond to Indigenous peoples' 'special characteristics' and hence provide them with equal standing when compared with non-Indigenous defendants.

6 Fraser (2004a: 125, 146) describes her use of the term 'deconstruction' as 'unorthodox' and denoting a 'specific type of institutional remedy for misrecognition' distinct from Jacques Derrida's theory of deconstruction.

7 Indigenous justice measures that challenge 'established forms of criminal justice' have also been described as 'innovative justice' (Daly and Marchetti 2012: 456).

(Fraser 1996: 30). It precludes a seesaw approach that tips from sympathetic to condemning portrayals of Indigenity because Indigenous people would be positioned to define the terms of their existence in the Australian legal system. The dominant institutional framework that recognizes the Other would give way to a parity of participation between Indigenous communities and the non-Indigenous community in the justice process. Hegel's 'identity model' provides that 'an ideal reciprocal relation between subjects' emerges where each subject sees the other 'both as its equal and also as separate from it' (Fraser 2000: 109). In a post-colonial society, especially one where Indigenous people have never ceded sovereignty, this requires that the state relinquishes control over Indigenous communities and works in cooperation with them to harness local Indigenous capacities.

The epistemic effect of a two-way recognition process would be to transform the inferior status of Indigenous people. The instrumental effect would be to strengthen Indigenous laws as well as to decarcerate Indigenous people from white institutions because they are no longer exclusively subjected to Anglo-Australian sentencing options, epitomized by the prison.[8] The strengthening of Indigenous laws would create more cohesive and law-abiding Indigenous societies. Indigenous organizations and law reform commissions over many years have noted that enhancing the place of Indigenous law in the Australian legal system would play a positive role in Indigenous communities (Aboriginal and Torres Strait Islander Commission 1995; Australian Law Reform Commission 1986: [517], hereinafter 'ALRC'; New South Wales Law Reform Commission 2000; Northern Territory Law Reform Committee 2003, hereinafter 'NTLRC'; Law Reform Commission of Western Australia 2006: 183, hereinafter 'LRCWA'). Warlpiri and Yolŋu people have described their laws as a bedrock in their societies. They have testified to the role of their laws in reducing crime and creating community harmony (Loy 2010; Gaymarani 2011: 283; Gaykamangu 2012: 248; Gondarra 2006: 43; see also ALRC 1986: [688]).

The state and judiciary's attempts to restrict Indigenous laws in the Northern Territory undermine the cohesiveness in these Indigenous communities. According to Goldflam (2012: 13), some Indigenous people turn away from aspects of customary law which are not tolerated by the mainstream. Where the more severe aspects of Indigenous law punishment are toned down, for example, it produces a 'Customary Law Lite' that lacks enforceability (2012: 13). Similarly, judicial recognition that deters Indigenous practices erodes the capacity of Indigenous communities to assert their laws on their own terms. Alternatively, empowering Indigenous communities in the justice process would fortify their laws, restore their governance structures and contribute to Indigenous healing.

8 Incarceration in white institutions is a form of Indigenous exclusion that has historically operated to control Indigenous Australians (see Chapter 2; and McCoy 1997: 611–12).

Transformative imaginings of Indigenous justice

A central tenant of a transformative approach to justice is the capacity for Indigenous societies to apply their laws and governance structures to their members. There are strong, lawful grounds for this position in a postcolonial society where Indigenous sovereignty was never ceded. Where such laws no longer have the capacity to govern Indigenous communities, Indigenous people should be able to partner with Anglo-Australian institutions to manage justice and dispute resolution processes. This requires engaging Indigenous people in a way that decentres postcolonial power. The application of a transformative justice paradigm to the Australian legal order is not a castle in the air.[9] Rather, it taps into governance structures and justice processes that already exist or have the potential to emerge in many Indigenous communities (see Blagg 2008). Legal pluralism in this sense is not essentialist, but allows for coexisting systems where Indigenous social practices are strengthened in their given 'social arenas' (Tamanaha 2000: 315). As Falzon (1998: 59) stated in this chapter's opening quote, transgressing limits 'introduces the new' and allows existing social structures to be renegotiated. Postcolonial criminologists show us that Indigenous authority already operates in 'liminal spaces' where Indigenous law and introduced law overlap (Blagg 2008; Cunneen 2011: 249).

Redressing the one-way recognition process requires vesting authority in Indigenous-owned structures, justice processes and individuals. In a postcolonial context, this requires decolonizing institutional patterns of Indigenous subordination by empowering Indigenous communities. Utilizing Indigenous justice involves strengthening *local* capacities in the particular Indigenous community. This section considers the diverse capacities within Indigenous communities and how they can provide for a transformative justice that collapses the recognition asymmetry.

Administration of Indigenous law punishment

Where Indigenous laws bind communities, including through the enforcement of Indigenous punishment systems, those punishment processes could be the lawful avenue for mediating and resolving matters to the satisfaction of the victim, the offender, their families and Indigenous community. Indigenous punishment, which primarily takes the form of exile, shaming, restitution and public acknowledgement and much more sparingly corporal punishment, would help restore balance in the community and engage community members in the criminal justice processes. On this premise, the Northern Territory Law Reform Committee (2003: 4) recommended Indigenous involvement in sentencing and the

9 Nonetheless, it is a bold strategy that is cognisant of legal narratives being embedded in broader social structures, cultural narratives and a history of colonial violence and injustice (see Cover 1983–4: 4).

administration of punishment. However, Indigenous punishment is only a small part of a much larger legal system that protects individuals and relationships, including with the land (Gaymarani 2011: 283). Respect for Indigenous legal systems more generally is integral to accommodating Indigenous punishment systems in a meaningful way (Gaykamangu 2012: 238).

Attributing responsibility to Indigenous people for identifying the entry points into the Anglo-Australian legal system would deconstruct the presumption of Anglo-Australian authority. The Indigenous community or victims may seek the protection of the courts. However, Indigenous involvement will be contingent on their acceptance of the court's jurisdiction, rather than it being mandated by the state. Warlpiri Elders, for example, have conveyed their acceptance of Anglo-Australian court processes, so long as 'traditional' punishment can be carried out to reconcile their community (Indigenous Law Centre 2010). Yolŋu Elder, Gaymarani, argues that non-Indigenous punishment can only have meaning when it is sanctioned by *Ngarra* law of Arnhem Land. This is articulated in the following quote:

> The Australian law will only be effective if a *Ngarra* law justice committee, made up of appropriate *dalkarramiri* [*Ngarra* law judge] and *jungay* [senior Yolŋu Elder], agrees to the extradition of a *Yolngu* offender to an Australian law court. The *Ngarra* law justice committee will listen to the offender's victim to see if he or she has a preference for the matter to be determined by *Ngarra* law or Australian law.
>
> (Gaymarani 2011: 300)

Participation of Indigenous people in justice institutions

Indigenous forms of punishment do not fit every Indigenous community. In Indigenous communities whose laws do not have the same punitive capacity, but in which strong authority structures exist, an Indigenous court or circle-sentence may be more appropriate for engaging Indigenous knowledges and values. This has been recommended by law reform commissions as an option for Indigenous communities provided they are instigated by the members of the Indigenous communities concerned (LRCWA 2006: 371; ALRC 1986: [1009]). Indigenous involvement in court sentencing can occur in the absence of community-owned justice processes, or to supplement such processes, and would allow for Indigenous community concerns to be projected in the punishment process. Gaymarani suggests that local courts could be constituted by Indigenous community members and apply Indigenous law:

> The people of Arnhem Land do not want the normal Court of Summary Jurisdiction. The Court of Summary Jurisdiction should always sit as a Community Court when in Arnhem Land. This *Ngarra* law should be the central component of the Community Court when it sits in Arnhem Land.

> This is one way that the Australian law and the *Ngarra* law can work side by side.
>
> (Gaymarani 2011: 299)

Throughout Australia, Indigenous courts have emerged over the past 15 years as an alternative for sentencing less serious Indigenous offenders.[10] They exist in small pockets and are not a wide-scale replacement of the lower courts, as proposed by Gaymarani. These courts, which operate outside the mainstream judicial system, galvanize Indigenous justice concepts by providing Indigenous Elders with a central role in the sentencing process (Daly and Marchetti 2012: 461). They are capable of challenging Anglo-Australian law and justice by bringing forward the views and sensibilities of the Indigenous domain. In this way, sentencing can better reflect the sentiments of Indigenous community members and avoid stereotypes (NTLRC 2003: 31). Daly and Marchetti's (2012: 436) research shows how Indigenous courts provide 'innovative justice' by incorporating Indigenous knowledge and modes of social control into the sentencing process. In this way, Indigenous courts 'bend and change the dominant perspective of "white law"' (Marchetti and Daly 2007: 429).

Indigenous courts, circle sentences and community justice groups entail Indigenous people having 'input' into sentencing decisions or providing 'advice' through consultations with Indigenous groups (Daly and Marchetti 2012: 462). In the Northern Territory, for example, when community courts operated before being disbanded for conflicting with legislative requirements for cultural evidence in sentencing,[11] respected persons would advise the magistrate on what they felt was an appropriate sentence before the court sat, or, alternatively, Elders would be involved in the sentencing process through talking to the offender about the impact of the crime and recommending a sentence after hearing sentencing submissions process. Thus, Indigenous people would exercise a degree of control over the procedure and outcome. In other jurisdictions, Elders tend to be only involved when appearing in the sentencing of select Indigenous offenders before

10 Since the early 1990s, separate Indigenous sentencing courts have formally emerged in New South Wales (circle sentencing), Queensland (Murri Courts), Victoria (Koori Courts) and South Australia (Nunga Courts). In some jurisdictions, this is supported by legislation, such as the Magistrates' Court Act 1989 (Vic) s. 4D and the Criminal Procedure Act 1986 (NSW) s. 348, or broadly under the Penalties and Sentences Act 1992 (Qld) s. 9(2)(p). In other jurisdictions there is no stable legislative basis, or legislation actually conflicts with the operation of community sentencing courts (such as in the Northern Territory, due to the legislative notice and form requirements for the admission of cultural evidence under the Sentencing Act 1995 (NT) s. 104A, as well as restrictions on cultural and customary law considerations in sentencing under the NTER Act (2007) s. 91). However, in 2012 the Queensland Murri Courts were abolished by the state government, indicating the weak premise of these courts even where legislation supports their operation.

11 In the Northern Territory, the Chief Magistrate recently declared community courts invalid because they do not meet notice and form requirements for the admission of Indigenous evidence under s. 104A of the Sentencing Act 1995 (NT).

them. In their robust form, Indigenous courts operate according to a 'transformative, culturally appropriate and politically charged participatory jurisprudence' (Marchetti 2010: 266). The involvement of Elders allows community members to feel a sense of ownership over the court process and for Indigenous views to be incorporated to reflect their dynamic culture rather than dominant institutions representing 'them' as frozen in the past (Marchetti and Daly 2012: 462, 469). In this respect, they engender a space for the views of Indigenous community members outside of the recognition space provided by the common law courts. However, despite the empowerment of Indigenous people at one level, on another level they do not have the capacity to enforce Indigenous laws or sanctions outside of the legislative regime (Marchetti and Daly 2007: 420–1). This precludes forms of Indigenous law punishment and supervisions of offenders by Indigenous community members (rather than corrections officers). As Rudin (2005: 99) states, Indigenous people must be given 'options and opportunities to develop processes that respond to the needs of [their Indigenous] community'. Critiques of the current system of Indigenous courts in Australia indicate where they stop short of providing transformative justice: final adjudication rests with a non-Indigenous magistrate;[12] Indigenous people do not have total control over the process, with the magistrate and lawyers continuing to be involved; it is usually only a small number of minor offenders who benefit from its jurisdiction; the sentencing options available to the court must come within the punishments prescribed by legislation; and they tend to operate in mainstream court complexes rather than in Indigenous spaces (Marchetti and Daly 2007: 420–1). Cunneen (2008a: 292) stipulates that for these processes to be effective it must not become another 'state-sponsored restorative justice program'. To some extent these concerns have been addressed by the Indigenous Justices of the Peace ('JP') system in Queensland, where the Indigenous JP is provided with full adjudication rights when presiding over minor sentencing matters involving Indigenous defendants (Allison *et al.* 2012). A variant of these courts can be seen in the peacemaking process on Mornington Island (in the Gulf of Carpentaria), where an Indigenous Peacemaker mediates matters, such as public nuisance, assaults and serious extended family disputes, in order to reconcile victims and offenders, rather than lay down punishment (Australian Government 2010). Gaykamangu (2012: 248) stresses that Indigenous law sentencing options need to be available to Indigenous courts, such as community work orders, exile from family, discipline by responsible Elders or the production of artwork by offenders, the proceeds of which are given to the victim of the crime.

Notwithstanding these concerns, Marchetti (2010: 271) argues that Indigenous courts, through their empowerment of Indigenous people and incorporation of

12 While some defendants have claimed that they would like the Elders to have more decision-making power, Elders have also expressed a view that they do not want to be responsible for the final decision imposed (Daly and Proietti-Scifoni 2009: 94). For a critical account of non-Indigenous control of Indigenous conferencing, see Blagg 1997: 496.

Indigenous perspectives and values, have the potential to be 'transformative' rather than merely 'restorative'. They provide Indigenous-controlled spaces that catalyze change in Anglo-Australian processes and to this extent they are an alternative mode of sentencing outside the limitations of the common law courts. This includes in family violence contexts, in which the transformative Indigenous court process can be cognisant of the 'subordinating experiences' of both offenders and victims (2010: 271). They can fashion appropriate penalties and allow the authority of the community to be reasserted. As Payne (2012) states, 'Indigenous courts are politically concerned with social change in race relations'. Furthermore, unlike in mainstream courts, the Indigenous sentencing court process involves Elders, as well as the families of both the victim and the offender. This removes the risk of the recognition of Indigenous circumstances being filtered through a 'white' lens.

Family violence and Indigenous involvement in healing

Transformative justice in family violence cases requires a broad set of Indigenous controlled strategies and programmes beyond what is available in the courts' sentencing repertoire. Cox *et al.* (2009: 151) stress that it is not possible to have justice without healing: 'If people don't heal, they will not be able to change their behaviours and will continue to be victims and perpetrators of violence'. Healing is a collective Indigenous experience that involves healing the victim, offender, families and the Indigenous community (in terms of recovering from the colonizer's oppression and violence). Communal healing is regarded as essential to addressing Indigenous family violence (Dodson 2007: 24; Calma 2007: 75). It entails the 'reconstruction of Indigenous society' through reviving Indigenous governance structures, laws and land ownership systems; investing in Indigenous cultural institutions; and respecting Indigenous authority structures (Dodson 2007: 24). These processes empower communities and reinforce respect for their laws and authority structures. It provides transformative justice by changing the postcolonial normative order.

Healing for Indigenous individuals can only be effective where it is self-determined by their community rather than confined to alienating Anglo-Australian institutions. In this way it enables Indigenous people to 'govern their own path of healing, to deal with past injustices, such as colonisation and its effects, in order to move into a future, which will sustain their livelihood and foster a just society' (Cox et al 2009: 151). Specific avenues available for promoting healing in Indigenous family violence cases include Indigenous peacemaking and reconciliation processes, support groups for the victim and offender of the same sex and culture,[13] and enforcement of Indigenous law punishment (which

13 This includes anti-violence programmes for Indigenous men, which Harry Blagg (2001a) has noted as being grounded in a distinctly Indigenous approach, such as focusing on intergenerational issues and mentoring of Indigenous youth by Elders, supporting young Aboriginal

condemns family violence). Cox *et al.* (2009: 160) demonstrate that healing can include everything from leadership and mentoring programmes and mothers' groups to artwork and sporting programmes for young men (also see Cox 2009). It extends to cultural women's camps or safe houses (*jilmi*) that are supported by the cooperation of Indigenous Elders and the police (Gaykamangu 2012: 248). These strategies show how Indigenous communities can redress oppression in its immediate and long-term, individual and collective forms.

Concluding observations

Judicial recognition of postcolonial Indigenous culture, disadvantage and resistance has had a troubled journey in the Northern Territory, New South Wales and Queensland. While earlier representations of Indigenous circumstances sought to level the punitive playing field by recognizing the ways in which these legitimate factors reduced culpability, later versions have regarded the offender as too colonized or too dysfunctional to be legitimate considerations for sentencing mitigation. In the late 1990s, the recognition pendulum swung from judicial sympathy to judicial disregard or condemnation. Either end of the pendulum is insufficient for Indigenous justice. This is because the pendulum pivots from institutions within the dominant order. The Anglo-Australian courts do not merely define the terms of recognition, but also reinstate their superiority over Indigenous systems and peoples.

The re-imagining of Indigeneity since the late 1990s has crystallized the will of courts to control and transform Indigenous communities in line with its normative order. Juxtaposed with greater punishment is a judicial message that non-Indigenous Australia will not accept Indigenous behaviours. This provides a control metaphor for the governance of Indigenous people and the dominance of the state. While the modes and terms of governance change over time, the management of Indigenous difference has taken on a particularly coercive disposition in recent years. Supported by moral panics and a postcolonial anxiety about the Indigenous Other, punitive controls have manifested in sentencing orders and sweeping policy changes in relation to Northern Territory Indigenous communities. The punitive impulse of the judiciary is matched with the coercive armoury of the state to regulate the risk of the Indigenous defendant and community. This assures the exclusive legal domain of the postcolonial state.

The higher courts' bifurcated interpretation of defendants' Indigenous communities as either culturally moribund or culturally depraved entrench a fiction of a homogenous 'white' order in Australia. At one end, the judicial imagining of Indigenous disappearance in the New South Wales courts is a powerful metaphor for the uncontested rule of postcolonial institutions. At the

fathers, creating men's 'meeting places' and healing camps and/or healing journeys and formulating local violence prevention strategies aimed at youth. See also Cunneen 2002.

other end, the judicial imagining of Indigenous dysfunctionality in remote Northern Territory communities is a counterpoint for the moral order of the wider 'white' community. It not only rules out the functionality of Indigenous cultures and laws, including Indigenous punishment, but also diminishes the legitimacy of Indigenous grievances and resistance to the Anglo-Australian order and its harmful subjugation of Indigenous peoples. The haunting legacy of colonization is dismissed by a view that the Indigenous community is to be blamed for its crime and dysfunction. The discourse of dysfunctionality in the courts is overlaid with messages of deterrence. In the parliaments it signals the need for coercive interventions and restrictions on Indigenous rights.

Dominant patterns of representation that deny the functionality of Indigenous communities impede their participation in governance (Fraser 2004: 29–30). For Indigenous people, their sustained capacity to play a restorative and disciplinary role over their offenders has been undermined by dominant institutions. However, it is because of this assault that the need for an alternative imagining of the criminal justice system's engagement with Indigenous people becomes more pressing. This requires a challenge to the 'unitary vision of the criminal law' that is premised on false claims to sovereignty (Cunneen 2011a: 314). Indigenous Australians have never relinquished sovereignty through negotiations and treaties with the colonizers. While claims of *terra nullius* have been debased in native title law, this has not resulted in recognition of rights to self-government. Opening up a discussion on sovereignty, power and authority, according to Cunneen (2011a: 314–15), would enable a negotiation to commence between Indigenous and non-Indigenous Australians in relation to the terms of engagement of Indigenous people within Australian governance and law. This can facilitate a common understanding of how Indigenous laws and practices offset the universalizing endeavour of non-Indigenous institutions. Ultimately, it can provide the foundation for a legal pluralist order that would transform the antimony imposed by the colonizer.

A transformative justice paradigm transcends judicial attempts to reconcile Anglo-Australian law with Indigenous law through lenient sentences that accommodate Indigenous law or harsh sentences that seek to deter or modify Indigenous law. This paradigm provides an innovative vehicle for Indigenous justice that is not contingent on recognition processes embedded in non-Indigenous institutions and values. Transformative justice promotes domains of Indigenous authority that strengthen the cohesiveness of Indigenous society and allow Indigenous cultures to survive and thrive. These domains can coexist with the non-Indigenous jurisdiction. As Blagg (2008) identifies, such coexistence already operates in a range of Australian hybrid spaces where Indigenous laws imbricate with non-Indigenous laws. Transformative techniques allow these spaces to flourish through the resurgence of Indigenous forms of justice.

Bibliography

International law sources

Indigenous and Tribal Peoples Convention, Opened for signature 27 June 1989, ILO C169 (entered into force 5 September 1991).

International Convention on the Elimination of All Forms of Racial Discrimination, Opened for Signature by General Assembly resolution 2106 (XX) 21 December 1965 (entered into force 4 January 1969).

UN Committee on the Elimination of Racial Discrimination (2010) Consideration of Reports Submitted by States Parties Under Article 9 of the Convention; Concluding Observations on Australia, CERD/C/AUS/CO/15-17, Seventy-seventh session, 13 September.

UN Declaration on the Rights of Indigenous Peoples (2007) Resolution adopted by the General Assembly 61/295, 13 September.

UN Human Rights Committee (2009) Consideration of Reports Submitted by States Parties Under Article 40 of the Covenant; Concluding Observations on Australia, CCPR/C/AUS/CO/5, Ninety-fifth session, 2 April.

Media sources

Abbott, T. (2006) 'The "New" Paternalism', *Online Opinion*, 28 June. Available http://www.onlineopinion.com.au/view.asp?article=4629 (accessed 8 January 2013).

Anon (1884) 'The Late Outrage by Natives at Alice Springs: The Perpetrators Pursued. Several Natives Shot Dead', *The Advertiser*, Adelaide, 17 September, p. 5.

Anon (1899) 'Native Cattle Stealers', *The Adelaide Advertiser*, 8 December, p. 4.

Anon (1899a) 'Treatment of Aborigines: "A Horrible Farce"', *The Advertiser*, Adelaide, 1 April, p. 6H.

Anon (1934) 'Death Sentence. Eight Aborigines. Judge's Comment. "Cold Blooded Murder"', *Sydney Morning Herald*, 31 May, p. 11.

Anon (1987) 'Police Hurt in Clash with Aborigines', *Australian Associated Press*, 16 August. Available on Factiva database (accessed 1 October 2012).

Anon (1987a) 'A Riot at Brewarrina', *Sydney Morning Herald*, 18 August, p. 16.

Anon (2004) 'Brogden's Riot Response: Bulldoze The Block', *Sydney Morning Herald*, 16 February. Available http://www.smh.com.au/articles/2004/02/16/1076779880553.html (accessed 4 January 2013).

Anon (2004a) 'No Excuses Can Exonerate Redfern Riot', *The Australian*, 18 February, p. 12.

Anon (2004b) 'Upholding the Law', *Daily Telegraph*, 20 February, p. 26.
Anon (2004c) 'Police "Deserve All They Get": Dead Teen's Mum', *Australian Associated Press*, 16 February.
Anon (2004d) 'Police Lost Everything in Island Riots, Says Union', *Australian Associated Press*, 29 November. Available on Factiva database (accessed 1 February 2012).
Anon (2010) 'Spearing "Would Bring Happiness"', *Alice Online*, 9 November. Available http://aliceonline.com.au/2010/11/09/spearing-would-bring-happiness/ (accessed 4 January 2013).
Anon (2010a) 'When Tribal Punishment is Just an Excuse for Crime', *The Australian*, 30 September, p. 15.
Anon (2010b) 'Let's Put Stop to Payback', *Northern Territory News*, 25 November, p. 12.
Barrett, S. (2004) 'Riot Controllers "Put Lives at Risk"', *The Australian*, 17 March, p. 5.
Bassi, R. (2012) 'Big Rally Says Still No Justice for TJ Hickey', *Green Left Weekly*, 18 February. Available http://www.greenleft.org.au/node/50066 (accessed 4 January 2013).
Bolt, A. (2002) 'Justice Gone Blind', *Herald Sun*, 24 October, p. 19.
(2009) 'It's So Hip to be Black', *Herald Sun*, 15 April, p. 22.
Brough, M. (2007) 'Commonwealth's Intervention into Aboriginal Communities in the Northern Territory', National Press Club Address, Canberra. Available http://www.formerministers.fahcsia.gov.au/2931/commonwealths-intervention-into-aboriginal-communities-in-the-northern-territory/ (accessed 4 January 2013).
Bullock, C. (2010) 'Old Law, New Ways', *Radio National – Background Briefing Transcript*, Australian Broadcasting Corporation, 21 November. Available http://www.abc.net.au/radionational/programs/backgroundbriefing/old-law-new-ways/2963368 (accessed 4 January 2013).
(2010a) 'Call to Modernise Tribal Punishment', *Background Briefing*, Australian Broadcasting Corporation News, 19 November. Available http://www.abc.net.au/news/stories/2010/11/19/3071131.htm?site=alicesprings (accessed 4 January 2013).
(2010b) 'Payback Out of Control in Central Australia', *Background Briefing*, Australian Broadcasting Corporation News, 12 November. Available http://www.abc.net.au/news/stories/2010/11/12/3064586.htm?site=alicesprings (accessed 4 January 2013).
Carlton, M. (2004) 'The Recipe for a Riot', *Sydney Morning Herald*, 21–22 February, p. 26.
Carrick, D. (2008) 'The Sentencing of Lex Wotton', *The Law Report Transcript*, Australian Broadcasting Corporation, 11 November. Available http://www.abc.net.au/radionational/programs/lawreport/the-sentencing-of-lex-wotton/3167052 (accessed 4 January 2013).
Carter, J. (1987) 'What If They Held a Riot and Nobody Came?', *Sydney Morning Herald*, 18 August, p. 18.
Chulov, M., Warne-Smith, D. and Colman, E. (2004) 'Rumour: The Spark that Fired Racial Tinderbox', *The Australian*, 17 February, p. 1.
Colman, E. (2004) 'Magistrate Refuses Bail for Alleged Riot Ringleader', *The Australian*, 25 February, p. 7.
Corder, M. (2004) 'Dead Boy's Aunt in the Dock over Sydney Riot', *The Independent* (London), 21 February, p. 31.
Devine, M. (2006) 'A Culture of Violence that Must Change', *Sydney Morning Herald*, 18 May, p. 1.
Duboudin, T. (1987) 'Five Hurt in Violent Clash with Police: Aborigines Protest over Deaths in Custody', *The Times*, 17 August. Available on Factiva database (accessed 1 February 2012).

Eastley, T. (2004) 'Teen's Death Sparks Redfern Riot', *AM Radio Transcript*, Australian Broadcasting Corporation, 16 February. Available http://www.abc.net.au/am/content/2004/s1045540.htm (accessed 4 January 2013).

(2004a) 'Qld Police Commissioner Defends Palm Island Response', *AM Radio Transcript*, Australian Broadcasting Corporation, 30 November. Available http://www.abc.net.au/am/content/2004/s1254473.htm (accessed 4 January 2013).

Editor (2006) 'One Law for All: Our Legal System Must Reinforce Australian Values', *The Australian*, 26 May, p. 19.

Everingham, S. (2010) '91 Yuendumu Residents in Police Safe House', *Australian Broadcasting Corporation News*, 16 September. Available http://www.abc.net.au/news/stories/2010/09/16/3014055.htm (accessed 4 January 2013).

Fife-Yeomans, J. (1988) 'Racial Anger Case Begins', *Sydney Morning Herald*, 26 July, p. 8.

Gondarra, D. (2006) 'Traditional Law is Keeping the Peace on Aboriginal Lands', Media Release 20, 1 November, p. 41. Available http://www.supremecourt.nt.gov.au/media/docs/commonwealth_intervention.pdf (accessed 8 January 2013).

(2011) 'Assent Law of the First People: Views from a Traditional Owner', *National Indigenous Times*, 3 March, p. 24.

Herbert, C. E. (1907) 'Northern Territory Natives: A Message from Mr. Herbert. The Treatment of the Blacks', *The Advertiser*, Adelaide, 19 April.

Hewett, T. (1987) 'Race Riots: More Towns Are at Risk', *Sydney Morning Herald*, 18 August, p. 1.

(1987a) 'Blood on the Street: The Night A Town Exploded', *Sydney Morning Herald*, 17 August, p. 1.

Hope, D. (1991) 'Call to Discipline Police Over Aborigine's Death', *Sydney Morning Herald*, 10 April, p. 2.

Howard, J. (2006) *Southern Cross Radio*, Sydney, 19 May.

(2007) 'Tony Jones Talks to Prime Minister John Howard', *Lateline Transcript*, Australian Broadcasting Corporation, 21 June. Available http://www.abc.net.au/lateline/content/2007/s1958609.htm (accessed 4 January 2013).

Johnson, A. (2010) 'No Change to NT Payback Stance', *Australian Broadcasting Corporation News*, 7 December. Available http://www.abc.net.au/news/2010-12-07/no-change-to-nt-payback-stance/2365368 (accessed 4 January 2013).

Jones, T. (2006) 'Paedophile Rings Operating in Remote Communities: Brough', *Lateline Transcript*, Australian Broadcasting Corporation, 16 May. Available www.abc.net.au/lateline/content/2006/s1640148.htm (accessed 4 January 2013).

(2006a) 'Crown Prosecutor Speaks Out about Abuse in Central Australia', *Lateline Transcript*, Australian Broadcasting Corporation, 15 May. Available http://www.abc.net.au/lateline/content/2006/s1639127.htm (accessed 4 January 2013).

Kelly, J. (2011) 'Abbott Urges Truant Fines for Aboriginal Parents Whose Children Don't Go to School', *The Australian*. Available http://www.theaustralian.com.au/national-affairs/abbott-urges-truant-fines-for-aboriginal-parents-whose-children-dont-go-to-school/story-fn59niix-1226046764113 (accessed 1 October 2012).

Kennedy, L., Pelly, M. and Totaro, P. (2004) 'Chased or Not, TJ Had Reasons to Run', *Sydney Morning Herald*, 17 February, p. 1.

Ketchell, M. (2004) '"They Were Saying They Would Kill Us": Police Tell of Terror', *Sunday Mail*, 28 November, p. 6.

Ketchell, M., Webster, D. and Dibben, K. (2004) 'Police Riot Terror', *Herald Sun*, 28 November, p. 30.

(2004a) 'How Rioters Set Trap for Police – Unarmed Officers Feared They Would Die as 300 Rampaged Trap for Police', *The Sunday Mail*, 28 November, p. 4.

Lamont, L. (2005) 'Rioter Loses Jail-Term Appeal', *Sydney Morning Herald*, 15 February, p. 5.

Levett, C. and Kennedy, L. (2004) 'Teen's Aunt to Miss Funeral as Bail Denied', *Sydney Morning Herald*, 21 February, p. 6.

Lewis, D. (1991) 'Funeral Riot: Jury Told to Ignore Cell Deaths Report', *Sydney Morning Herald*, 13 April, p. 6.

(1991a) 'Blacks' Behaviour has Deteriorated: Brewarrina Riot Judge', *Sydney Morning Herald*, 9 May, p. 3.

(1991b) 'Two Found Guilty Over Brewarrina Funeral Riot', *Sydney Morning Herald*, 17 April, p. 3.

Lineham, S. and Seeney, H. (2004) 'Palm Island Explodes: Anarchy on Palm Island on Knife's Edge Overnight', *Townsville Bulletin*, 27 November, p. 1.

Liston, G. (2010) 'Criminology Expert Questions Child Abuse Taskforce', Australian Broadcasting Corporation, Darwin, 7 June. Available http://www.abc.net.au/news/stories/2010/06/07/2920541.htm?site=darwin&section=news (accessed 4 January 2013).

Mancuso, R. and Connolly, S. (2004) 'Palm Island Erupts: Buildings Burn, Police Threatened', *Australian Associated Press*, 26 November. Available on Factiva database (accessed 1 February 2012).

Marshall, A. (2004) 'Aboriginal Riot in Sydney Injures 40 Police', *Australian News Commentary*, 20 February. Available http://australian-news.net/Redfern_riots.htm (accessed 4 January 2013).

Martin, B. (2005) 'Opinion: In Defence', *Northern Territory News/Sunday Territorian*, 19 August, p. 12.

(2006) 'Speech to the South Australian Press Club', Adelaide, 15 September. Available http://www.supremecourt.nt.gov.au/media/20060915cjmartin_sa_pressclub1.html (accessed 4 January 2013).

Melbourne Correspondent (1904) 'Western Australian Slavery: A Disclaimer by Dr. Rentoul', *The Advertiser*, Adelaide, 25 April, p. 5.

Merritt, C. (2006) 'I Got It Wrong on Tribal Rape Sentence: Chief Justice', *The Australian*, 24 May, p. 1.

Miranda, C. (2004) 'Setting the Stage for a Violent Showdown', *Daily Telegraph*, 17 February, p. 2.

Moon, K. and Munckton, S. (2004) 'Redfern "Riot": Black Youth Fight Back', *Green Left Weekly*, 25 February. Available http://www.greenleft.org.au/node/30460 (accessed 4 January 2013).

Morrell, S. (2005) 'Girl Let Down by Laws', *Herald-Sun* (Sydney), 22 August, p. 18.

Murdoch, L. (2009) 'NT Alcohol Laws a Waste: Police', *The Age*, 12 March, p. 8.

(2010) 'NT Police Reject Tribal Law in Clan War', *The Age*, 24 November, p. 3.

(2010a) 'Traditional Law Can Be Used for Disputes, Says MP', *Sydney Morning Herald*, 30 December, p. 4.

Murdoch, L. and Skelton, R. (2011) 'Rivers of Grog Still Taxing Communities', *Sydney Morning Herald*, 23 May, p. 8.

Murray, P. (2010) 'Why Do We Stand Silent on Tribal Punishment?', *The West Australian*, 16 February, p. 20.

Neill, R. and Schliebs, M. (2010) 'Aboriginal Fighting "Could Go on 20 years"', *The Australian*, 24 November, p. 9.

O'Brien, K. (2006) 'Australian Law Should Apply to All: Brough', *7.30 Report Transcript*, Australian Broadcasting Corporation, 23 May. Available http://www.abc.net.au/7.30/content/2006/s1645722.htm (accessed 4 January 2013).

Pavey, A. (2004) 'Beattie Defends Police Tactics in Island Riot', *Australian Associated Press*, 29 November. Available on Factiva database (accessed 1 February 2012).

Penberthy, D. and Kamper, A. (2004) 'Flashpoint – Redfern . . . Sydney . . . 1am . . . February 16 . . . 2004 – The Redfern Riots', *Daily Telegraph*, 17 February, p. 1.

Priest, T. (2004) 'Stop the Social Engineering and Empower Sydney Police', *The Australian*, 18 February, p. 13.

Skelton, R. (2006) 'Shame in Nation's Dead Heart', *The Sydney Morning Herald*, 20 May, p. 26.

Smith, S. (2006) 'Sexual Abuse Reported in Indigenous Community', *Lateline Transcript*, Australian Broadcasting Corporation, 21 June. Available http://www.abc.net.au/lateline/content/2006/s1668773.htm (accessed 4 January 2013).

Spielmann, P. J. (1994) 'Aborigines Deal Out Rough Justice in the Bush', *Australian Associated Press*, 8 August, Available on Factiva database (accessed 1 February 2012).

Squires, N. (2005) 'Aborigines Seek Return of Tribal Justice', *The Daily Telegraph* (Sydney), 6 June, p. 13.

(2005a) 'Aborigines Call for Return to "Payback"; Many Say They Prefer Short, Sharp Shock of Tribal Justice to Months or Years in Jail', *New Zealand Herald*, 1 June, p. 4.

Steketee, M. (2008) 'Mainstream Must Reach Aborigines', *The Australian*, 27 March, p. 16.

Tatz, C. (1996) 'Opinion: Black Search for Meaning', *The Age*, 5 January, p. 11.

Tingle, L. (2007) 'Brough Justice: Assimilate Or Be Damned', *Australian Financial Review*, 10 August, p. 87.

Toohey, P. (2001) 'Tribal Payback Reduces Jail Term', *The Australian*, 17 May, p. 3.

(2002) 'Victim Trapped between Two Worlds', *The Australian*, 9 October, p. 1.

(2002a) 'Custom Alone Can't Overturn Basic Rights', *The Australian*, 10 October, p. 10.

(2002b) 'Black, White and Blurred', *The Australian*, 12 October, p. 21.

(2002c) 'Indigenous Minister Condemns Judge in Aboriginal Promised Bride Case', *The Australian*, 17 October, p. 9.

Totaro, P., Levett, C. and Geesche, J. (2004) 'Alcohol, Heat, Grief Triggered the Riot', *Sydney Morning Herald*, 17 February, p. 1.

Williams, G. (1988) 'Boney on Police: "I'm Just Frightened of Them Bastards"', *Sydney Morning Herald*, 10 February, p. 7.

Williams, G. and Cordell, M. (1987) 'No Way He Would Kill Himself, Says Aboriginal's Family', *Sydney Morning Herald*, 8 August, p. 1.

(1987a) 'Man "Too Drunk" to Hang Himself', *Sydney Morning Herald*, 10 August, p. 8.

Willoughby, S. (2007) 'Solidarity for Hurley: Incensed Coast Cops in Protest', *Gold Coast Bulletin*, 31 January, p. 4.

Young, P. D. (2005) 'Promised Brides' Sex Ban', *Sunday Mail* (Brisbane), 28 August, p. 16.

Zinn, C. (1997) 'Aborigines Win Back the Right to Swift Justice', *The Guardian* (London), 5 December, p. 19.

Parliamentary debates

Aagaard, J. (2004) 'Question on Child Protection', *Northern Territory Parliamentary Debates*, Ninth Assembly, First Session, Parliamentary Record No. 21, 17 August.

Ah Kit, J. (2002) *Debates: Ninth Assembly, First Session*, Parliamentary Record No. 3, Northern Territory Legislative Assembly, 7 March.

Bell, N. (1995) 'Sentencing Bill (Serial 85) – Second Reading in Continuation, in Committee, Third Reading', *Northern Territory Parliamentary Record*, Seventh Assembly First Session, No. 14, 22 August.

Braham, L. (2003) 'Presentation and Second Reading Speech: Sentencing Amendment Bill (Serial 126)', *Northern Territory Parliamentary Debates*, Ninth Assembly, First Session, Parliamentary Record No. 10, 18 February.

Brough, M. (2007) 'Second Reading Speech, Social Security and Other Legislation Amendment (Welfare Payment Reform) Bill 2007', *Parliamentary Debates: House of Representatives Official Hansard*, Commonwealth of Australia, No. 11, 7 August.

(2007a) 'Second Reading Speech: Northern Territory National Emergency Response Bill 2007', *Parliamentary Debates: House of Representatives Official Hansard*, Commonwealth of Australia, No. 11, 7 August.

Burke, B. (1996) 'Ministerial Statement: Criminal Justice System and Victims of Crime', *Northern Territory Parliamentary Record*, Seventh Assembly, First Session, No. 24, 20 August.

(1996a) 'Sentencing Amendment Bill (Serial 186) Work Health Amendment Bill (Serial 189) Juvenile Justice Amendment Bill (Serial 188) Prisons (Correctional Services) Amendment Bill (Serial 187) – Presentation and Second Reading, Debate Adjourned', *Northern Territory Parliamentary Record*, Seventh Assembly, First Session, No. 27, 17 October.

Carney, J. (2003) 'Criminal Code Amendment Bill (No. 2)', *Northern Territory Second Reading Speeches*. Available http://www.austlii.edu.au/au/legis/nt/bill_srs/ccab22003232/srs.html (accessed 4 January 2013).

Ellison, C. (2006) 'Second Reading Speech: Crimes Amendment (Bail and Sentencing) Bill', *Parliamentary Debates: The Senate*, Commonwealth of Australia, 8 November.

Finch, F. (1995) 'Sentencing Bill (Serial 85) – Presentation and Second Reading, Debate Adjourned', *Northern Territory Parliamentary Record*, Seventh Assembly First Session, No. 10, 18 May.

MacDonald, S. (2006) 'Second Reading Speech Crimes Amendment (Bail and Sentencing) Bill', *Parliamentary Debates: The Senate*, Commonwealth of Australia, No. 10, 14 September.

McCarthy, M. (2011) 'Justice (Corrections) and Other Legislation Amendment Bill 2011', *Northern Territory Second Reading Speeches*, Northern Territory Parliament, 5 May. Available http://www.austlii.edu.au/au/legis/nt/bill_srs/jaolab2011508/srs.html (accessed 4 January 2013).

Underwood, R. H. (1906) *Western Australian Parliamentary Debates*, No. 30, Perth: Government Printer.

Unpublished archival materials

Askins, F. T. (1965) *Dark - Night. What of the Dawn: History Story of Australian (Northern Territory) Natives, 1905–1965*, Unpublished, Archive File, Mortlock Library: D5135 (Lit Ms).

Bennett, H. G. (1819) *Letter to Viscount Sidmouth, Secretary of State for the Home Department, on the Transportation Laws, the State of the Hulks, and of the Colonies in New South Wales*, London: J. Ridgeway.

Bleakley, J. W. (1929) *The Aborigines and Half-Castes of Central Australia and North Australia 1928*, Report to the Parliament of the Commonwealth of Australia, Canberra.

d'Abbs, P. (1994) *Interview with Harry Giese*, Darwin, Archive File, Northern Territory Archives Service: NTRS 226, TS 755.

Driver, A. R. (1949) Correspondence to the Secretary, Department of the Interior, 6 July, Archive File, National Archives (Darwin): CA1070, F1 43/24.

Kelsey, D. (1938) *Research Papers on the History and Personal Experiences of Kelsey in the Northern Territory*, vol. 5, Archive File, Mortlock Library (SA): D3422(T).

McCaffery, R. K. (1953) *Maintenance Payment to Dependants of Aboriginal Employees on Pastoral Properties*, Archive File, National Archives (Darwin): CRS F1 1953/307.

Marsh, R. (1954) 'Maintenance of Aboriginal Dependants on Pastoral Leases', Memorandum from the Assistant Secretary, Department of Territories, No. 51/1634, February, Archive File, National Archives (Canberra): A452/54; 1955/303.

Northern Territory Office of the Government Resident (1929) *Finding of the Board of Enquiry Concerning the Killing of Natives in Central Australia by Police Parties, and Other Matters*, Alice Springs, Commonwealth of Australia, 18 January, Archive File, National Library of Australia: ANL MS744.

Published materials, theses and oral presentations

Aas, K. F. (2005) *Sentencing in the Age of Information*, London: Glasshouse Press.

Aboriginal and Torres Strait Islander Commission (1995) *Recognition, Rights and Reform*, A Report to Government on Native Title Social Justice Measures, Canberra: ATSIC.

Aboriginal and Torres Strait Islander Social Justice Commissioner (2011) *Social Justice Report*, Sydney: Australian Human Rights Commission.

Aboriginal Legal Rights Movement (2006) 'Submission to the Inquiry into the Crime Amendment (Bail and Sentencing) Bill 2006', Submission no. 7, 26 September.

Aborigines Select Committee, *Report of the 1899 Select Committee of the Legislative Council on the Aborigines Bill: Minutes of Evidence*, South Australian Parliamentary Papers, no. 77, 8 November, Auth. C. E. Bristow, Adelaide: Government Printer.

Adjin-Tettey, E. (2007) 'Sentencing Aboriginal Offenders: Balancing Offenders' Needs, Victims and Society's Interests and Decolonization of Aboriginal Peoples', *Canadian Journal of Women and the Law* 19(1): 179.

Adorno, T. W., Frenkel-Brunswik, E., Levinson, D. J. and Sanford, R. N. (1950) *The Authoritarian Personality*, vols 1 and 2, New York: Harper.

Agamben, G. (1998) *Homo Sacer: Sovereign Power and Bare Life*, trans. D. Heller-Roazen, Stanford: Stanford University Press.

Agozino, B. (2004) 'Imperialism, Crime and Criminology: Towards the Decolonisation of Criminology', *Crime, Law and Social Change* 41(4): 343.

Allard, T. (2010) 'Understanding and Preventing Indigenous Offending', *Indigenous Justice Clearinghouse Research Brief*, no. 9. Available http://www.indigenousjustice.gov.au/briefs/brief009.pdf (accessed 4 January 2013).

Allison, F., Cunneen, C., Loban, H., Luke, G. and Munro, K. (2012) 'Sentencing and Punishment in the Indigenous Justices of the Peace Courts', *Australian Indigenous Law Review* 16(1): 15.

Altman, J. (2007) 'The Howard Government's Northern Territory Intervention: Are Neo-paternalism and Indigenous Development Compatible?', *Centre for Aboriginal Economic Policy Research*, Topical Issue No. 16/2007.

Amankwah, H. A. (1994) 'Post-*Mabo*: The Prospect of the Recognition of a Regime of Customary (Indigenous) Law in Australia', *University of Queensland Law Journal* 18(1): 15.

Anderson, B. (1983) *Imagined Communities: Reflections on the Origin and Spread of Nationalism*, London: Verso.

Anderson, K. J. (1993) 'Constructing Geographies: "Race", Place and the Making of Sydney's Aboriginal Redfern', in P. Jackson and J. Penrose (eds) *Constructions of Race, Place and Nation*, Minneapolis: University of Minnesota Press.

(1999) 'Reflections on Redfern', in E. Stratford (ed.) *Australian Cultural Geographies*, Melbourne: Oxford University Press.

Ang, I. (1999) 'Racial/Spatial Anxiety: "Asia" in the Psycho-geography of Australia Whiteness', in G. Hage and R. Couch (eds) *The Future of Australian Multiculturalism: Reflections on the Twentieth Anniversary of Jean Martin's The Migrant Presence*, Sydney: Research Institute for Humanities and Social Sciences, University of Sydney.

Anghie, A. (2004) *Imperialism, Sovereignty and the Making of International Law*, Cambridge: Cambridge University Press.

Anthony, T. (2003) 'Postcolonial Feudal Hauntings of Northern Australian Cattle Stations', *Law Text Culture* 7: 277.

(2007) 'Unmapped Territory: Indigenous Stolen Wages on Cattle Stations', *Australian Indigenous Law Review* 11(1): 4.

(2007a) 'Reconciliation and Conciliation: The Irreconcilable Dilemma of the 1965 "Equal" Wage Case for Aboriginal Station Workers', *Labour History* 93(11): 15.

(2009) 'The Return to the Legal and Citizenship Void: Indigenous Welfare Quarantining in the Northern Territory and Cape York', *Balayi: Culture, Law and Colonialism* 10: 28.

(2010) 'Governing Crime in the Intervention', *Law in Context* 27(2): 90.

(2012) 'The Northern Territory Intervention: The Ongoing Story of Withheld Indigenous Money', *Ngiya: Talk the Law* 3: 2.

Anthony, T. and Anthony, D. (2008) 'Psychologising Criminals and the Frankfurt School's Critique', in T. Anthony and C. Cunneen (eds) *Critical Criminology Companion*, Sydney: Hawkins Press.

Anthony, T. and Blagg, H. (2012) *Addressing the "Crime Problem" of the Northern Territory Intervention: Alternate Paths to Regulating Minor Driving Offences in Remote Indigenous Communities*, Report to the Criminology Research Council, CRC 38/09-10.

Anthony, T. and Chapman, R. (2008) 'Unresolved Tensions: Warlpiri Law, Police Powers and Land Rights', *Indigenous Law Bulletin* 7(5): 9.

Armitage, A. (1995) *Comparing the Policy of Aboriginal Assimilation: Australia, Canada, and New Zealand*, Vancouver: University of British Columbia Press.

Ashworth, A. (2002) 'Sentencing', in M. Maguire, R. Morgan and R. Reiner (eds) *Oxford Handbook of Criminology*, 3rd edn, Oxford: Oxford University Press.

(2005) *Sentencing and Criminal Justice*, 4th edn, Cambridge: Cambridge University Press.

Atherfold, J. (2006) 'Redfern: The "Riot" and the Reporting', *Australian Studies in Journalism* 17: 41.

Atkinson, J. (2002) *Trauma Trails – Recreating Song Lines: The Transgenerational Effects of Trauma in Indigenous Australia*, Melbourne: Spinifex.

(2006) 'Traditional Violence and Bullsh*t Law', *New Matilda*, 27 September. Available http://newmatilda.com/2006/09/27/traditional-violence-and-bullsh*t-law (accessed 4 January 2013).

(2006a) 'Violence against Aboriginal Women: Reconstitution of Community Law – the Way Forward', *Indigenous Law Bulletin* 27(6): 13.

(2006b) 'Book Review – a Fatal Conjunction: Two Laws Two Cultures', *Indigenous Law Bulletin* 6(20): 20.

Attwood, B. (2009) *Possession: Batman's Treaty and the Matter of History*, Melbourne: Miegunyah Press.

Austin, T. (1988) 'Looking Back', in V. Dixon (ed.) *Looking Back*, Darwin: Historical Society of Northern Territory.

Australian Bureau of Statistics (2009) *Prisoners in Australia*, no. 4517.0, Canberra. Available http://www.ausstats.abs.gov.au/Ausstats/subscriber.nsf/0/A570D4363D75FE30CA257687001D5128/$File/45170_2009.pdf (accessed 4 January 2013).

(2011) *Prisoners in Australia*, no. 4517.0, Canberra: Commonwealth of Australia. Available http://www.ausstats.abs.gov.au/Ausstats/subscriber.nsf/0/7B05CD44A0E2FC8ACA25795F000DBD0F/$File/45170_2011.pdf (accessed 8 January 2013).

(2011a) Census Fact Sheet 2011. Available http://www.abs.gov.au/websitedbs/d3310114.nsf/4a256353001af3ed4b2562bb00121564/7a566d5e3cc24297ca25784500107ae0!OpenDocument (accessed 8 January 2013).

(2011b) *Regional Statistics, Northern Territory, Mar 2011*, no. 1362.7. Available http://www.abs.gov.au/ausstats/abs@.nsf/Latestproducts/1362.7Feature%20Article1Mar%202011?opendocument&tabname=Summary&prodno=1362.7&issue=Mar%202011&num=&view= (accessed 8 January 2013).

(2011c) 'Demographic, Social and Economic Characteristics Overview: Aboriginal and Torres Strait Islander People and Where They Live', *The Health and Welfare of Australia's Aboriginal and Torres Strait Islander Peoples, Oct 2010*, no. 4704.0, Available http://www.abs.gov.au/AUSSTATS/abs@.nsf/lookup/4704.0Chapter210Oct+2010 (accessed 8 January 2013).

(2012) *Recorded Crime – Offenders Australia 2010–11*, no. 4519.0. Available http://www.ausstats.abs.gov.au/Ausstats/subscriber.nsf/0/0D38AEF648B5C1EECA25799E000E3B15/$File/45190_2010-11.pdf (accessed 8 January 2013).

Australian Government (2010) 'Making Peace on Mornington Island', *Closing the Gap*, 1 December. Available: http://www.indigenous.gov.au/stories/country/80_making_peace_on_mornington_island (accessed 1 April 2010).

Australian Law Reform Commission (1986) *The Recognition of Aboriginal Customary Laws*, Final Report, no. 31, Canberra: Australian Government Publishing Service.

(2006) 'Submission to the Inquiry into the Crime Amendment (Bail and Sentencing) Bill 2006', Submission no. 1, 25 September.

Australian Law Reform Commission and New South Wales Law Reform Commission (2010) *Family Violence – A National Legal Response*, Summary Report, Commonwealth of Australia.

Baker, J. (2001) 'The Scope for Reducing Indigenous Imprisonment Rates', *Contemporary Issues in Crime and Justice*, no. 55, Sydney: New South Wales Bureau of Crime Statistics and Research.

Balbus, I. D. (1973) *The Dialectics of Legal Repression*, New York: Russell Sage Foundation.

Barker, J. (2006) 'Recapturing the History of Brewarrina Mission', Woganurra Aboriginal Co-op. Available http://www.environment.nsw.gov.au/resources/heritagebranch/heritage/funding/projectbremission.pdf (accessed 8 January 2013).

Barnes, B. (1988) 'You Can Go Back to Your Place', in P. Marshall (ed.) *Raparapa Kularr Martuwarra . . . All Right, Now We Go 'Side the River, along that Sundown Way: Stories from Fitzroy River Drovers*, Broome: Magbala Books.
Barthes, R. (1972) *Mythologies*, trans. A. Lavers, London: J. Cape.
Bauman, Z. (2000) *Liquid Modernity*, Cambridge: Polity Press.
Becker, H. S. (1991) *Outsiders: Studies in the Sociology of Deviance*, New York: Free Press.
Behrendt, L. (1993) 'Aboriginal Women and the White Lies of the Feminist Movement', *Australian Feminist Journal* 1: 27.
(1994) 'Aboriginal Urban Identity: Preserving the Spirit, Protecting the Traditional in Non-traditional Settings', *Australian Feminist Law Journal* 4: 56.
(2002) 'Aboriginal Women and the Criminal Justice System', *Judicial Officers Bulletin* 14(6): 41.
(2005) 'The 2004 Clare Burton Memorial Lecture – Law Stories and Life Stories: Aboriginal Women, the Law and Australian Society', *Australian Feminist Studies* 20(47): 245.
(2006) 'Politics Clouds Issues of Culture and "Customary Law"', *Proctor* July: 14.
Behrendt, L. and Vivian, A. (2010) 'Indigenous Self-Determination and the Charter of Human Rights and Responsibilities: A Framework for Discussion', Occasional Paper, Melbourne: Victorian Equal Opportunity Human Rights Commission.
Behrendt, L. and Watson, N. (2008) 'A Response to Louis Nowra', *Alternative Law Journal* 33(1): 45.
Bell, L. A. (2010) *Storytelling for Social Justice: Connecting Narrative and the Arts in Antiracist Teaching*, New York: Routledge.
Bentham, J. (1962) 'Principals of Penal Law', in J. Bowring (ed.) *The Works of Jeremy Bentham*, New York: Russell and Russell.
Berger, P. and Luckmann, T. (1966) *The Social Construction of Reality: A Treatise in the Sociology of Knowledge*, New York: Anchor Books.
Bhabha, H. K. (1990) *Nation and Narration*, New York: Routledge.
(1994) *The Location of Culture*, London: Routledge.
Biber, K. (2004) 'Being/Nothing: Native Title and Fantasy Fulfilment', *Indigenous Law Journal* 3: 1.
Bielefeld, S. (2003) 'The Culture of Consent and Traditional Punishments under Customary Law', *Southern Cross University Law Review* 7: 142.
Birch, T. (2004) '"Who Gives a Fuck about White Society Anymore": A Response to the Redfern Riot', *Overland* 175: 18.
Bird, J. (1988) 'They Can't Break Us Down', in P. Marshall (ed.) *Raparapa Kularr Martuwarra . . . All Right, Now We Go 'Side the River, along that Sundown Way: Stories from Fitzroy River Drovers*, Broome: Magbala Books.
Blackstone, W. (1979) *Commentaries*, vol. 1, facsimile edn 1765–9, Chicago, IL: University of Chicago Press.
Blagg, H. (1997) 'A Just Measure of Shame? Aboriginal Youth and Conferencing in Australia', *British Journal of Criminology* 37(4): 481.
(2001) 'Aboriginal Youth and Restorative Justice: Critical Notes from the Australian Frontier', in A. Morris, G. Maxwell and G. M. Maxwell (eds) *Restorative Justice for Juveniles: Conferencing, Mediation and Circles*, Oxford: Hart Publishing.
(2001a) *Pilot Counselling Programs for Mandated and Non-Mandated Indigenous Men: Research and Program Development*, Full Report, Perth: Crime Research Centre, University of Western Australia.
(2002) 'Restorative Justice and Aboriginal Family Violence', in H. Strang and J. Braithwaite (eds) *Restorative Justice and Family Violence*, Cambridge: Cambridge University Press.

(2008) *Crime Aboriginality and the Decolonisation of Justice*, Sydney: Hawkins Press.

(2008a) 'Colonial Critique and Critical Criminology: Issues in Aboriginal Law and Aboriginal Violence', in T. Anthony and C. Cunneen (eds) *The Critical Criminology Companion*, Sydney: Hawkins Press.

(2012) 'Re-imagining Youth Justice: Cultural Contestation in the Kimberley Region of Australia since the 1991 Royal Commission into Aboriginal Deaths in Custody', *Theoretical Criminology* 16(4): 481.

Blagg, H., Morgan, N., Cunneen, C. and Ferrante, A. (2005) *Systemic Racism as a Factor in the Over-representation of Aboriginal People in the Criminal Justice System*, Report to the Equal Opportunity Commission and Aboriginal Justice Forum, Melbourne.

Blumer, H. (1969) *Symbolic Interactionism: Perspective and Method*, Englewood Cliffs, NJ: Prentice-Hall.

Bolton, G. C. (1981) 'Black and White after 1897', in C. T. Stannage (ed.) *A New History of Western Australia*, Nedlands: University of Western Australia Press.

(1982) 'Aborigines in Social History: An Overview', in R. M. Berndt (ed.) *Aboriginal Sites, Rights and Resource Development*, Perth: University of Western Australia Press.

Bond, C. E. W. and Jeffries, S. (2011) 'Indigeneity and the Judicial Decision to Imprison: A Study of Western Australia's Higher Courts', *British Journal of Criminology* 51: 256.

(2012) 'Indigeneity and the Likelihood of Imprisonment in Queensland's Adult and Children's Courts', *Psychiatry, Psychology and Law* 19(2): 169.

Bond, C. E. W., Jeffries, S. and Weatherburn, D. (2011) 'How Much Time? Indigenous Status and the Sentenced Imprisonment Term Decision in New South Wales', *Australian & New Zealand Journal of Criminology* 44(2): 272.

Borrows, J. (2002) *Recovering Canada: The Resurgence of Indigenous Law*, Toronto: University of Toronto Press.

Bourdieu, P. (1987) 'The Force of Law: Towards a Sociology of the Juridical Field', *Hastings Law Journal* 38(5): 814.

(1991) *Language and Symbolic Power*, trans. G. Raymond and M. Adamson, Cambridge: Polity Press.

Box, S. (2003) 'Crime, Power and Ideological Mystification', in E. McLaughlin, J. Muncie and G. Hughes (eds) *Criminological Perspectives*, 2nd edn, London: Sage Publications.

Brady, W. and Carey, M. (2000) '"Talkin' Up Whiteness": A Black and White Dialogue', in J. Docker and G. Fischer (eds) *Race, Colour and Identity in Australia and New Zealand*, Sydney: University of New South Wales Press.

Braithwaite, J. (1989) *Crime, Shame and Reintegration*, Cambridge: Cambridge University Press.

Brennan, S., Williams, G., Behrendt, L. and Strelein, L. (2005) *Treaty*, Sydney: Federation Press.

Brewarrina Aboriginal Health Service Limited (2010) 'About Brewarrina'. Available http://www.bahsl.com.au/index.php/bahsl-the-community/about-brewarrina/ (accessed 5 January 2013).

Briscoe, G. (2003) *Counting, Health and Identity: A History of Aboriginal Health and Demography in Western Australia and Queensland 1900–1940*, Canberra: Aboriginal Studies Press.

Broadhurst, R. (1987) 'Imprisonment of the Aborigine in Western Australia, 1957–85', in K. Hazlehurst (ed.) *Ivory Scales – Black Australians and the Law*, Sydney: University of New South Wales Press.

(1997) 'Aborigines and Crime in Australia', *Crime and Justice* 21: 407.

(2002) 'Crime and Indigenous People', in A. Graycar and P. Grabosky (eds) *Handbook of Australian Criminology*, New York: Cambridge University Press.

Brogden, M. (1987) 'Law and Criminal Labels: The Case of the French Métis in Western Canada', *Journal of Human Justice* 1(2): 13.
Brown, D. (1989) 'What Truth?', *Legal Service Bulletin* 14(4): 161.
(2005) 'Continuity, Rupture, Or Just One More of the "Volatile and Contradictory"? Glimpses of New South Wales' Penal Practice Behind and Through the Discursive', in J. Pratt, D. Brown, S. Hallsworth, M. Brown and W. Morrison (eds) *The New Punitiveness: Trends, Theories, Perspectives*, Cullompton: Willan.
Brown, K. (2007) 'Customary Law: Sex with Under-age "Promised Wives"', *Alternative Law Journal* 32(1): 11.
Buchan, B. (2008) *Empire of Political Thought*, London: Pickering and Chatto.
Buchanan, G. (1933) *Packhorse and Waterhole: With the First Overlanders to the Kimberleys*, Sydney: Angus & Robertson.
Burke, R. H. (2005) *An Introduction to Criminological Theory*, 2nd edn, Cullompton: Willan.
Calma, T. (2007) 'Integration of Customary Law into the Australian Legal System', *Law in Context* 25(1): 74.
Carter, P. (2007) 'Public Space: Its Mythopoetic Foundations and the Limits of the Law', *Griffith Law Review* 16(2): 430.
(2010) *The Road to Botany Bay: An Exploration of Landscape and History*, Minneapolis: University of Minnesota Press.
Central Australian Legal Aid Service and North Australian Aboriginal Justice Agency (2010) 'The Northern Territory Emergency Response ("the Intervention") and the Impact on the Criminal Justice System and Aboriginal Offenders', *23rd Annual Australian and New Zealand Society of Criminology Conference*, Alice Springs, 28 September.
Charon, J. M. (2007) *Symbolic Interactionism: An Introduction, an Interpretation, an Integration*, 9th edn, Upper Saddle River NJ: Pearson Education.
Chesterman, J. and Galligan, B. (1997) *Citizens without Rights: Aborigines and Australian Citizenship*, Cambridge: Cambridge University Press.
Chesterman, J. and Villaflor, G. (2000–1) 'Mr Neal's Invasion: Behind an Indigenous Rights Case', *Australian Journal of Law and Society* 15: 90.
Christie, N. (1986) 'The Ideal Victim', in E. A. Fattah (ed.) *From Crime Policy to Victim Policy: Reorienting the Justice System*, Basingstoke: Macmillan.
Clyne, R. (1987) *Colonial Blue: A History of the South Australian Police Force 1836–1916*, Adelaide: Wakefield Press.
Cohen, S. (1985) *Visions of Social Control: Crime, Punishment and Classification*, Cambridge: Polity Press.
(2002) *Folk Devils and Moral Panics*, 3rd edn, New York: Routledge.
Cornell, S. (2012) 'Paths to Indigenous Self-Determination: Rights and Governance in Four English-settler Societies', Public lecture at the University of Sydney, School of Social and Political Sciences, Department of Sociology and Social Policy, 18 July.
Cover, R. M. (1983–4) 'Foreword: *Nomos* and Narrative', *Harvard Law Review* 97: 4.
Cowlishaw, G. (1991) 'Inquiring into Aboriginal Deaths in Custody: The Limits of a Royal Commission', *Journal for Social Justice Studies* 4: 101.
(2004) *Blackfellas, Whitefellas, and the Hidden Injuries of Race*, Malden, MA: Blackwell.
(2009) *The City's Outback*, Sydney: University of New South Wales Press.
Cox, D. (2009) 'Aboriginal Healing Project', Indigenous Family Violence Forum, Mackay, Queensland. Available http://www.noviolence.com.au/public/forum2009/dorindacox.pdf (accessed 8 January 2013).
Cox, D., Young, M. and Bairnsfather-Scott, A. (2009) 'No Justice without Healing: Australian Aboriginal People and Family Violence', *Australian Feminist Law Journal* 30: 151.

Craigie, B. (1992) 'Aboriginal People and the Criminal Justice System in the 1990s', in C. Cunneen (ed.) *Aboriginal Perspectives on Criminal Justice*, Sydney: Institute of Criminology, University of Sydney.

Crenshaw, K. (1991) 'Mapping the Margins: Intersectionality, Identity Politics, and Violence against Women of Colour', *Stanford Law Review* 43(6): 1255.

Cunneen, C. (1989) 'Constructing a Law and Order Agenda: Conservative Populism and Aboriginal People in NSW', *Aboriginal Law Bulletin* 1(38): 6.

(1990) *Aboriginal/Police Relations in Redfern with Special Reference to the Police Raid of 8 February 1990*, Sydney: Human Rights and Equal Opportunities Commission.

(1992) 'Judicial Racism', *Aboriginal Law Bulletin* 2(58): 9.

(1999) 'Zero Tolerance Policing: How Will it Affect Indigenous Communities?', *Indigenous Law Bulletin* 4(19): 7.

(2001) *Conflict, Politics and Crime: Aboriginal Communities and the Police*, Sydney: Allen & Unwin.

(2002) 'Preventing Violence against Indigenous Women through Programs which Target Men', *University of New South Wales Law Journal* 25(1): 242.

(2007) 'Riot, Resistance and Moral Panic: Demonising the Colonial Other', in S. Poynting and G. Morgan (eds) *Outrageous! Moral Panics in Australia*, Hobart: ACYS Publishing.

(2008) 'Changing the Neo-Colonial Impacts of Juvenile Justice', *Current Issues in Criminal Justice* 20(1): 43.

(2008a) 'Understanding Restorative Justice through the Lens of Critical Criminology', in T. Anthony and C. Cunneen (eds) *The Critical Criminology Companion*, Sydney: Hawkins Press.

(2010) 'Fear: Crime and Punishment', *Dialogue* 29(2): 44.

(2011) 'Postcolonial Perspectives for Criminology', in M. Bosworth and C. Hoyle (eds) *What is Criminology?*, Oxford: Oxford University Press.

(2011a) 'Indigeneity, Sovereignty, and the Law: Challenging the Processes of Criminalization', *The South Atlantic Quarterly* 110(2): 309.

Cunneen, C. and Robb, T. (1987) *Criminal Justice in North-West New South Wales*, Sydney: New South Wales Bureau of Crime Statistics and Research.

Curthoys, A. (1999) 'An Uneasy Conversation: Multicultural and Indigenous Discourses', in G. Hage and R. Couch (eds) *The Future of Australian Multiculturalism: Reflections on the Twentieth Anniversary of Jean Martin's The Migrant Presence*, Sydney: Research Institute for Humanities and Social Sciences, University of Sydney.

Dagistanli, S. (2007) *Boys Like Them: The Role of the Courts in Moral Panics around "Muslim" Gang Rape*, unpublished PhD thesis, University of Western Sydney.

(2007a) '"Like a Pack of Wild Animals": Moral Panics around "Ethnic" Gang Rape in Sydney', in S. Poynting and G. Morgan (eds) *Outrageous! Moral Panics in Australia*, Hobart: ACYS.

Daly, K. (1994) *Gender, Crime, and Punishment*, New Haven: Yale University Press.

Daly, K. and Marchetti, E. (2012) 'Innovative Justice Processes: Restorative Justice, Indigenous Justice, and Therapeutic Justice', in M. Marmo, W. De Lint and D. Palmer (eds) *Crime and Justice: A Guide to Criminology*, 4th edn, Sydney: Lawbook.

Daly, K. and Proietti-Scifoni, G. (2009) *Defendants in the Circle: Nowra Circle Court, the Presence and Impact of Elders, and Re-offending*, Brisbane: School of Criminology and Criminal Justice, Griffith University.

Davis, M. and McGlade, H. (2005) *International Human Rights Law and the Recognition of Aboriginal Customary Law*, Background Paper 10, Aboriginal Customary Laws Project 94, Law Reform Commission of Western Australia.

Day, A., Nakata, M. and Project Team (2008) 'Implications for the Delivery of Anger Management Programs', in A. Day, M. Nakata and K. Howells (eds) *Anger and Indigenous Men: Understanding and Responding to Violent Behaviour*, Sydney: Federation Press.

Delgado, R. (2000) 'Story-Telling for Oppositionists and Others: A Plea for Narrative', in R. Delgado and J. Stefancic (eds) *Critical Race Theory: The Cutting Edge*, Philadelphia: Temple University Press.

Denzin, N. K. (2001) 'Symbolic Interactionism, Poststructuralism and the Racial Subject', *Symbolic Interaction* 24(2): 243.

Derrida, J. (1978) *Writing and Difference*, Chicago: University of Chicago Press.

(1989–90) 'Force of Law: The "Mystical Foundation of Authority"', trans. M. Quaintance, *Cardozo Law Review* 11: 920.

(2009) *The Beast and the Sovereign*, trans. G. Bennington, Chicago: University of Chicago Press.

Dillon, M. (2007) 'National Security and the Failed State in Remote Australia', Austral Policy Forum 07-01A, Melbourne: RMIT.

Dillon, M. and Westbury, N. (2007) *Beyond Humbug: Transforming Government Engagement with Indigenous Australia*, Adelaide: Seaview Press.

Dodson, M. (1994) 'The Wentworth Lecture: The End in the Beginning: Re(de)finding Aboriginality', *Australian Aboriginal Studies* 1: 2.

(1994a) 'The End in the Beginning re(De)finding Aboriginality', The Wentworth Lecture, The Australian Institute of Aboriginal and Torres Strait Islander Studies (Original Speech).

Dodson, P. (2007) 'Whatever Happened to Reconciliation?', in J. Altman and M. Hinkson (eds) *Coercive Reconciliation: Stabilise, Normalise, Exit*, Melbourne: Arena Press.

Donovan, P. F. (1981) *A Land Full of Possibilities: A History of South Australia's Northern Territory*, Brisbane: University of Queensland Press.

Dorsett, S. (2002) '"Since Time Immemorial": A Story of Common Law Jurisdiction, Native Title, and the Case of Tanistry', *Melbourne University Law Review* 26(1): 32.

Douglas, H. (2002) 'Justice Kriewaldt, Aboriginal Identity and the Criminal Law', *Criminal Law Journal* 26: 204.

(2004) 'Assimilation, Lutheranism and the 1950s Justice of Kriewaldt', *Australian Journal of Legal History* 8: 285.

(2005) *Legal Narratives of Indigenous Existence: Crime, Law, and History*, unpublished PhD thesis, University of Melbourne.

(2005a) 'Customary Law, Sentencing and the Limits of the State', *Canadian Journal of Law and Society* 20(1): 141.

(2005b) '"She Knew What Was Expected of Her": The White Legal System's Encounter with Traditional Marriage', *Feminist Legal Studies* 13: 181.

(2009) *Aboriginal Australians and the Criminal Law: History, Policy, Culture*, Saarbrucken: VDM Verlag.

Downes, D. and Rock, P. (2007) 'Symbolic Interactionism', in D. Downes and P. Rock (eds) *Understanding Deviance*, 5th edn, Oxford: Oxford University Press.

Duff, R. A. (1998) 'Dangerousness and Citizenship', in A. Ashworth and M. Wasik (eds) *Fundamentals of Sentencing Theory: Essays in Honour of Andrew von Hirsch*, Oxford: Clarendon Press.

Duff, R. A. and Garland, D. (1994) *A Reader on Punishment*, Oxford: Oxford University Press.

Durkheim, E. (1933) *The Division of Labor in Society*, Glencoe: Free Press.

(1973) *Moral Education: A Study in the Theory and Application of the Sociology of Education*, New York: Free Press.

(1982) *The Rules of Sociological Method*, New York: Free Press.

Dwyer, P. (2008) 'Last Drinks: Correspondence', *Quarterly Essay* 31: 87.

Easton, S. and Piper, C. (2005) *Sentencing and Punishment: The Quest for Justice*, Oxford: Oxford University Press.

Edmonds, P. (2010) *Urbanizing Frontiers: Indigenous Peoples and Settlers in 19th-century Pacific Rim Cities*, Vancouver: University of British Columbia Press.

Edney, R. (2005) 'Just Deserts in Post-Colonial Society: Problems in the Punishment of Indigenous Offenders', *Southern Cross University Law Review* 9: 73.

(2006) 'The Retreat from Fernando and the Erasure of Indigenous Identity in Sentencing', *Indigenous Law Bulletin* 6(17): 8.

Edney, R. and Bagaric, M. (2007) *Australian Sentencing: Principles and Practice*, Melbourne: Cambridge University Press.

Eggington, D. and Allingham, K. (2006) 'Move on Laws: A New Mechanism for Police Control', *Indigenous Law Bulletin* 6(23): 18.

Eggleston, E. (1976) *Fear, Favour or Affection: Aborigines and the Criminal Law in Victoria, South Australia and Western Australia*, Canberra: Australian National University Press.

Elder, B. (2003) *Blood on the Wattle: Massacres and Maltreatment of Aboriginal Australians since 1788*, 3rd edn, Sydney: New Holland Publishers.

Elias, N. (1978) *The Civilizing Process: The Development of Manners-changes in the Code of Conduct and Feeling in Early Modern Times*, vol. I, New York: Urizen Books.

Ellinghaus, K. (2003) 'Absorbing the "Aboriginal Problem": Controlling Interracial Marriage in Australia in the Late 19th and Early 20th Centuries', *Aboriginal History* 27: 183.

Faine, J. (1993) *Lawyers in the Alice: Aboriginals and Whitefellas' Law*, Sydney: Federation Press.

Falzon, C. (1998) *Foucault and Social Dialogue: Beyond Fragmentation*, London: Routledge.

Fanon, F. (1967) *Black Skin, White Masks*, New York: Grove Press.

Feeley, M. M. (1992) *The Process is the Punishment: Handling Cases in a Lower Criminal Court*, New York: Russell Sage.

Findlay, M. (2006) *Criminal Law: Problems in Context*, 2nd edn, Melbourne: Oxford University Press.

Finnane, M. (2001) '"Payback", Customary Law and Criminal Law in Colonised Australia', *International Journal of the Sociology of Law* 29: 293.

(2006) 'The Tides of Customary Law', *ANZLH E-Journal* 1.

Finnane, M. and McGuire, J. (2001) 'The Uses of Punishment and Exile: Aborigines in Colonial Australia', *Punishment and Society* 3(2): 279.

Finnane, M. and Paisley, F. (2010) 'Police Violence and the Limits of Law on a Late Colonial Frontier: The "Borroloola Case" in 1930s Australia', *Law and History Review* 28(1): 141.

Fisher, M. (1985) 'Casenote on *R v Charlie Limbiari Jagamara*', *Aboriginal Law Bulletin* 1(12): 11.

Fitzgerald, J. (2009) 'Why Are Indigenous Imprisonment Rates Rising?', *Crime and Justice Statistics*, Issue Paper No. 41, Sydney: NSW Bureau of Crime Statistics and Research.

Fitzgerald, R. (1986) *A History of Queensland: From the Dreaming to 1915*, Brisbane: University of Queensland Press.

Fleury-Steiner, B. D., Dunn, K. and Fleury-Steiner, R. (2009) 'Governing through Crime as Commonsense Racism: Race, Space, and Death Penalty "Reform" in Delaware', *Punishment and Society* 11(1): 5.

Flynn, M. (1994) 'Go Directly to Gaol!', *Alternative Law Journal* 19(5): 211.
(2004) 'Fernando and the Sentencing of Indigenous Offenders', *Judicial Officers Bulletin* 16(9): 67.
(2005) 'Not "Aboriginal Enough" for Particular Consideration when Sentencing', *Indigenous Law Bulletin* 6(9): 15.
Flynn, M. and Stanton, S. (1997) 'Another Failed Sovereignty Claim: *Thorpe v Commonwealth of Australia (No. 3)*', *Indigenous Law Bulletin* 4(7): 19.
Fogelson, R. M. (1968) 'Violence as Protest', in R. H. Connery (ed.) *Urban Riots: Violence and Social Change*, Proceedings of the Academy of Political Science, vol. XXIX, no. 1, Academy of Political Science, Columbia University.
Foley, G. (2001) *Black Power in Redfern 1968–1972*, The Koori History Website. Available http://www.kooriweb.org/foley/essays/essay_1.html (accessed 8 January 2013).
Forbes-Boyte, K. (2009) 'Whiteout? Gentrification and Colonialism in Inner-City Sydney', *City* 13(1): 153.
Ford, L. (2006) 'Empire and Order on the Colonial Frontiers of Georgia and New South Wales', *Itinerario: Geographies of Empire* 30: 96.
(2010) *Settler Sovereignty: Jurisdiction and Indigenous People in America and Australia, 1788–1836*, Cambridge, MA: Harvard University Press.
Foucault, M. (1979) *Discipline and Punish: The Birth of the Prison*, trans. A. Sheridan, New York: Vintage Books.
(1980) *Power/Knowledge: Selected Interviews and Other Writings 1972–1977*, C. Gordon (ed.), New York: Pantheon Books.
(1981) *The History of Sexuality*, vol. 1, trans. R. Hurley, Harmondsworth: Penguin.
(1991) 'Governmentality', in G. Burchell, C. Gordon and P. Miller (eds) *The Foucault Effect: Studies in Governmentality*, London: Harvester.
(2007) *Security, Territory, Population: Lectures at the College de France 1977–78*, trans. G. Burchell, Basingstoke: Palgrave Macmillan.
Fougere, C. (2006) 'Customary Law and International Human Rights: *The Queen v GJ*', *Law Society Journal* 44(7): 42.
Franklin, J. (2008) 'The Cultural Roots of Aboriginal Violence', *Quadrant* 52(11): 22.
Fraser, N. (1995) 'From Redistribution to Recognition? Dilemmas of Justice in a "Post-Socialist" Age', *New Left Review* 212: 68.
(1996) 'Social Justice in the Age of Identity Politics: Redistribution, Recognition, and Participation', Lecture delivered at the Tanner Lectures on Human Values, Stanford University. Available http://tannerlectures.utah.edu/lectures/documents/Fraser98.pdf (accessed 8 January 2013).
(1997) *Justus Interruptus: Critical Reflections on the 'Postsocialist' Condition*, New York: Routledge.
(2000) 'Rethinking Recognition', *New Left Review* 3: 107.
(2004) 'Integrating Redistribution and Recognition: Problems in Moral Philosophy', in N. Fraser and A. Honneth (eds) *Redistribution or Recognition?: A Political-philosophical Exchange*, New York: Verso.
(2004a) 'Institutionalizing Democratic Justice: Redistribution, Recognition, and Participation', in S. Benhabib and N. Fraser (eds) *Pragmatism, Critique, Judgment: Essays for Richard J. Bernstein*, Cambridge, MA: Massachusetts Institute of Technology.
Fromm, E. (1963) *The Dogma of Christ and Other Essays on Religion, Psychology and Culture*, Oxford: Routledge & Kegan Paul.
Fryer-Smith, S. (2002) *Aboriginal Benchbook for Western Australian Courts*, Carlton: Australian Institute of Judicial Administration.

Funnell, N. (2005) 'Non-lethal Intelligence: Strike Force Coburn and the Police Response to the Redfern Riot', *Indigenous Law Bulletin* 6(10): 4.

Gargett, A. (2005) 'A Critical Media Analysis of the Redfern Riot', *Indigenous Law Bulletin* 6(10): 8.

Garland, D. (2001) *The Culture of Control: Crime and Social Order in Contemporary Society*, Oxford: Oxford University Press.

(2004) 'Beyond the Culture of Control', *Critical Review of International Social and Political Philosophy* 7(2): 160.

Gaykamangu, J. G. (2012) 'Ngarra Law: Aboriginal Customary Law from Arnhem Land', *Northern Territory Law Journal* 2: 236.

Gaymarani, G. P. (2011) 'An Introduction to the Ngarra Law of Arnhem Land', *Northern Territory Law Journal* 1: 283.

Geertz, C. (1985) *The Interpretation of Cultures*, New York: Basic Books.

Glowczewski, B. and Wotton, L. (2008) *Warriors for Peace: The Political Condition of the Aboriginal People as Viewed from Palm Island*, Montpellier: Indigène Editions.

Goffman, E. (1958) *The Presentation of Self in Everyday Life*, Edinburgh: University of Edinburgh, Social Sciences Research Centre.

Goldflam, R. (2012) 'The (Non-)Role of Aboriginal Customary Law in Sentencing', *Uluru Criminal Law Conference*, 31 August–1 September, Legalwise Seminars.

Goode, E. and Ben-Yehuda, N. (1994) 'Moral Panics: Culture, Politics, and Social Construction', *Annual Review of Sociology* 20: 149.

Gore, C. and Pratten, D. (2003) 'The Politics of Plunder: The Rhetorics of Order and Disorder in Southern Nigeria', *African Affairs* 102: 211.

Gosford, B. (2010) 'The Oz, Yuendumu and "Tribal Punishment" – Dangerous Myths about Customary Law', *Crikey* (Sydney), 18 October. Available http://www.crikey.com.au/2010/10/18/the-oz-yuendumu-and-tribal-punishment-dangerous-myths-about-customary-law/ (accessed 5 January 2013).

Graham, K. (1999) 'Aboriginal Marginalisation and Racism in the Juvenile Justice System', Paper presented at the Children and Crime: Victims and Offenders Conference convened by the Australian Institute of Criminology, 17–18 June, Brisbane. Available http://www.aic.gov.au/media_library/conferences/children/graham.pdf (accessed 10 January 2013).

Gray, P. (2005) 'The Politics of Risk and Young Offenders' Experiences of Social Exclusion and Restorative Justice', *British Journal of Criminology* 45(6): 938.

Gray, S. (2005a) 'The State of Things in the Territory: Literalism, Principle and Policy in Northern Territory Criminal Law', *Criminal Law Journal* 29: 37.

(2007) 'The Elephant in the Drawing Room: Slavery and the Stolen Wages Debate', *Australian Indigenous Law Review* 11(1): 30.

Gray, T., Burgess, S. and Hinton, M. (2008) 'Indigenous Australians in Sentencing', in E. Johnston, M. Hinton and D. Rigney (eds) *Indigenous Australians and the Law*, 2nd edn, New York: Routledge-Cavendish.

Green, N. (1995) *The Forrest River Massacres*, Fremantle: Fremantle Arts Centre Press.

Greer, G. (2008) *On Rage*, Melbourne: Melbourne University Press.

Gribble, Rev. J. B. (1884) *'Black But Comely'. Or, Glimpses of Aboriginal Life in Australia*, London: Morgan and Scott.

Guha, R. (1998) *Dominance without Hegemony: History and Power in Colonial India*, Cambridge, MA: Harvard University Press.

Gunn, J. (1990) *We of the Never-Never*, Sydney: Arrow.

Haebich, A. (1992) *For Their Own Good: Aborigines and Government in the Southwest of Western Australia 1900–1940*, Nedlands: University of Western Australia Press.

(2000) *Broken Circles: Fragmenting Indigenous Families 1800–2000*, Fremantle: Fremantle Arts Centre Press.

Hage, G. (1998) *White Nation: Fantasies of White Supremacy in a Multicultural Society*, Sydney: Pluto Press.

(2003) *Against Paranoid Nationalism: Searching for Hope in a Shrinking Society*, Sydney: Pluto Press.

Hall, S., Critcher, C., Jefferson, T., Clarke, J. and Roberts, B. (1978) *Policing the Crisis: Mugging, the State, and Law and Order*, London: Macmillan.

Harman, K. E. (2008) *Aboriginal Convicts: Race, Law, and Transportation in Colonial New South Wales*, unpublished PhD thesis, University of Tasmania.

Harris, C. (1995) 'Whiteness as Property', in K. Crenshaw, N. Gotanda, G. Peller and K. Thomas (eds) *Critical Race Theory*, New York: The New Press.

Harrison, B. (1978) 'The Myall Creek Massacre', in I. McBryde (ed.) *Records of Time Past*, Canberra: Australian Institute of Aboriginal Studies.

Hartman, S. V. (1997) *Scenes of Subjection: Terror, Slavery, and Self-making in Nineteenth-century America*, New York: Oxford University Press.

Hasluck, P. (1953) *Native Welfare in Australia*, Perth: Patterson Brokenshaw.

(1988) *Shades of Darkness: Aboriginal Affairs 1925–1965*, Melbourne: Melbourne University Press.

Havemann, P. (2005) 'Denial, Modernity and Exclusion: Indigenous Placelessness in Australia', *Macquarie Law Journal* 5: 57.

Hay, D. (1975) 'Property, Authority and the Criminal Law', in D. Hay, P. Linebaugh, J. G. Rule, E. P. Thompson and C. Winslow (eds) *Albion's Fatal Tree: Crime and Society in Eighteenth-century England*, New York: Pantheon Books.

Heiss, A. (2012) *Am I Black Enough For You?*, Sydney: Random House.

Herbert, C. E. (1905) *Annual Report of the Government Resident*, Port Darwin.

Hindess, B. (1996) *Discourses of Power: From Hobbes to Foucault*, Oxford: Blackwell.

Hogarth, J. (1971) *Sentencing as a Human Process*, Toronto: University of Toronto Press.

Hogg, R. (2001) 'Penality and Modes of Regulating Indigenous People in Australia', *Punishment and Society* 3(3): 355.

(2005) 'Policing the Rural Crisis', *Australian & New Zealand Journal of Criminology* 38(3): 340.

(2008) 'Resisting a "Law and Order" Society', in T. Anthony and C. Cunneen (eds) *The Critical Criminology Companion*, Sydney: Hawkins Press.

Hooper, C. (2008), *The Tall Man: Death and Life on Palm Island*, Melbourne: Hamish Hamilton.

House of Representatives (2006), 'Revised Explanatory Memorandum: Crimes Amendment (Bail and Sentencing) Bill 2006', The Parliament of the Commonwealth of Australia.

Howard-Wagner, D. (2008) 'Legislating away Indigenous Rights', *Law Text Culture* 12(1): 45.

(2010) 'The State's "Intervention", in Indigenous Affairs in the Northern Territory: Governing the Indigenous Population through Violence, Abuse and Neglect', in C. Browne and J. McGill (eds) *Violence in France and Australia: Disorder in the Post-colonial Welfare State*, Sydney: University of Sydney Press.

(2010a) 'From State of Denial to State of Emergency: Governing Australian Indigenous Communities through the Exception', in D. Fassin and M. Pandolfi (eds) *Contemporary*

States of Emergency: The Politics of Military and Humanitarian Interventions, New York: Zone Publishing.

Hoy, D. C. (1986) 'Power, Repression, Progress: Foucault, Lukes, and the Frankfurt School', in D. C. Hoy (ed.) *Foucault: A Critical Reader*, Oxford: Basil Blackwell.

Hudson, B. (1987) *Justice through Punishment: A Critique of the 'Justice' Model of Corrections*, Hampshire: Macmillan Education.

(1999) 'Punishment, Poverty and Responsibility: The Case for a Hardship Defence', *Social and Legal Studies* 8: 583.

(2006) 'Punishing Monsters, Judging Aliens: Justice at the Borders of Community', *Australian & New Zealand Journal of Criminology* 39(2): 232.

(2006a) 'Balancing the Ethical and the Political: Normative Reflections on the Institutionalization of Restorative Justice', in I. Aertsen, T. Daems and L. Robert (eds) *Institutionalizing Restorative Justice*, Portland: Willan.

(2006b) 'Beyond White Man's Justice: Race, Gender and Justice in Late Modernity', *Theoretical Criminology* 10(1): 29.

Huggins, J. (1987–8) '"Firing on in the Mind": Aboriginal Women Domestic Servants in the Inter-war Years', *Hecate* 13(2): 5.

Hughes, H. (2007) *Lands of Shame: Aboriginal and Torres Strait Islander 'Homelands' in Transition*, Sydney: Centre for Independent Studies.

Human Rights and Equal Opportunities Commission (2006) 'Submission to the Inquiry into the Crime Amendment (Bail and Sentencing) Bill 2006', Submission no. 5, 27 September.

Hume, L. (1991) 'Them Days: Life on an Aboriginal Reserve 1892–1960', *Aboriginal History* 15(1): 4.

Hunt, J. and Smith, D. (2007) *Indigenous Community Governance Project: Year Two Research Findings*, Working Paper 36, Canberra: Centre for Aboriginal Economic Policy Research.

Hunter, C. (2005) 'Palm Island: The Truth behind the Media Portrayal – an Interview with Erykah Kyle, Chairperson of the Palm Island Aboriginal Council', *Indigenous Law Bulletin* 6(12): 16.

Hunyor, J. (2007) 'Custom and Culture in Bail and Sentencing: Part of the Problem or Part of the Solution?', *Indigenous Law Review* 6(29): 8.

Indigenous Law Centre (2010) *Bush Law: An Open Forum*, 17 March, University of New South Wales, Sydney.

Jackson, R. (2004) 'Submission to the Inquiry into Issues Relating to Redfern/Waterloo', Indigenous Social Justice Association submission no. 91, 29 September.

Jackson, S. and Hardy, F. (2010) 'The Impact of Mandatory Sentencing on Indigenous Offenders', Paper presented to the Sentencing Conference 2010, Canberra: Australian National University. Available http://njca.anu.edu.au/Professional%20Development/programs%20by%20year/2010/Sentencing%202010/Papers/Jackson-Hardy%20.pdf (accessed 8 January 2013).

JanMohammed, A. R. (1985) 'The Economy of Manichean Allegory: The Function of Racial Difference in Colonialist Literature', in H. L. Gates Jr. (ed.) *"Race," Writing and Difference*, Chicago: University of Chicago Press.

Jeffries, S. and Bond, C. (2009) 'Does Indigeneity Matter? Sentencing Indigenous Offenders in South Australia's Higher Courts', *Australian & New Zealand Journal of Criminology* 42(1): 47.

Johannsen, K. G. (1992) *A Son of 'The Red Centre': Memoirs and Anecdotes of the Life of Road Train Pioneer and Bush Inventor of the Northern Territory of Australia*, Morphettville: K. Johannsen.

Johns, G. (2011) *Aboriginal Self-Determination: The Whiteman's Dream*, Melbourne: Connor Court Publishing.

Kenny, R. (2008) 'Tricks or Treats?: A Case for Kulin Knowing in Batman's Treaty', *History Australia* 5(2): 38.1.

Kidd, R. (1997) *The Way We Civilise: Aboriginal Affairs – the Untold Story*, Brisbane: University of Queensland.

(2003) 'Abuse of Trust: The Government as Banker in Queensland', *Indigenous Law Bulletin* 5(26): 13.

Kimm, J. (2004) *A Fatal Conjunction: Two Laws Two Cultures*, Sydney: Federation Press.

Kowald, M. and Johnston, R. (1992) *You Can't Make it Rain: The Story of the North Australian Pastoral Company 1877–1991*, Brisbane: Boolarong Publications with North Australian Pastoral Company.

Kristeva, J. (1991) *Strangers to Ourselves*, trans. L. S. Roudiez, New York: Columbia University Press.

Kritzer, H. (2007) 'Towards a Theorization of Craft', *Social and Legal Studies* 16: 321.

Lacan, J. (1977) *Écrits: A Selection*, trans. Alan Sheridan, London: Tavistock.

Lacey, N. (1988) *State Punishment: Political Principles and Community Values*, London: Routledge.

(2002) 'Legal Constructions of Crime', in M. Maguire, R. Morgan and R. Reiner (eds) *The Oxford Handbook of Criminology*, Oxford: Oxford University Press.

Langton, M. (1981) 'Urbanizing Aborigines: The Social Scientists' Great Deception', *Social Alternatives* 2(2): 16.

(1993) 'Rum, Seduction and Death: "Aboriginality" and Alcohol', *Oceania* 63(3): 195.

Law Council of Australia (2006) 'Submission to the Inquiry into the Crime Amendment (Bail and Sentencing) Bill 2006', Submission no. 3, 26 September.

Law Reform Commission of Western Australia (2006) *Aboriginal Customary Laws*, Final Report, Project 94.

Lawford, E. (1988) 'Crowbar saved my life', in P. Marshall (ed.) *Raparapa Kularr Martuwarra . . . All Right, Now We Go 'Side the River, along that Sundown Way: Stories from Fitzroy River Drovers*, Broome: Magbala Books.

Little, J. (2010) 'Journalism, Creative Non-fiction and Australia's Black History: The Tall Man and Cross-cultural Source Relationships', *Australian Journalism Review* 32(2): 47.

Locke, J. (1924) *Two Treatises on Government*, Book II, London: Everyman's Library.

Lombroso, C. (1876/2006) *Criminal Man*, trans. M. Gibson and N. H. Rafter, Durham, NC: Duke University Press.

Loos, N. (1991) 'From Church to State: The Queensland Government Take-overs of Anglican Missions in North Queensland', *Aboriginal History* 15(1): 73.

Loy, D. (2010) *Bush Law*, Message Stick Transcript, Australian Broadcasting Corporation, 28 March. Available http://www.abc.net.au/tv/messagestick/stories/s2855782.htm (accessed 5 January 2013).

Lucas, D. (1995) 'Breaking the Silence that Silences: A Time of Challenge and Change in Aboriginal/Police Relations, the 1960s and 1970s', *Current Issues in Criminal Justice* 7(1): 44.

Luke, G. and Cunneen, C. (1998) *Sentencing Aboriginal People in the Northern Territory: A Statistical Analysis*, Sydney: Institute of Criminology, Sydney University Law School.

Mackenzie, G., Stobbs, N. and Thomas, M. (2007) '"What Really Happened" Versus "What We Can Prove": Tension between the Roles of Coroner and DPP in Queensland', *Indigenous Law Bulletin* 6(24): 6.

Maddison, S. (2009) *Black Politics: Inside the Complexity of Aboriginal Political Culture*, Sydney: Allen & Unwin.

Mals, P., Howells, K., Day, A. and Hall, G. (2008) 'Indigenous Service Providers' Perspectives on Anger Programs', in A. Day, M. Nakata and K. Howells (eds) *Anger and Indigenous Men: Understanding and Responding to Violent Behaviour*, Sydney: Federation Press.

Marchetti, E. (2010) 'Indigenous Sentencing Courts and Partner Violence: Perspectives of Court Practitioners and Elders on Gender Power Imbalances During the Sentencing Hearing', *Australian & New Zealand Journal of Criminology* 43(2): 263.

Marchetti, E. and Daly, K. (2007) 'Indigenous Sentencing Courts: Towards a Theoretical Jurisprudential Model', *Sydney Law Review* 29(3): 415.

McAuliffe, C. (2009) 'Book Review: *Cities of Whiteness*', *Annals of the Association of American Geographers* 99(3): 627.

McCausland, R. (2008) 'Indigenous Trauma, Grief and Loss', in A. Day, M. Nakata and K. Howells (eds) *Anger and Indigenous Men: Understanding and Responding to Violent Behaviour*, Sydney: Federation Press.

McCoy, C. (1997) 'Review Essay: Sentencing (and) the Underclass', *Law & Society Review* 31: 589.

McDougall, S. (2006) *Palm Island: Future Directions*, Resource Officer Report. Available http://www.link.asn.au/downloads/papers/indeginous/p_in_14.pdf (accessed 8 January 2013).

McGlade, H. (2006) 'Aboriginal Women, Girls and Sexual Assault: The Long Road to Equality within the Criminal Justice System', *ACSSA Newsletter* 12: 6. Available http://www.aifs.gov.au/acssa/pubs/newsletter/n12pdf/n12_4.pdf (accessed 8 January 2013).

(2012) *Our Greatest Challenge: Aboriginal Children and Human Rights*, Canberra: Aboriginal Studies Press.

McGrath, A. (1987) *'Born in the Cattle': Aborigines in Cattle Country*, Sydney: Allen & Unwin.

McIntyre, G. (2005) *Aboriginal Customary Law: Can it be Recognised?*, Background Paper 9, Aboriginal Customary Laws Project 94, Law Reform Commission of Western Australia.

McLaughlin, R. (1996) 'Some Problems and Issues in Recognition of Indigenous Customary Law', *Aboriginal Law Bulletin* 3(82): 4.

Mead, G. H. and Morris, C. W. (1934) *Mind, Self and Society from the Standpoint of a Social Behaviourist*, Chicago: University of Chicago Press.

Melossi, D. (2000) 'Changing Representations of the Criminal', *British Journal of Criminology* 40(2): 296.

Meyer, J. and O'Malley, P. (2005) 'Missing the Punitive Turn? Canadian Criminal Justice, "Balance" and Penal Modernism', in J. Pratt, D. Brown, S. Hallsworth, M. Brown and W. Morrison (eds) *The New Punitiveness: Trends, Theories, Perspectives*, Cullompton: Willan.

Mickler, S. (1992) 'Visions of Disorder: Aboriginal People and Youth Crime Reporting', *Cultural Studies* 6(3): 322.

Mildren, D. (1994) 'The Administration of Justice in the Northern Territory during the War Years', *Journal of Northern Territory History* 5: 21.

(1996) 'The Role of the Legal Profession and the Courts in the Evolution of Democracy and Aboriginal Self-Determination in the Northern Territory in the Twentieth Century', *Journal of Northern Territory History* 7: 47.

(2003) *Aboriginal Sentencing*, Paper presented to the Seventh Colloquium of the Judicial Conference of Australia Inc, Darwin, 30 May–1 June. Available http://www.jca.asn.au/attachments/mildren03.doc (accessed 5 January 2013).

(2008) 'Customary Law: Is it Relevant?', *Northern Territory Law Journal* 1(2): 69.

(2008a) 'Aboriginals in the Criminal Justice System', *Adelaide Law Review* 29: 7.

(2011) *Big Boss Fella – All Same Judge: A History of the Supreme Court of the Northern Territory*, Sydney: Federation Press.

Mills, J. (2011) 'The Justice Gulf in the Centre', *New Matilda*, 2 February. Available http://newmatilda.com/2011/02/02/justice-gulf-centre (accessed 5 January 2013).

Moreton-Robinson, A. (2003) 'I Still Call Australia Home: Indigenous Belonging and Place in a White Postcolonising Society' in S. Ahmed, C. Castada, A. Fortier and M. Sheller (eds) *Uprootings/Regroundings: Questions of Home and Migration*, Oxford: Berg.

Morris, B. (1997) 'Racism, Egalitarianism and Aborigines', in G. Cowlishaw and B. Morris (eds) *Race Matters: Indigenous Australians and 'Our' Society*, Canberra: Aboriginal Studies Press.

(2001) 'Policing Racial Fantasy in the Far West of New South Wales', *Oceania* 71(3): 242.

(2005) 'Crisis in Identity: Aborigines, Media, the Law and Politics – Civil Disturbance in an Australian Town', *Critique of Anthropology* 25(1): 59.

Moses, D. (2000) 'An Antipodean Genocide? The Origins of the Genocidal Moment in the Colonization of Australia', *Journal of Genocide Research* 2(1): 89.

Motha, S. (1998) '*MABO* – Encountering the Epistemic Limit of the Recognition of Difference', *Griffith Law Review* 7(1): 79.

(2005) 'The Failure of "Postcolonial" Sovereignty in Australia', *Australian Feminist Law Journal* 22: 107.

(2007) 'Reconciliation as Dominion', in S. Veitch (ed.) *Law and the Politics of Reconciliation*, Edinburgh: Ashgate.

Muncie, J. (2006) 'Governing Young People: Coherence and Contradiction in Contemporary Youth Justice', *Critical Social Policy* 26(4): 770.

Musharbash, Y. (2009) *Yuendumu Everyday: Contemporary Life in Remote Aboriginal Australia*, Canberra: Aboriginal Studies Press.

Napaljarri, P. R. and Cataldi, L. (trans.) (2003) *Warlpiri Dreamings and Histories: Yimikirli – Newly Recorded Stories from the Aboriginal Elders of Central Australia*, Walnut Creek, CA: AltaMira Press.

National Inquiry into the Separation of Aboriginal and Torres Strait Islander Children from Their Families (1997) *Bringing Them Home: Report of the National Inquiry into the Separation of Aboriginal and Torres Strait Islander Children from Their Families*, Sydney: Human Rights and Equal Opportunity Commission. Available http://www.humanrights.gov.au/pdf/social_justice/bringing_them_home_report.pdf (accessed 8 January 2013).

New South Wales Law Reform Commission (2000) *Sentencing: Aboriginal Offenders*, Final Report, no. 96, Sydney: NSWLRC.

Nicholson, J. (1999) 'The Sentencing of Aboriginal Offenders', *Criminal Law Journal* 23: 85.

(2012) 'Sentencing Aboriginal Offenders – A Judge's Perspective', *Uluru Criminal Law Conference*, 31 August–1 September, Legalwise Seminars.

Norrie, A. (2001) *Crime, Reason and History: A Critical Introduction to Criminal Law*, 2nd edn, London: Butterworths.

North Australian Aboriginal Justice Agency (2008) 'Submission to the Northern Territory Emergency Response Review Board', Submission no. 105. Available http://www.nterreview.gov.au/subs/nter_review_report/105_naaja/105_NAAJA_6.htm (accessed 10 January 2013).

Northern Territory Department of Justice (2008) *Correctional Services: Statistical Summary 2007–2008*, Darwin: Office of Crime Prevention.

(2009) *Correctional Services: Statistical Summary 2008–2009*, Darwin: Office of Crime Prevention.

(2010) *Annual Report 2009–10*, Darwin: Northern Territory Government. Available http://www.nt.gov.au/justice/docs/depart/annualreports/doj_areport_2009_2010.pdf (accessed 8 January 2013).

Northern Territory Emergency Response Review Board (2008) *Report of the NTER Review Board*, Canberra: Commonwealth of Australia.

Northern Territory Government (2011) 'Major Remote Towns: Properly Planned and Designed Towns', Department of Regional Development and Indigenous Advancement. Available http://www.drdia.nt.gov.au/regional_services (accessed 8 January 2013).

Northern Territory Law Reform Committee (2003) *Report of the Committee of Inquiry into Aboriginal Customary Law*, Final Report, Darwin: NTLRC.

(2003a) *Aboriginal Communities and Aboriginal Law in the Northern Territory*, Background Paper No. 1, Inquiry into Aboriginal Customary Law, Darwin: NTLRC.

Northern Territory Police, Fire and Emergency Services (2003–10) *Annual Reports*, Darwin: Northern Territory Government.

Northern Territory Road Safety Taskforce (2006) *Safer Road Use: A Territory Imperative*, Report – Key Findings. Darwin: AGPS.

Northern Territory Supreme Court (2009) 'Sentencing Principles'. Available http://www.supremecourt.nt.gov.au/documents/sentencing_principles.pdf (accessed 8 January 2013).

Nowra, L. (2007) *Bad Dreaming: Aboriginal Men's Violence against Women and Children*, Melbourne: Pluto Press.

O'Connell, S. (2006) 'Aboriginal Customary Law under Siege', *National Indigenous Legal Conference*, Sydney, 22–23 September.

O'Conner, I. (1993) 'Aboriginal Child Welfare Law, Policies and Practices in Queensland: 1865–1989', *Australian Social Work* 46(3): 11.

O'Malley, P. (1996) 'Indigenous Governance', *Economy and Society* 25(3): 310.

(2004) 'The Uncertain Promise of Risk', *Australian & New Zealand Journal of Criminology* 37(3): 323.

O'Shane, P. (1992) 'Aborigines and the Criminal Justice System', in C. Cunneen (ed.) *Aboriginal Perspectives on Criminal Justice*, Sydney: Institute of Criminology, University of Sydney.

(1999) 'Back to the Future: Aboriginal Imprisonment Rates and Other Experiences', *Flinders Journal of Law Reform* 3(2): 127.

Office of the Aboriginal and Torres Strait Islander Social Justice Commissioner (1996) *Indigenous Deaths in Custody 1989 to 1996*, A Report for the Aboriginal and Torres Strait Islander Commission, Sydney: Human Rights and Equal Opportunities Commission.

Omeri, S. (2006) 'Considering Aboriginality', *Law Society Journal* August: 74.

Ormesher, P. (1995) 'The Background of Redfern: Assimilation, Post-assimilation and Australian Racism', *Nelen Yubu* 59: 16.

Palmer, E. (1903) *Early Days in North Queensland*, Classics edn, Sydney: Angus & Robertson.

Payne, J. (2012) 'Aboriginal Sentencing Courts', *Uluru Criminal Law Conference*, 31 August–1 September, Legalwise Seminars.

Payne, S. (1990) 'Aboriginal Women and the Criminal Justice System', *Aboriginal Law Bulletin* 1(46): 9.

Pearson, N. (2007) 'White Guilt, Victimhood and the Quest for a Radical Centre', *Griffith Review* 16: 11.

Pedersen, H. and Woorunmurra, B. (2000) *Jandamarra and the Bunuba Resistance*, Broome: Magabala Books.

Pilkington, J. (2009) *Aboriginal Communities and the Police's Taskforce Themis: Case Studies in Remote Aboriginal Community Policing in the Northern Territory*, Darwin: North Australian Aboriginal Justice Agency and Central Australian Legal Aid Service.

Pitty, R. (1994) 'Brewarrina Riot: The Hidden History', *Aboriginal Law Bulletin* 3(70): 9.

Pollock, G. (1988) *Vision and Difference*, New York: Routledge.

Porter, R. (2009) 'From Community Housing to Public Housing in Northern Territory Remote Aboriginal Communities: The Policy Context', DKCRC Working Paper 44, Desert Knowledge CRC, Alice Springs.

Povinelli, E. (2002) *The Cunning of Recognition: Indigenous Alterities and the Making of Australian Multiculturalism*, Durham, NC: Duke University Press.

Pratt, J. (2005) 'Elias, Punishment, and Decivilization', in J. Pratt, D. Brown, M. Brown, S. Hallsworth and W. Morrison (eds) *The New Punitiveness: Trends, Theories, Perspectives*, Cullompton: Willan.

(2008) 'Penal Populism and the Contemporary Role of Punishment', in T. Anthony and C. Cunneen (eds) *The Critical Criminology Companion*, Sydney: Hawkins Press.

Presdee, M. (2000) *Cultural Criminology and the Carnival of Crime*, London: Routledge.

Queensland Government (2011) *Aboriginal and Torres Strait Islander Missions and Reserves in Queensland*. Available http://www.slq.qld.gov.au/__data/assets/pdf_file/0018/82602/missions_and_reserves.pdf (accessed 8 January 2013).

Queensland Police Union (2005) *Police Journal*, July, Brisbane: Queensland Police Union of Employees.

Read, P. (2007) 'Murder, Revenge and Reconciliation on the North Eastern Frontier', *History Australia* 4(1): 09.1.

Redfern Residents for Reconciliation (2012) 'Redfern Oral History Timeline'. Available http://www.redfernoralhistory.org/Timeline/Timeline/tabid/239/Default.aspx (accessed 5 January 2013).

Reid, G. (1990) *A Picnic with the Natives: Aboriginal-European Relations in the Northern Territory to 1910*, Melbourne: Melbourne University Press.

Reynolds, H. (1982) *The Other Side of the Frontier: Aboriginal Resistance to the European Invasion of Australia*, Ringwood: Penguin.

(1996) *Aboriginal Sovereignty: Reflections on Race, State and Nation*, Sydney: Allen & Unwin.

Richards, K. (2009) *Juveniles' Contact with the Criminal Justice System in Australia*, Canberra: Australian Institute of Criminology.

Roach, K. (2009) 'One Step Forward, Two Steps Back: *Gladue* in the Courts of Appeal', *Criminal Law Quarterly* 54: 470.

Roberts, J. V., Stalans, L. J., Indermaur, D. and Hough, M. (2003) *Penal Populism and Public Opinion: Lessons from Five Countries*, New York: Oxford University Press.

Rolls, E. (1984) *A Million Wild Acres: 200 years of Man and an Australian Forest*, Ringwood: Penguin.
Rolls, M. (2001) 'The Meaninglessness of Aboriginal "Cultures"', *Balayi: Culture Law and Colonialism* 2(1): 7.
Ross, K. and Taylor, J. (2000) 'The Relative Social and Economic Status of Indigenous People in Bourke, Brewarrina and Walgett', Working Paper No. 8/2000, Canberra: Centre for Aboriginal Economic Policy Research.
Rowley, C. D. (1970) *The Destruction of Aboriginal Society: Aboriginal Policy and Practice*, vol. I, Canberra: Australian National University Press.
Rowse, T. (1987) 'Were You Ever Savages? Aboriginal Insiders and Pastoralists' Patronage', *Oceania* 58(2): 82.
(1990) 'Enlisting the Warlpiri', *Continuum: Journal of Media & Cultural Studies* 3(2): 174.
(1992) 'Strehlow's Strap: Functionalism and Historicism in Colonial Ethnography', in B. Attwood and J. Arnold (eds) *Power, Knowledge and Aborigines*, Clayton: La Trobe University Press in association with National Centre for Australian Studies, Monash University.
(1998) *White Flour, White Power: From Rations to Citizenship in Central Australia*, Cambridge: Cambridge University Press.
(2011) 'Global Indigenism: A Genealogy of a Non-Racial Category', in A. Holland and B. Brookes (eds) *Rethinking the Racial Moment: Essays on the Colonial Encounter*, Newcastle upon Tyne: Cambridge Scholars.
Royal Commission into Aboriginal Deaths in Custody (RCIADIC) (1991) *National Report*, Canberra: Australian Government Publishing Service.
Rudin, J. (2005) 'Aboriginal Justice and Restorative Justice', in E. Elliott and R. Gordon (eds) *New Directions in Restorative Justice: Issues, Practice, Evaluation*, Cullompton: Willan.
Rusden, G. W. (1883) *History of Australia*, vol. III, Melbourne: G. Robertson.
Rutherford, J. (2000) *The Gauche Intruder: Freud, Lacan and the White Australian Fantasy*, Melbourne: Melbourne University Press.
Sadurski, W. (1985) 'Distributive Justice and the Theory of Punishment', *Oxford Journal of Legal Studies* 5(1): 47.
Said, E. (1978) *Orientalism: Western Conceptions of the Orient*, Harmondsworth: Penguin.
(1994) *Culture and Imperialism*, London: Vintage.
Sanson-Fisher, R. (1978) 'Aborigines in Crime Statistics: An Interaction between Poverty and Detectors', *Australian & New Zealand Journal of Criminology* 11(2): 7.
Scraton, P. (2007) *Power, Conflict and Criminalisation*, London: Routledge.
Select Committee on Aboriginal Tribes (1837) *Report of the Parliamentary Select Committee on Aboriginal Tribes (British Settlements)*, London: William Ball. Available http://archive.org/stream/reportparliamen00britgoog#page/n6/mode/2up (accessed 5 January 2013).
Select Committee on The Aborigines Bill (1899) *Report of the 1899 Select Committee of the Legislative Council on The Aborigines Bill: Minutes of Evidence*, South Australian Parliamentary Papers, no. 77, 8 November, Auth. C. E. Bristow, Adelaide: Government Printer.
Shapiro, M. (1972) 'Toward a Theory of *Stare Decisis*', *Journal of Legal Studies* 1(1): 125.
Shaw, W. (2000) 'Ways of Whiteness: Harlemising Sydney's Aboriginal Redfern', *Australian Geographical Studies* 38(3): 291.
(2003) '(Post)Colonial Encounters: Gendered Racialisations in Australian Courtrooms', *Gender, Place & Culture* 10(4): 315.
(2006) 'Decolonizing Geographies of Whiteness', *Antipode* 38(4): 851.
(2007) *Cities of Whiteness*, Malden, MA: Wiley-Blackwell.

(2009) 'Riotous Sydney: Redfern, Macquarie Fields, and (My) Cronulla', *Environment and Planning D: Society and Space* 27: 425.

Silver, A. (1976) 'The Demand for Order in Civil Society', in D. J. Bordua (ed.) *The Police: Six Sociological Essays*, New York: John Wiley.

Simon, J. (2001–2) 'Governing through Crime Metaphors', *Brooklyn Law Review* 67(4): 1035.

(2007) *Governing through Crime: How the War on Crime Transformed American Democracy and Created a Culture of Fear*, New York: Oxford University Press.

Skyring, F. (2011) *Justice: A History of the Aboriginal Legal Service of Western Australia*, Perth: University of Western Australia Publishing.

Smandych, R. and Linden, R. (1995) 'Co-existing Forms of Native and Private Justice: An Historical Study of the Canadian West', in K. M. Hazelhurst (ed.) *Legal Pluralism and the Colonial Legacy: Indigenous Experiences of Justice in Canada, Australia and New Zealand*, Aldershot: Avebury Press.

Snowball, L. and Weatherburn, D. (2006) 'Indigenous Over-representation in Prison: The Role of Offender Characteristics', *Contemporary Issues in Crime and Justice: Crime and Justice Bulletin*, no. 99, Sydney: NSW Bureau of Crime Statistics and Research.

(2007) 'Does Racial Bias in Sentencing Contribute to Indigenous Overrepresentation in Prison?', *Australian and New Journal of Criminology* 40(3): 272.

Southwood, S. (2007) 'Equality of the Law and the Sentencing of Aboriginal Offenders under the Sentencing Act (NT)', Paper presented at the Law Council of Australia Conference – Rule of Law: The Challenges of a Changing World, Brisbane, 1 September. Available http://www.lawcouncil.asn.au/fms/speeches/Rule%20of%20Law/Session%205%20Stephen%20Southwood.pdf (accessed 8 January 2013).

Spark, C. (2003) 'Documenting Redfern: Representing Home and Aboriginality on The Block', *Continuum: Journal of Media & Cultural Studies* 17(1): 33.

Spiers-Williams, M. (2011) 'The Impossibility of Community Justice Whilst There is Intervention', *Fifth Annual Australian and New Zealand Critical Criminology Conference*, James Cook University, Cairns, 7–8 July.

Spivak, G. C. (1985) 'The Rani of Sirmur: An Essay in Reading the Archives', *History and Theory* 24(3): 247.

(1988) 'Can the Subaltern Speak', in C. Nelson and L. Grossberg (eds) *Marxism and the Interpretation of Culture*, London: Macmillan.

(1996) *The Spivak Reader: Selected Works of Gayatri Chakravorty Spivak*, D. Landry and G. MacLean (eds), London: Routledge.

Standing Committee on Legal and Constitutional Affairs (2006) *Unfinished Business: Indigenous Stolen Wages*, Canberra: Department of Senate.

Steering Committee for the Review of Government Service Provision (2009) *Report on Government Services 2009*, Canberra: Productivity Commission.

Strelein, L. (2003) '*Members of the Yorta Yorta Aboriginal Community v Victoria* [2002] HCA 58 (12 December 2002) – Comment', in J. Weir (ed.) *Land, Rights, Laws: Issues of Native Title*, Native Title Research Unit, *Australian Institute of Aboriginal and Torres Strait Islander Studies* 2(21): 1.

Strike Force Coburn (2004) *Final Report – Part A: Analysis – Redfern Local Area Command Civil Unrest 15–16 February 2004*, New South Wales Police.

Stubbs, J. (2008) 'Critical Criminological Research', in T. Anthony and C. Cunneen (eds) *The Critical Criminology Companion*, Sydney: Hawkins Press.

Sutton, P. (2001) 'The Politics of Suffering: Indigenous Policy in Australia since the 1970s', *Anthropological Forum* 11(2): 125.

(2009) *The Politics of Suffering: Indigenous Australia and the End of the Liberal Consensus*, Melbourne: Melbourne University Publishing.

Tamanaha, B. (2000) 'A Non-Essentialist Version of Legal Pluralism', *Journal of Law and Society* 27(2): 296.

(2008) 'Understanding Legal Pluralism: Past to Present, Local to Global', *Sydney Law Review* 30(3): 375.

Tata, C. (2007) 'Sentencing as Craftwork and the Binary Epistemologies of the Discretionary Decision Process', *Social and Legal Studies* 16(3): 425.

Tata, C. and Hutton, N. (1998) 'What "Rules" in Sentencing? Consistency and Disparity in the Absence of "Rules"', *International Journal of the Sociology of Law* 26: 339.

Thomson, J. (ed.) (1989) *Reaching Back: Queensland Aboriginal People Recall Early Days at Yarrabah Mission*, Canberra: Aboriginal Studies Press.

Thomson, N., MacRae, A., Brankovich, J., Burns, J., Catto, M., Gray, C., Levitan, L., Mailing, C., Potter, C., Ride, K., Stumpers, S. and Urquhart, B. (2012) *Overview of Australian Indigenous Health Status 2011*, Perth: Australian Indigenous Health*InfoNet*. Available http://www.healthinfonet.ecu.edu.au/overview_2012.pdf (accessed 8 January 2013).

Thorpe, B. (1992) 'Aboriginal Employment and Unemployment: Colonised Labour', in C. Williams with B. Thorpe (eds) *Beyond Industrial Sociology: The Work of Men and Women*, Sydney: Allen & Unwin.

Tonry, M. (1995) *Malign Neglect: Race, Crime and Punishment in America*, New York: Oxford University Press.

Toohey, P. (2005) 'Age of Contempt', *The Bulletin* 123(34), 23 August. Available on Factiva database (accessed 1 February 2012).

(2007) 'Hard Law, Hard Love', *The Bulletin* 125(27), 2 July. Available on Factiva database (accessed 1 February 2012).

(2008) 'Last Drinks: The Impact of the Northern Territory Intervention', *Quarterly Essay* 30: 1.

Travers, M. (2006) 'Understanding Talk in Legal Settings: What Law and Society Studies Can Learn from a Conversation Analyst', *Law & Social Inquiry* 31: 447.

Tully, J. (2008) *Public Philosophy in a New Key*, vol. 1: Democracy and Civic Freedom, Cambridge: Cambridge University Press.

Turner-Walker, J. (2011) *Clash of the Paradigms: Night Patrols in Remote Central Australia*, unpublished Masters of Criminal Justice thesis, University of Western Australia.

Valverde, M. (1996) '"Despotism" and Ethical Liberal Governance', *Economy and Society* 25(3): 357.

van Krieken, R. (2004) 'Legal Reasoning as a Field of Knowledge Production: Luhmann, Bourdieu and Law's Autonomy', Presented at the Annual Meeting of the Law and Society Association. Available http://ses.library.usyd.edu.au/bitstream/2123/967/1/legal%20reasoning.pdf (accessed 8 January 2013).

Van Marle, F. and Maruna, S. (2010) 'Ontological Insecurity and "Terror Management"', *Punishment and Society* 12(1): 7.

Von Hirsch, A. (2004) 'Scaling Punishments: A Reply to Julia Davis', in C. Tata and N. Hutton (eds) *Sentencing and Society: International Perspectives*, Aldershot: Ashgate.

Walker, J. (1987) 'Prison Cells with Revolving Doors: A Judicial or Societal Problem', in K. M. Hazelhurst, *Ivory Scales: Black Australia and the Law*, Sydney: University of New South Wales Press.

Walker, J. and McDonald, D. (1995) 'The Over-representation of Indigenous People in Custody in Australia', *Trends and Issues in Crime and Criminal Justice*, no. 47, Canberra: Australian Institute of Criminology.

Walsh, T. and Taylor, M. (2007) 'You're Not Welcome Here: Police Move-on Powers and Discrimination Law', *University of New South Wales Law Journal* 30(1): 151.

Watson, I. (2007) 'Aboriginal Women's Laws and Lives: How Might We Keep Growing the Law?', *Australian Feminist Law Journal* 26: 95.

(2008) 'The "Recognition" of Cultural Background in Indigenous Sentencing', Paper presented to the Sentencing Conference National Judicial College of Australia, ANU College of Law, Canberra. Available http://njca.anu.edu.au/Professional%20 Development/programs%20by%20year/2008/Sentencing%20Conference%20 2008/papers/watson.pdf (accessed 8 January 2013).

(2009) 'Aboriginality and the Violence of Colonialism', *Borderlands e-journal*, 8(1): 1. Available http://www.borderlands.net.au/vol8no1_2009/iwatson_aboriginality.pdf (accessed 8 January 2013).

Watson, John (1988) 'We Know This Country', in P. Marshall (ed.) *Raparapa Kularr Martuwarra ... All Right, Now We Go 'Side the River, along that Sundown Way: Stories from Fitzroy River Drovers*, Broome: Magbala Books.

Watson, Joanne (1993) *Becoming Bwgcolman: Exile and Survival on Palm Island Reserve, 1918 to the present*, unpublished PhD thesis, University of Queensland.

(1995) '"We Couldn't Tolerate Any More": The Palm Island Strike of 1957', *Labour History* 69: 149.

(2010) *Palm Island: Through a Long Lens*, Canberra: Aboriginal Studies Press.

Watson, N. (2011) 'Aboriginal and Torres Strait Islander Identities', in A. Cadzow and J. Maynard (eds) *Nelson Aboriginal Studies*, Melbourne: Nelson Cengage Learning.

Watson, V. (2009a) 'From the "Quiet Revolution" to "Crisis" in Australian Indigenous Affairs', *Cultural Studies Review* 15(1): 88.

Weatherburn, D., Snowball, L. and Hunter, B. (2006) 'The Economic and Social Factors Underpinning Indigenous Contact with the Justice System: Results from the 2002 NATSISS', *Contemporary Issues in Crime and Justice: Crime and Justice Bulletin*, no. 104, Sydney: New South Wales Bureau of Crime Statistics and Research.

(2008) 'Predictors of Indigenous Arrest: An Exploratory Study', *Australian & New Zealand Journal of Criminology* 41(2): 307.

White, J. (1997) 'Power/Knowledge and Public Space: Policing the "Aboriginal Towns"', *Australian & New Zealand Journal of Criminology* 30(3): 275.

White, R. and Perrone, S. (1997) *Crime and Social Control: An Introduction*, Melbourne: Oxford University Press.

Wild, R. and Anderson, P. (2007) *Ampe Akelyernemane Meke Mekarle 'Little Children Are Sacred'*, Report of the Northern Territory Board of Inquiry into the Protection of Aboriginal Children from Sexual Abuse, Northern Territory Government.

Williams, P. (1997) *Seeing a Color-Blind Future: The Paradox of Race*, BBC Reith Lecture Series, London: Virago Press.

Williams, V. (2003) *The Approach of Australian Courts to Aboriginal Customary Law in the Areas of Criminal, Civil and Family Law*, Background Paper 1, Aboriginal Customary Laws Project 94, Law Reform Commission of Western Australia.

Willshire, W. H. (1896) *The Land of the Dawning: Being Facts Gleaned from Cannibals in the Australian Stone Age*, Adelaide: W. K. Thomas & Co.

Wilson, P. R. (1982) *Black Deaths, White Hands*, Sydney: Allen & Unwin.

Wohlan, C. (2005) *Aboriginal Women's Interests in Customary Law Recognition*, Background Paper 13, Aboriginal Customary Laws Project 94, Law Reform Commission of Western Australia.

Woodroffe, D. (2006) *Aboriginal Customary Law and the Sentencing Discretion by Courts in the Northern Territory*, National Indigenous Legal Conference, Sydney, 22–23 September.

Wootten, H. (1991) 'Report of the Inquiry into the Death of Lloyd James Boney', Royal Commission into Aboriginal Deaths in Custody, Canberra: Australian Government Publishing Service.

Yeo, S. (1994) 'Native Criminal Jurisdiction after *Mabo*', *Current Issues in Criminal Justice* 6(1): 9.

Young, S. (2008) *The Trouble with Tradition: Native Title and Cultural Change*, Sydney: Federation Press.

Zagar, C. (ed.) (1990) *Growing up Walgett: Young Members of the Walgett Aboriginal Community Speak Out*, Canberra: Aboriginal Studies Press.

Zdenkowski, G. (1994) 'Customary Punishment and Pragmatism – Some Unresolved Dilemmas: *The Queen v Wilson Jagamara Walker*', *Aboriginal Law Bulletin* 3(68): 26.

(1999) 'Mandatory Imprisonment of Property Offenders in the Northern Territory', *University of New South Wales Law Journal* 22(1): 302.

(2000) 'Limiting Sentencing Discretion: Has There Been a Paradigm Shift?', *Current Issues in Criminal Justice* 12(1): 58.

Žižek, S. (2007) 'Ego Ideal and Superego: Lacan as Viewer of *Casablanca*', in S. Žižek, *How to Read Lacan*. Available http://www.lacan.com/zizraphael.htm (accessed 5 January 2013).

Index